Digital Drawing for Beginners and Intermediates with Adobe Photoshop

From simple forms to complicated objects

Stephanie Lane

Keywords: photoshop, photoshop elements 2018, photoshop digital painting, adobe photoshop elements 2018, photoshop cc 2018 book, photoshop 2018 for dummies, photoshop books 2018, adobe photoshop cc classroom in a book 2018, drawing photoshop, drawing in photoshop.

Table of Contents

Disclaimer

While all attempts have been made to verify the information provided in this book, the author does assume any responsibility for errors, omissions, or contrary interpretations of the subject matter contained within. The information provided in this book is for educational and entertainment purposes only. The reader is responsible for his or her own actions and the author does not accept any responsibilities for any liabilities or damages, real or perceived, resulting from the use of this information.

The trademarks that are used are without any consent, and the publication of the trademark is without permission or backing by the trademark owner. All trademarks and brands within this book are for clarifying purposes only and are the owned by the owners themselves, not affiliated with this document.

Introduction

Learning how to draw is a continuous process. Learning, or even mastering, one medium should not be your only goal. It is not enough that you are good at just one kind of drawing, you should strive to learn more and improve your art and skills further.

Adobe Photoshop is a great tool not just for total beginners but also for those who are transitioning from traditional tools and mediums to the digital ones.

Adobe Photoshop

Adobe Photoshop is one of the newer mediums being used by graphic artists and designers all over the world. It is a very versatile tool that gives you the freedom to express your thoughts and feelings into the piece or work that you are creating. It is the medium that allows you create stunning, realistic, three-dimensional images that will not only give joy and delight to those who see your art but also gives you the ability to improve your art while using it. Since Photoshop is a digital medium, you can make as many mistakes or edits as you want just to make your piece better.

Device to Use

Photoshop is a program that has already spread throughout the world and, by extension, to all the devices that have recently been developed can install it. This means that you do not have to be in one place, or need a personal computer, to create amazing works of art.

Desktop

The first, and most widely used, version of Photoshop is those that are built for desktop or laptop computers. This version is the most complete and has all the tools you need to create images. This is also where most users make their art. The great thing about Photoshop, both for desktop and mobile, is that all works can be integrated without any changes made to the piece.

Mobile Gadgets

Most tablets and mobile phones have the capability to install the Adobe Photoshop App. This app turns the mobile device into a Photoshop Workspace which you can use to create and draw. You can even integrate the mobile device, especially tablets, to act as a second screen when working on a piece. You can also use it as a pad when using a stylus pen to make drawing and making art in Photoshop feel more natural and it will also give you greater control over your piece.

Learning the Basics

Circle

1. Make a new layer by pressing Ctrl + Shift + N. Click the Right Mouse Button on the Selection Tool and choose the Ellipse Selection Tool. Create a perfect circle by holding the Shift Key and dragging the mouse until you get the desired size of the circle.

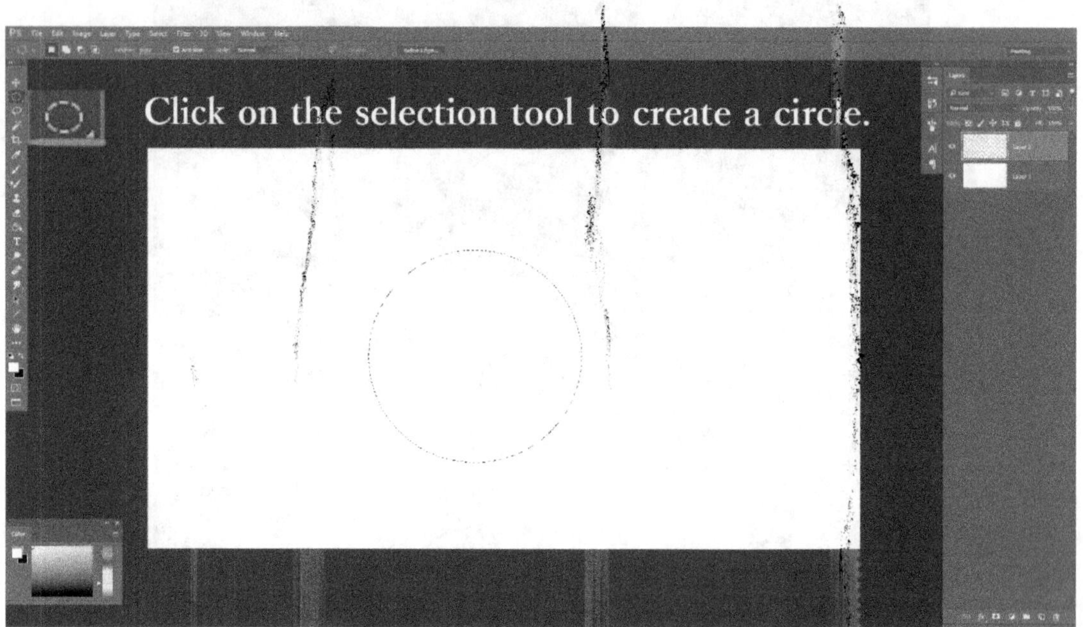

2. Select the Paint Bucket Tool and choose a color. This can be any color of your choice. Click on the selection to fill it with the color.

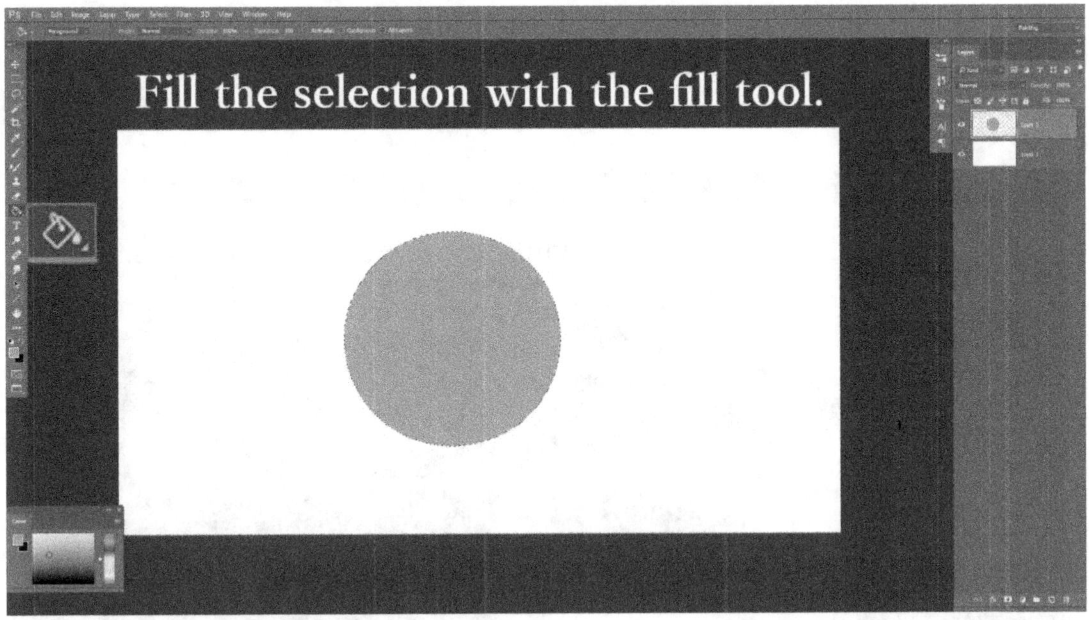

3. Pull up the colors window and choose a color darker than the color you selected earlier. Select the Paint Brush Tool and press the Right Mouse Button anywhere on the Workspace. This will pull up the Brushes Window. Choose a soft brush and increase the Hardness to 100%. Draw a partial circle on the middle of the selection to create a three dimensional effect on it.

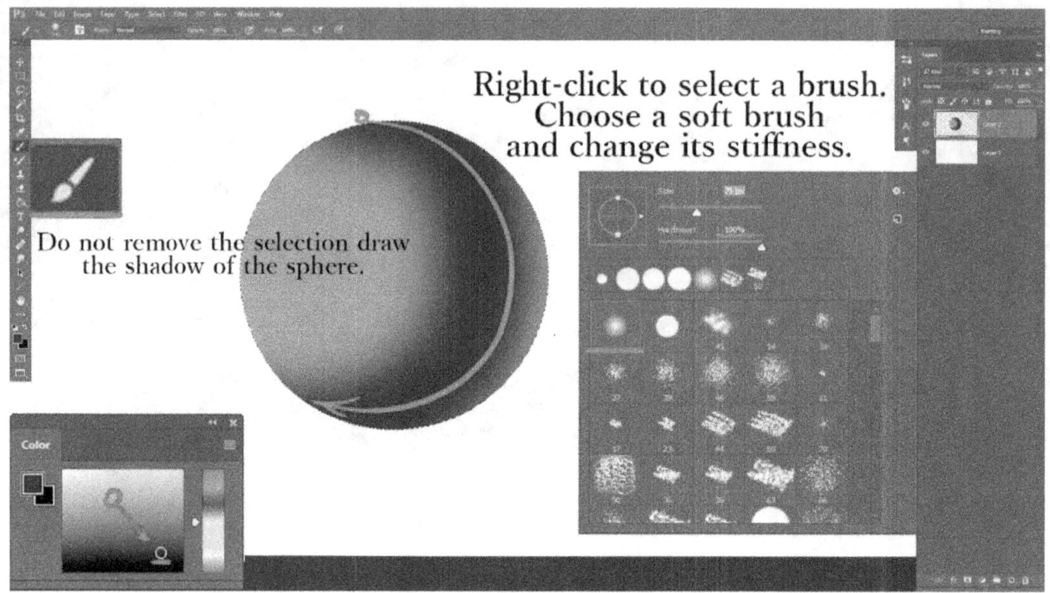

4. This should be the drawn area. Notice that there are parts of the circle that are dark and light. The larger light area is where the light source hits the object. The smaller one is called the reflex. Always keep in mind the direction of your light source. This will add realism and coherence to the whole piece.

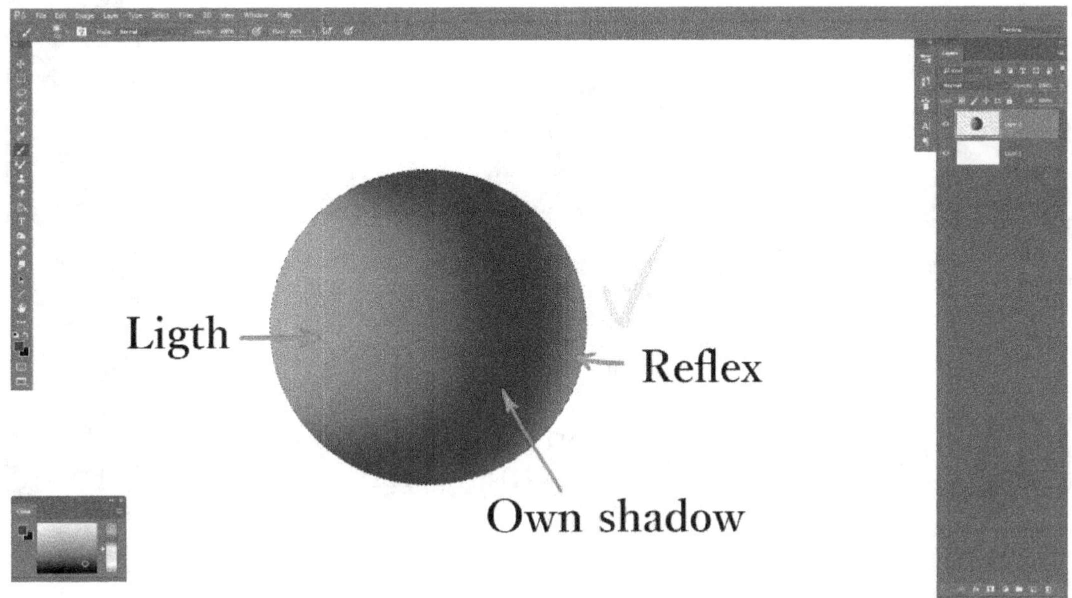

5. Select the Dodge Tool and change its Range to Midtones and its Exposure to 8%. Click on the center of the large area of light to add an effect of a bright light hitting the circle.

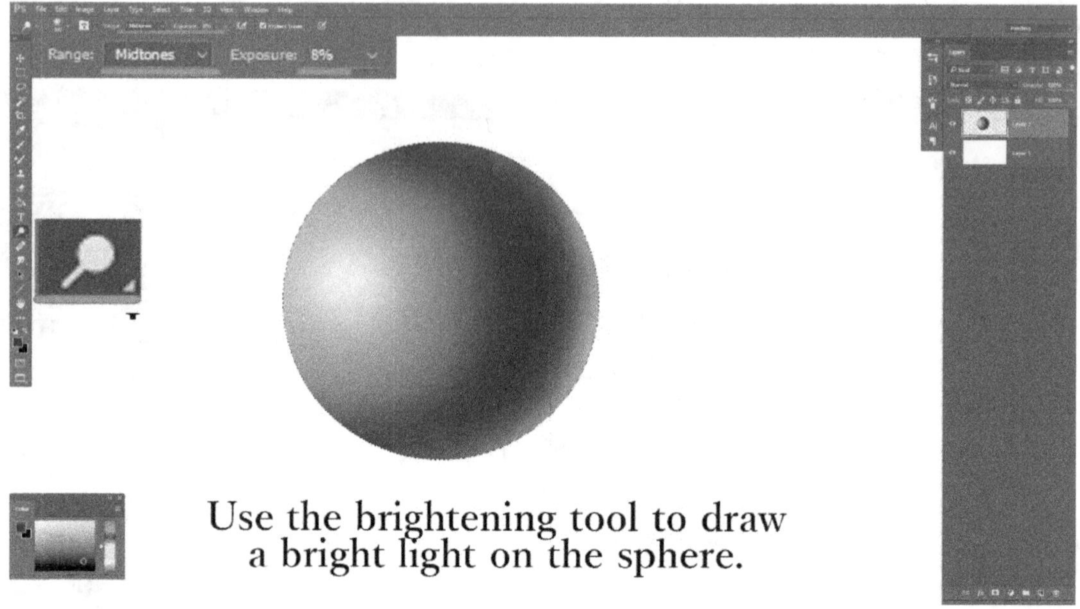

Use the brightening tool to draw
a bright light on the sphere.

6. Select the Brush Tool again and press the Right Mouse Button on the Workspace. Scroll down on the Brushes Window and select the brush texture that you want to use.

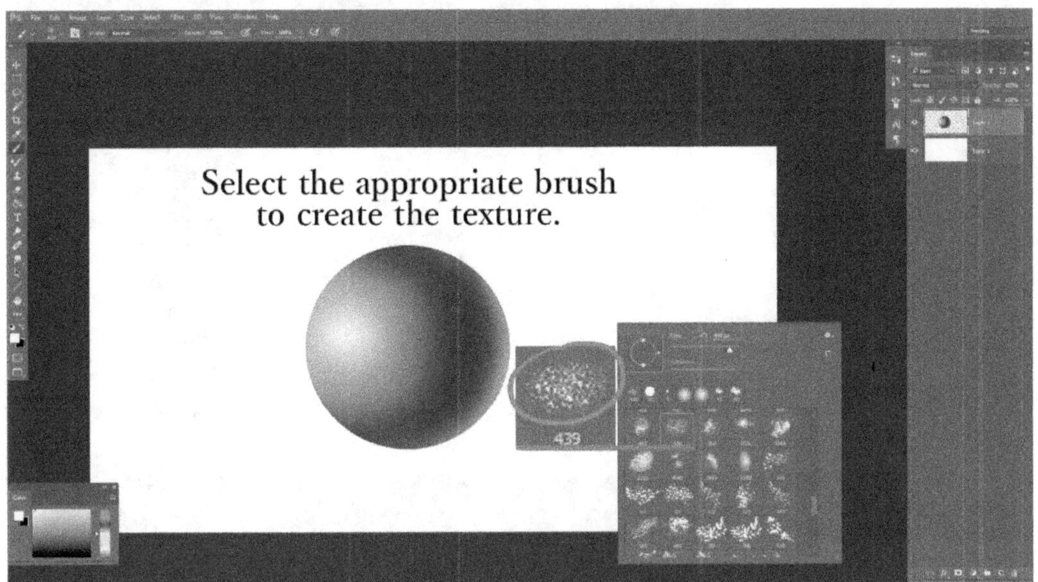

7. Make another layer and draw the texture. Make sure to cover the whole sphere with the desired texture.

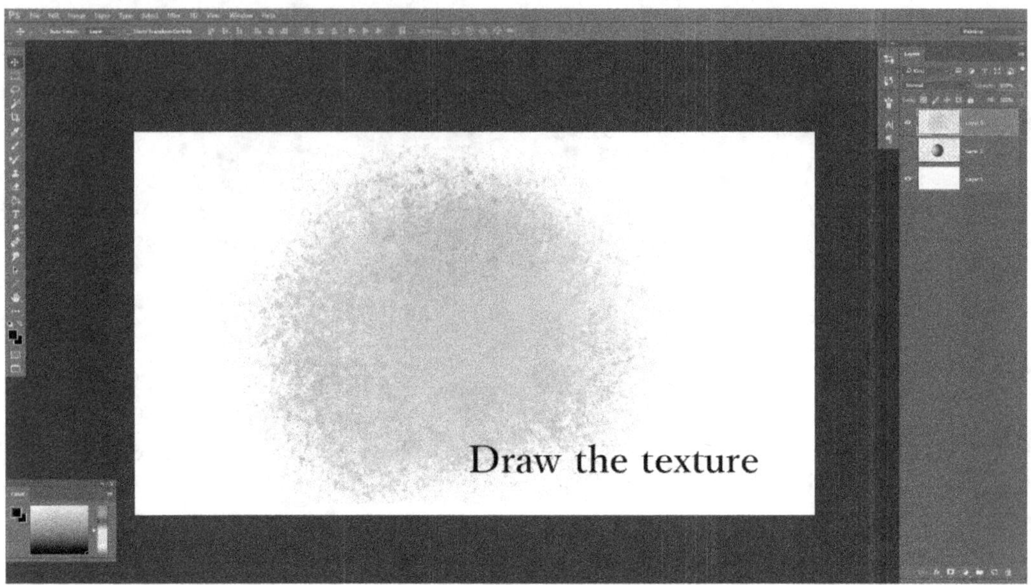

8. While still on the texture's layer, select 'Filter' from the Menu Bar. On the dropdown menu, select 'Liquify...'

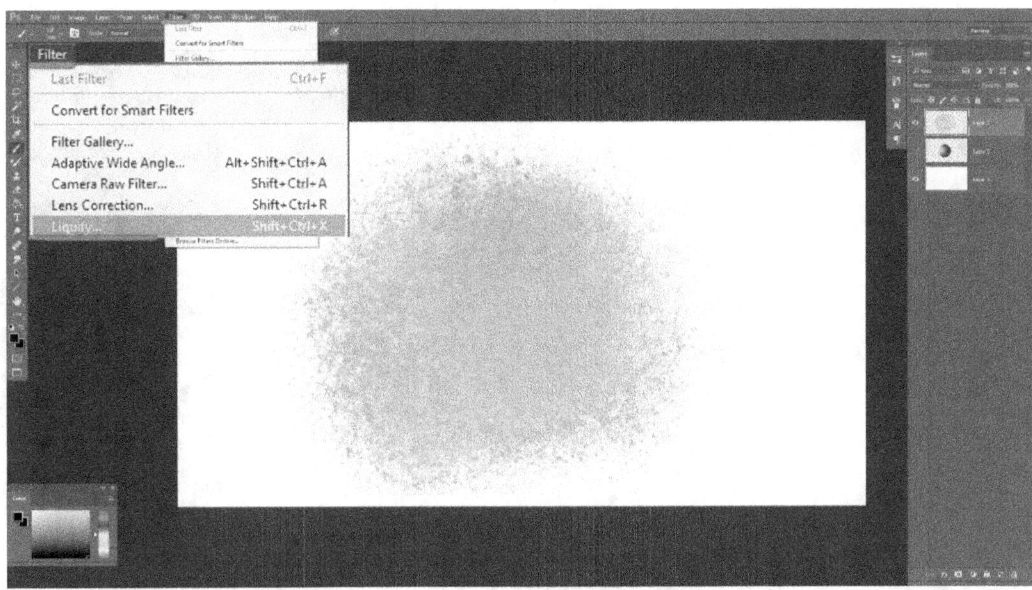

9. While on the Liquify Window, select the Bloat Tool and create a circle of the same or similar size to the circle. Once the desired size is defined, click "OK" on the side bar.

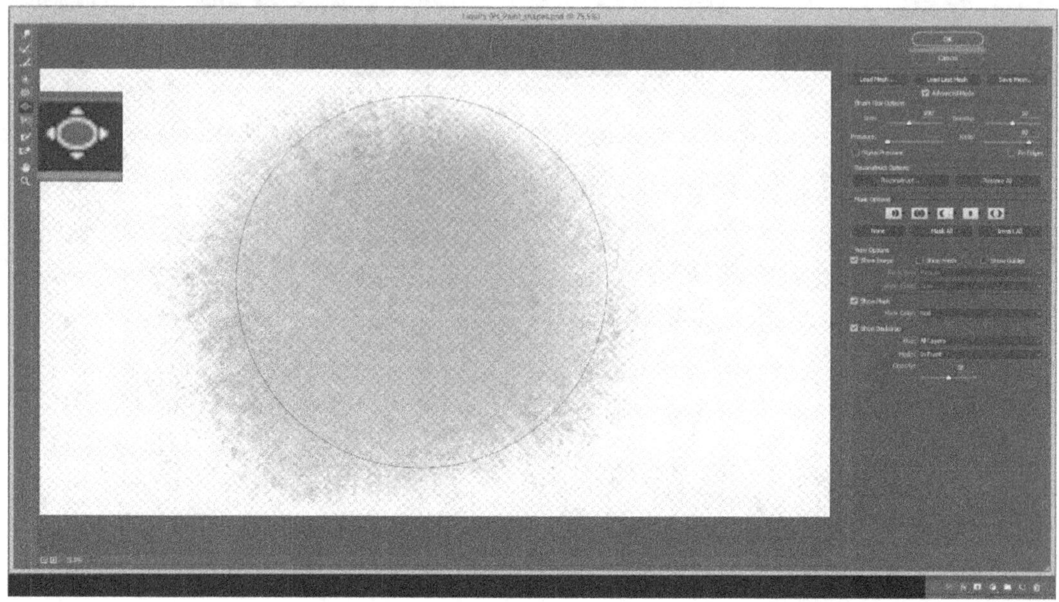

10. Press Ctrl+T on the texture and deform it to match the shape of the circle exactly.

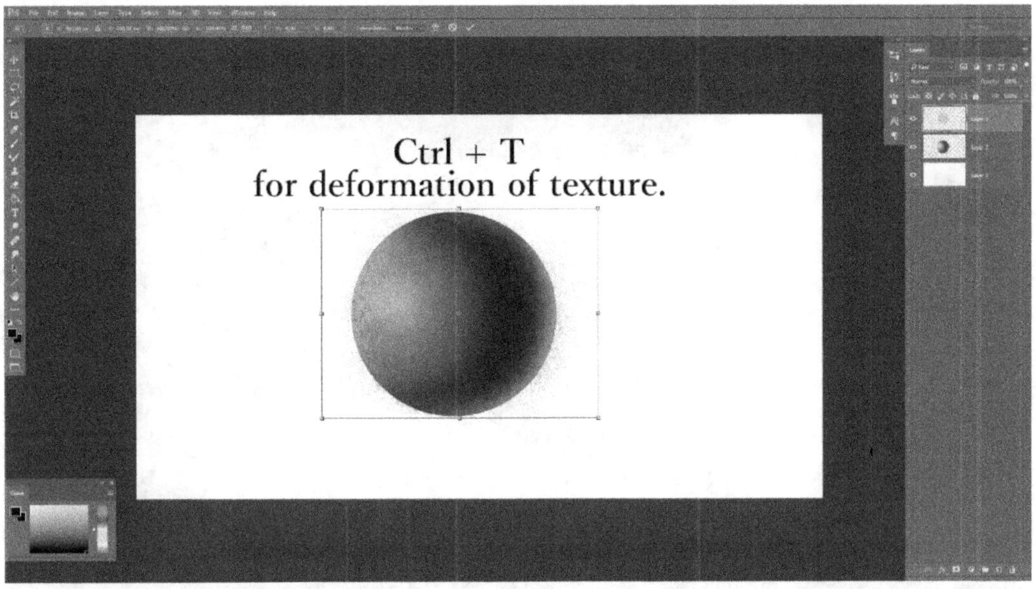

11.   Hide the layer of the texture. Select the layer of the sphere and apply the Gaussian Blur to it. To apply the filter, go to Filter>Blur>Gaussian Blur...

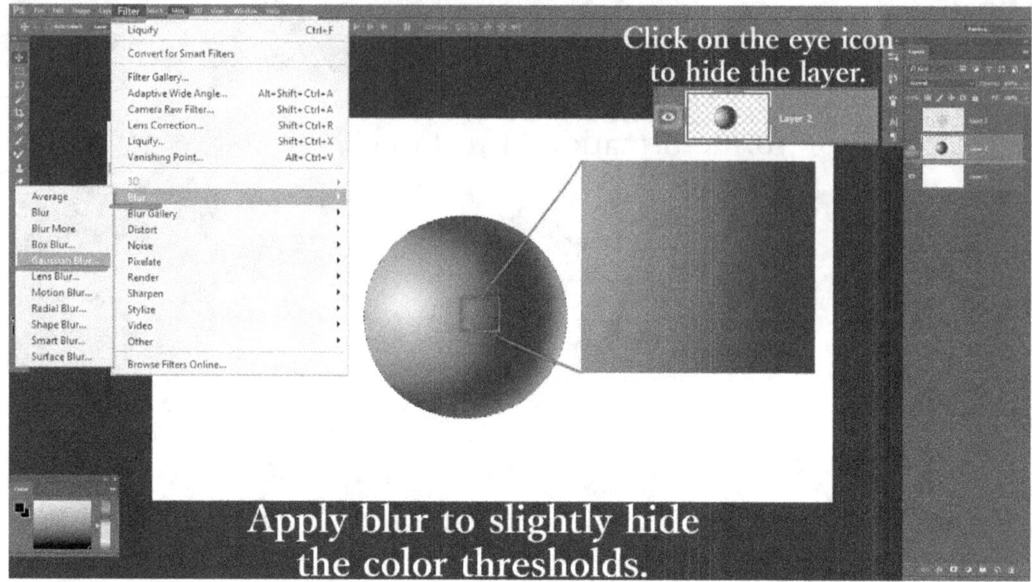

12. Adjust the Gaussian Blur's radius to 10.0.

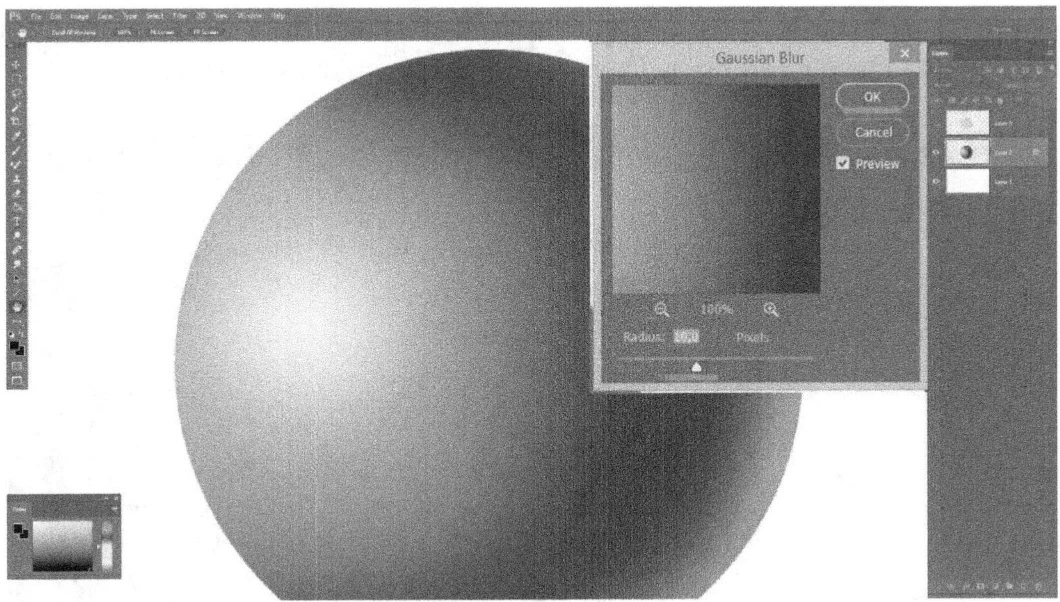

13. Make the layer of the texture visible again by clicking the Eye Icon next to the layer icon. While on the texture's layer, click on the icon of the sphere's layer to make a selection around it. Press Shift+Ctrl+I to select the inverse of the selection. Press Del to delete excess parts of the texture.

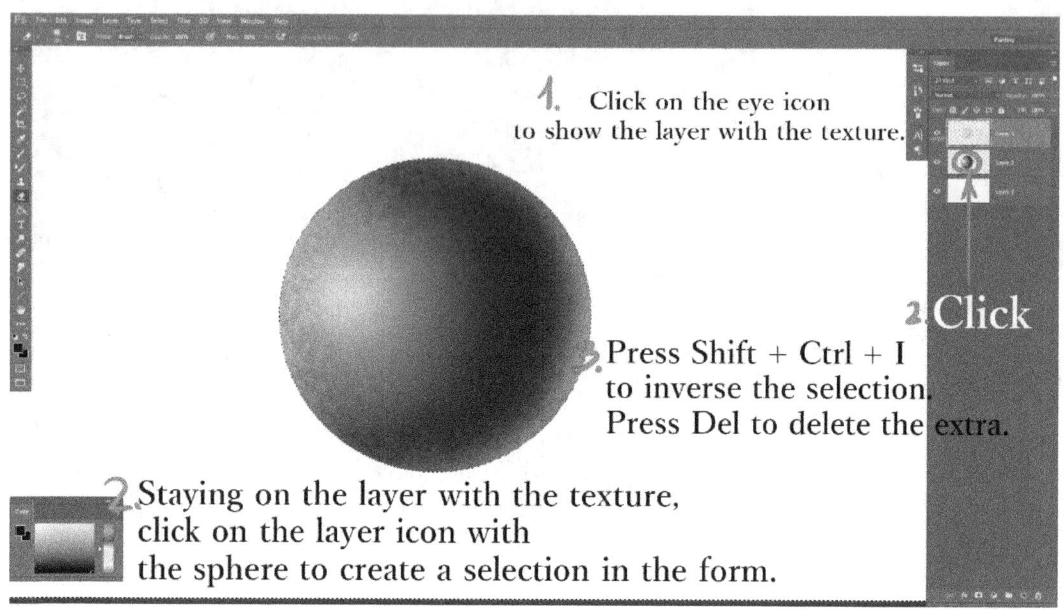

14. Select the layers for both the sphere and the texture and merge them by clicking the Right Mouse Button and selecting Merge Layers.

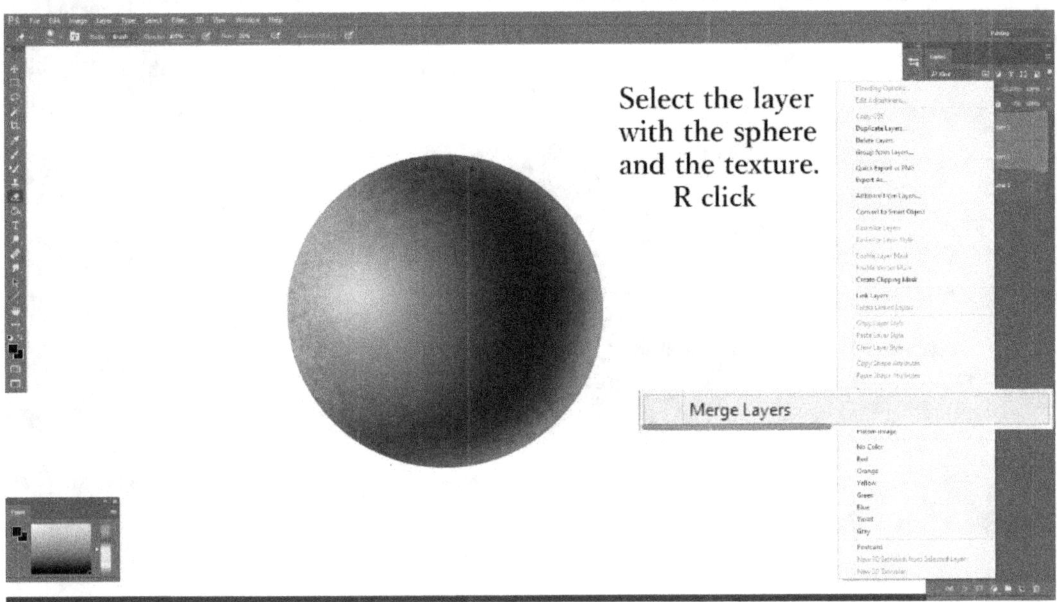

15. Press Ctrl+T to rotate the sphere to the desired light direction.

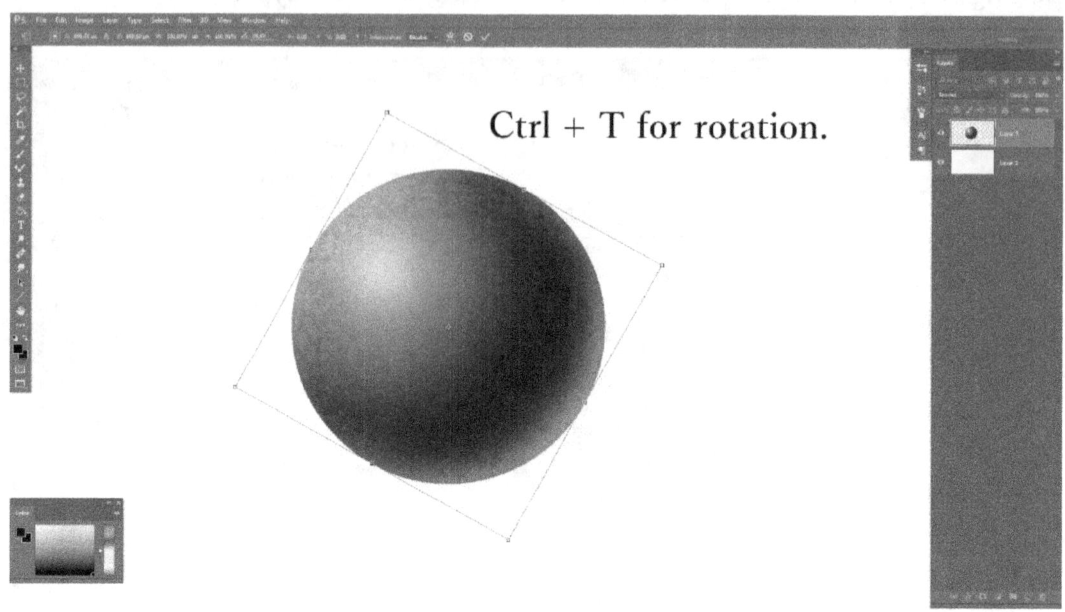

16. Create a new layer. This is for the sketches. Draw a sketch of the details you want to add to the sphere.

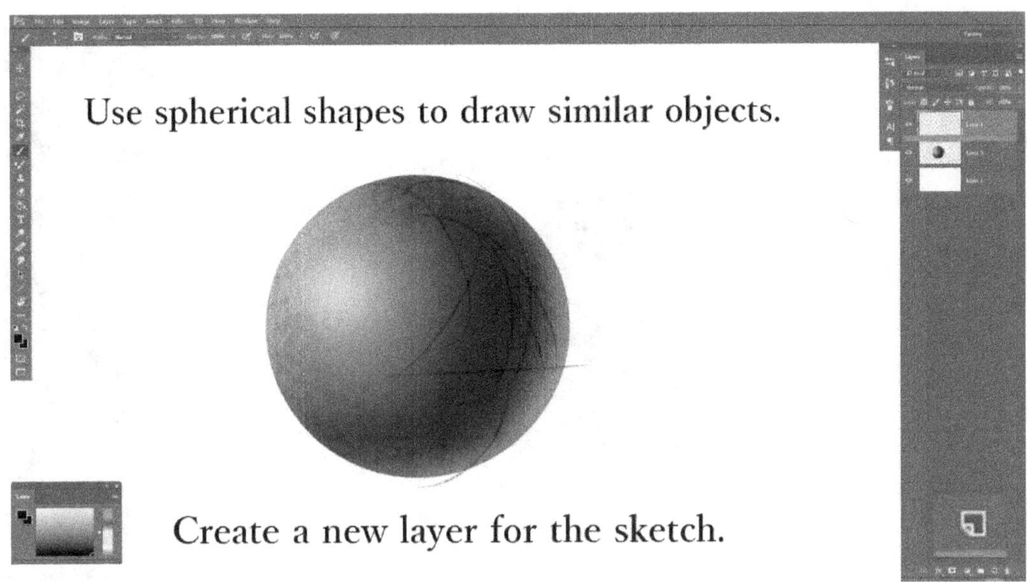

17. Draw other details. Make sure to draw spherical sketches to make the drawings similar.

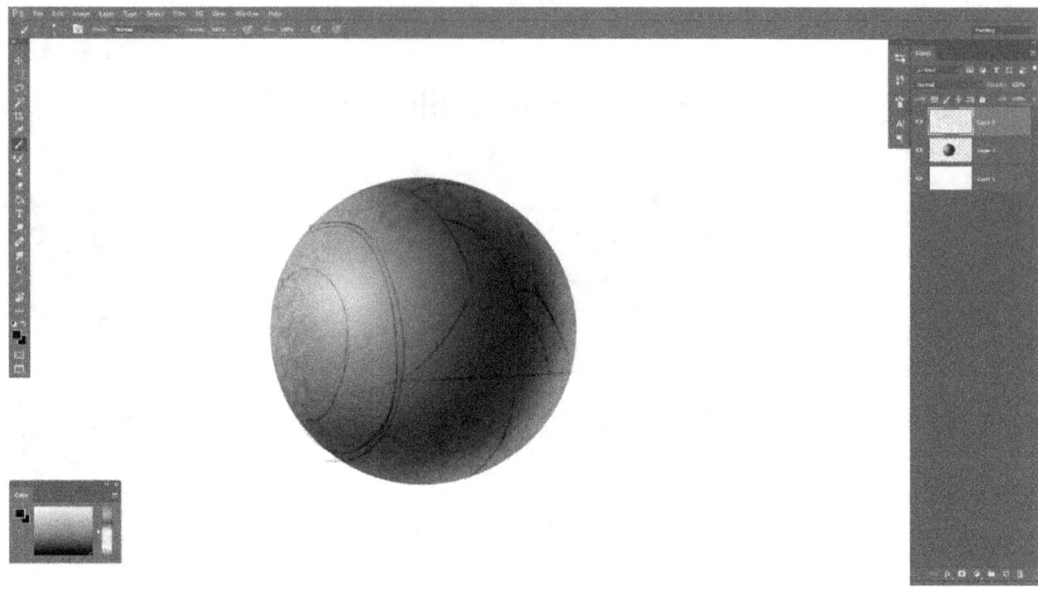

18. To make drawing easier, you can hold the R Key to rotate the whole canvas.

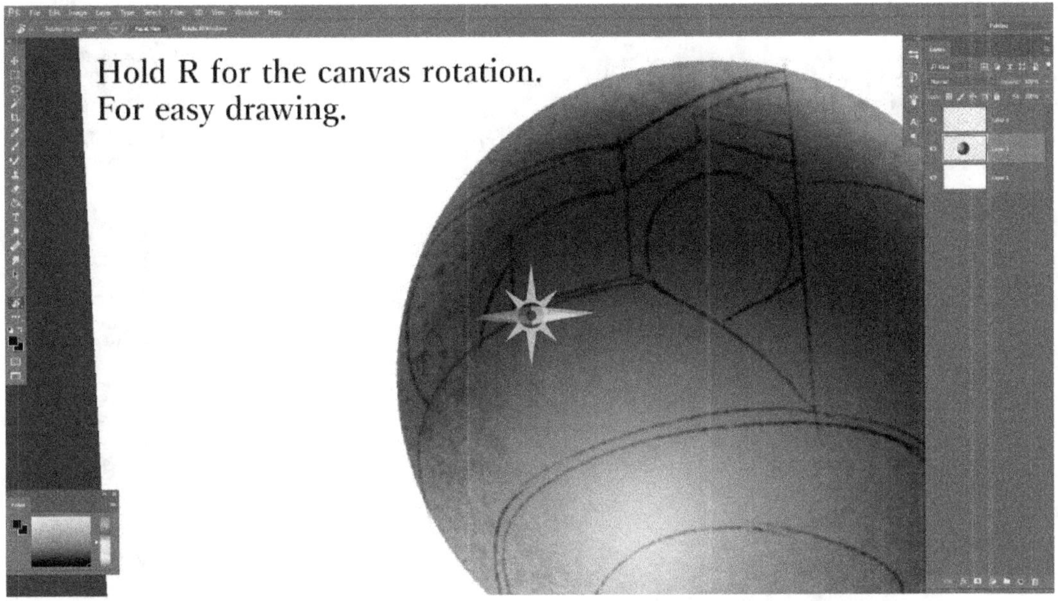

19. Select the sphere's layer and choose the Eraser Tool. Erase any parts of the sphere that may be removed based on the sketch that you made.

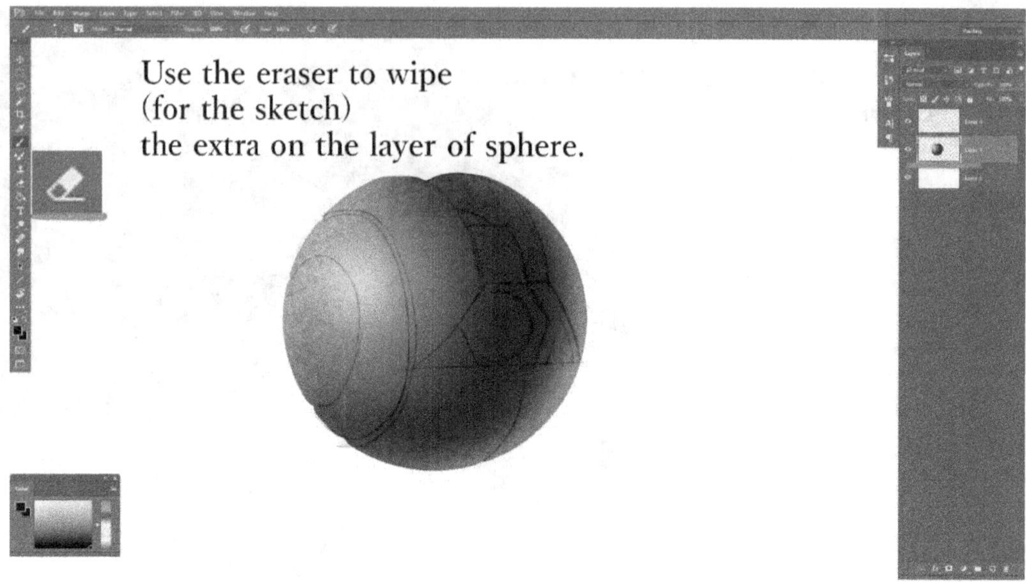

20. Select the layer of the sketch and add more details to it if needed.

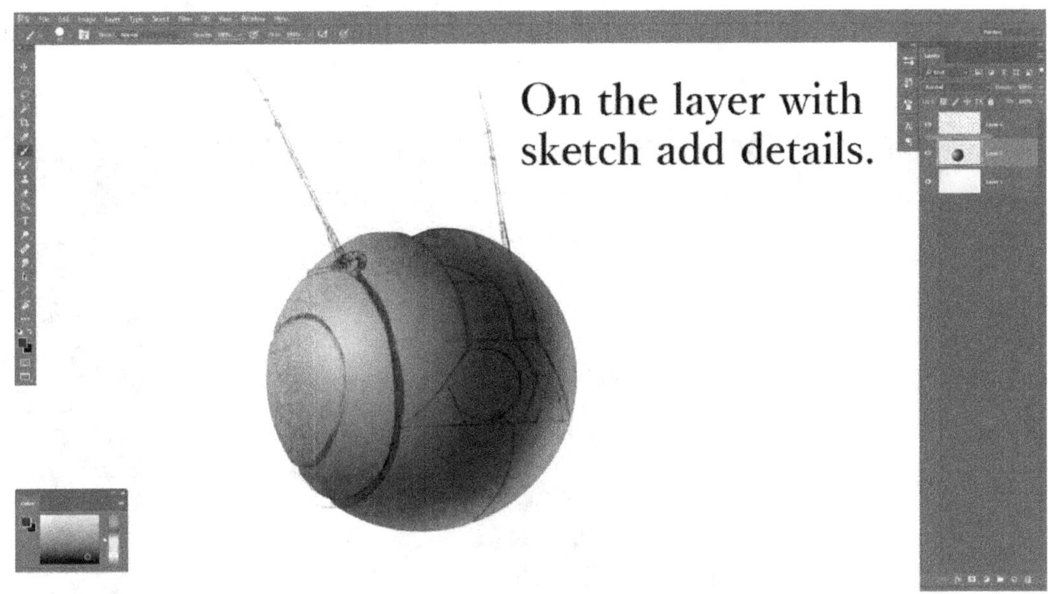

21. Lock the layer of the sphere. With the Brush Tool, draw illuminated areas and the shadows of the parts of the sphere that correspond with the sketch. This will add an effect of the sphere having carved out or lower sections.

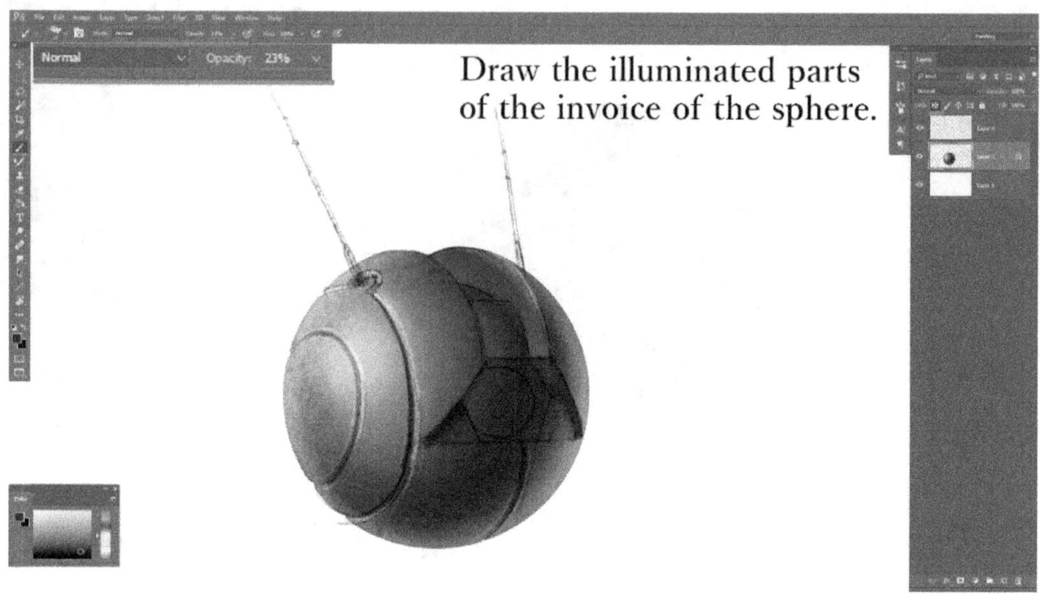

22. On the layer of the sphere, draw shadows and shapes on the sketch. Mark the highlights and the shadows.

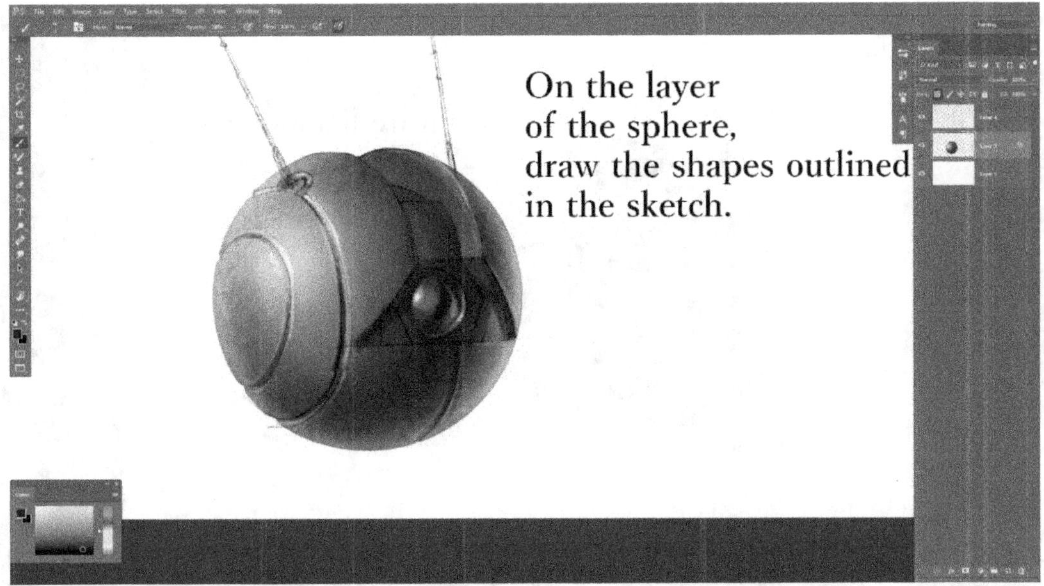

23. Select a different color. Draw on the sphere to mark the location and areas that are illuminated by light sources.

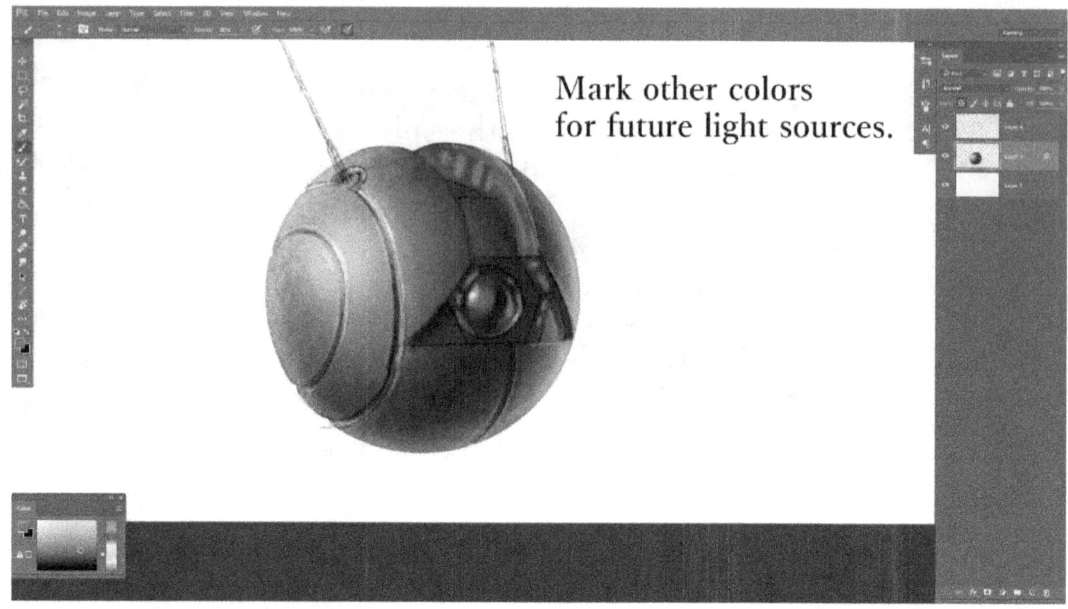

24. Draw the reflexes of the light sources.

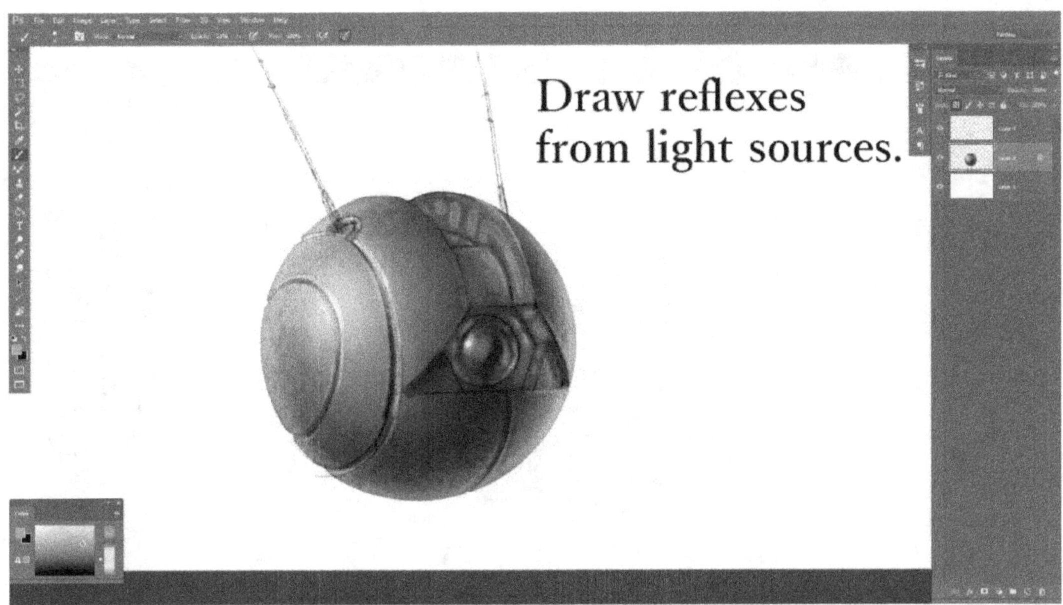

25. Draw and color in some more details. You may also choose to combine the layers of the sketch and the sphere.

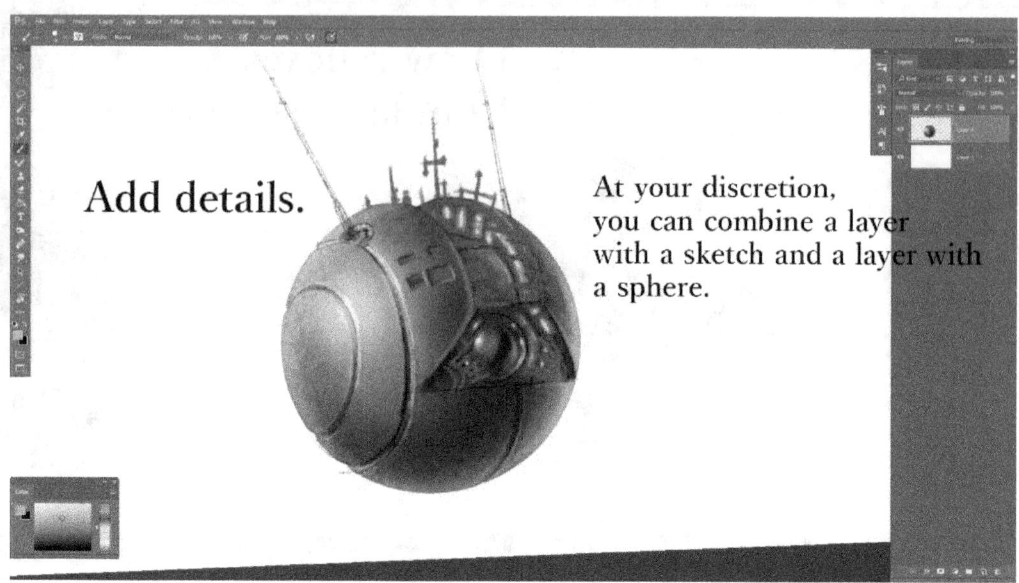

26. Add highlights that simulate the sparkle of metal and add the reflections of light as well.

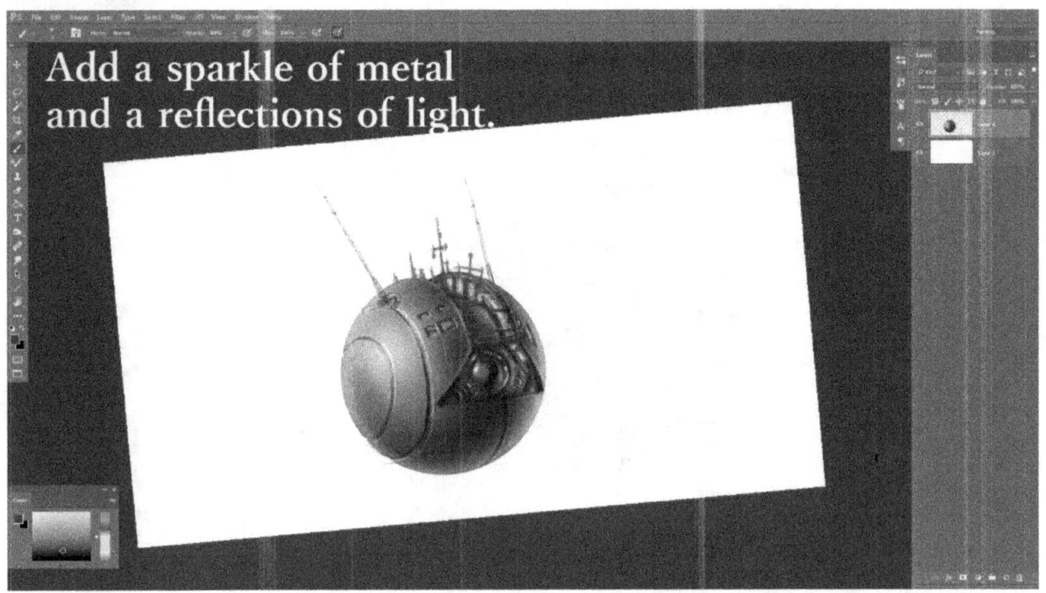

27. Add highlights to the details.

28. Draw the antenna by drawing an area similar to the shading of a cylinder. Make the shadings and colors longer. Press Ctrl+T and deform the cylinder to make the top end narrower. Press Ctrl+T again and elongate the whole shape. Add the light sources.

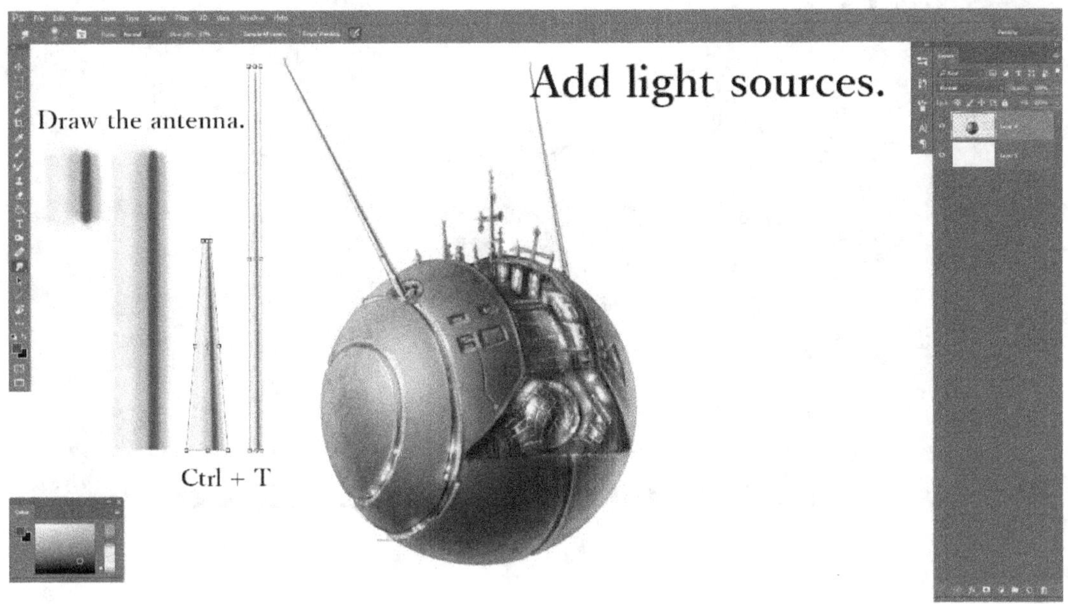

29. Crop the Canvas size by either selecting the Crop Tool or pressing the C Key.

30. The finished piece is.

Square

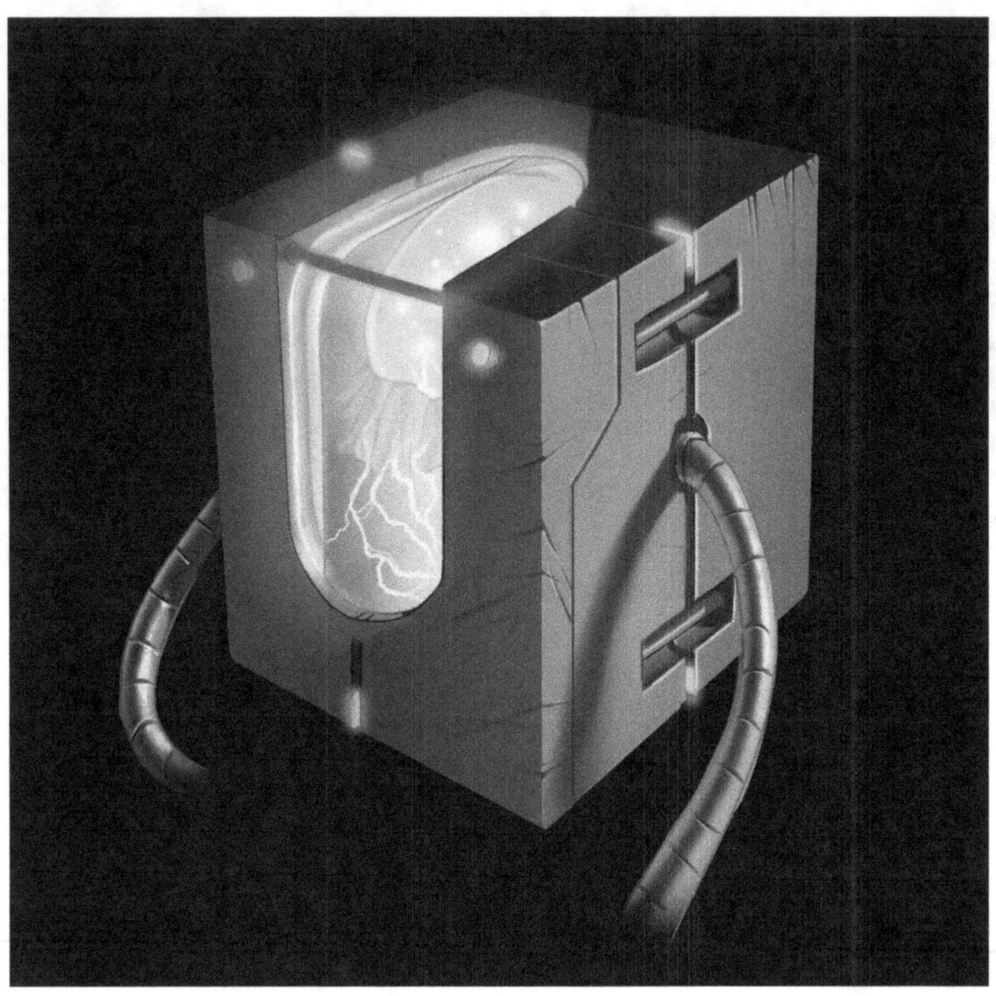

1. Create a New Layer. Choose the Selection Tool and mark a square area.
Make the area a perfect square by holding the Shift Key while drawing it.

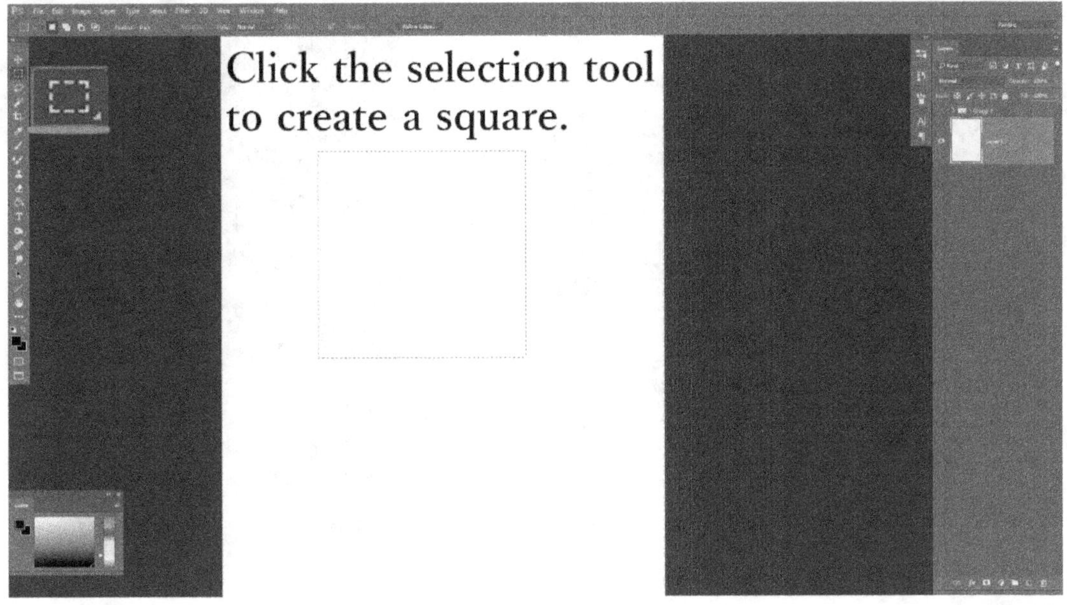

2. Choose the Pain Bucket Tool and fill the area with color.

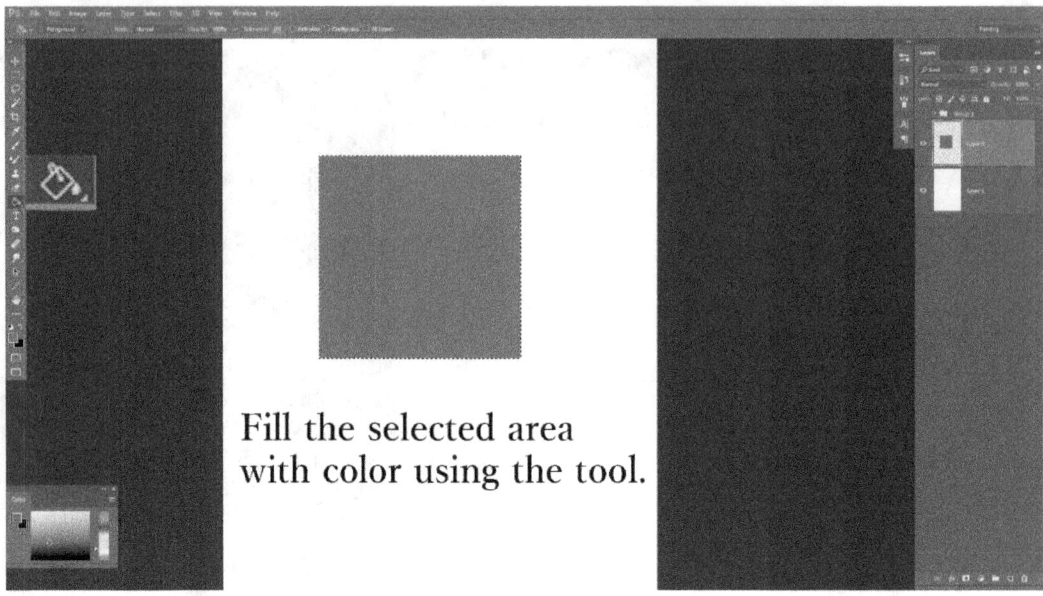

3. Press Ctrl+T and deform the square to the shape of a diamond.

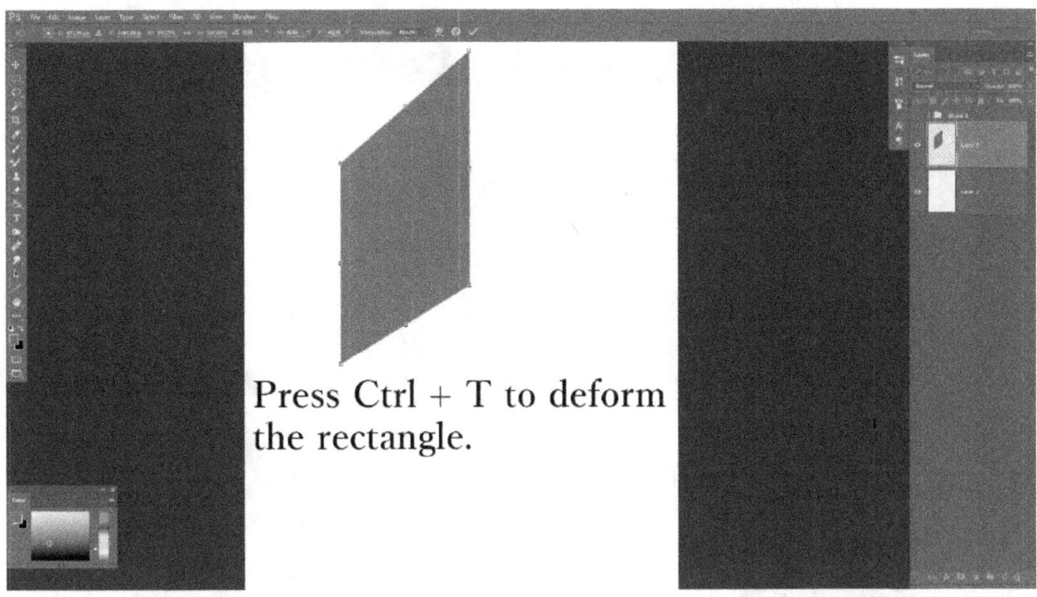

4. Make another layer and press Ctrl+T. Press the Right Mouse Button and select "Flip Horizontal" on the menu.

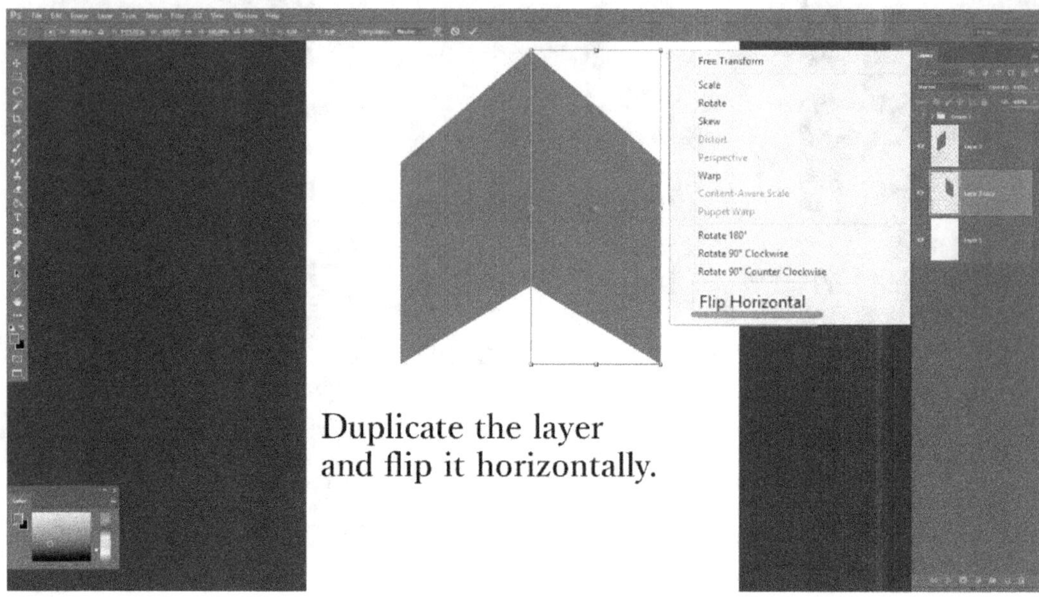

Duplicate the layer
and flip it horizontally.

5. Press Ctrl+T on the new shape and transform it to the desired shape.

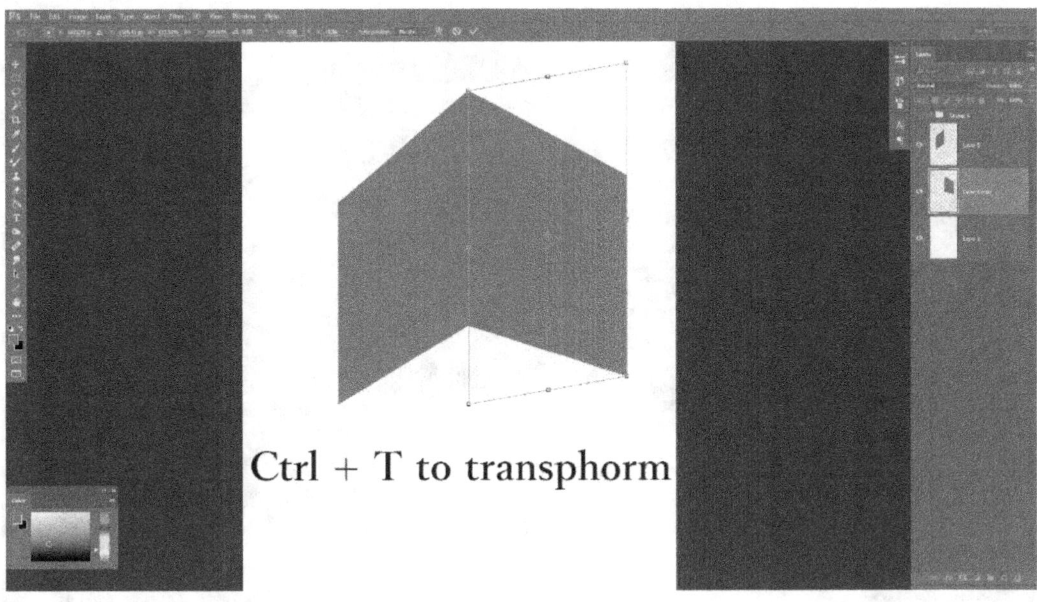

6. Press Ctrl+L and pull up the Levels Window. Change the middle level to 0.64.

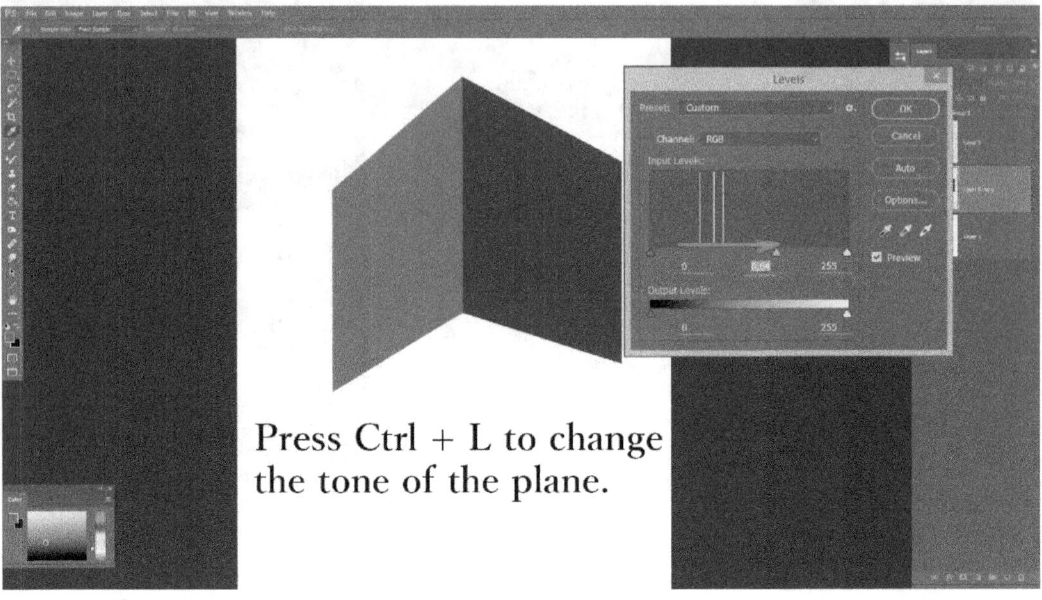

Press Ctrl + L to change the tone of the plane.

7. Copy the darker layer. Rotate the shape and deform it to fit the overall shape. Make this new layer darker y adjusting its levels.

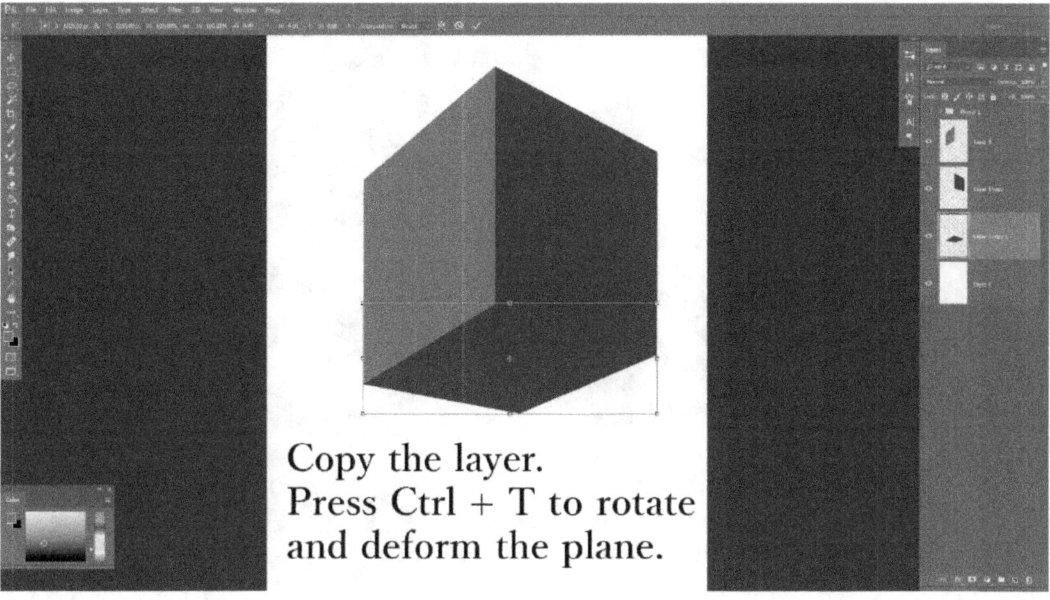

8. Select all three layers. While they are selected, press the Right Mouse
Button and select "Merge Layers" on the menu.

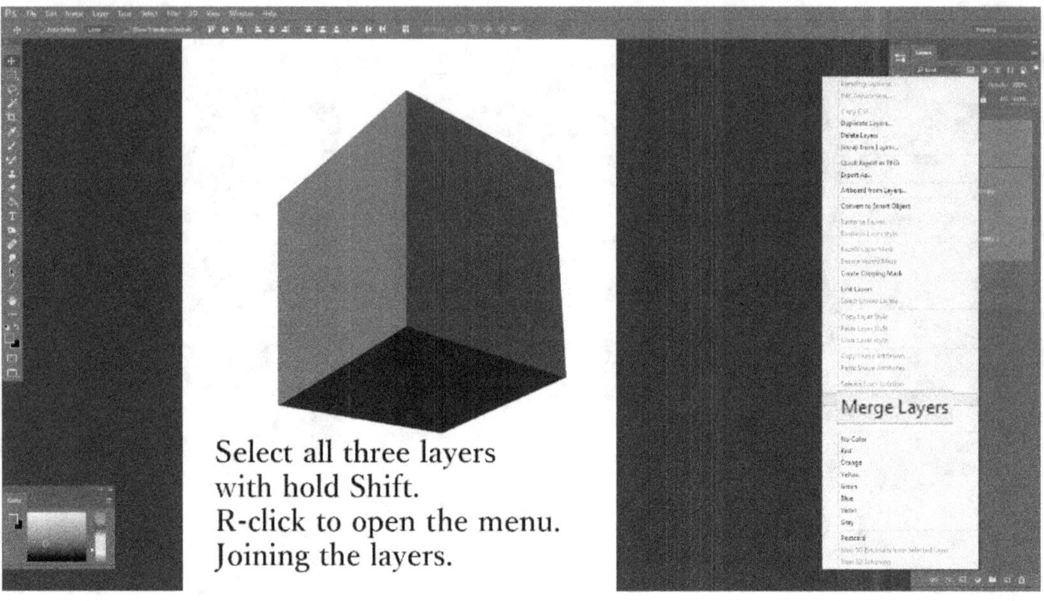

Select all three layers
with hold Shift.
R-click to open the menu.
Joining the layers.

9. You can change the shape's color by pressing Ctrl+U to pull up the Hue/Saturation Window and adjusting the Hue and Saturation of the object.

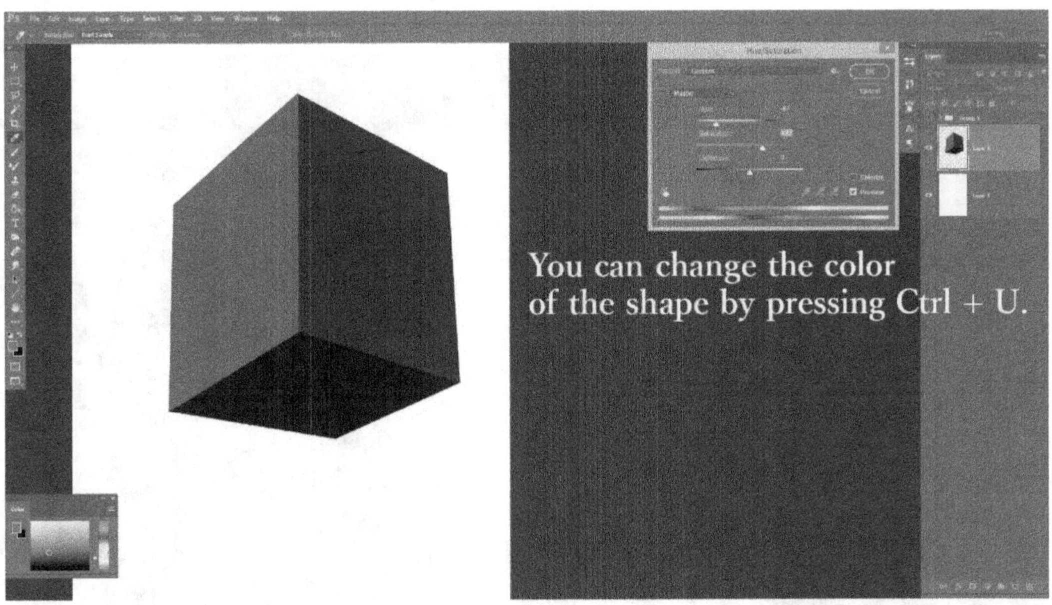

10. We will show you another way of drawing the same shape. Draw four vertical lines similar to the ones shown above using the Brush Tool. To make sure that the lines are really straight, hold the Shift Key while drawing the lines.

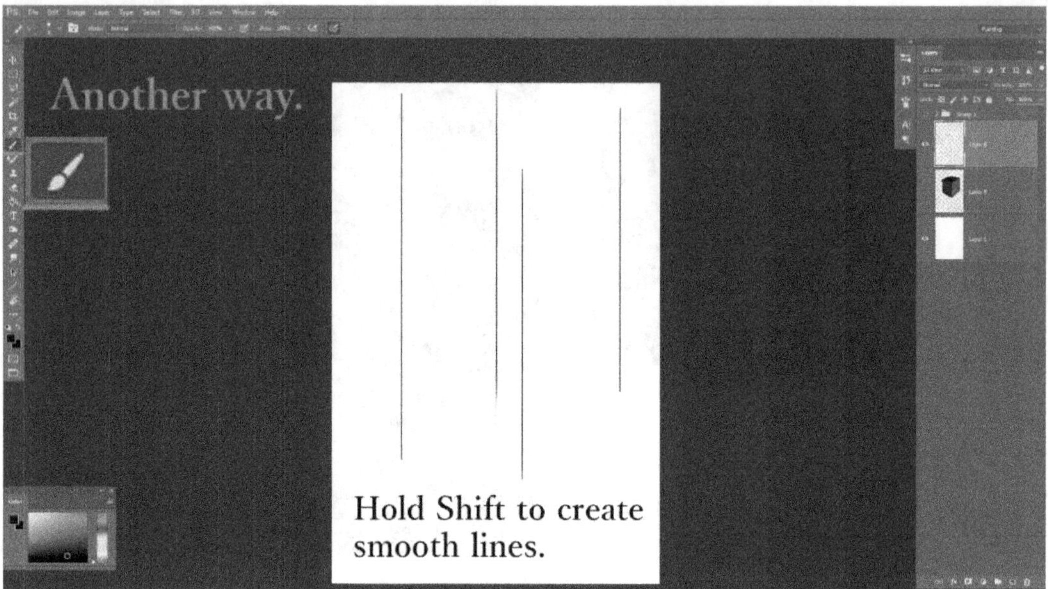

11.   Press Ctrl+T to deform the shape. Create a perspective effect.

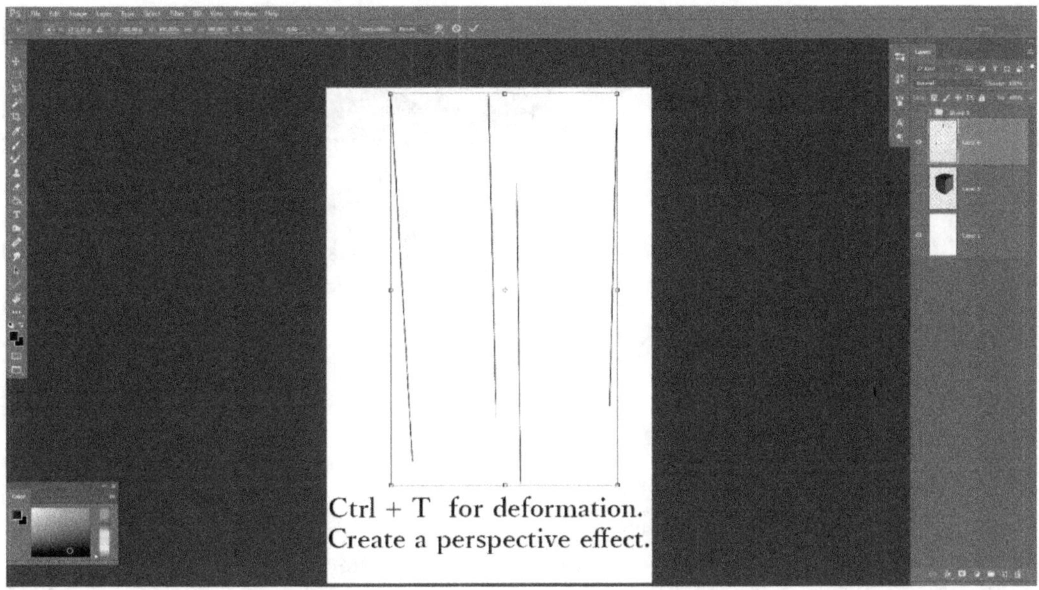

12. Using the same way, draw the horizontal edges of the cube.

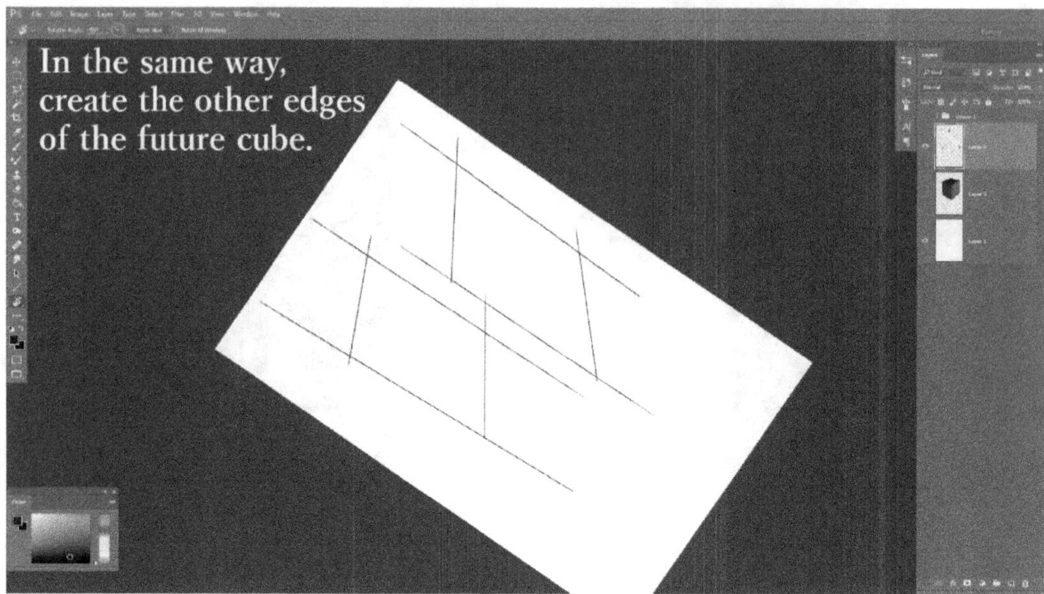

13. If needed, press the R Key to rotate the canvas and make the drawing the shape more comfortable.

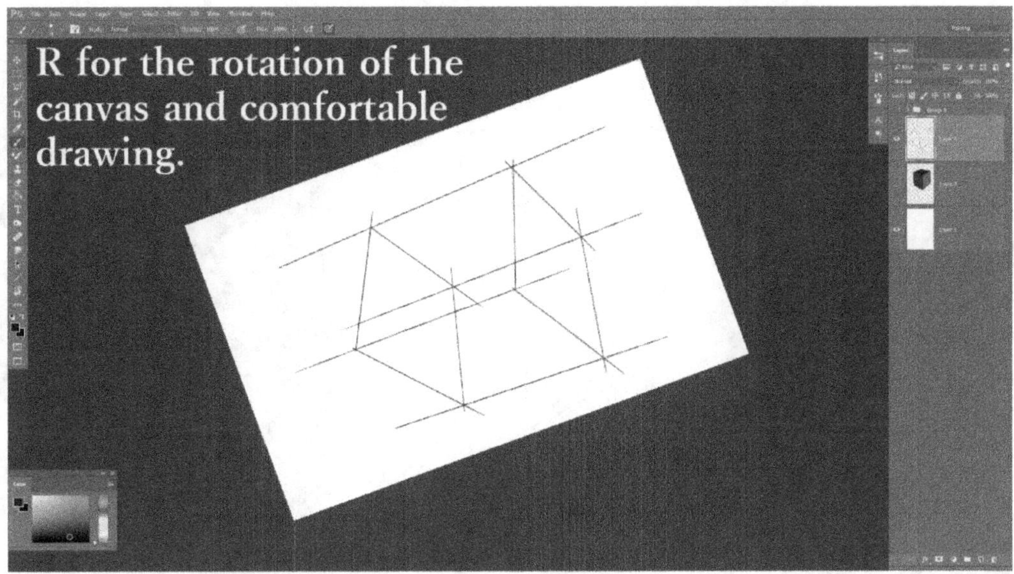

14. Choose the Eraser Tool and remove any extra or excess lines on the shape.

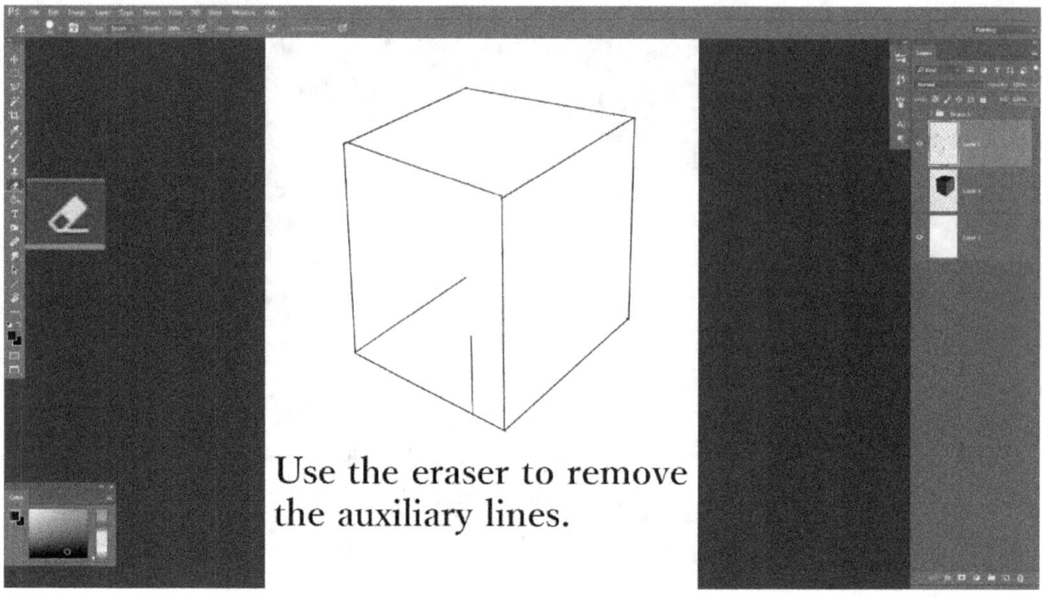

15. To color the shape in, click on an empty face of the cube while the Magic
Wand Tool is selected. This will mark an area that you can fill with color.
Use the Paint Bucket Tool to paint the area with the desired color.

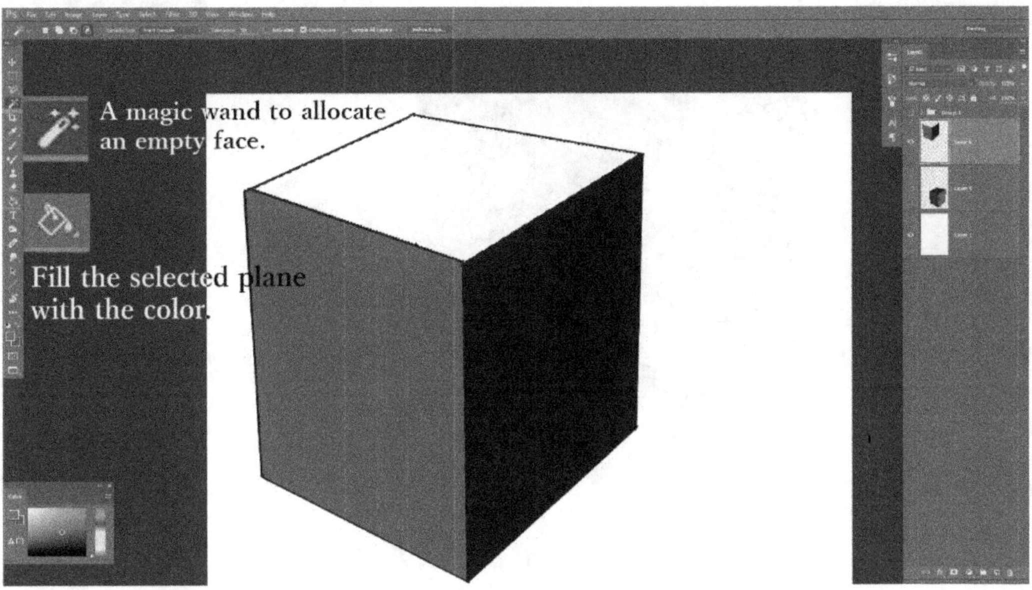

16. The whole cube filled with color.

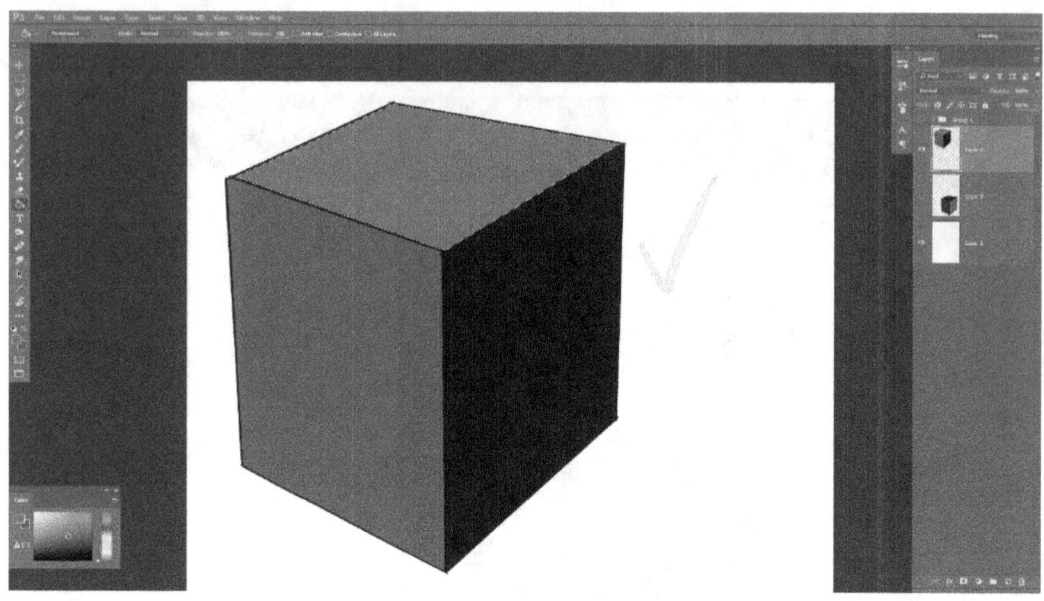

17. The two different methods of drawing the cube are.

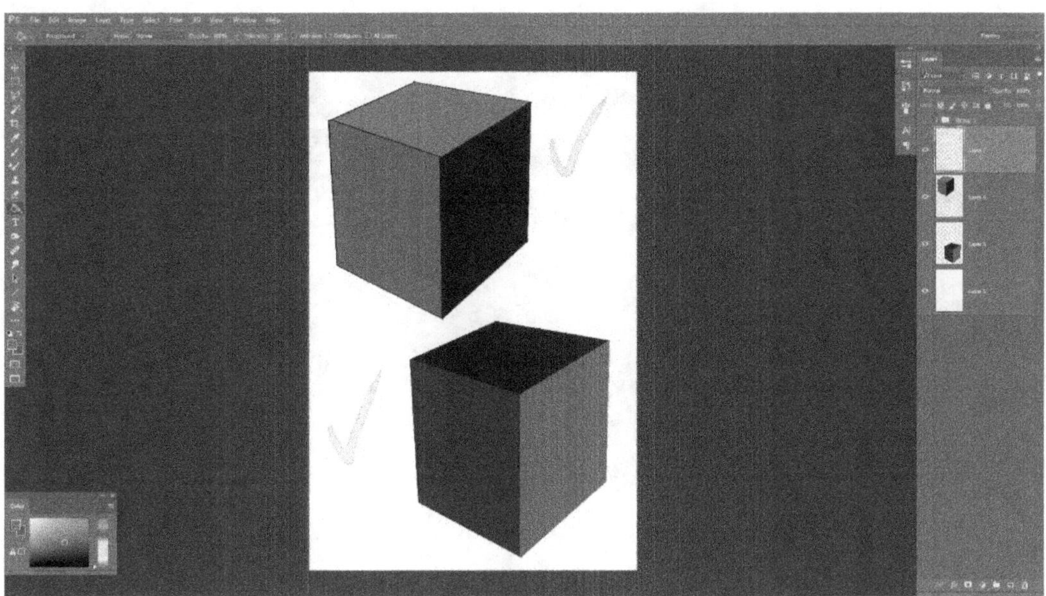

18. Press Ctrl+L and adjust the middle level to 1.99.

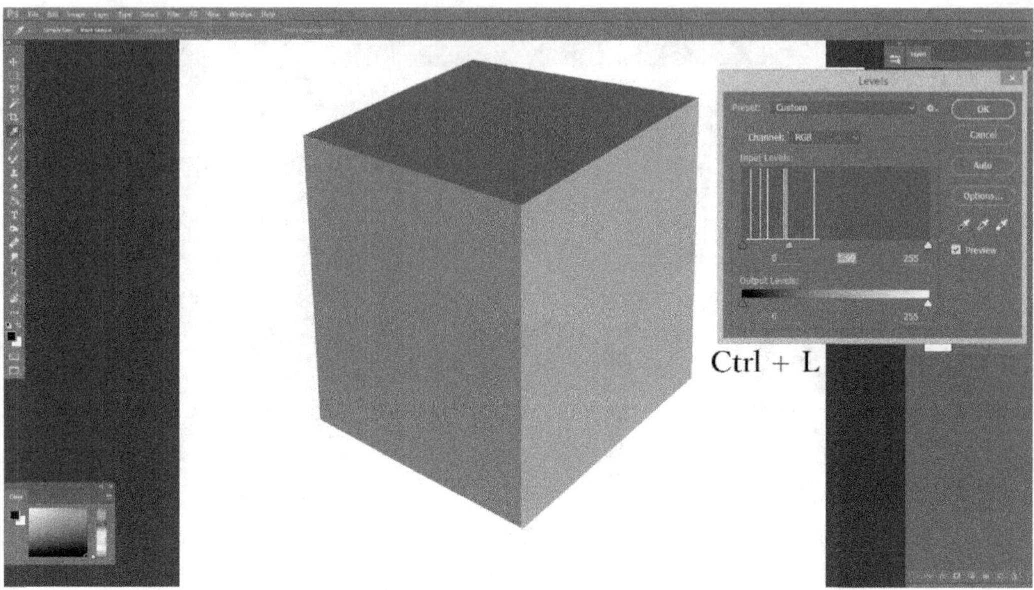

19. Make another layer for the sketch. Draw details for the cube using the skill to draw things that are similar in shape.

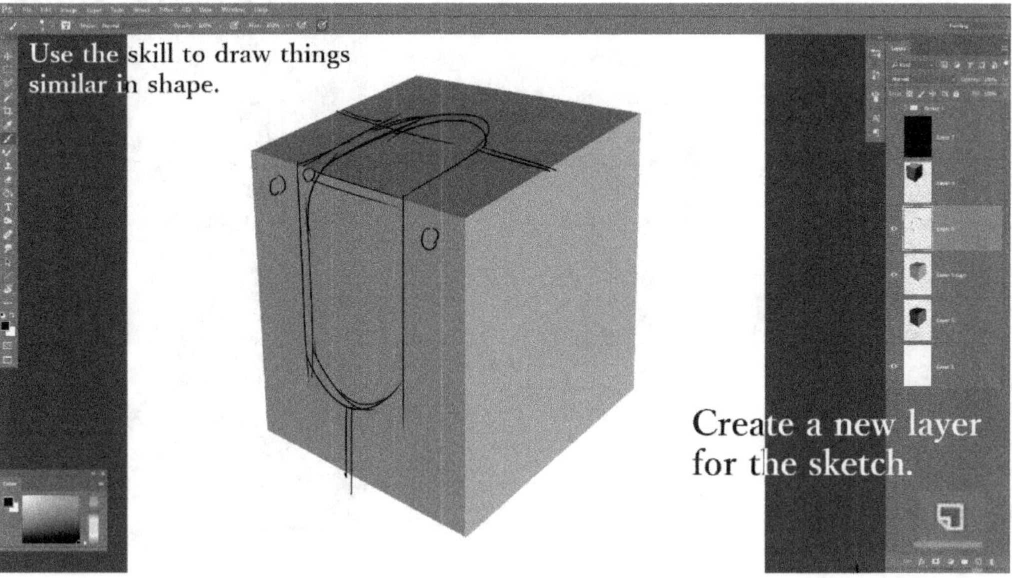

20. Draw more details to the piece.

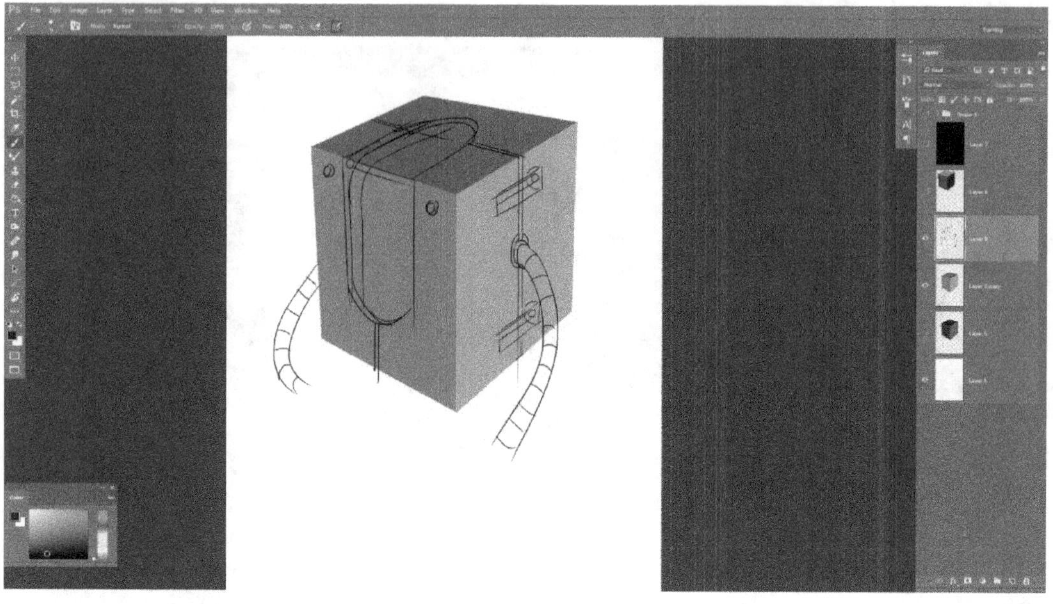

21. Select the Brush Tool and paint the color of one face to a part that is carved out. To apply the same color to this area hold the Alt Key and click on the desired color to copy it. Paint this over the defined area.

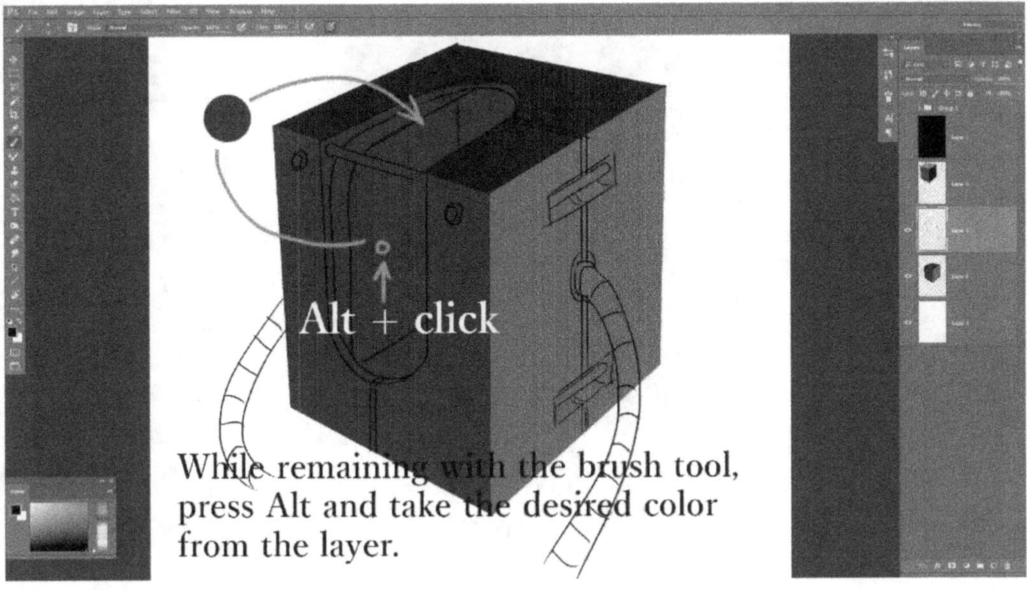

22. With the Polygonal Lasso Tool, mark a selection around the specific area.

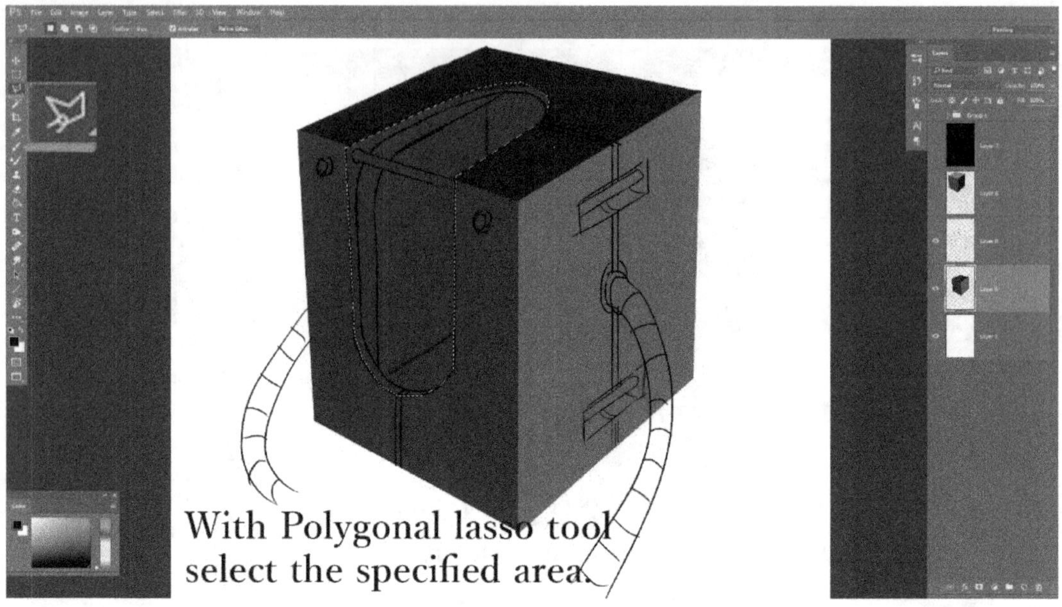

23. Change the area's color by adjusting its Hue. You can do this by pressing Ctrl+U and changing the Hue levels to +180.

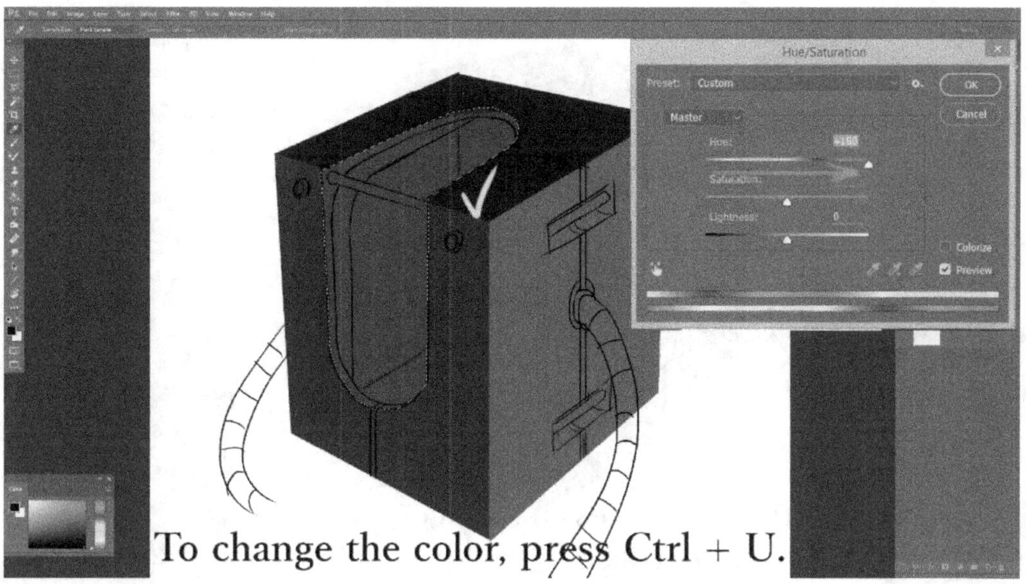

24. Select the Dodge Tool. Change the parameters to Midtones Range and 100% Exposure. Highlight the areas that are lighted by a light source.

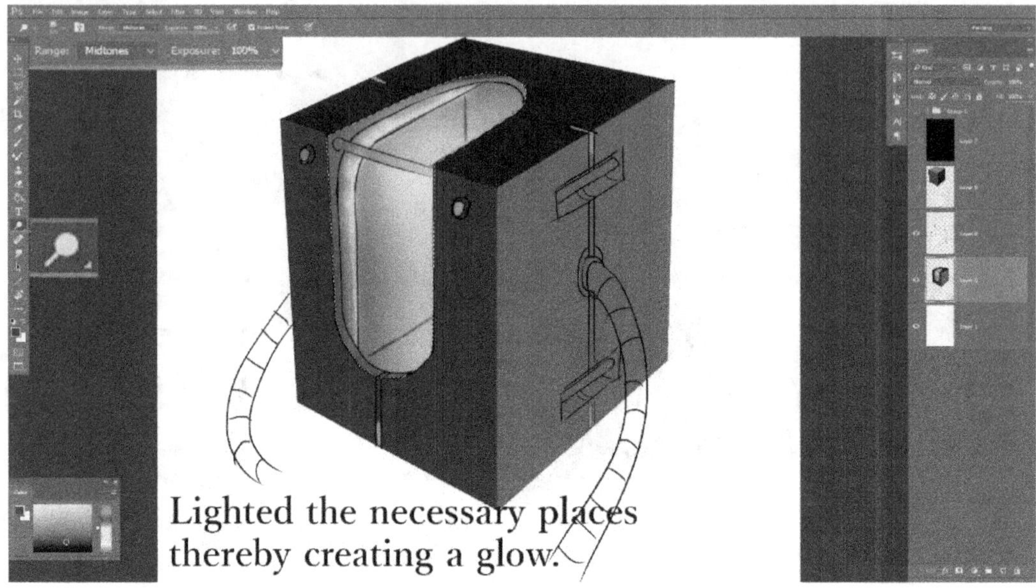

Lighted the necessary places thereby creating a glow.

25. Using the Smudge and Burn Tools, draw scratches on the cube's surface. Do this by making a line from one area to another with the Smudge Tool. With the Dodge Tool, draw the highlights on the scratch. Make another Smudge to make the reflex of the scratch.

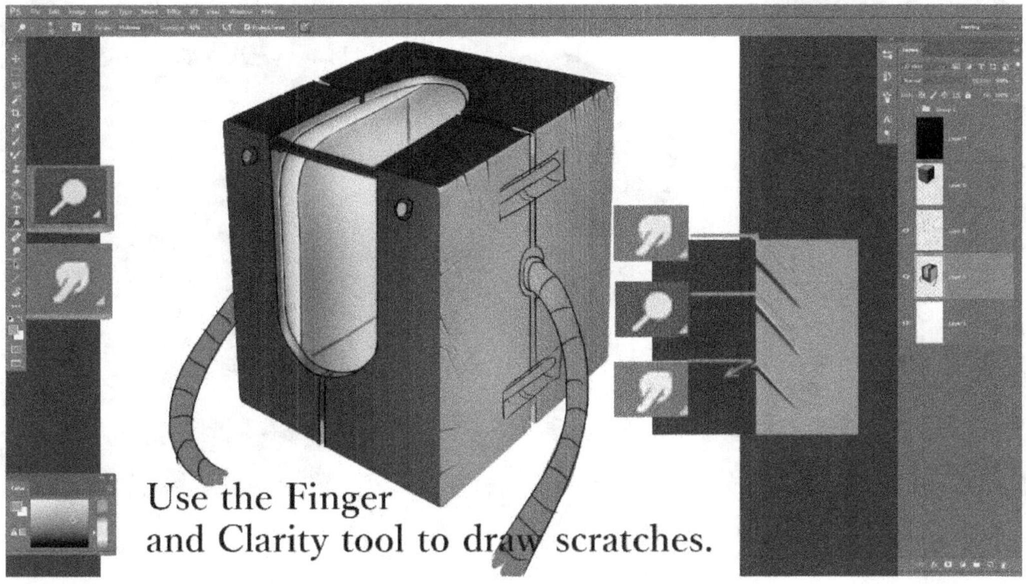

26. Draw the highlights and shadows of recessed areas on the cube. These areas use the same method for drawing cylindrical shapes.

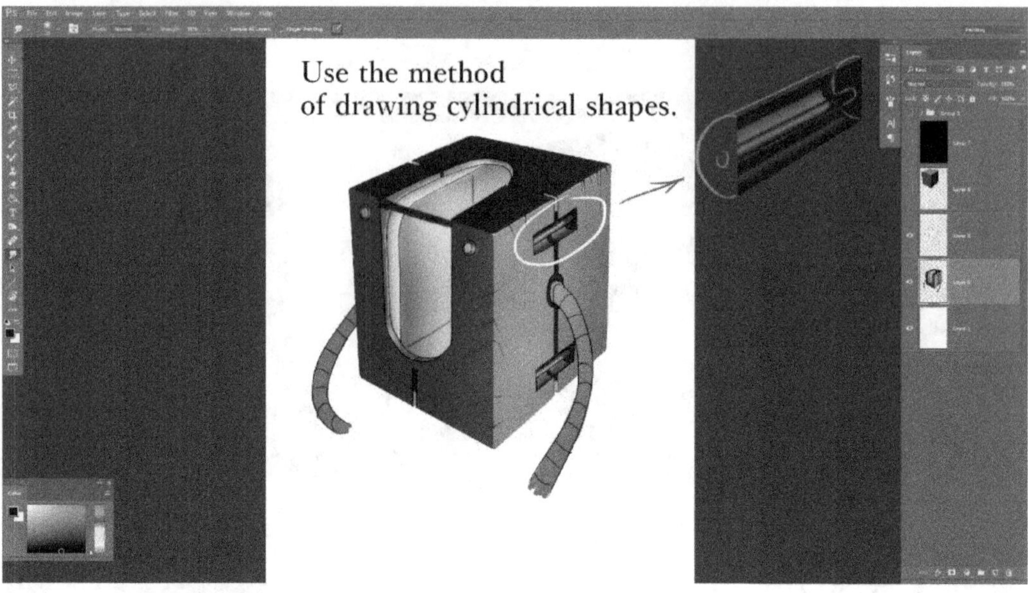

27. Add glow elements to the cube.

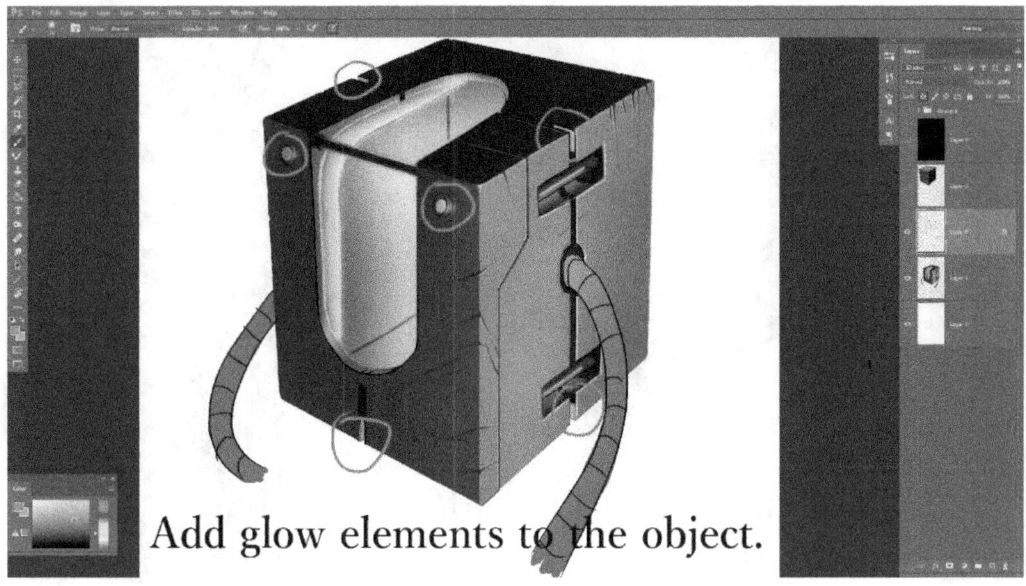

28. Draw the shadows of the pipes by using the Burn Tool.

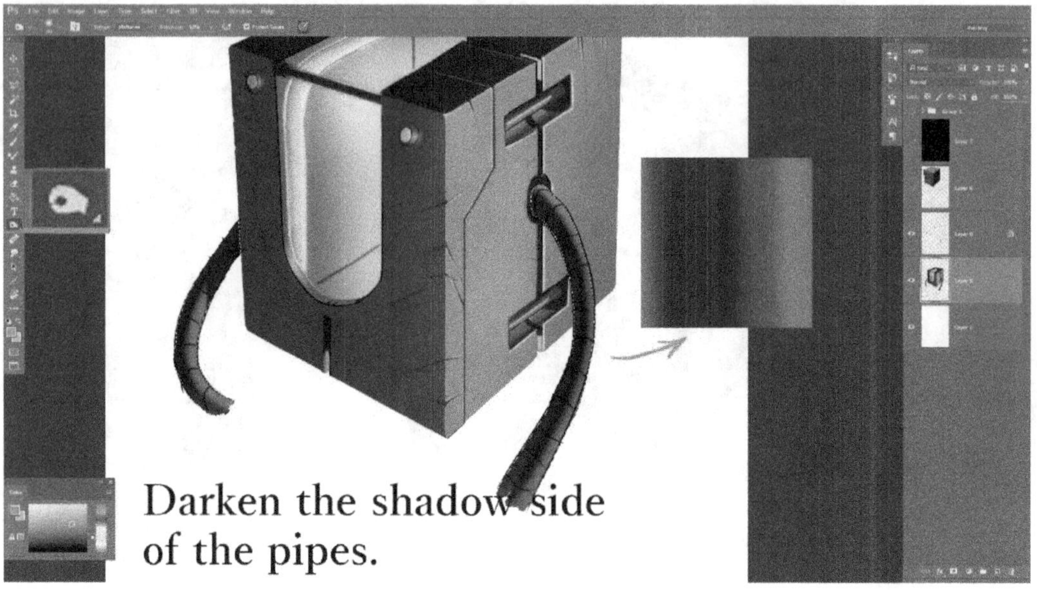

29. With the Dodge Tool, highlight the illuminated areas of the pipe.

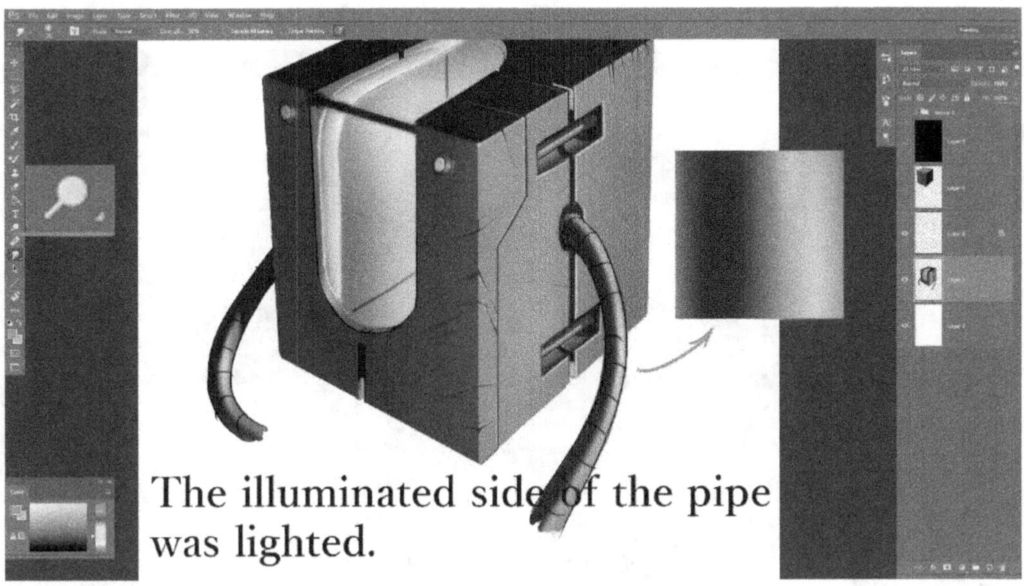

30. Using the Smudge Tool, make the pipe appear corrugated by smudging perpendicular to the pipe's shape. Make a new layer and draw a sketch.

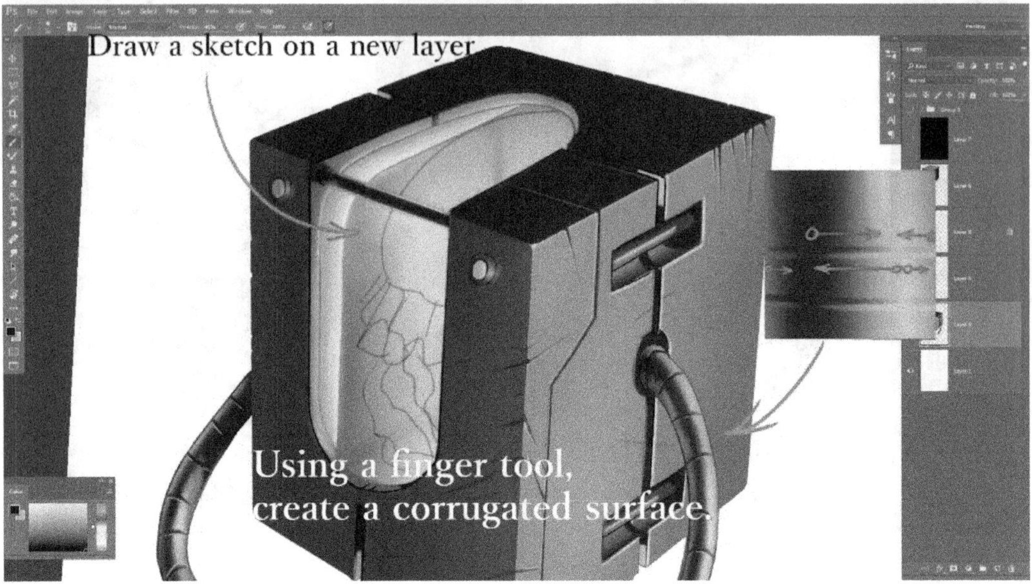

31. Color in the sketch. Draw lightning and electric sparks to it as well.

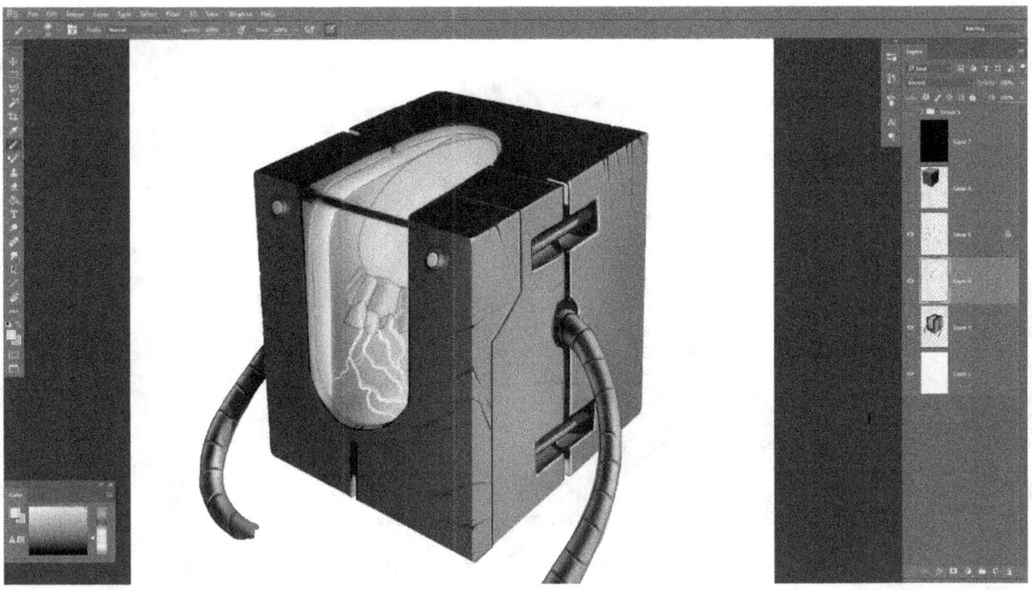

32. With bright tones, draw a glow on the inside of the recessed area.

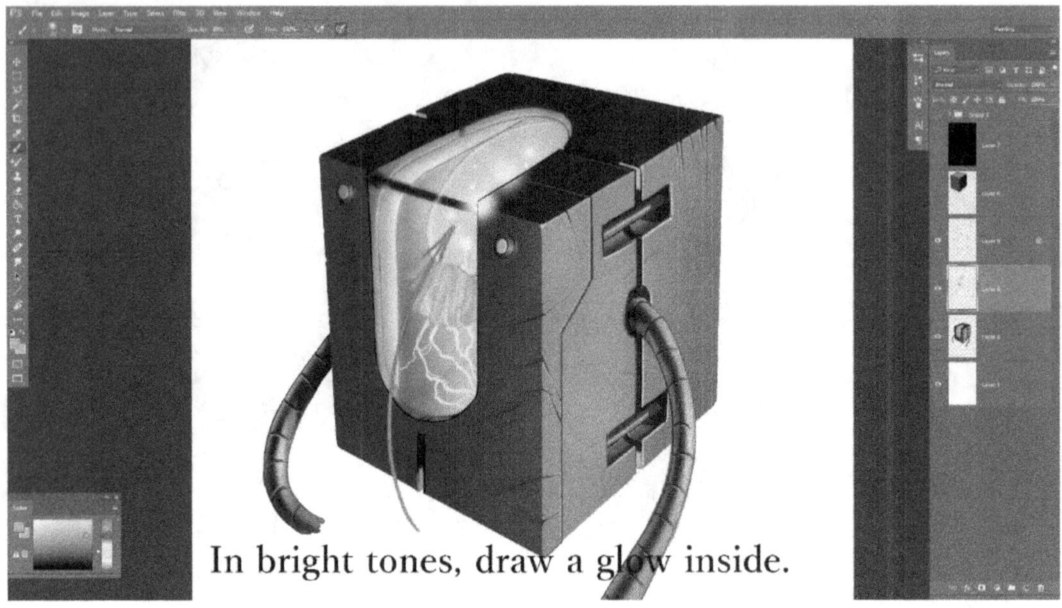

In bright tones, draw a glow inside.

33. Draw the reflex of the colors and erase any excess parts of the layer.

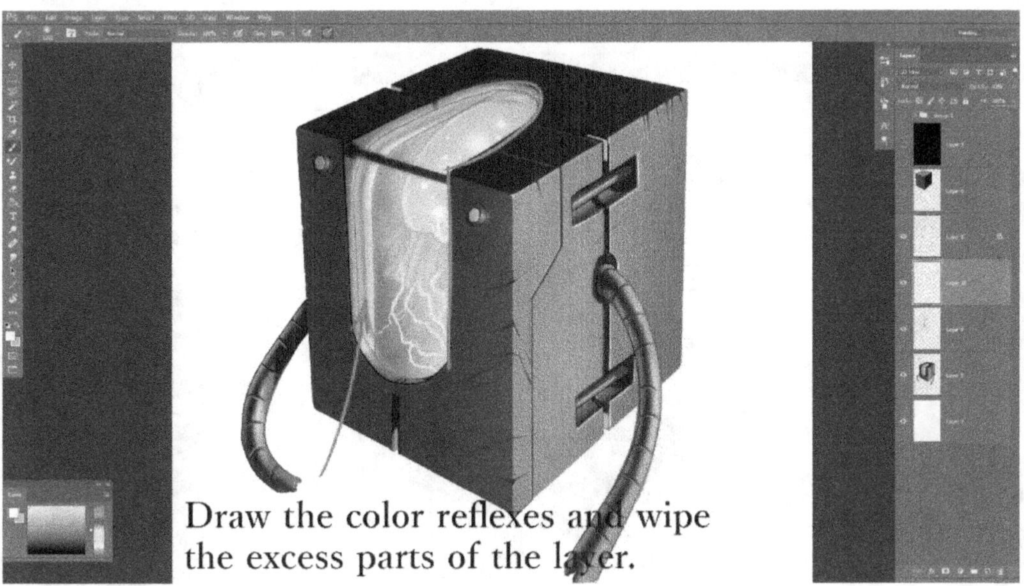

34. Draw a light on the layer using the Brush Tool. Use a very low Opacity value to achieve this effect. Wipe off any excess areas using the Eraser Tool.

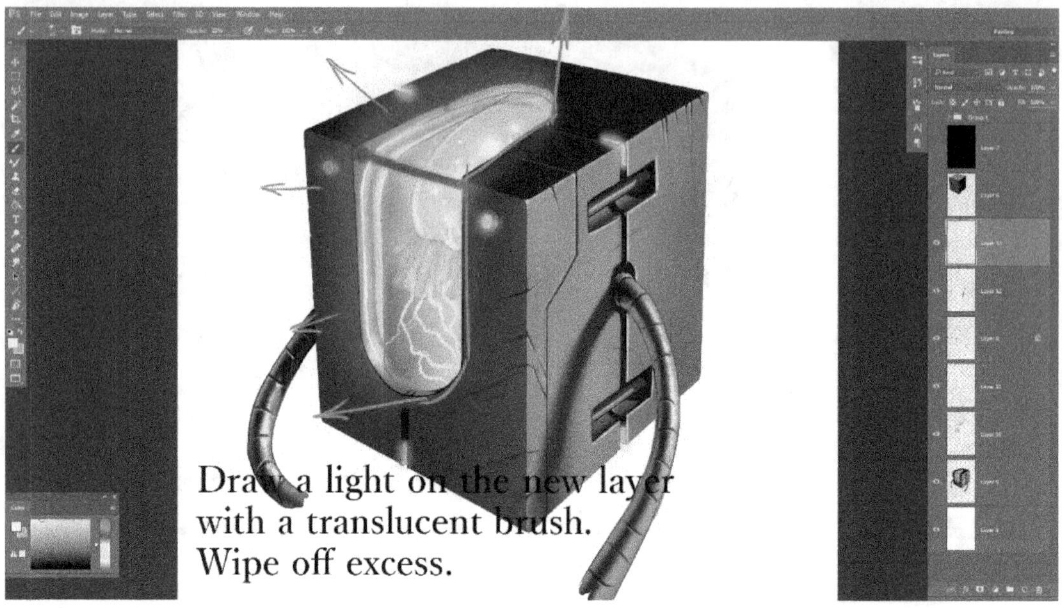

Pyramid

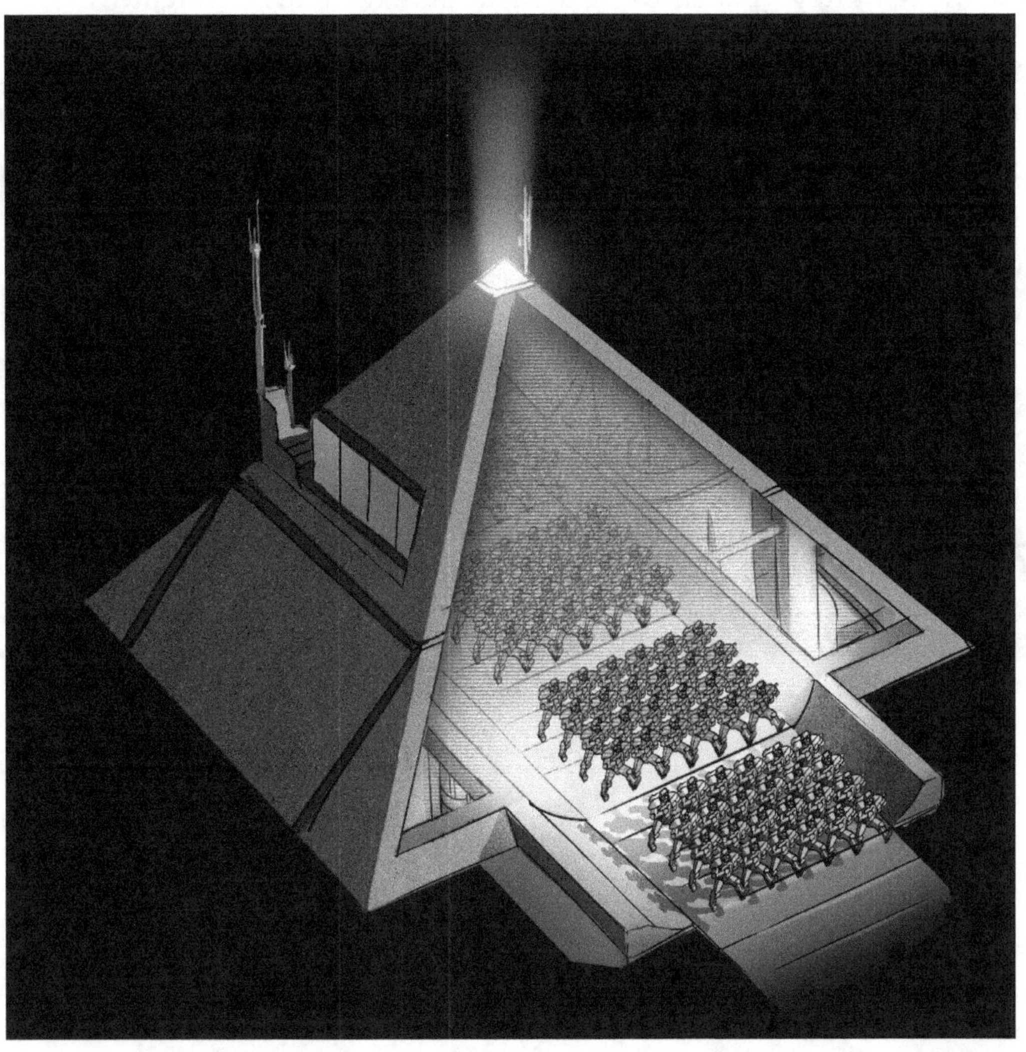

1. Make a new layer. With the Brush Tool, draw a straight line at an angle. Hold the Shift Key while drawing to make sure the line is straight.

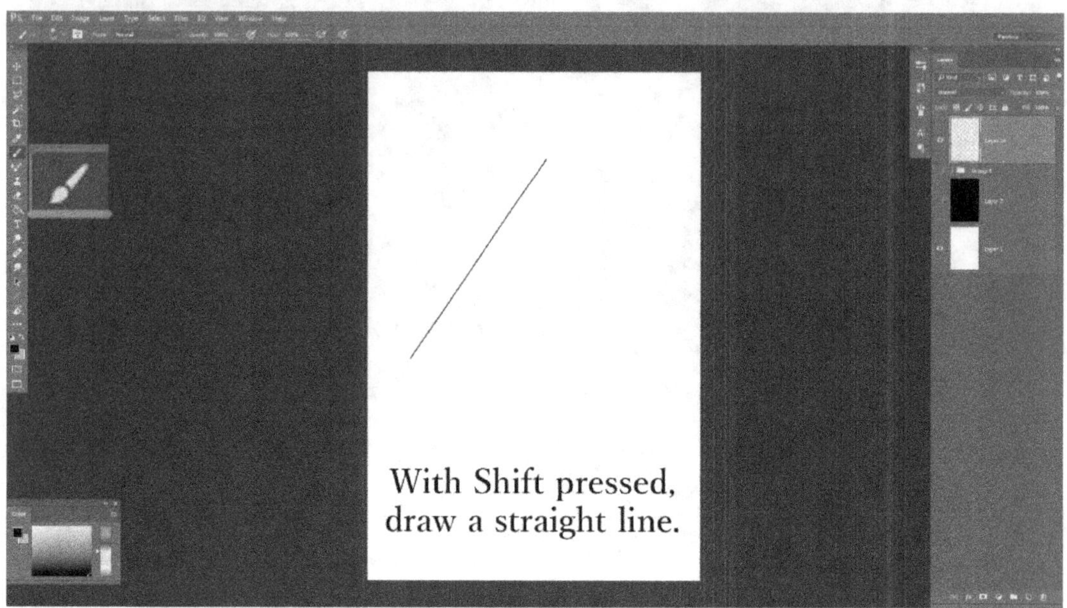

2. Draw two more lines at different angles in the same manner to create a pyramid shape.

3. Draw the edges of the pyramid's base using the same method.

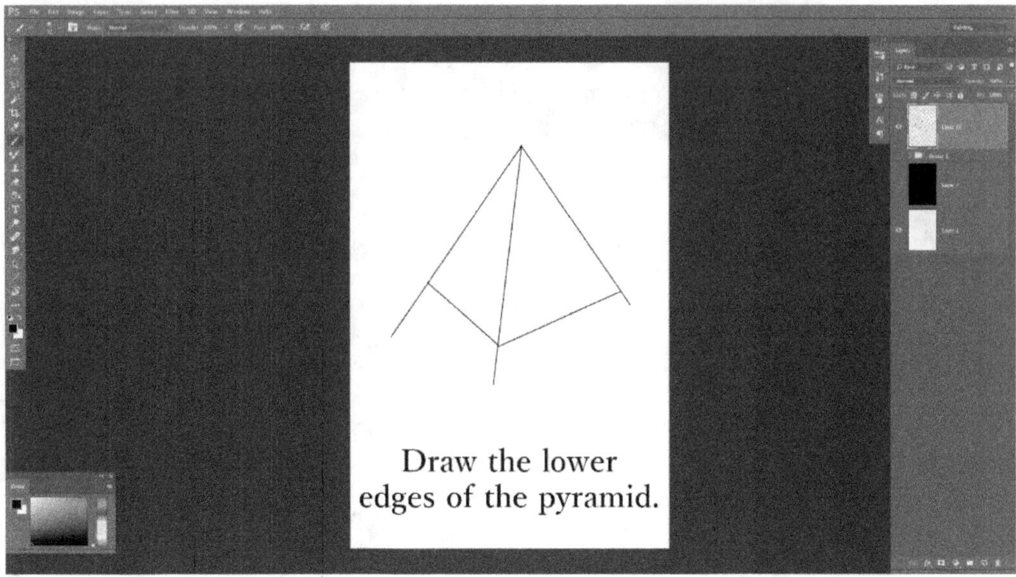

4. Remove any excess lines using the Eraser Tool. Press Ctrl+T and adjust the size of the pyramid. Make it taller and larger.

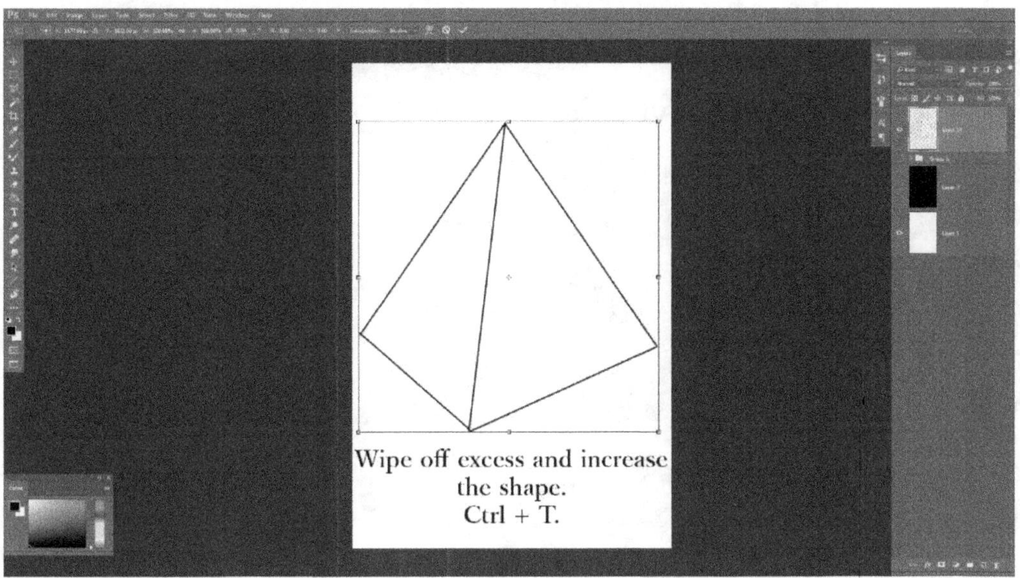

5. Make another layer below the drawing of the pyramid. Color the areas with a light and dark color corresponding to the light and dark areas of the pyramid.

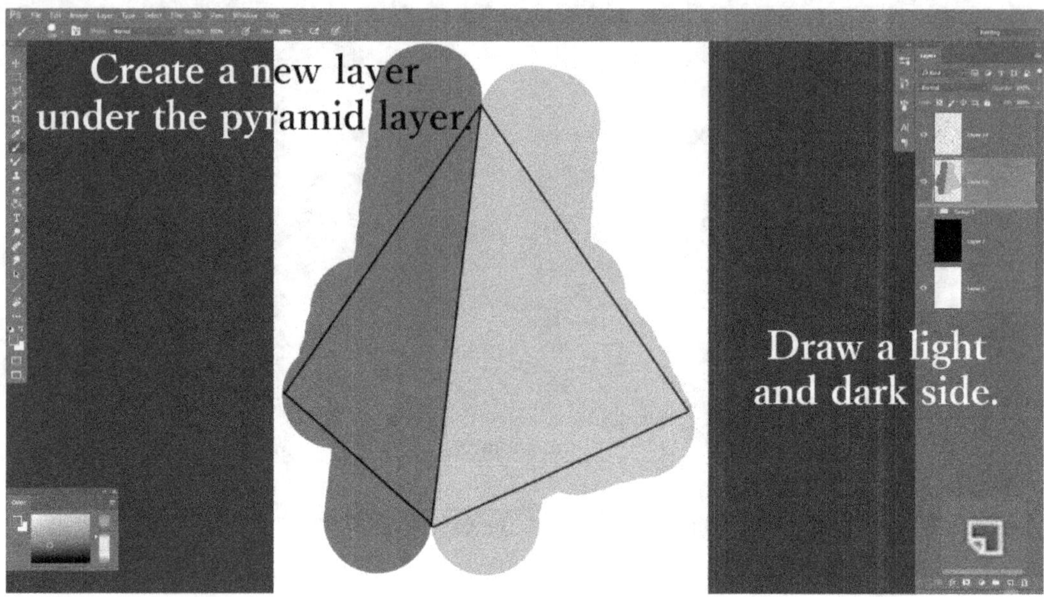

6. Using the Eraser Tool, remove any excess areas of color.

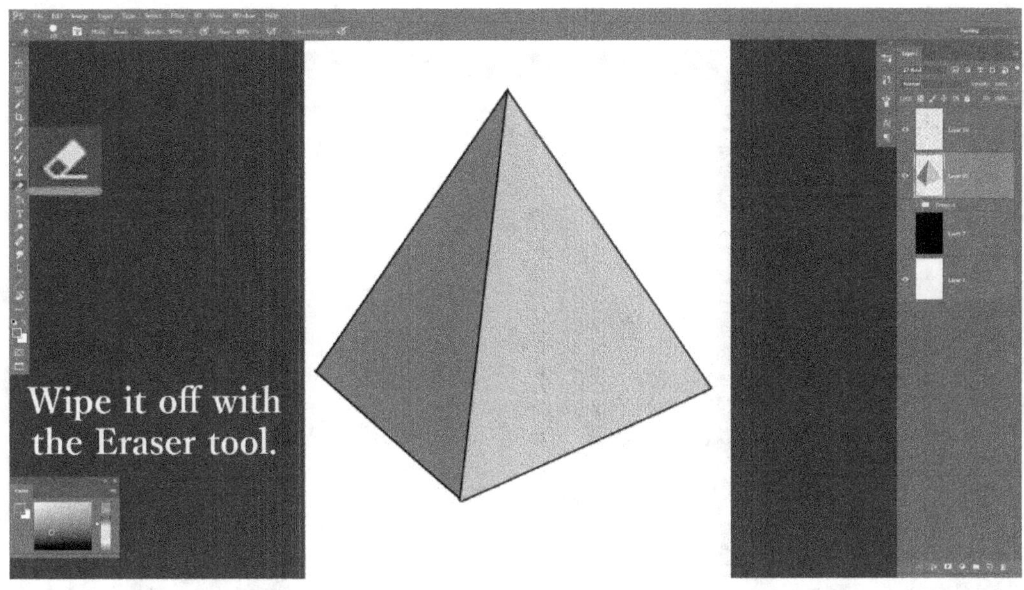

7. Lock the layer of the drawing. Paint over the lines of the sketch with a color the same as the area next to it.

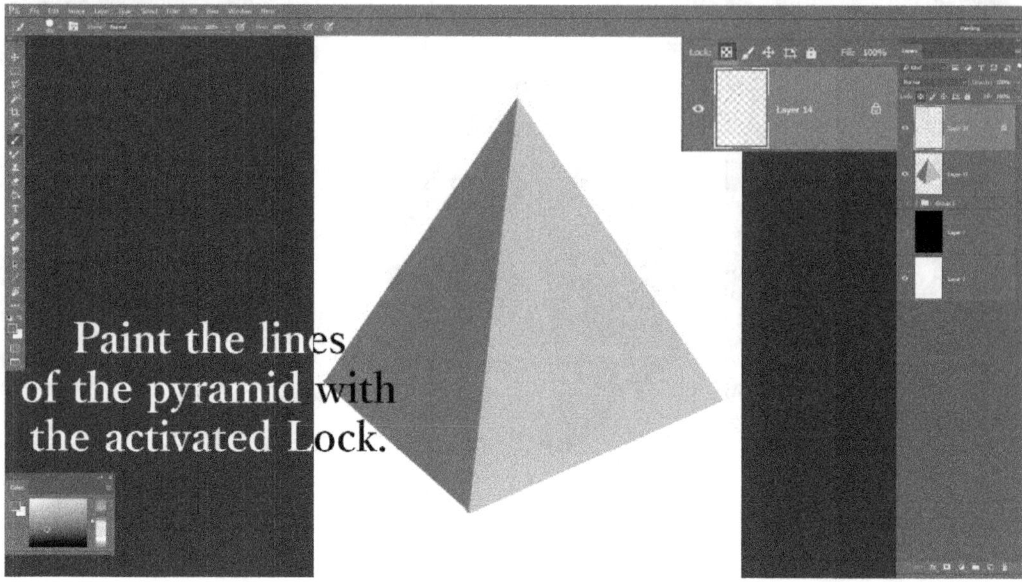

8. Press the C Key to reduce the canvas size.

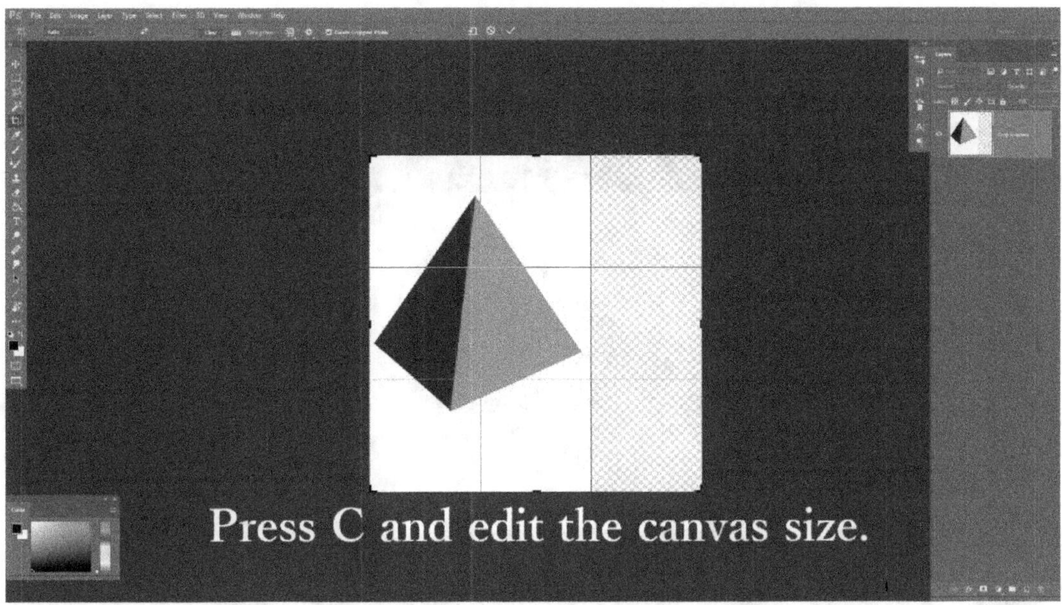

9. Press Ctrl+T and deform the pyramid. Adjust the size of its base while holding down the Crtl, Shift, and Alt Keys.

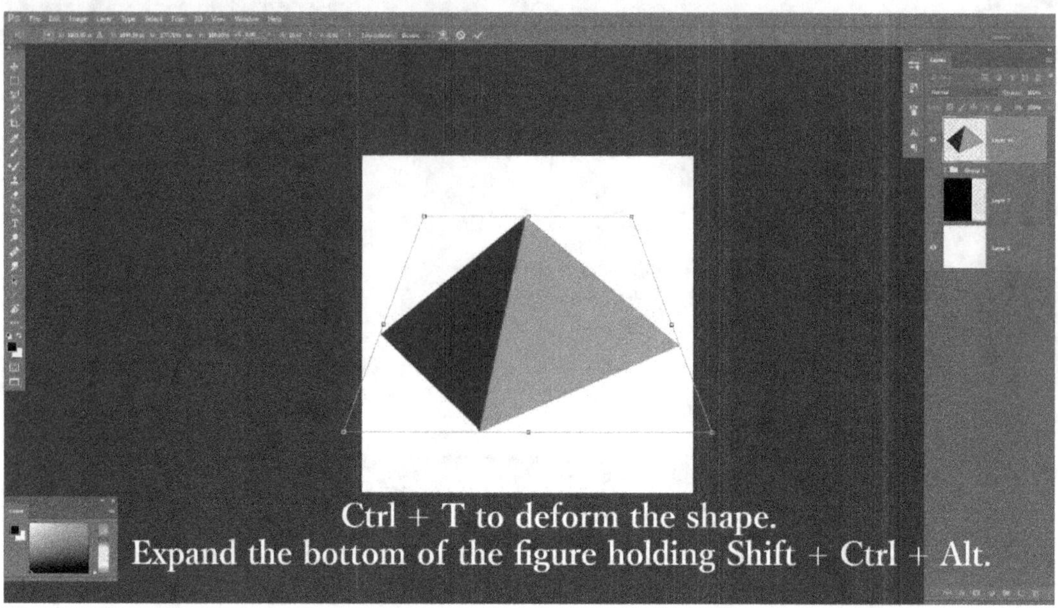

10. Make another layer for the sketch. Draw details and shapes for the pyramid. Make sure to use similar shapes. Draw in other details and adjust the shape of the pyramid using a combination of different tools.

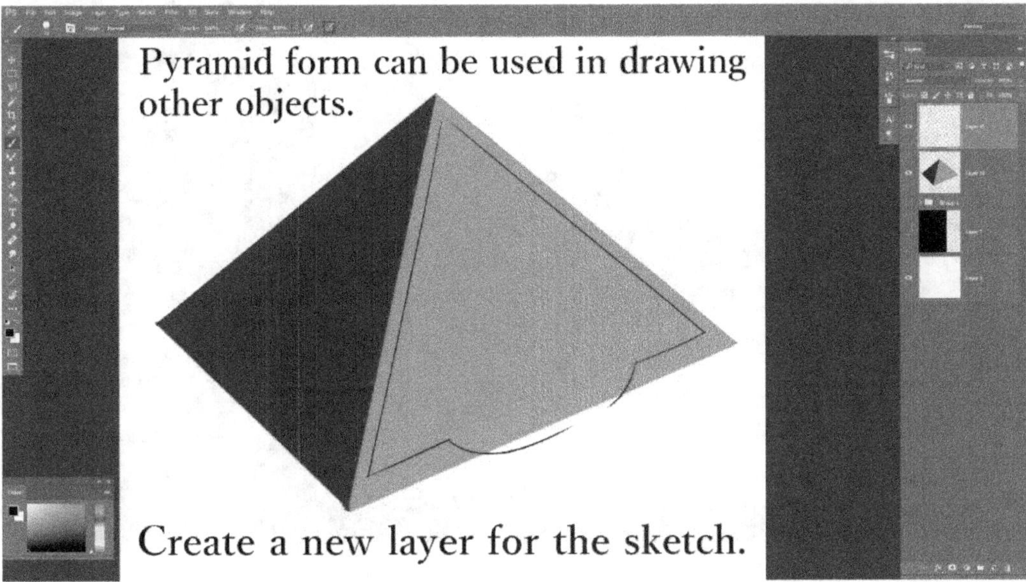

11. Mark the shadows and penumbrae of the details with the appropriate colors.

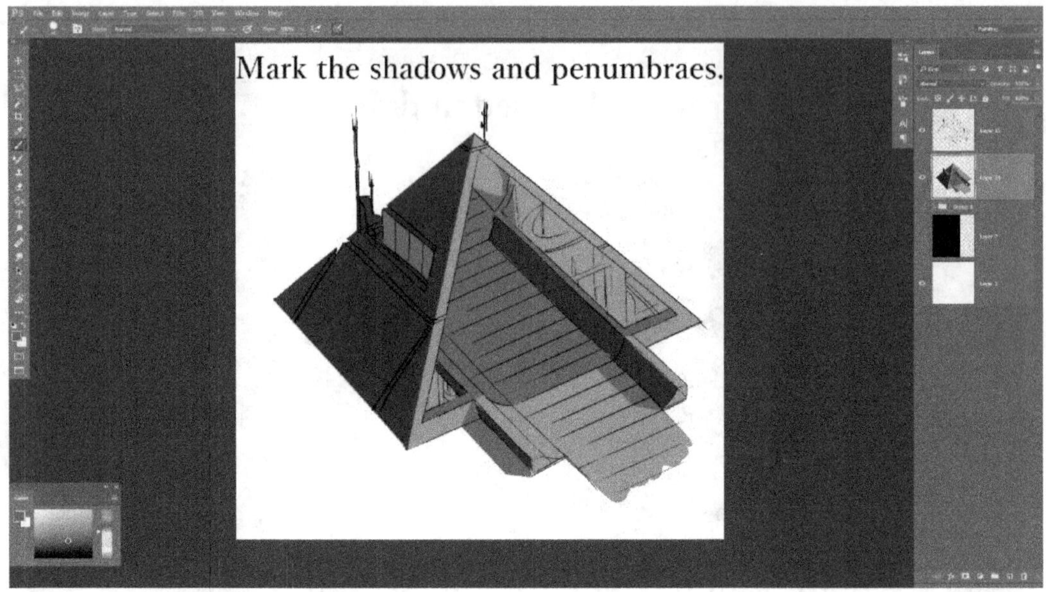

12. Make another layer. On this layer draw a sketch of a figure. You can choose what level of details you want to add to this sketch.

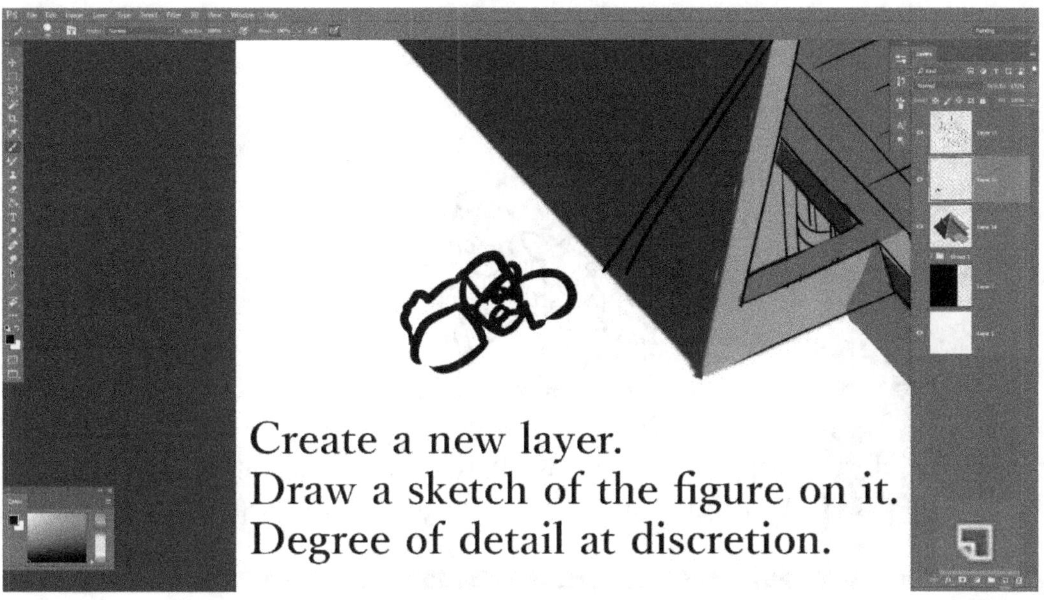

13. When the sketch of the figure is finished, copy the layer and arrange the figures. Merge all the layers together.

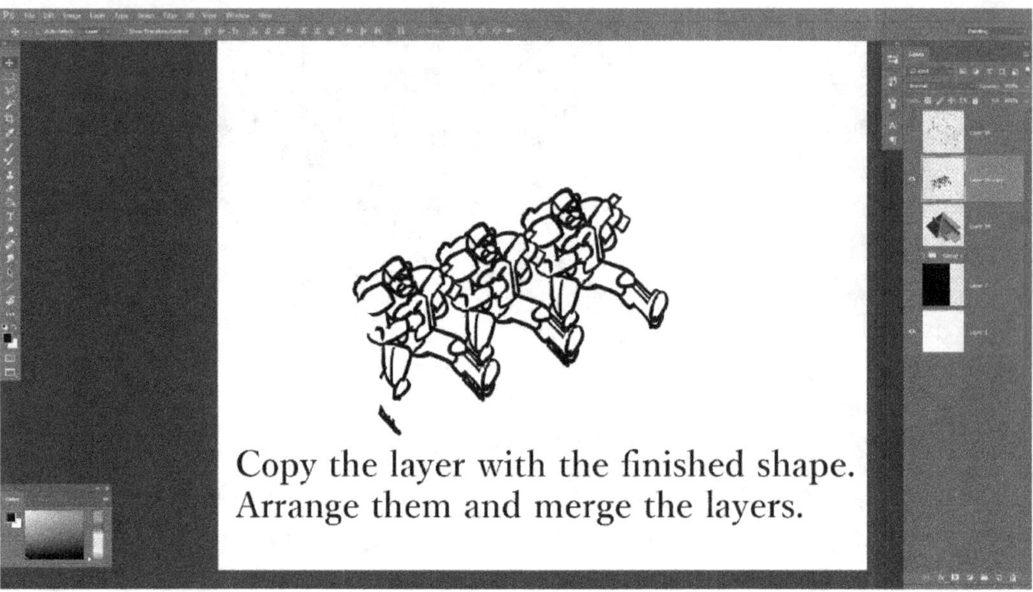

14. Make another layer and paint its lights and shadows. Copy the layer and dock it with the layer of the sketch.

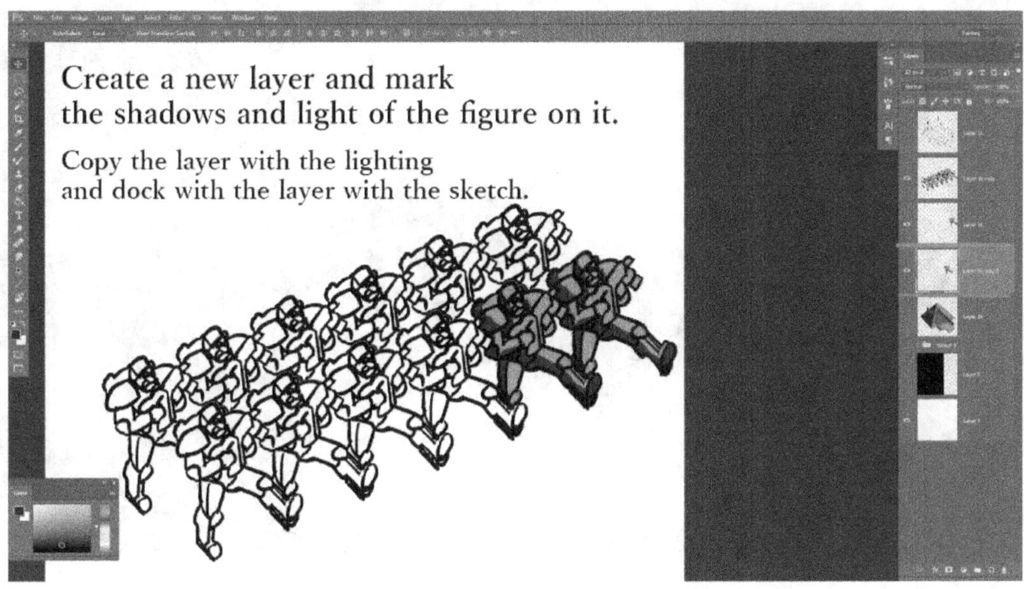

15. Apply the same method until all the figures are colored.

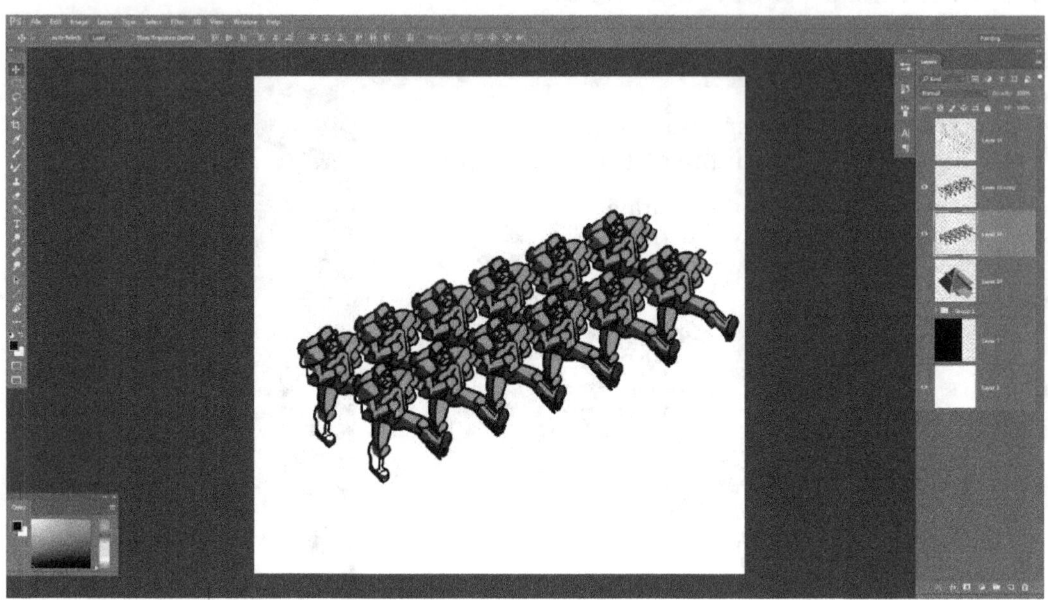

16. Copy and merge the layers until the desired number of figures is achieved.

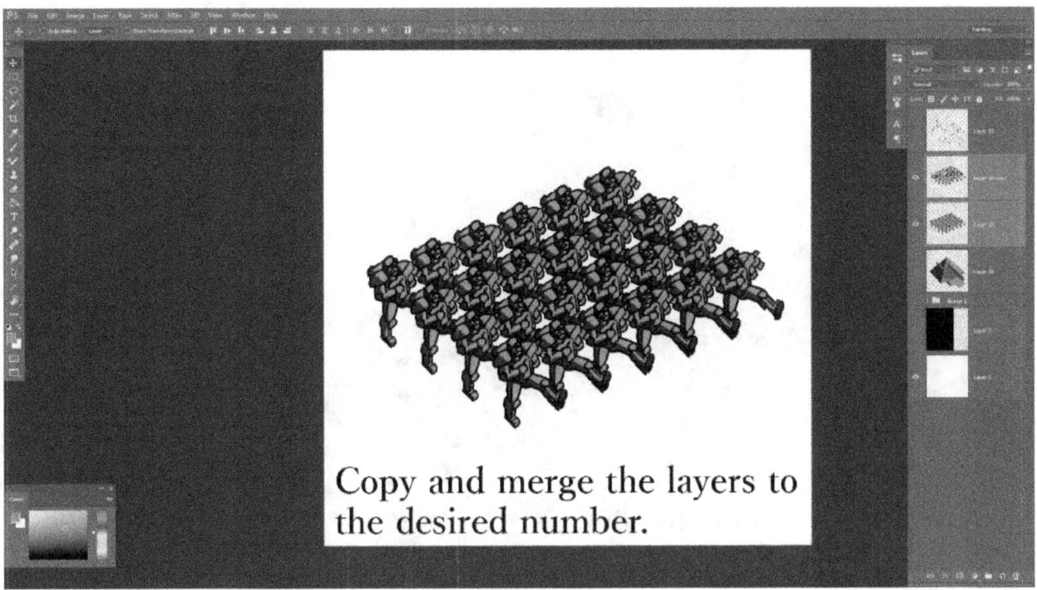

17. Copy the figures again and arrange them according to the layout of the pyramid. Merge all the layers of the figures together.

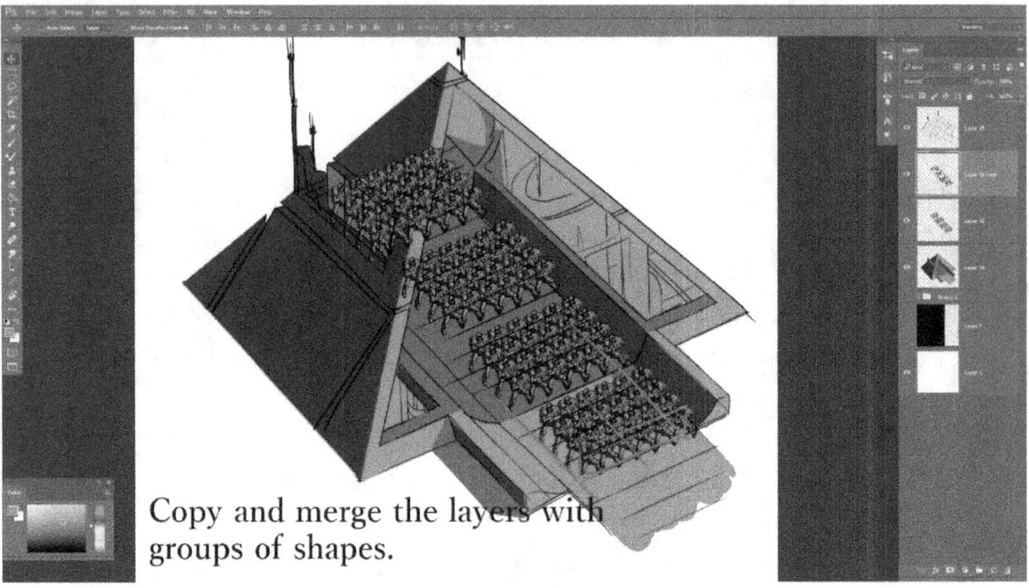

Copy and merge the layers with groups of shapes.

18. Use the Eraser Tool to remove any excess figures.

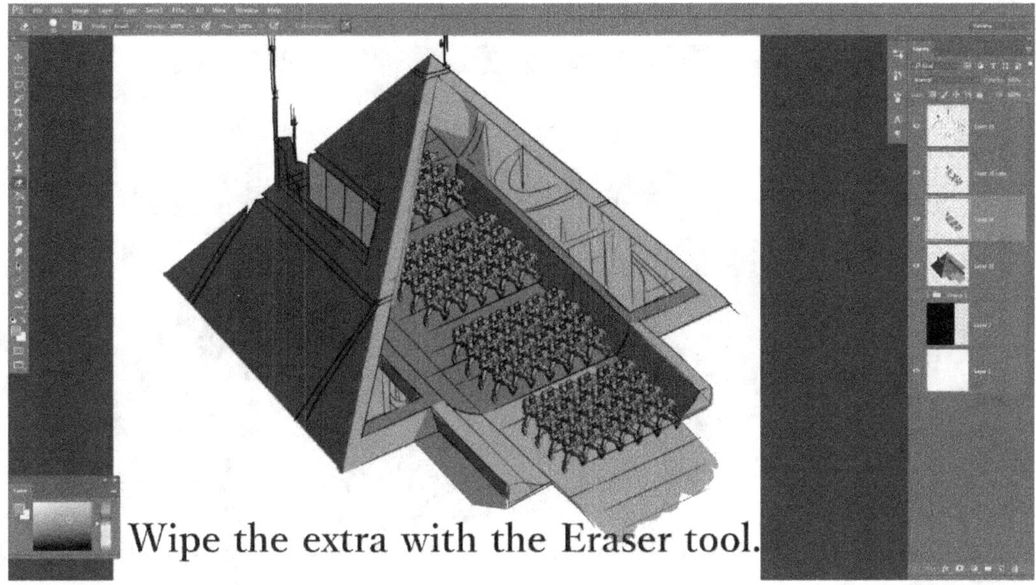

19. With the Brush Tool, Paint is over the areas that are in the shade to create a shadow effect. Draw the shadows of the figures not shaded as well.

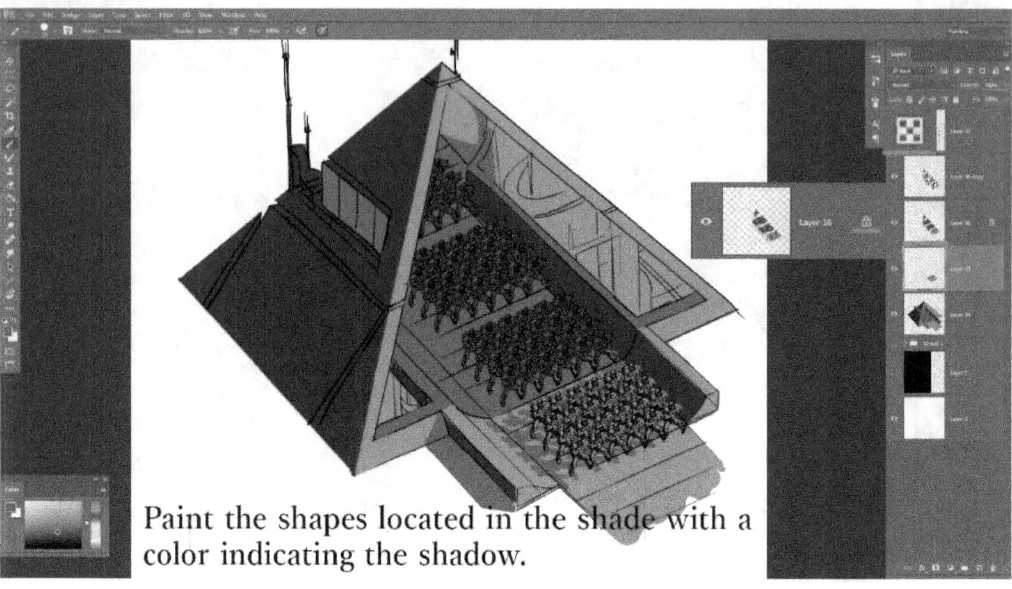

Paint the shapes located in the shade with a color indicating the shadow.

20. Select the layer of the pyramid. Using the Polygonal Selection Tool, mark is out an area as shown.

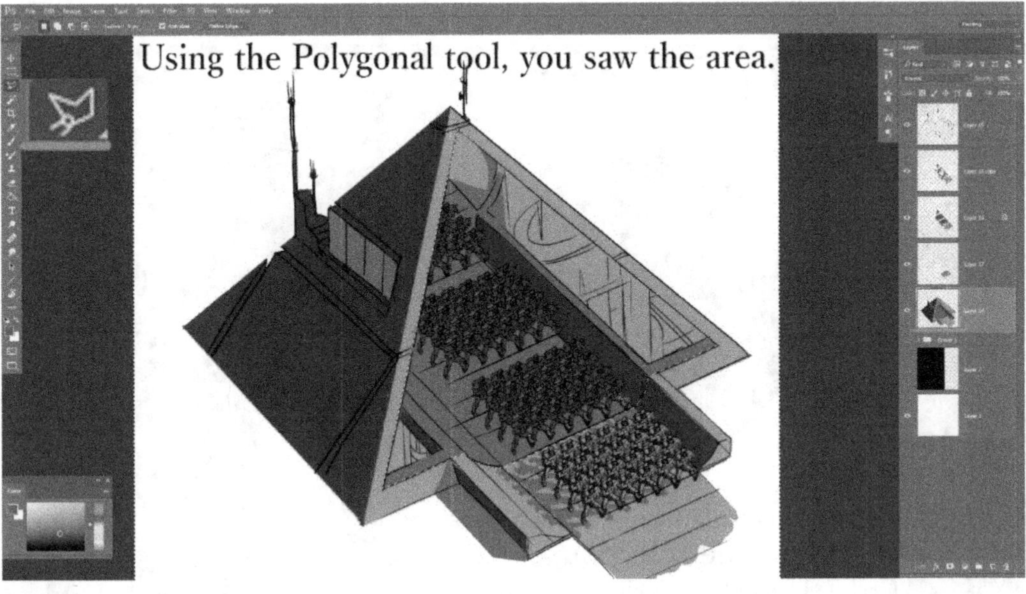

21. Press Ctrl+Shift+I to select the inverse. Press Ctrl+U to pull up the Hue/Saturation Window. Change the Hue and Saturation of the selected area to change its color.

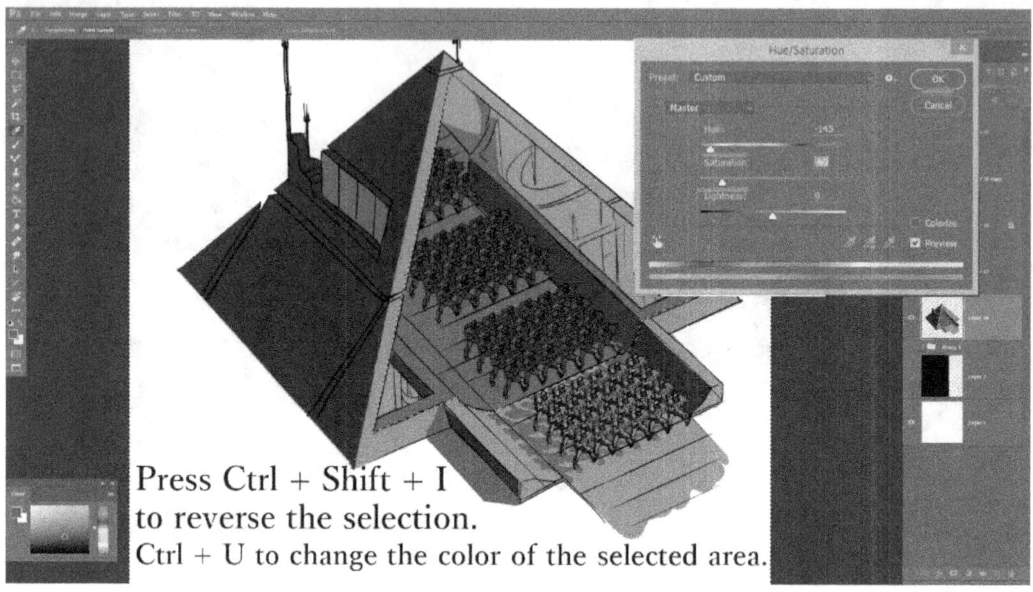

22. Press Ctrl+L to pull up the Levels Window. Change the lower level to 19.

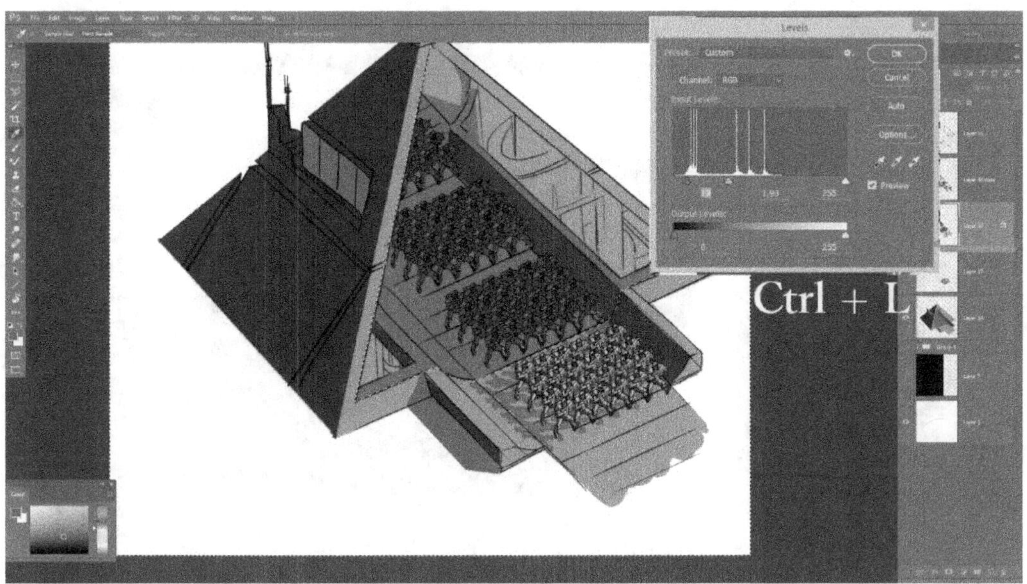

23. Press Ctrl+Shift+I to invert the selection. Make a new layer and fill it with black. Select Filter and choose "Filter Gallery…" from the menu.

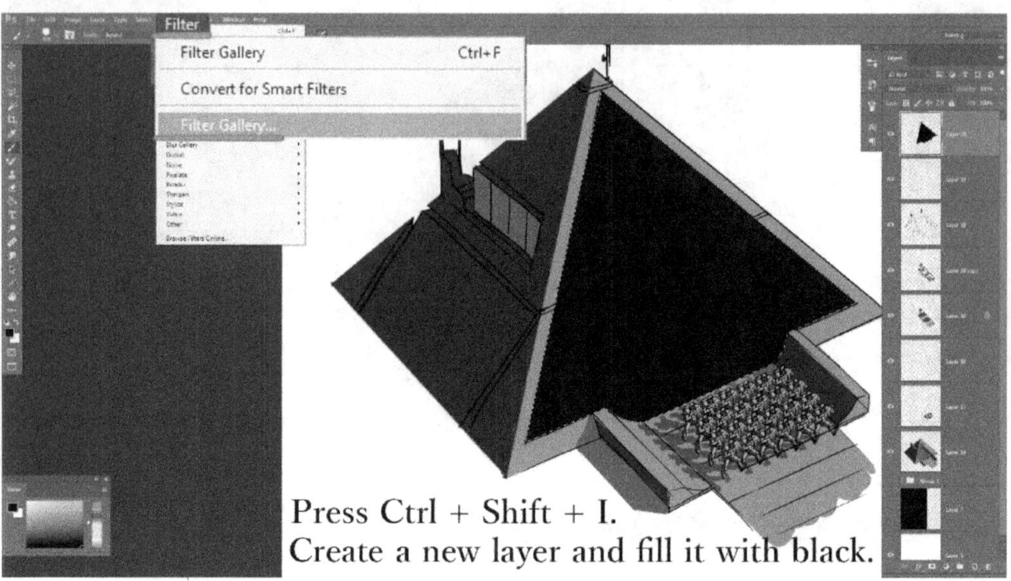

24. This will open the Filter Gallery on a separate window. From the sidebar, under the "Artistic" folder, chose "Film Grain" and click "OK".

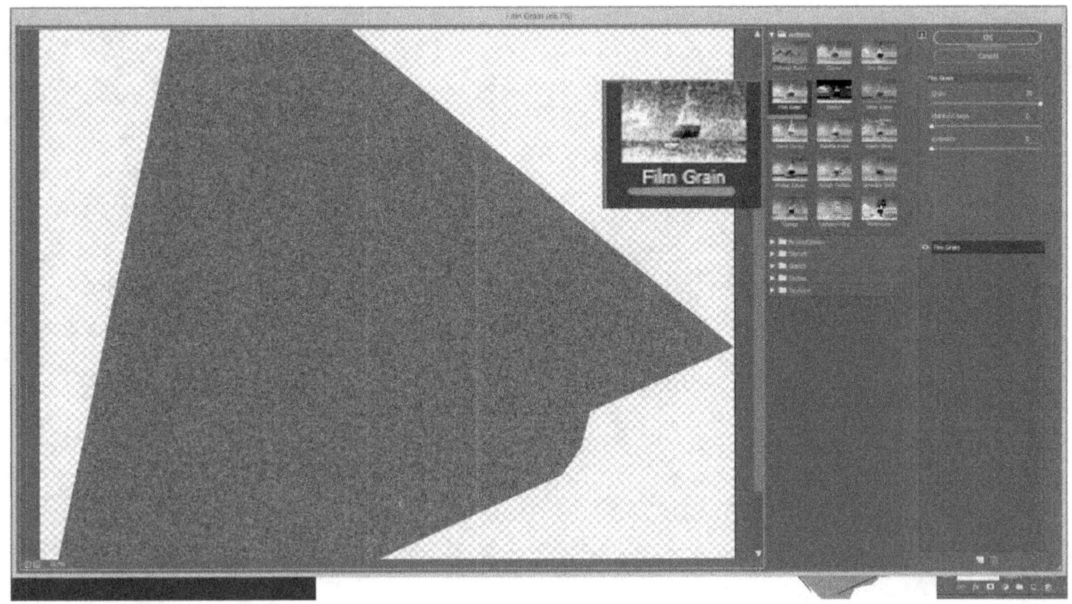

25. On the same window, from the "Sketch" folder, select "Halftone Pattern". Change the size to 3 and click "OK".

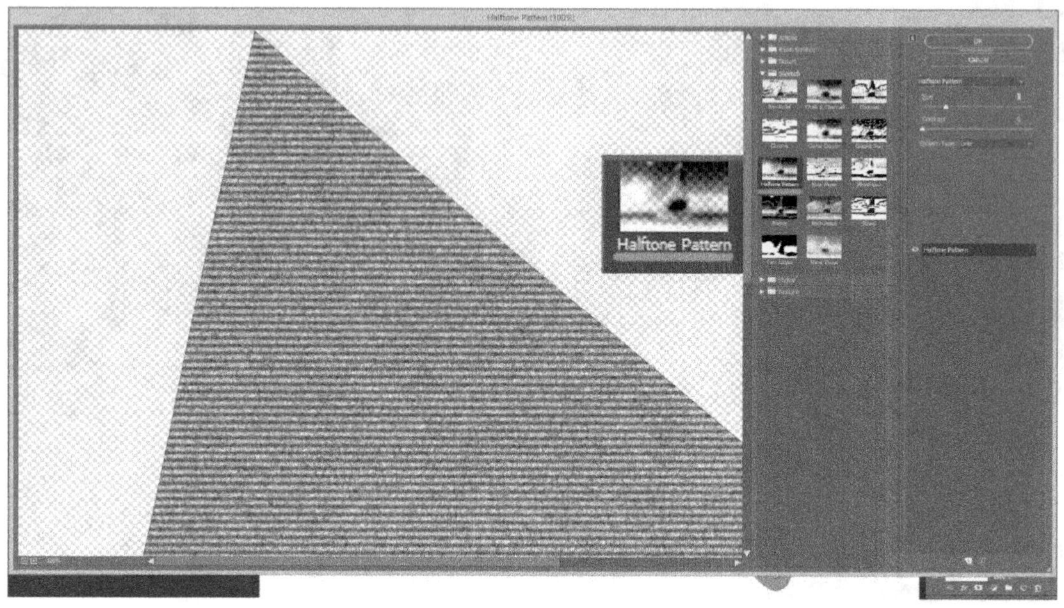

26. Add the Divide modifier to the selected layer. To do this, click on the Layer Modifier menu located on the top of the layer sidebar. Choose "Divide" from the drop-down menu.

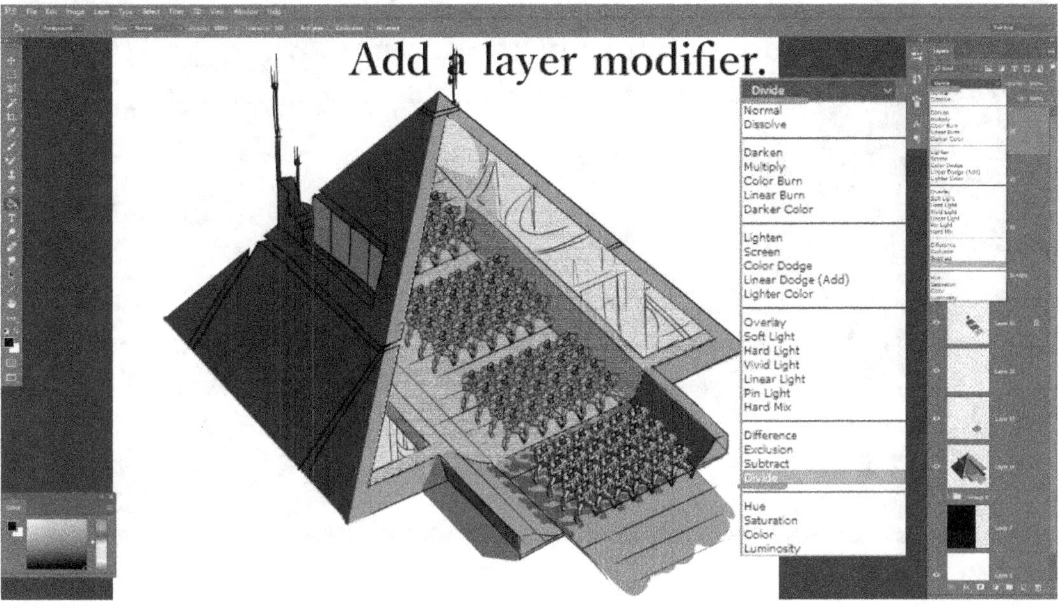

27. Download an image of a texture and add it to the program. Make sure to do this on a new layer.

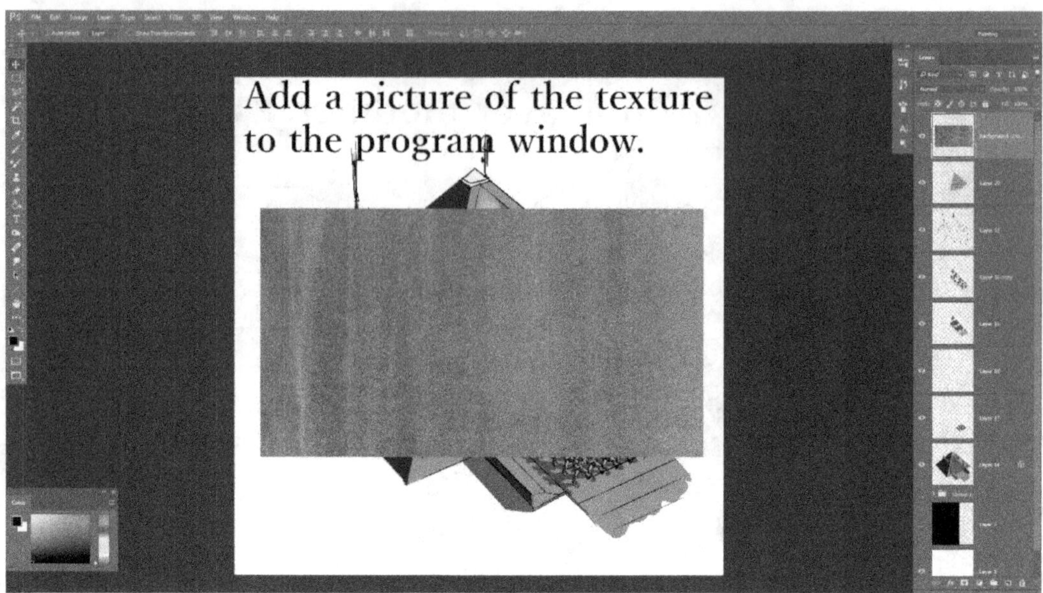

28. Copy the layer of the image. Press Ctrl+T to adjust the shape of the image.

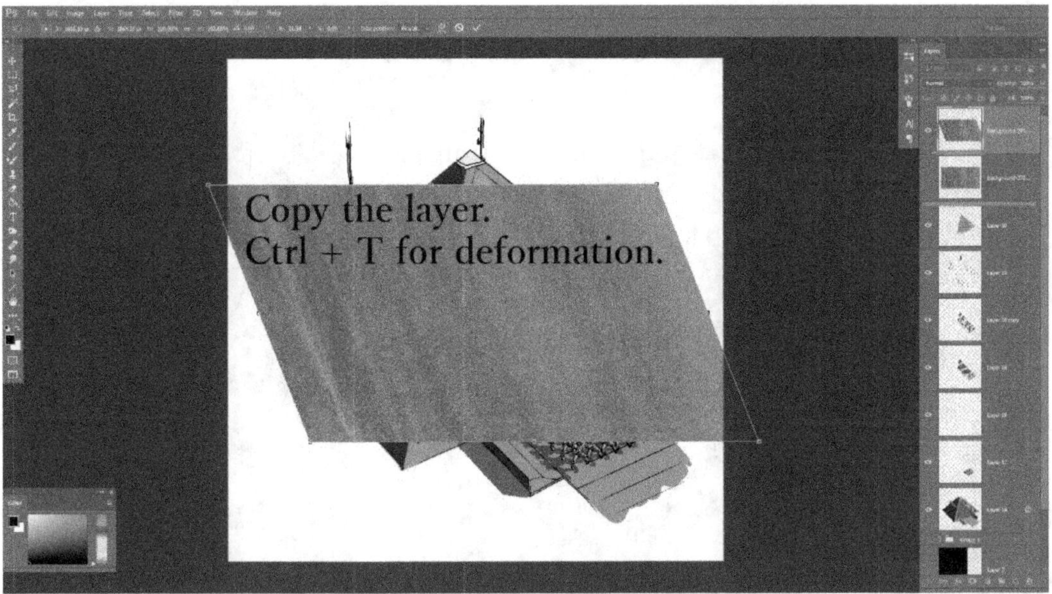

29. Adjust the shape of the image to fit the pyramid. Change the layer's Opacity to 52%. Use the Eraser Tool to remove any excess parts of the image.

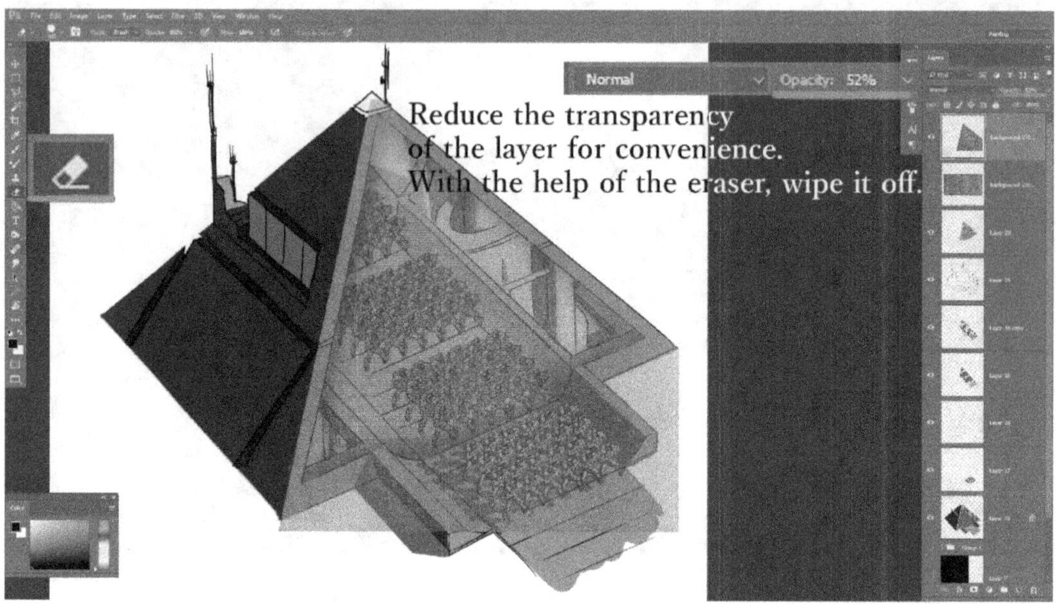

30. Apply the same method to the other surfaces of the pyramid. With the texture's layer selected, change its modifier to "Vivid Light".

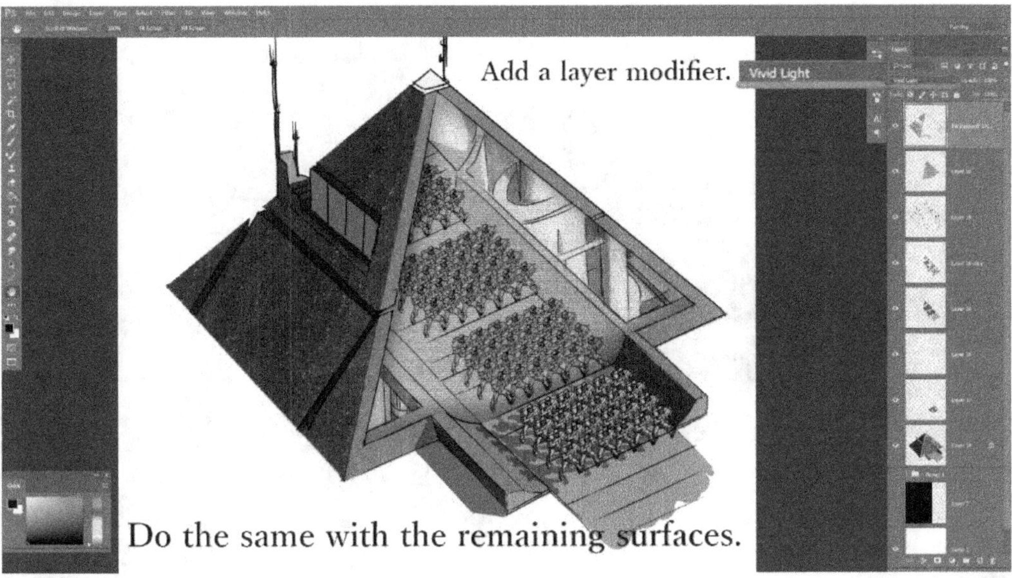

31. Press Ctrl+U to bring up the Hue/Saturation Window. Adjust the Saturation to -79.

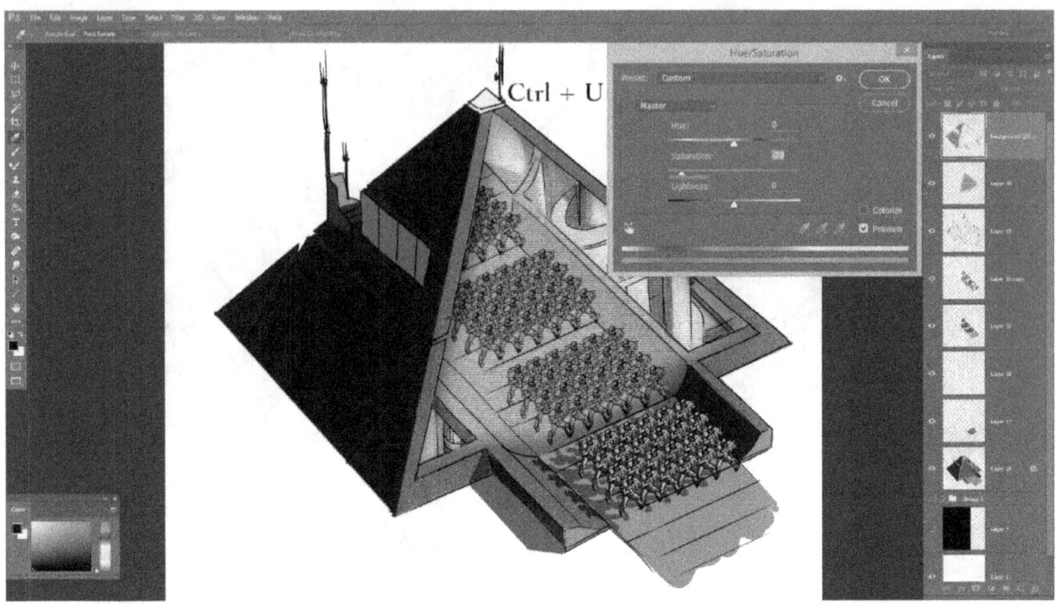

32. Press Ctrl+L to bring up the Levels Window. Adjust the Middle level to 1.64.

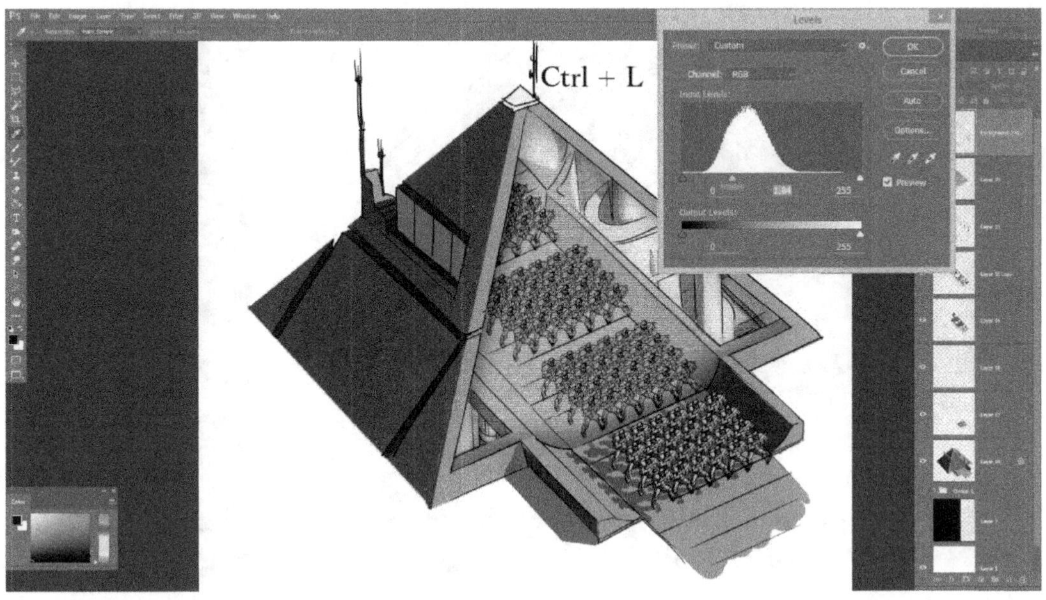

33. Make another layer. Select the Paint Brush Tool and choose a soft brush. Paint a cloud over the figures on the ramp.

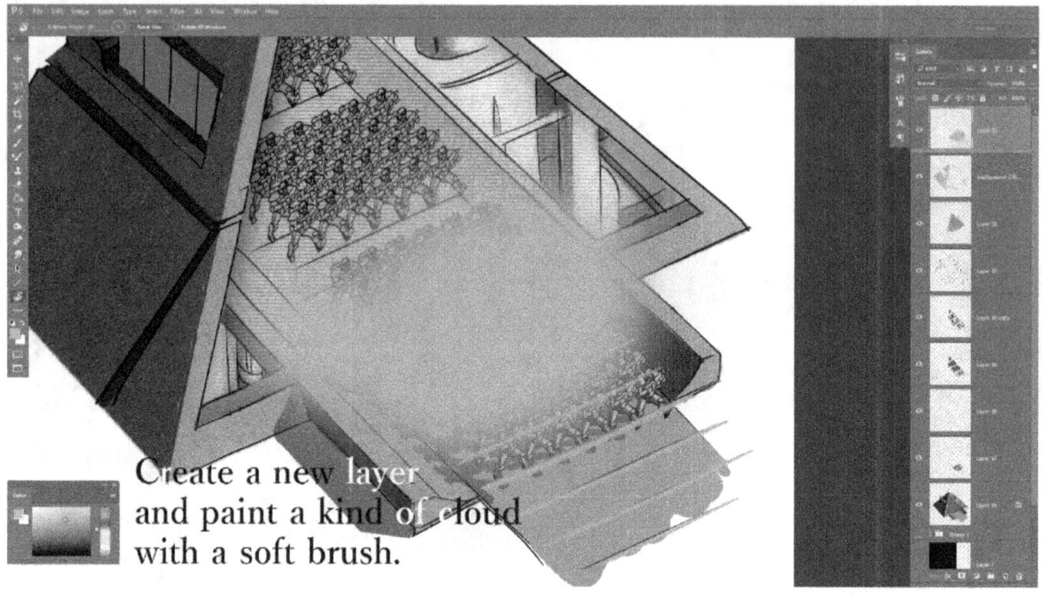

34. Change this layer's modifier to "Color Dodge".

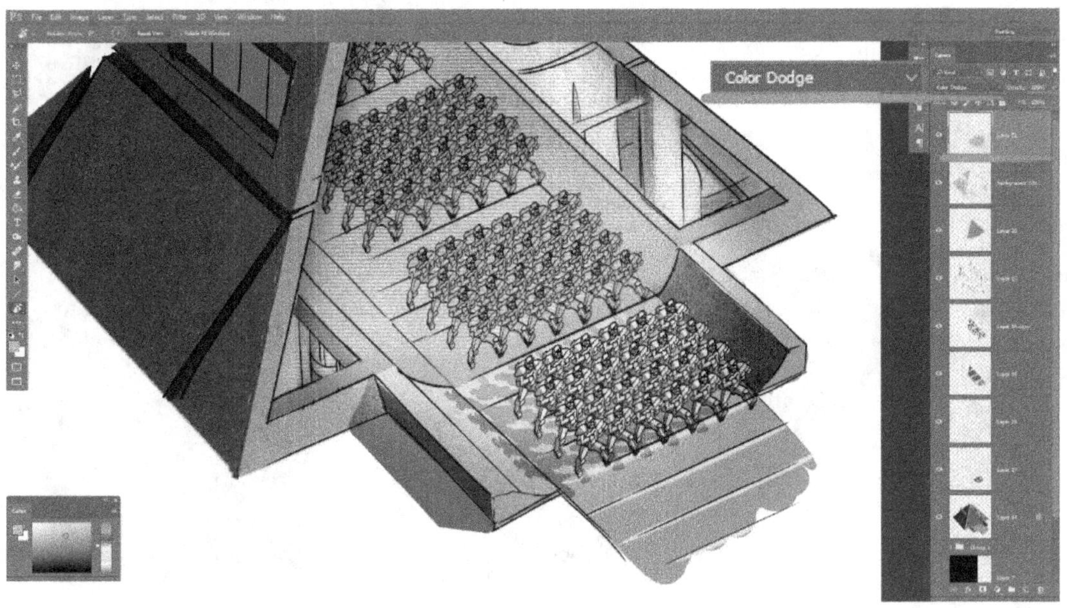

35. Select the Polygonal Lasso Tool and mark an area as shown.

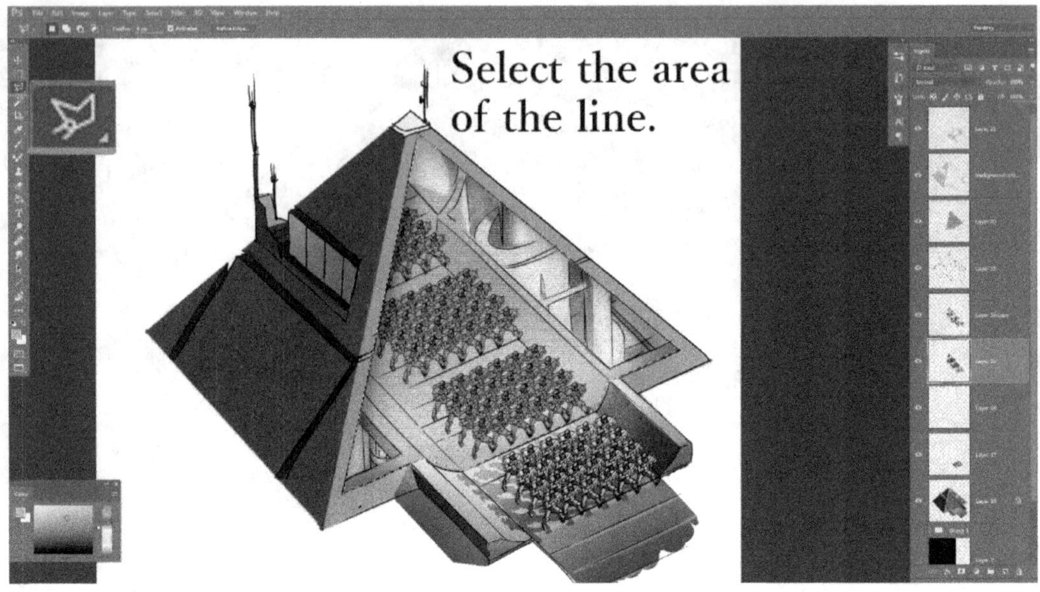

36. Use the Eraser tool and remove a bit of the top of the sketch of the figures on the ramp.

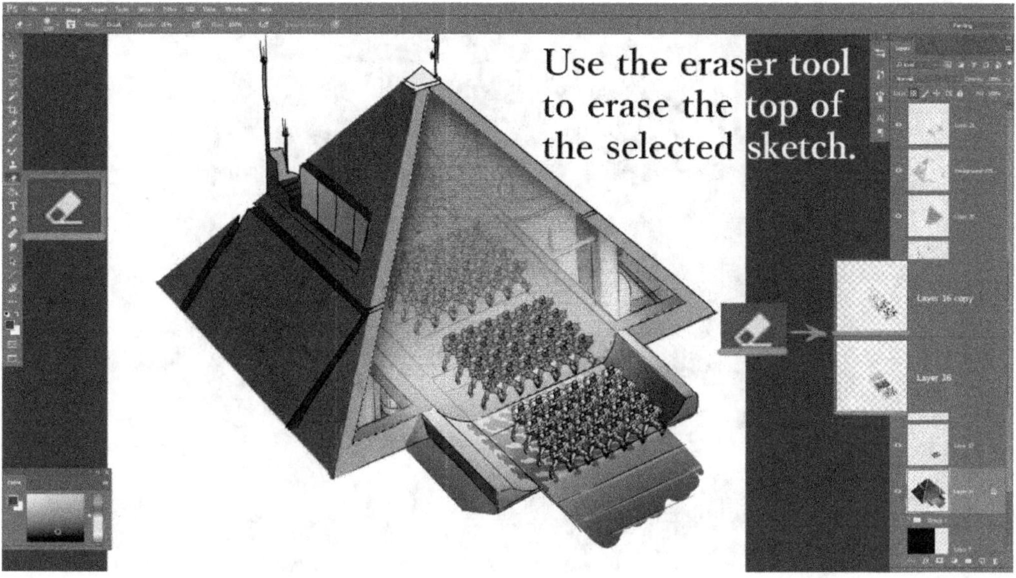

37. Make a new layer and fill it with black. Move this layer under all the drawings.

38. Make a new layer and place it on top of all the other layers. Paint a vertical line with a soft brush using the Brush Tool. Choose a light color for this step.

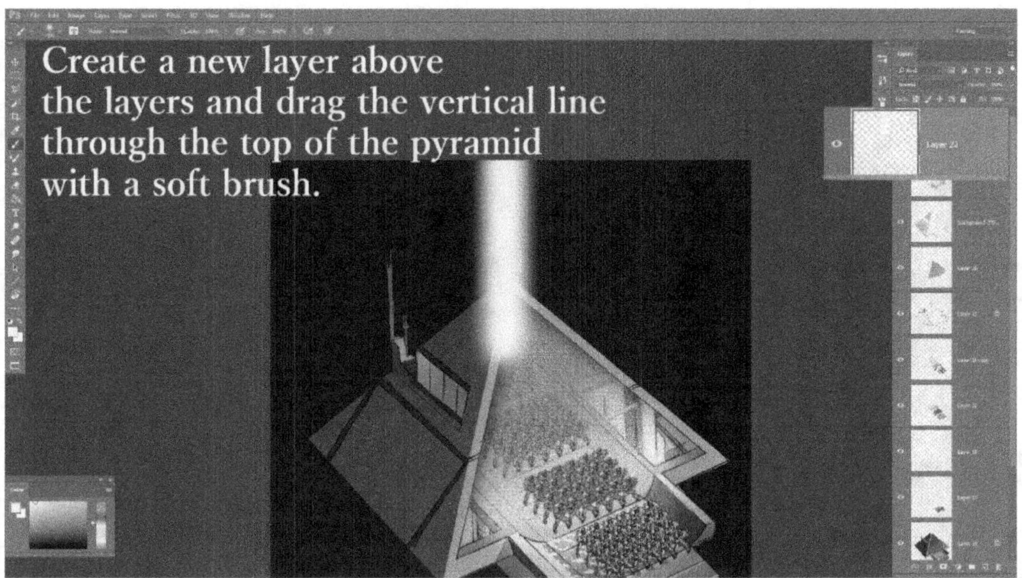

39. Click on the Eraser Tool and remove excess parts of the light beam. Use a large soft brush for the top of the beam and a small soft brush for the bottom and sides.

40. The finished image is.

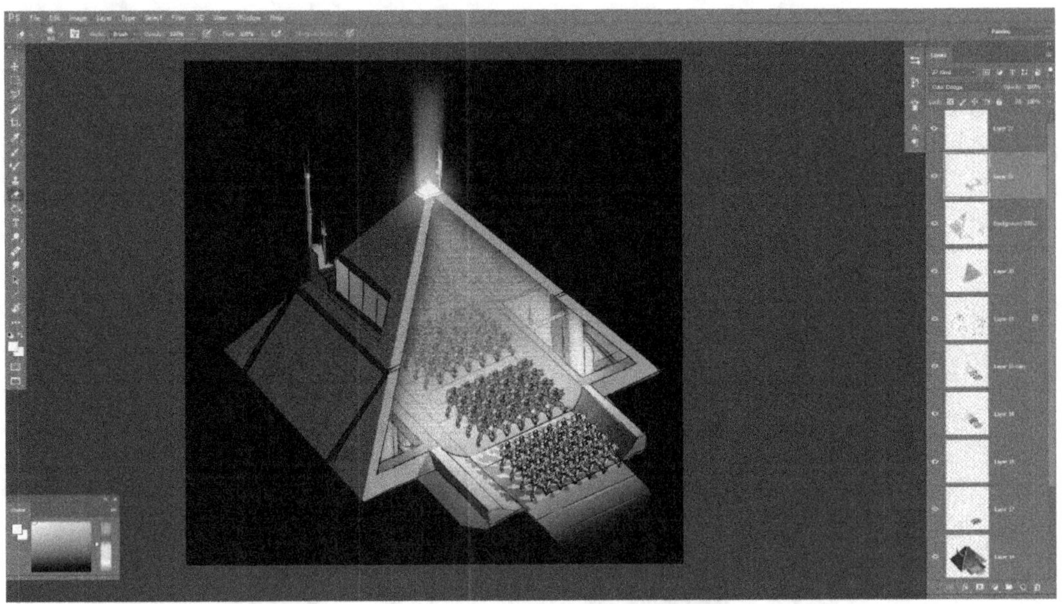

Cone

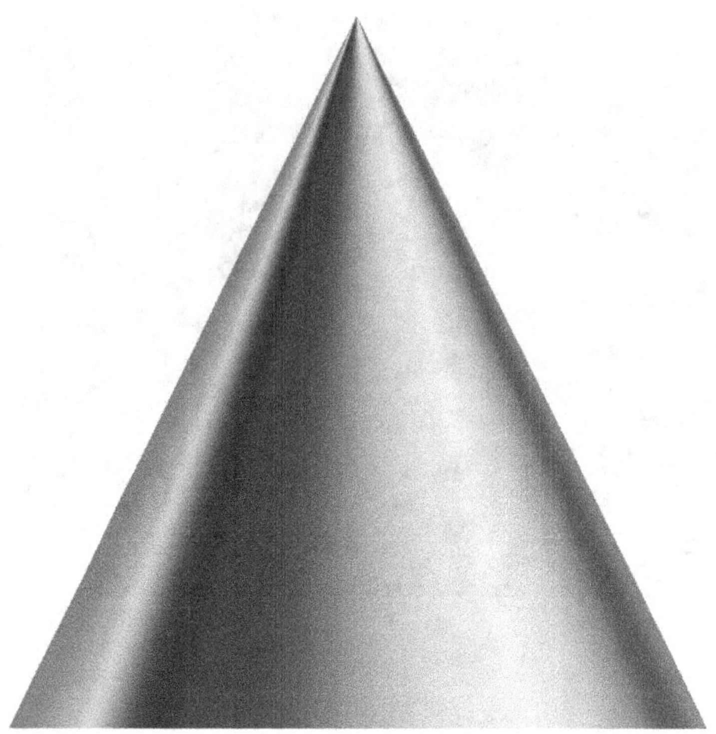

1. Make a new layer. Select the Rectangular Selection Tool and create a square area.

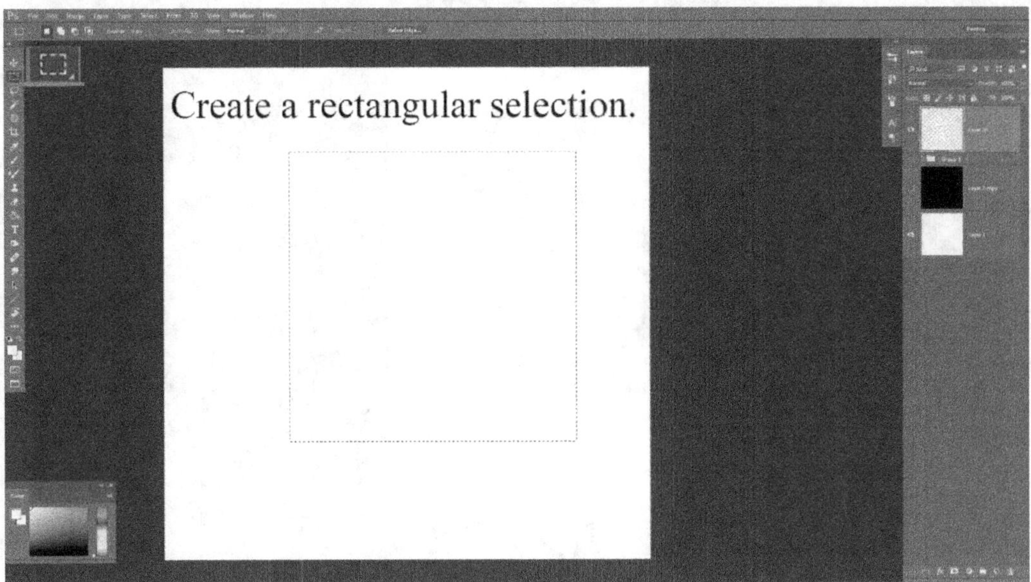

2. Fill the shape with a color using the Paint Bucket Tool.

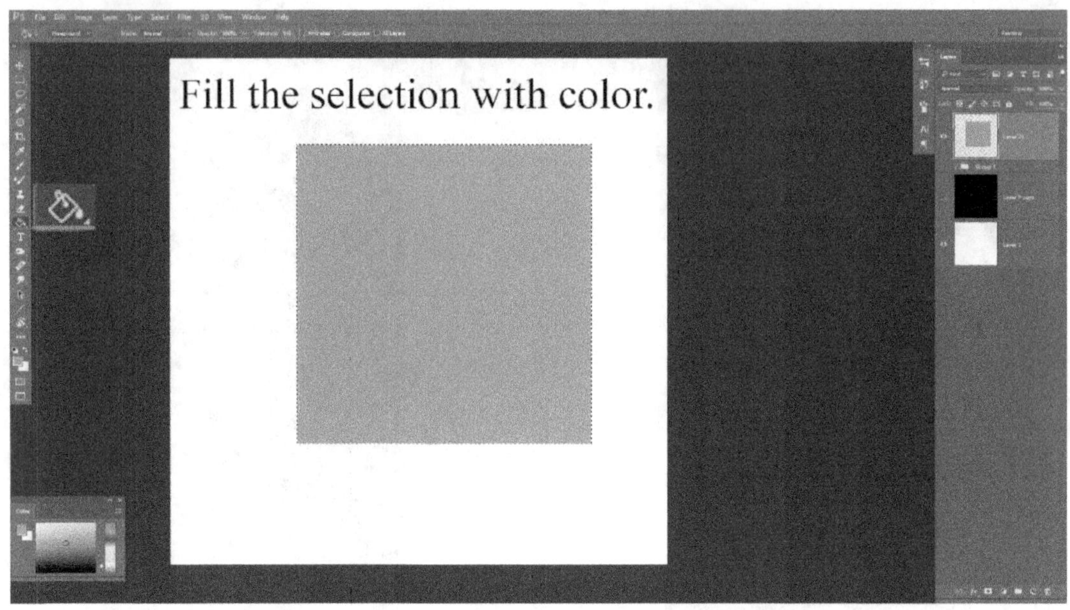

3. Lock the layer of the square. Change the Mode and Opacity of the Brush Tool to Color Dodge and 55%, respectively. Paint highlights on the square.

4. Select the Burn Tool and darken areas of the shadow to create contrast.

5. Use the Dodge Tool and draw a light line to give the shape more shine. Make sure the Range is on Midtones and the Exposure is at 68%.

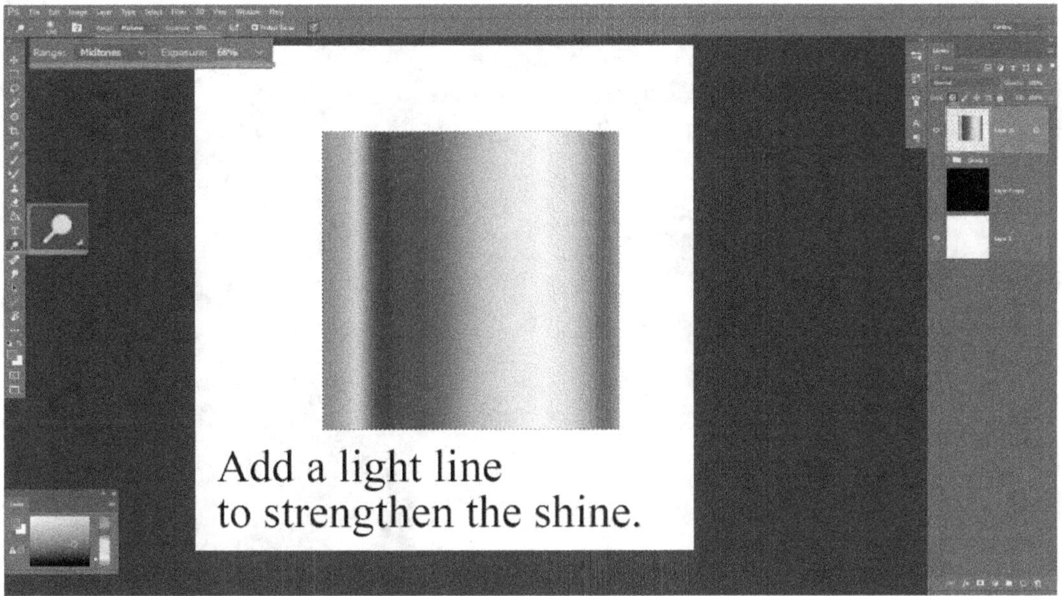

6. Press Ctrl+T to bring up the transformation box. Hold the Ctrl, Alt, and Shift Keys while dragging one of the upper corners of the box. Drag it to the middle point.

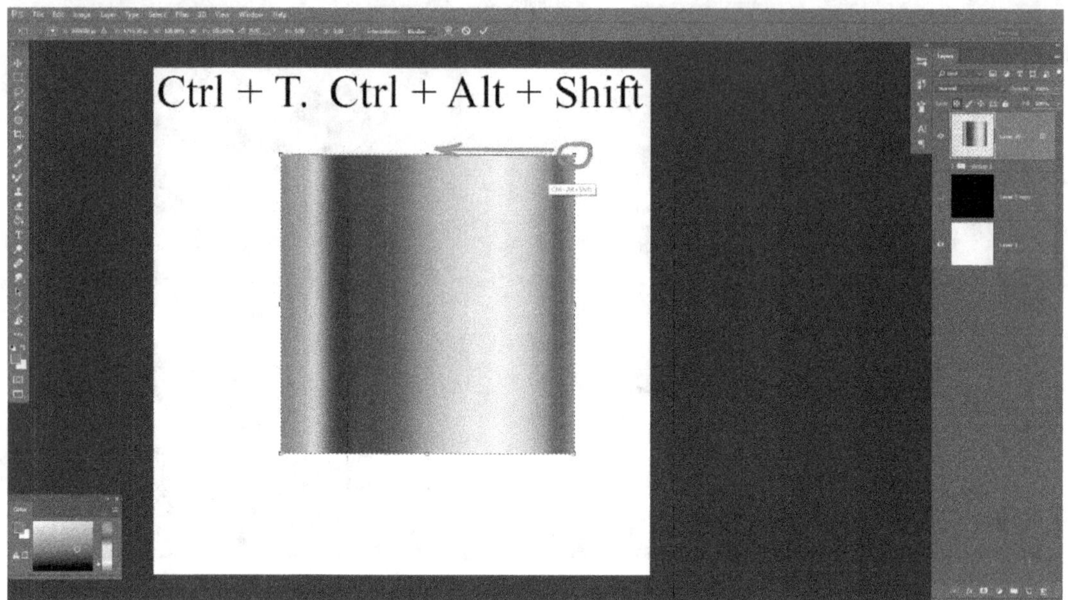

7. This step should create a triangle similar to the one above.

8. Make a new layer. On this layer, mark out a square using the Rectangular
Selection Tool.

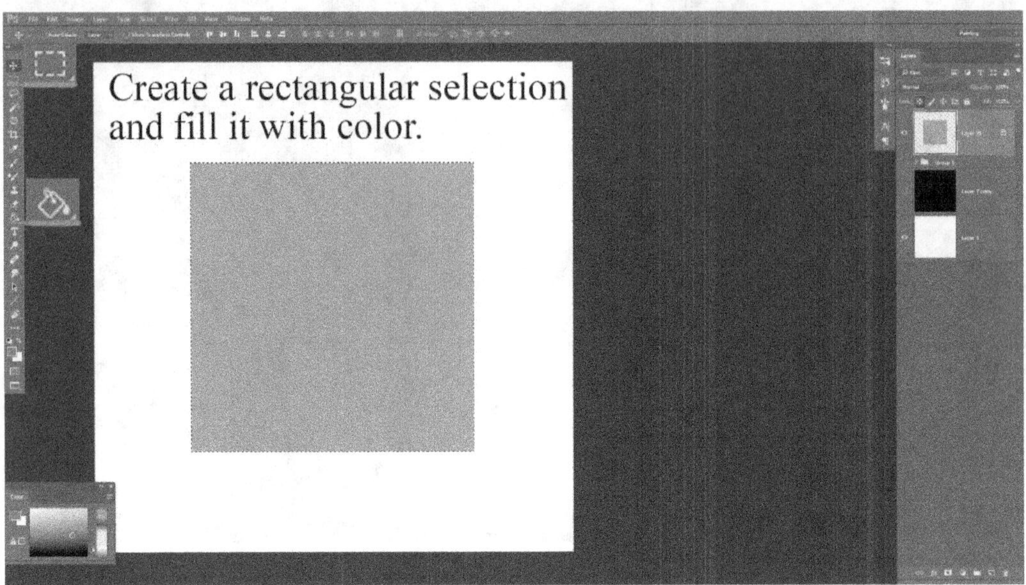

9. Create an oval with the same width as the square at the bottom of it. Use the Elliptical Selection Tool.

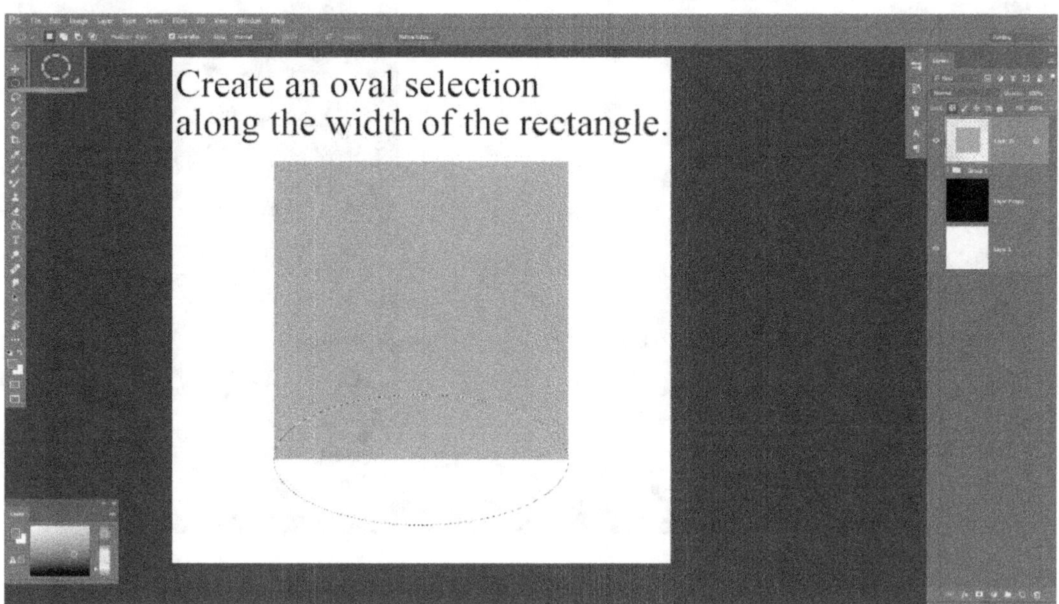

10. Fill the oval with the same color as the square.

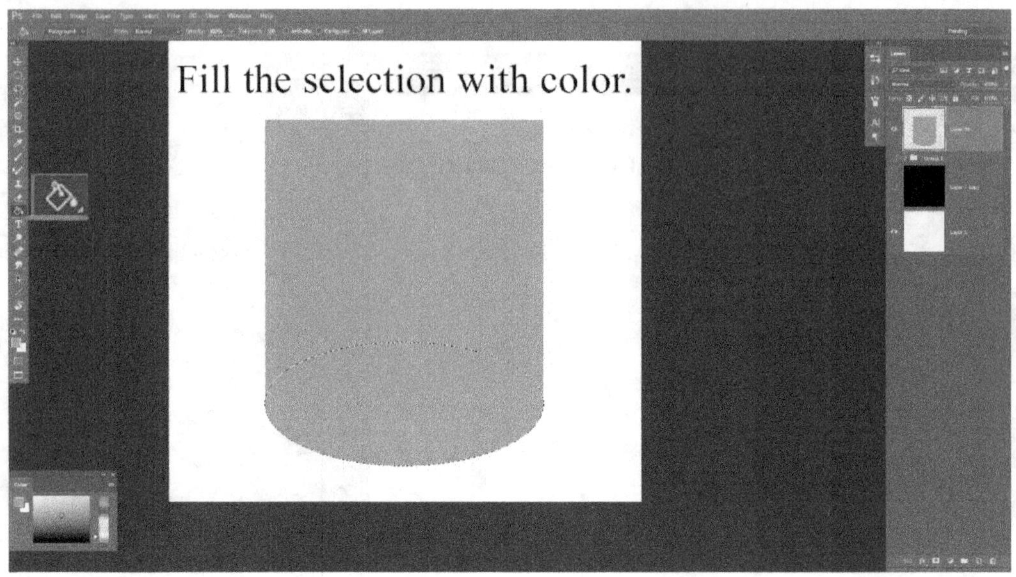

11.   Merge the two layers together. Make a gloss on the surface using the Burn and Dodge Tools. Draw these shadows and highlights in the same way that you would on a cylinder.

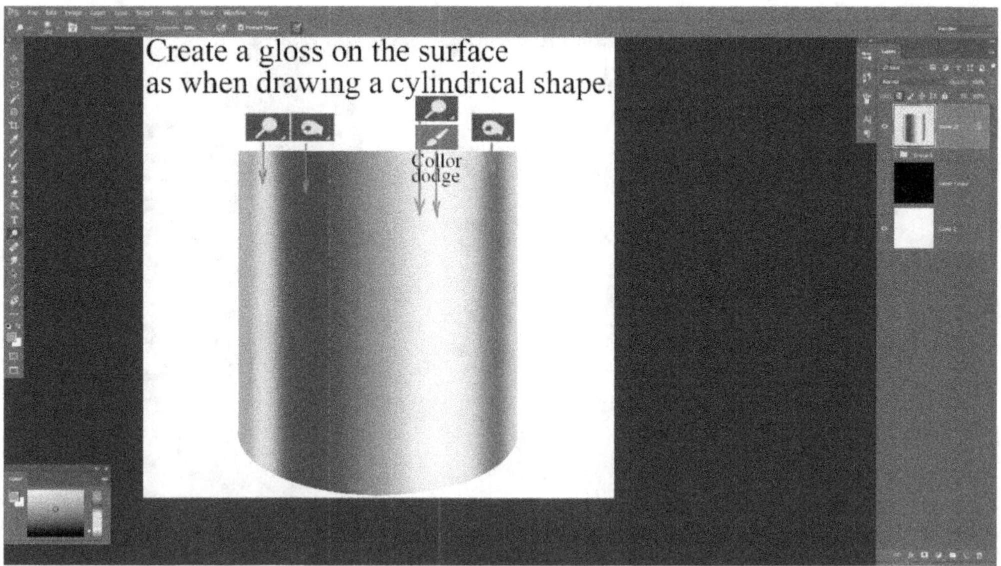

12. Press Ctrl+T to open the transformation box. Hold the Ctrl, Alt, and Shift keys while dragging one of the top corners of the box towards the middle.

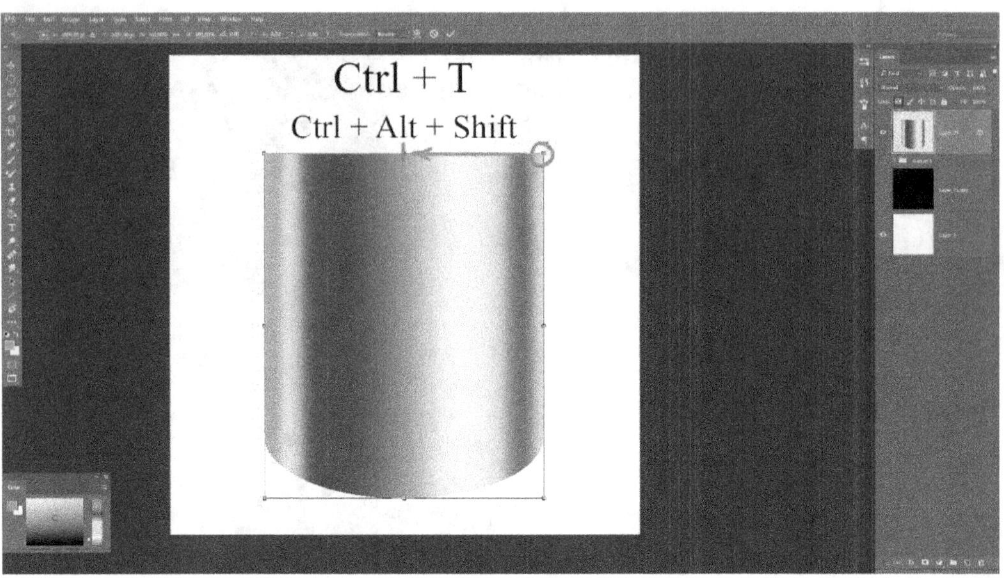

13. Press the Enter Key to apply the transformation.

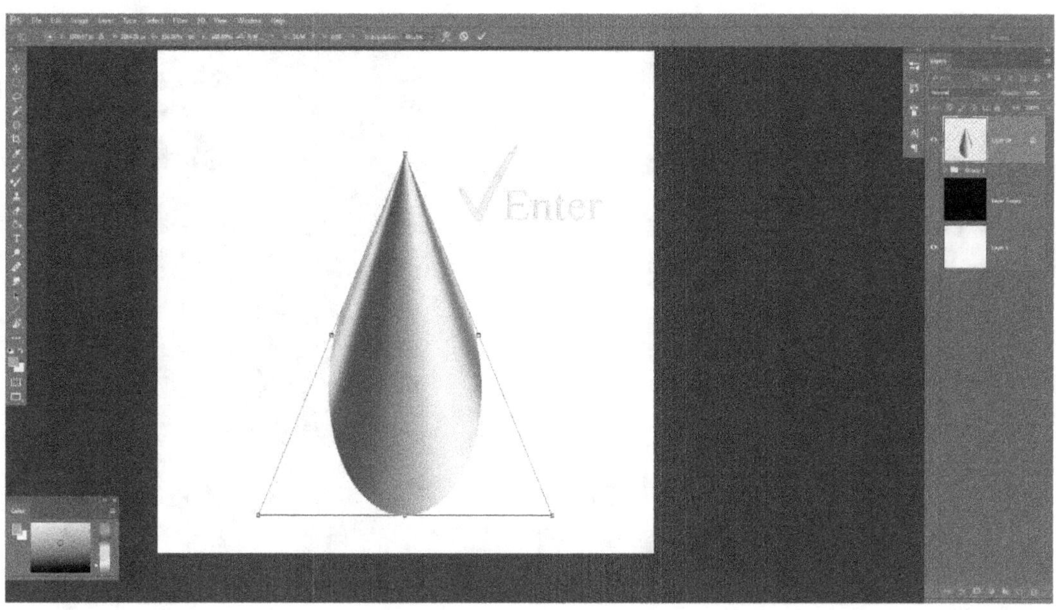

14. Press Ctrl+T and adjust the box to compress the shape vertically.

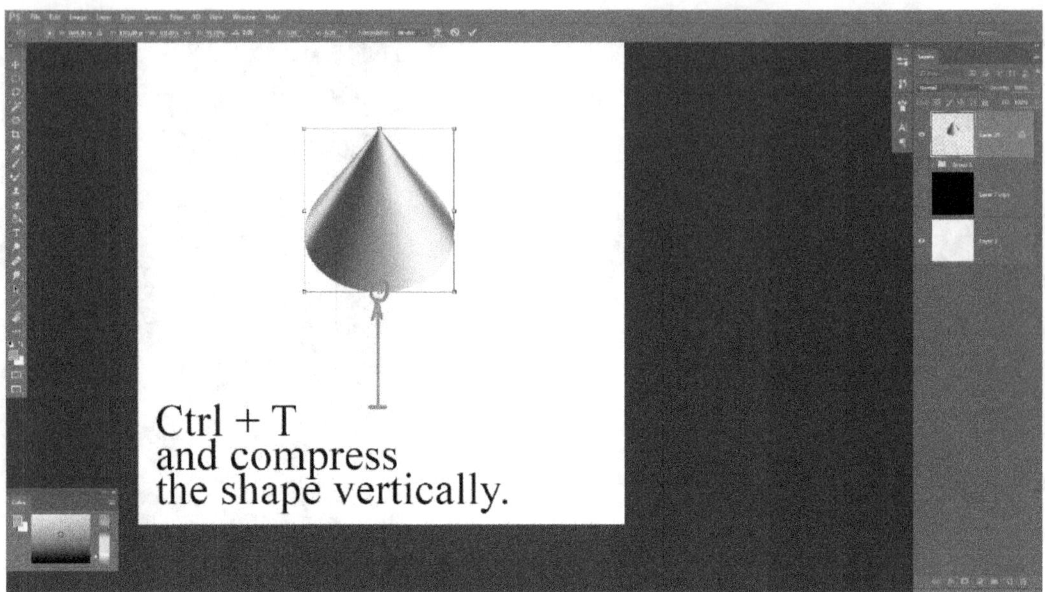

15. Make a new layer. Draw the object's shadow.

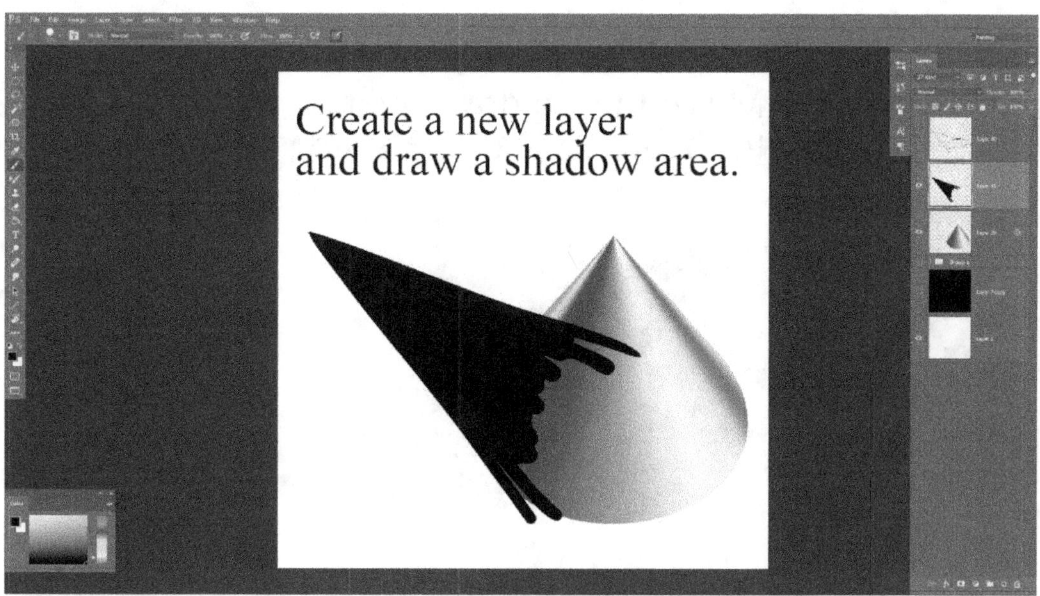

16. Move the layer of the shadow below that of the cone.

17. Use the Lasso Tool to mark out an area at the top of the shadow. With the area selected, click the Right Mouse Button to pull up the dropdown menu. Select "Feather..." from this menu.

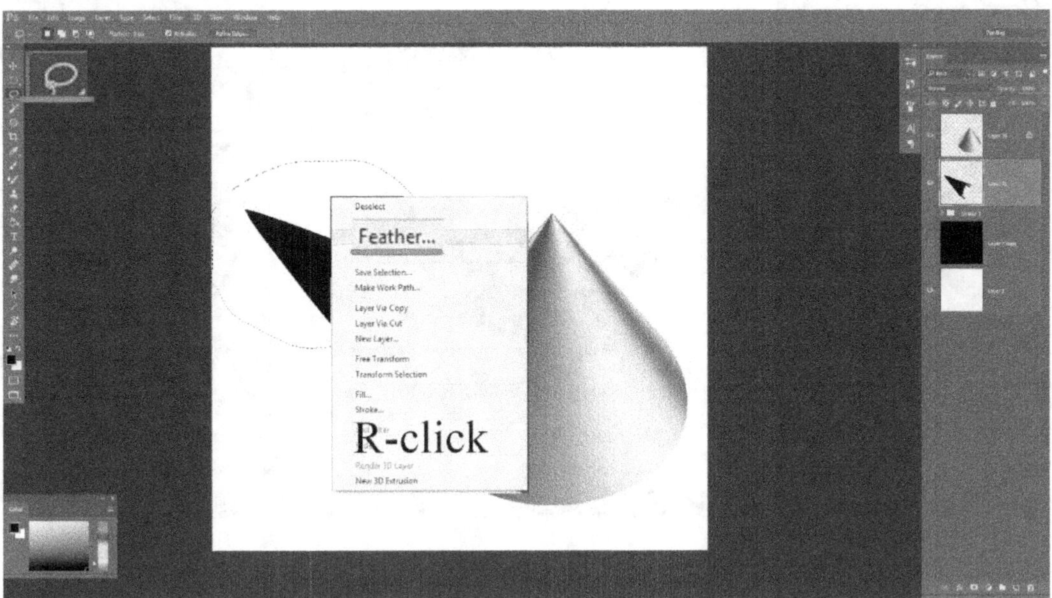

18. Set the Feather Radius to 120.

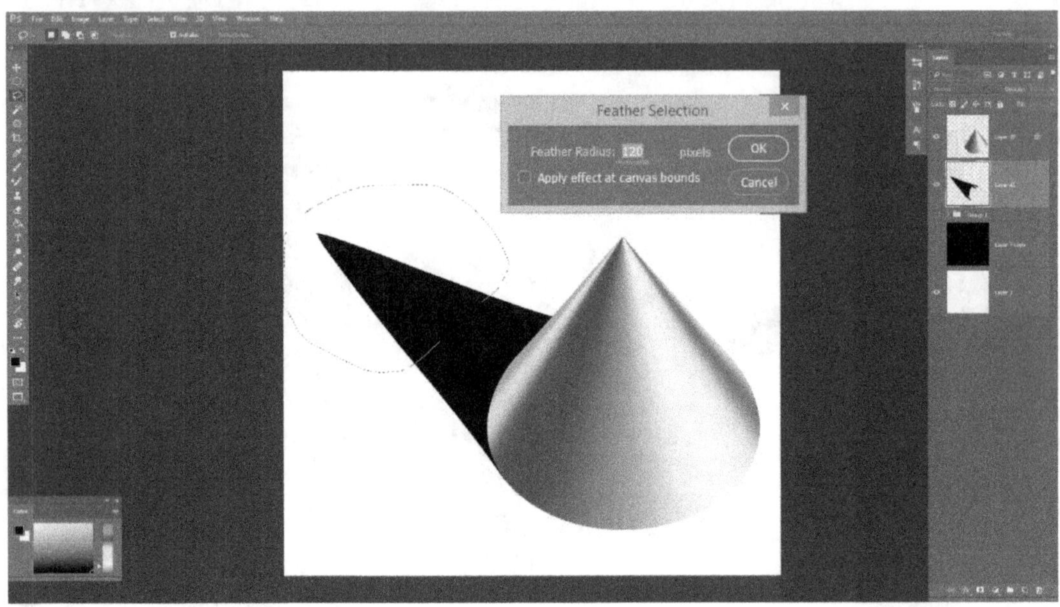

19. With the area still selected, click on the "Filter" menu. Choose "Blur" from the menu and select "Gaussian Blur..."

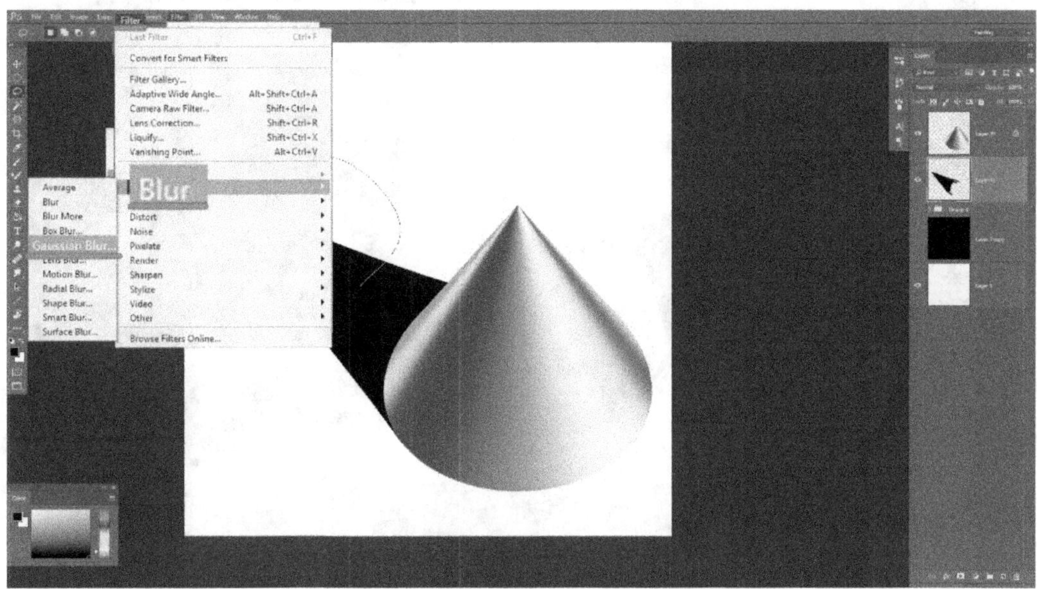

20. Adjust the radius of the Gaussian Blur to 20.8.

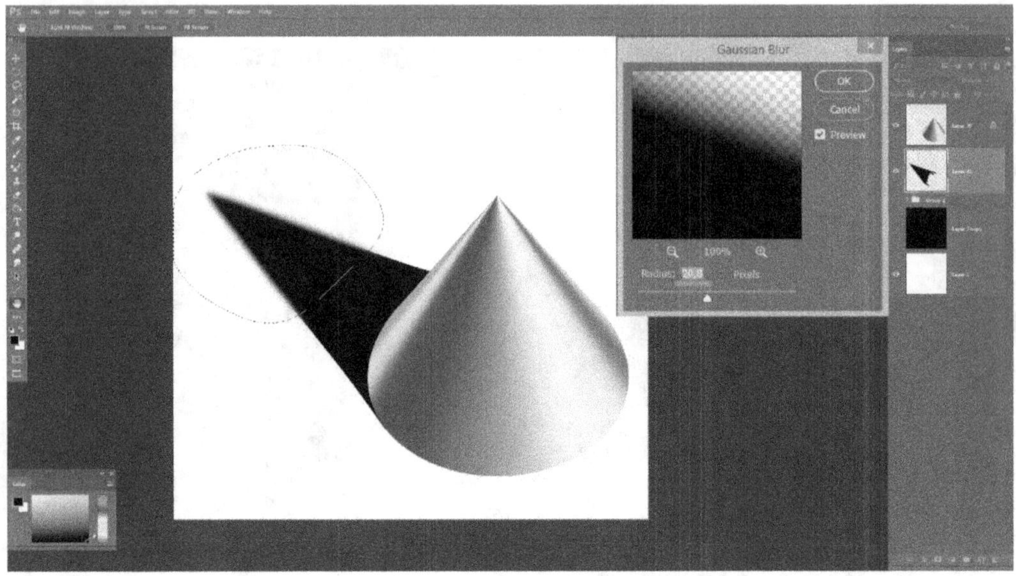

21. Create another selection using the Lasso Tool, this time make the area larger. Click the Right Mouse Button and select Feather from the menu again. Set the Feather Radius to 60.

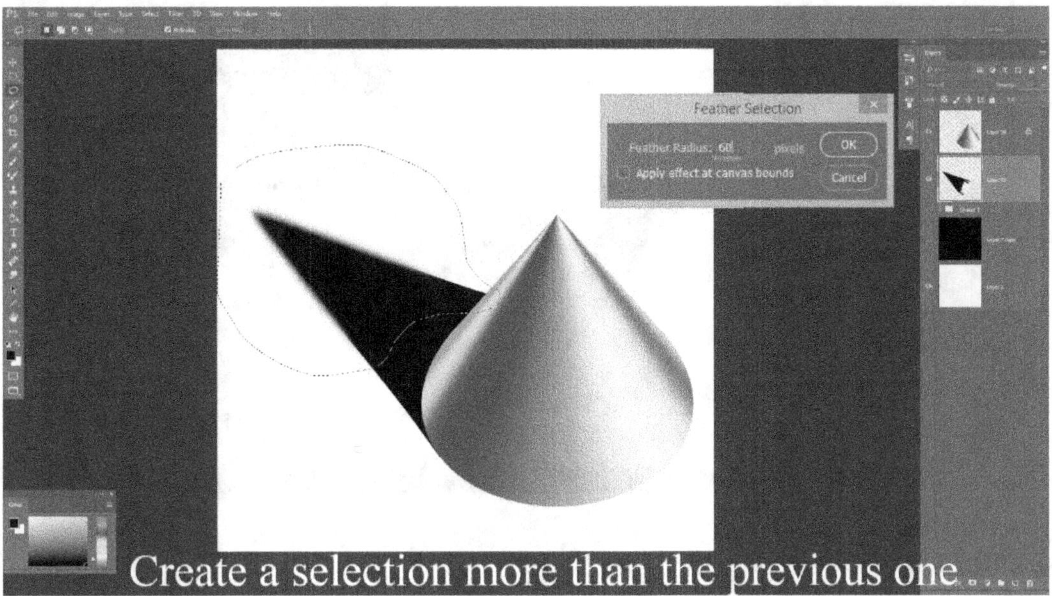

22. Apply the Gaussian Blur to the new selected area. Set the Radius to 13.9.

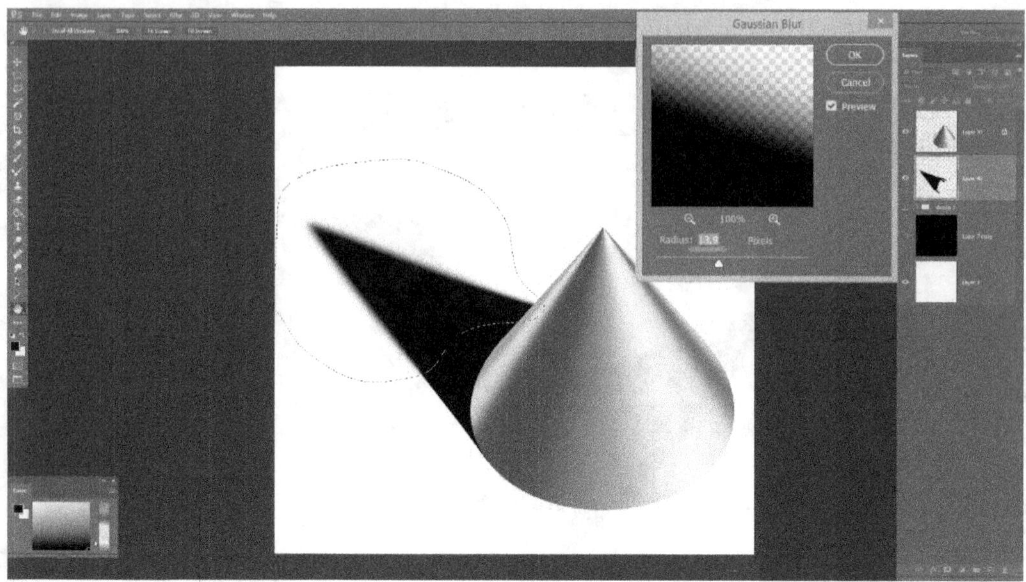

23. Choose the Eraser Tool and use a soft brush.

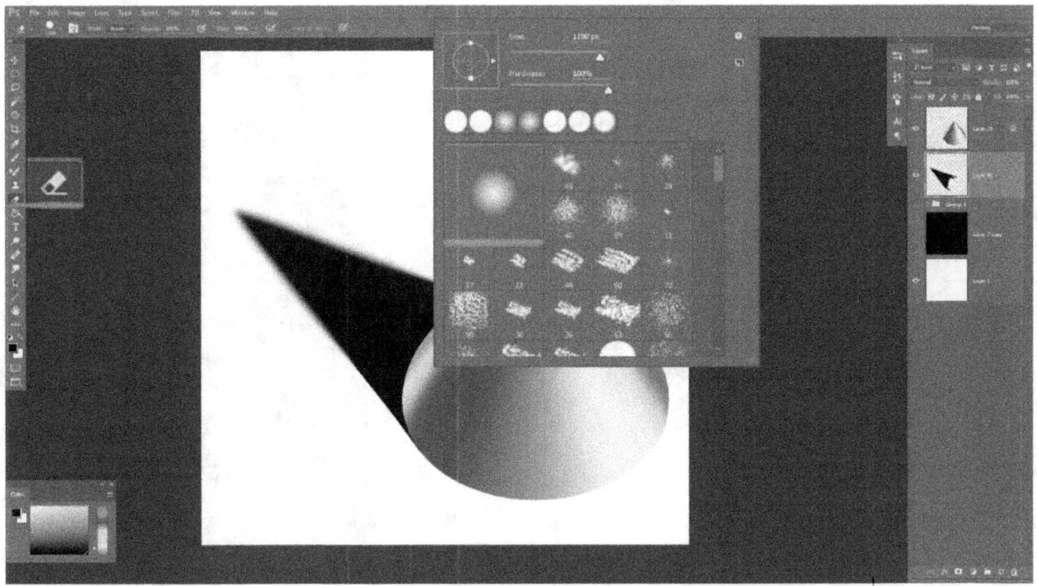

24. Erase a far part of the shadow.

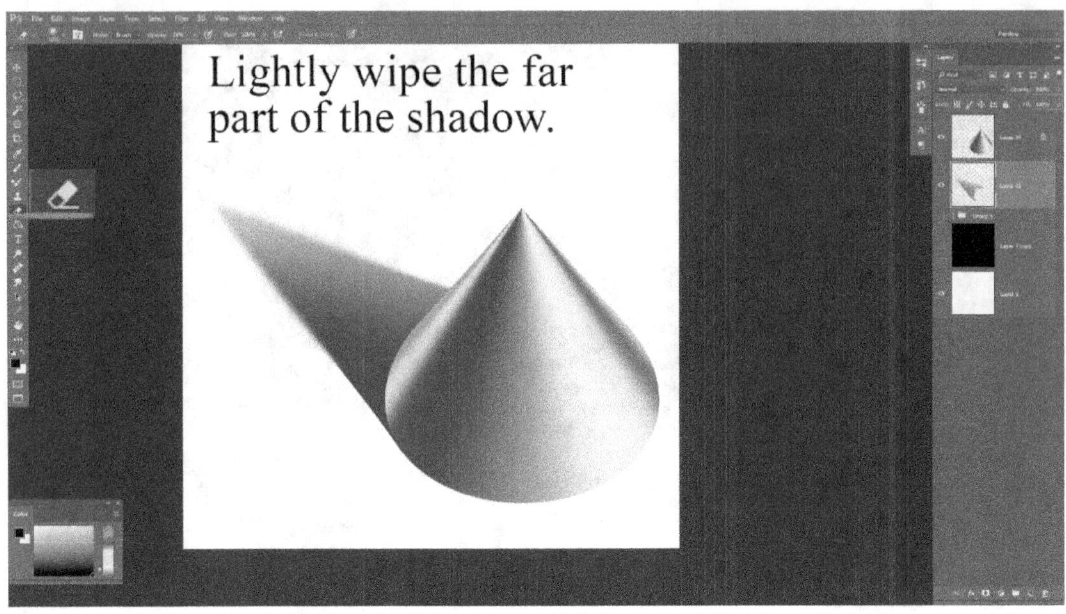

25. Lock the shadow's layer. With the Brush Tool paint is over the shadow with a color darker than the cone.

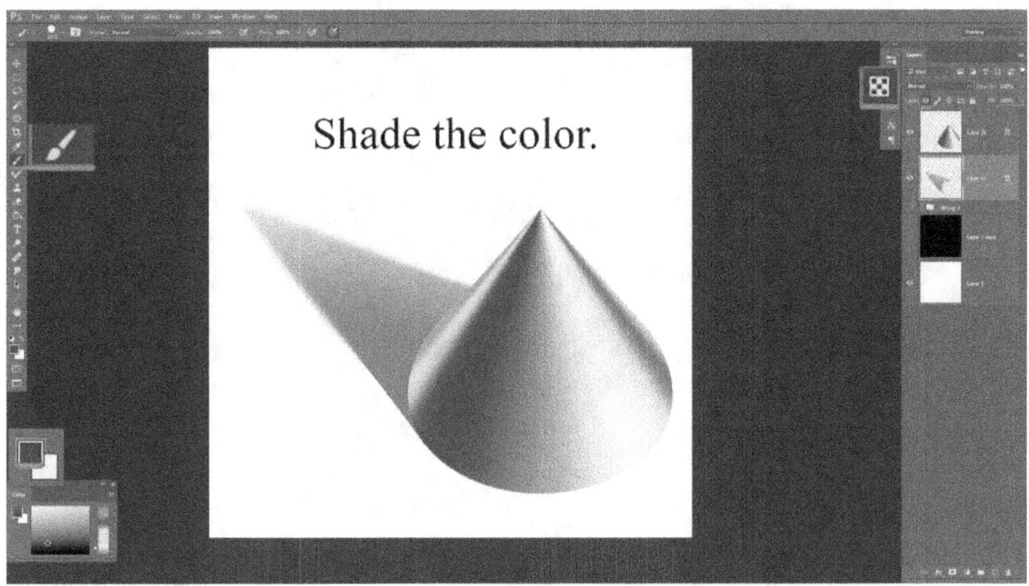

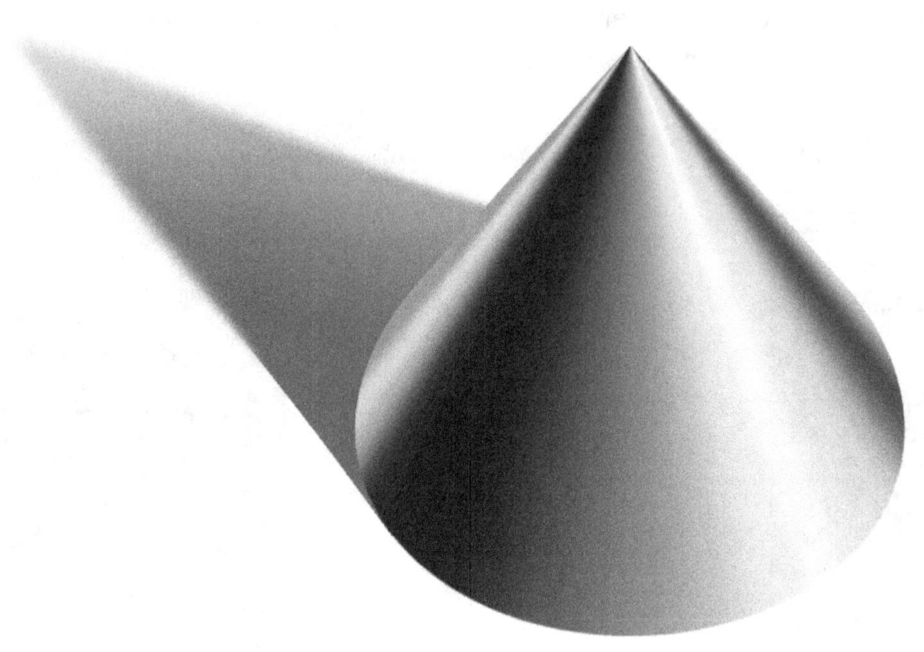

26. Press Ctrl+U to open up the Hue/Saturation Window. Change the Saturation to -91.

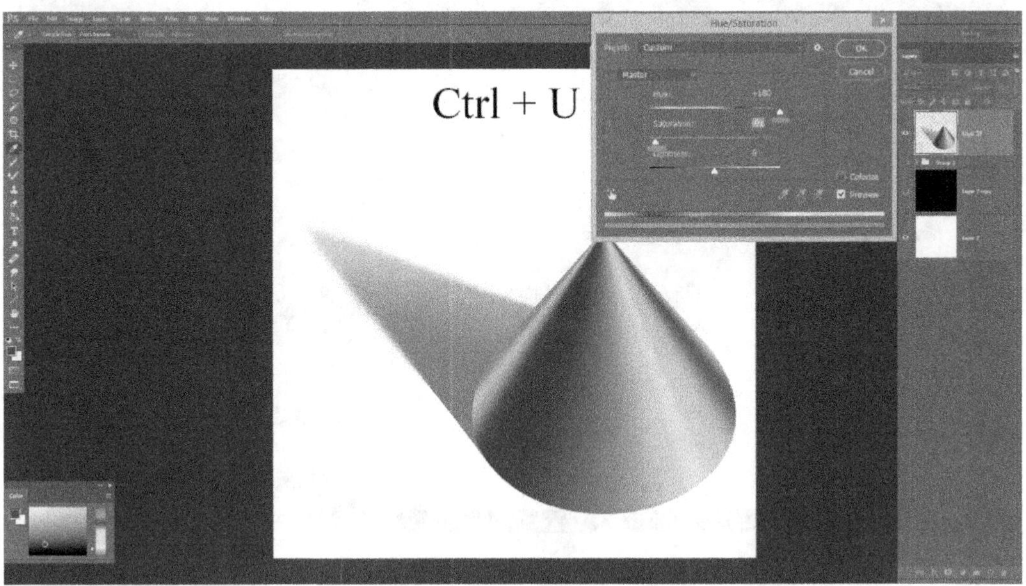

27. Press Ctrl+L and change the middle level to 1.15.

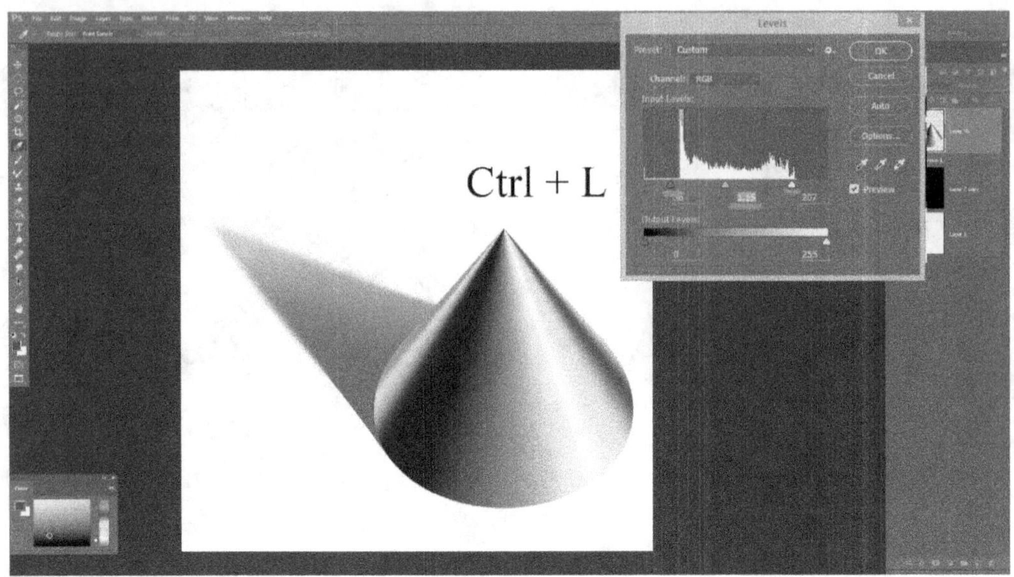

Cylindrical Cup

1. On a new layer, mark out a rectangle using the Rectangular Selection
Tool.

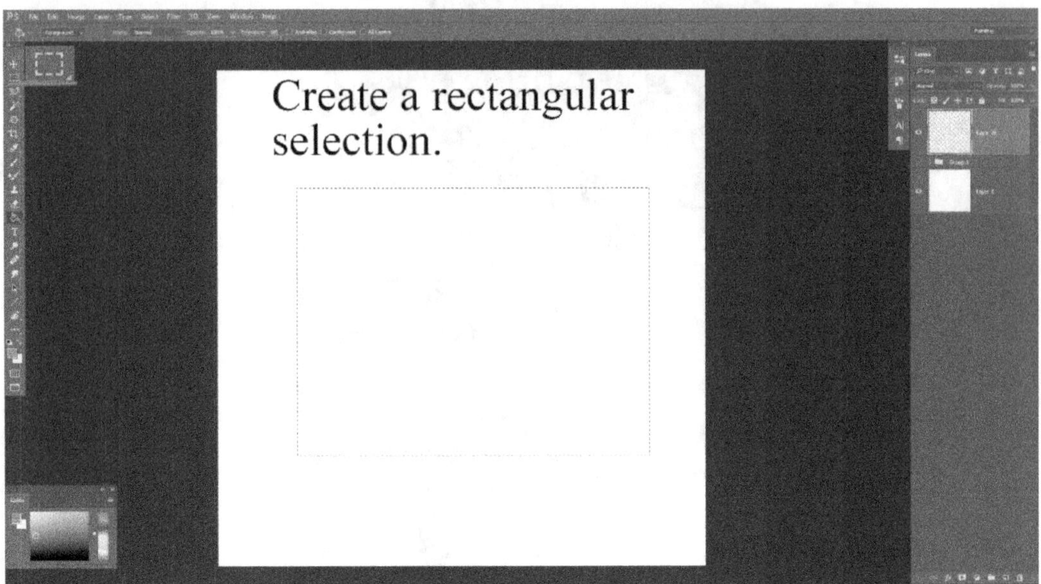

2. Fill the shape with color using the Paint Bucket Tool.

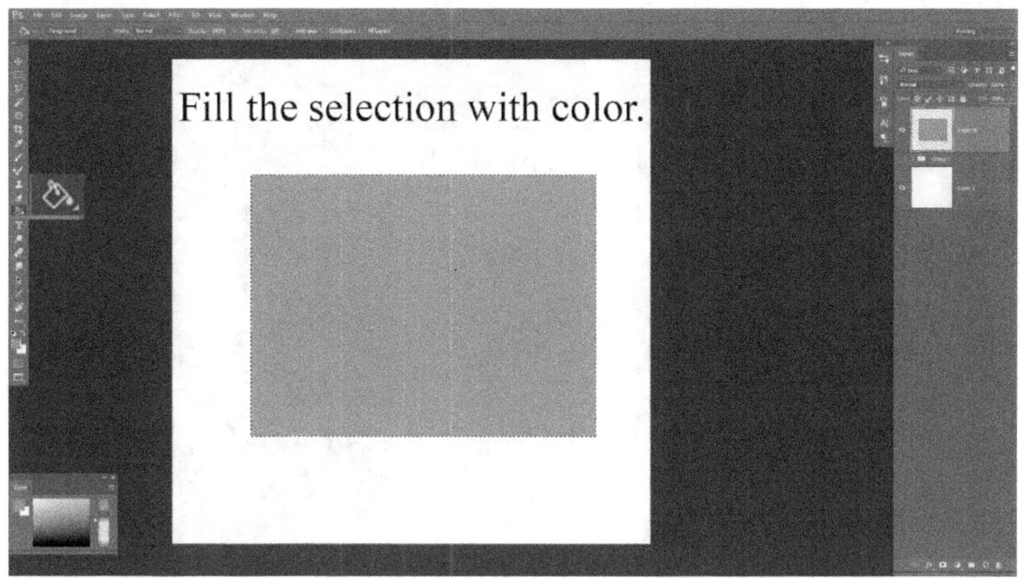

3. Copy the layer of the rectangle. To do this, just drag the rectangle's layer while pressing down on the Ctrl and Alt Keys.

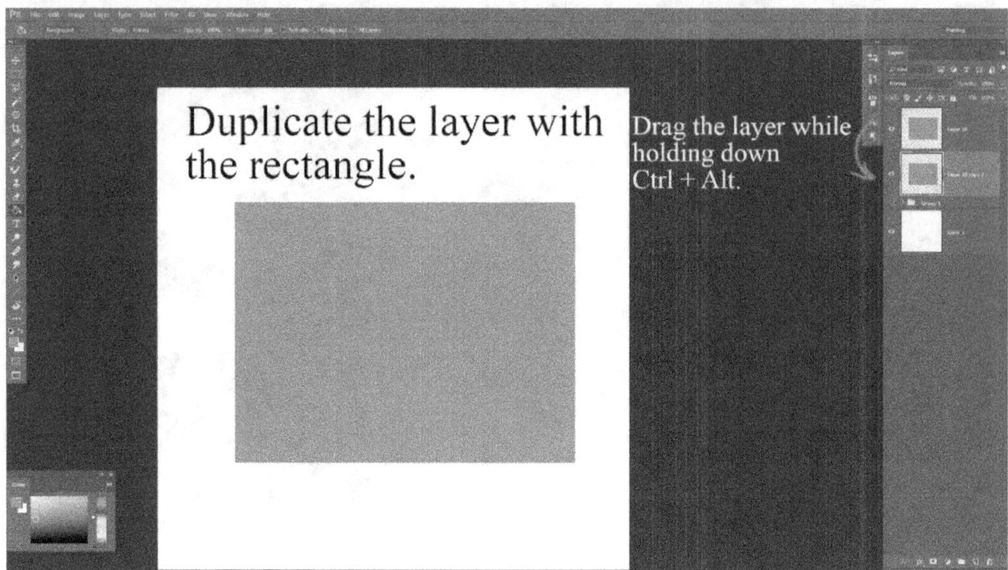

4. Hide the two layers of the rectangles. Make a new layer and draw an oval selection using the Elliptical Selection Tool.

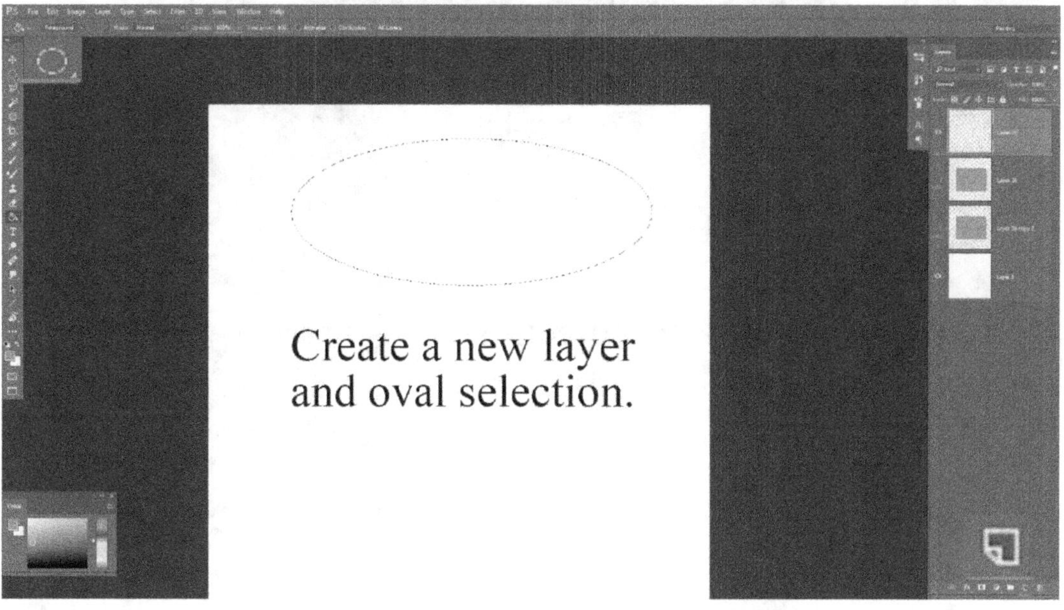

5. Fill the oval with the same color as the rectangles.

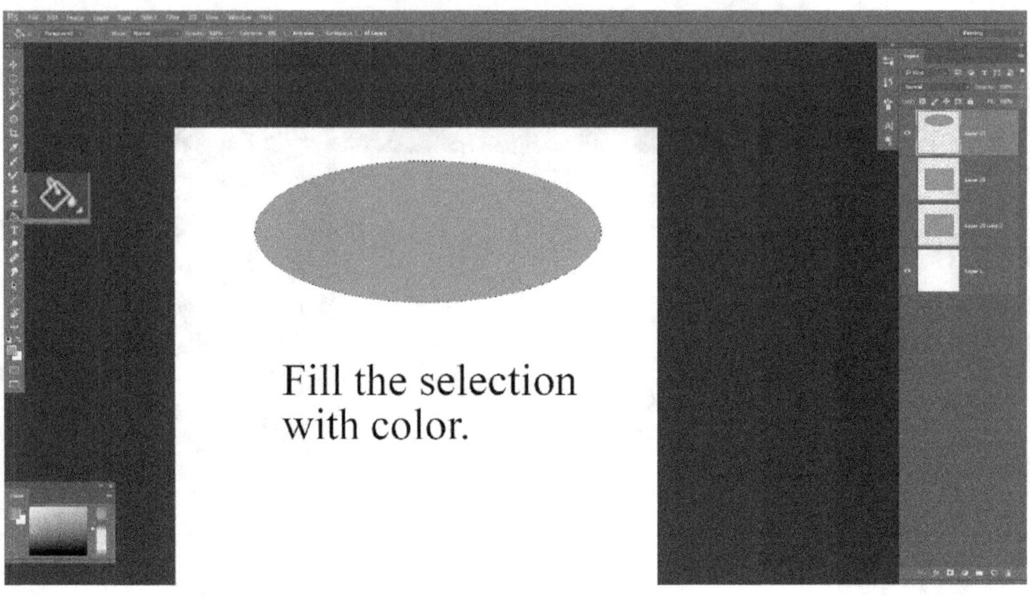

6. Press Ctrl+L to open the Levels window. Adjust the middle level to 0.64.

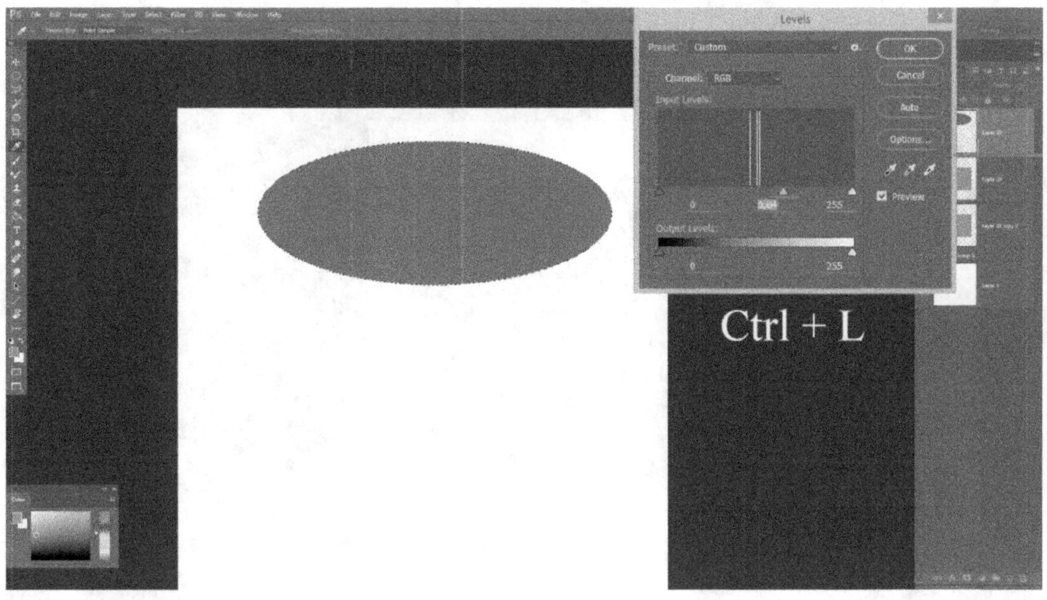

7. Make all the layers visible. Move one of the layers of the rectangles on top of the oval. Move the shapes to align them.

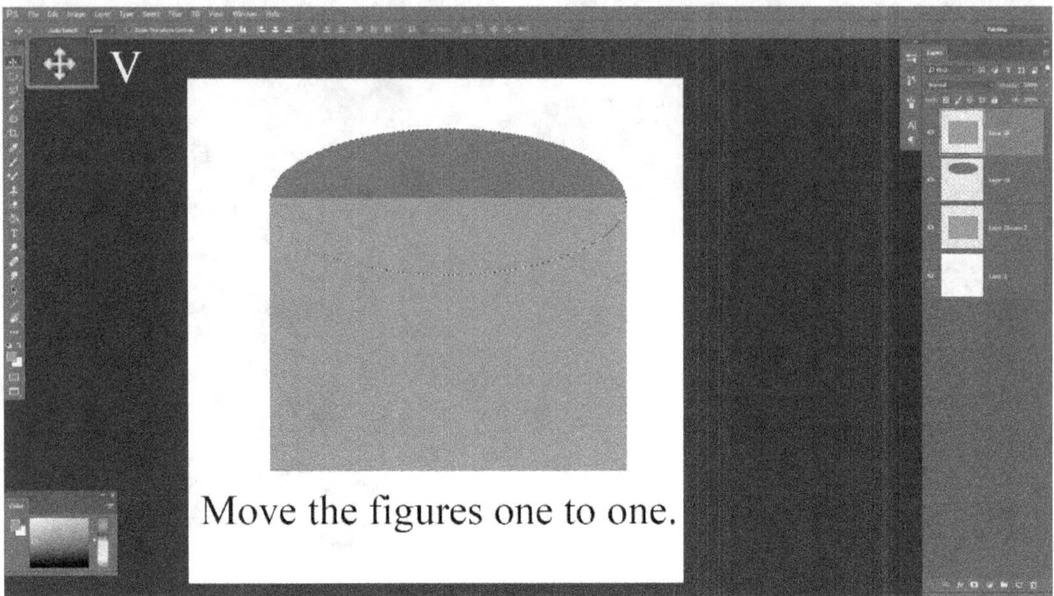

8. Without removing the oval's selection, click on the rectangle's layer and press the Del Key to remove an area of the rectangle.

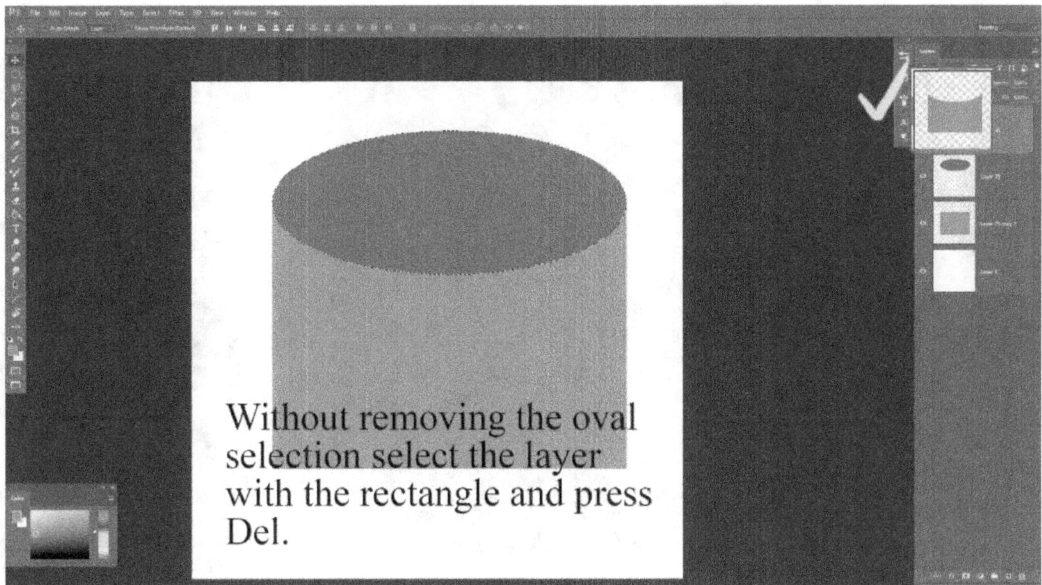

9. Copy the layer of the oval and move the copy to the bottom of the rectangle.

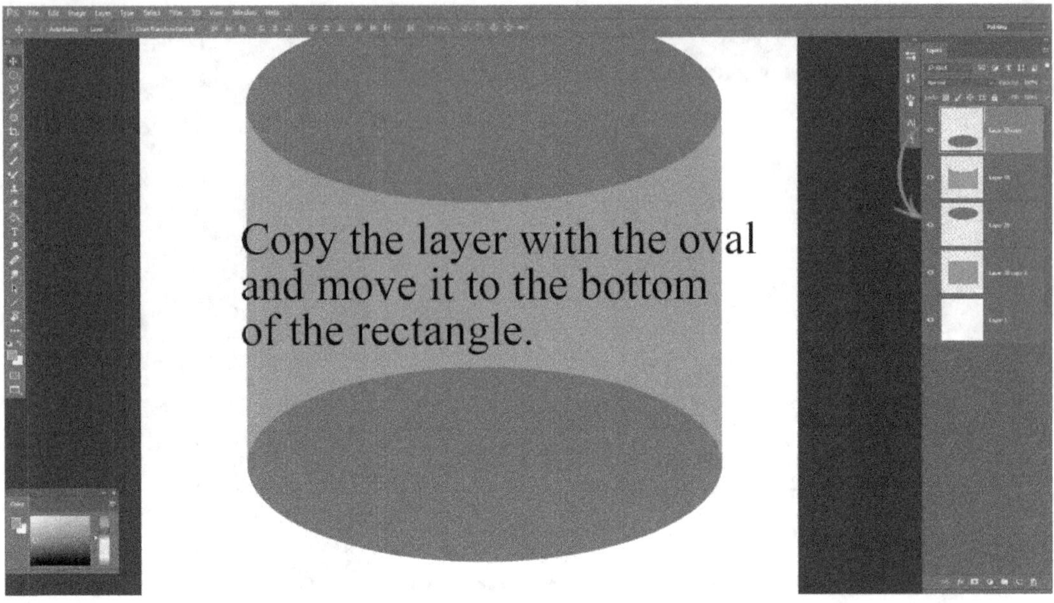

10. Press Ctrl+T to open the transformation box. Stretch the oval vertically.

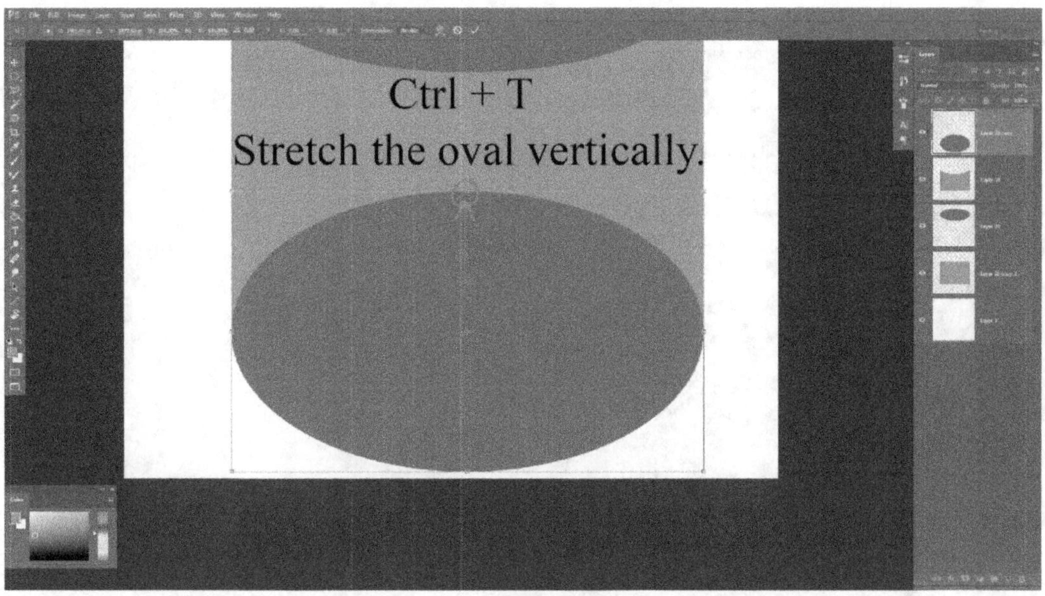

11. Lock the lower oval's layer. Select the Brush Tool and fill the oval with the same color as the rectangle.

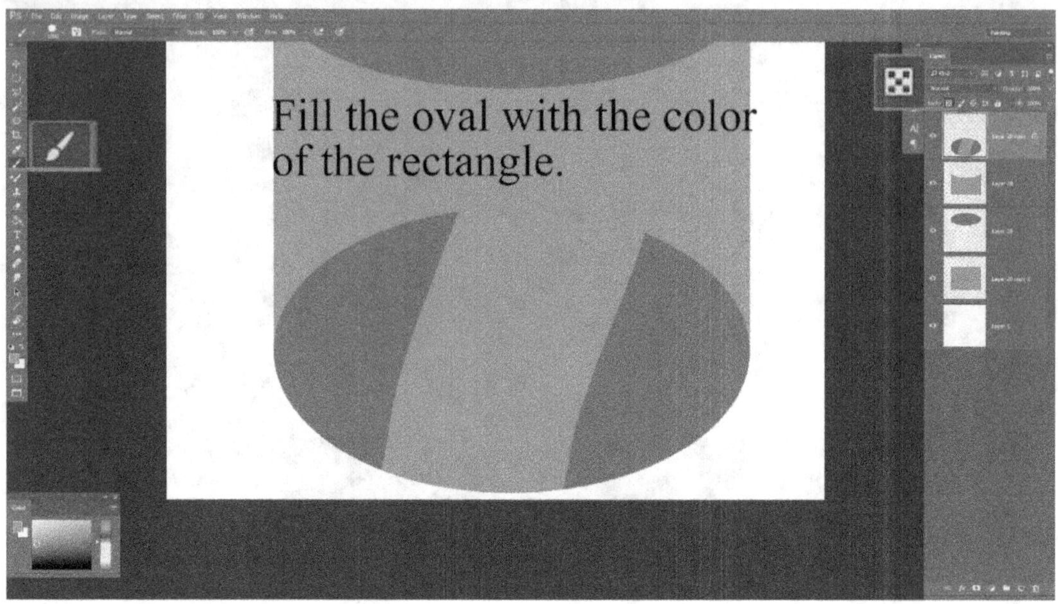

12. The finished basic cylindrical shape is.

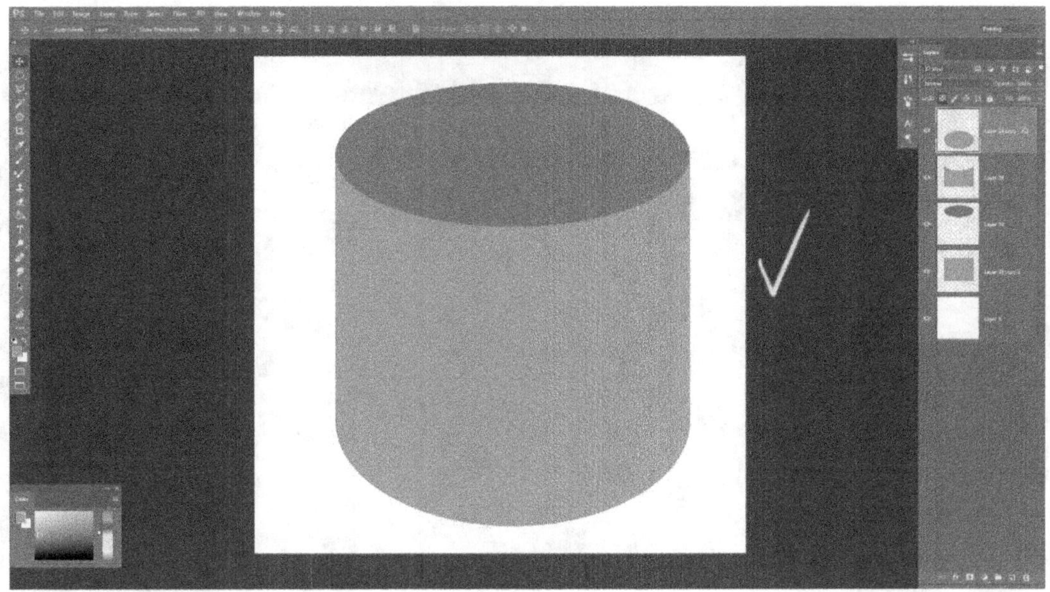

13. Press Ctrl+T to open the transformation box. Increase the upper oval's size slightly by dragging the corners of the transformation box outward.

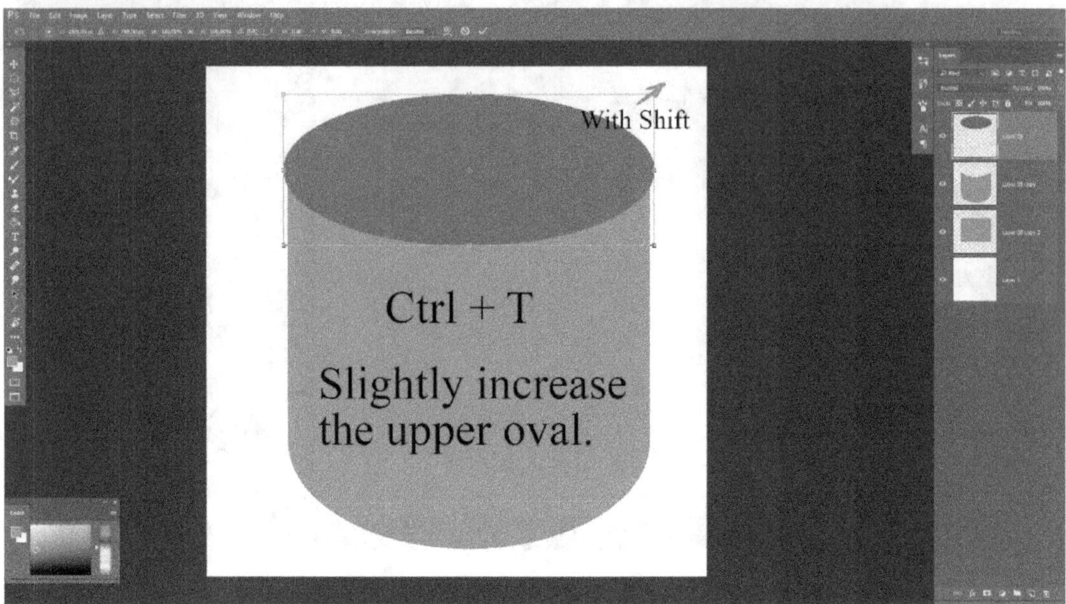

14. Select the layer of the bottom of the "cup". Click the Dodge Tool and set its parameters for Range and Exposure to Midtones and 100%, respectively. Pressing down on the Shift Key, draw a vertical line on the side of the "cup".

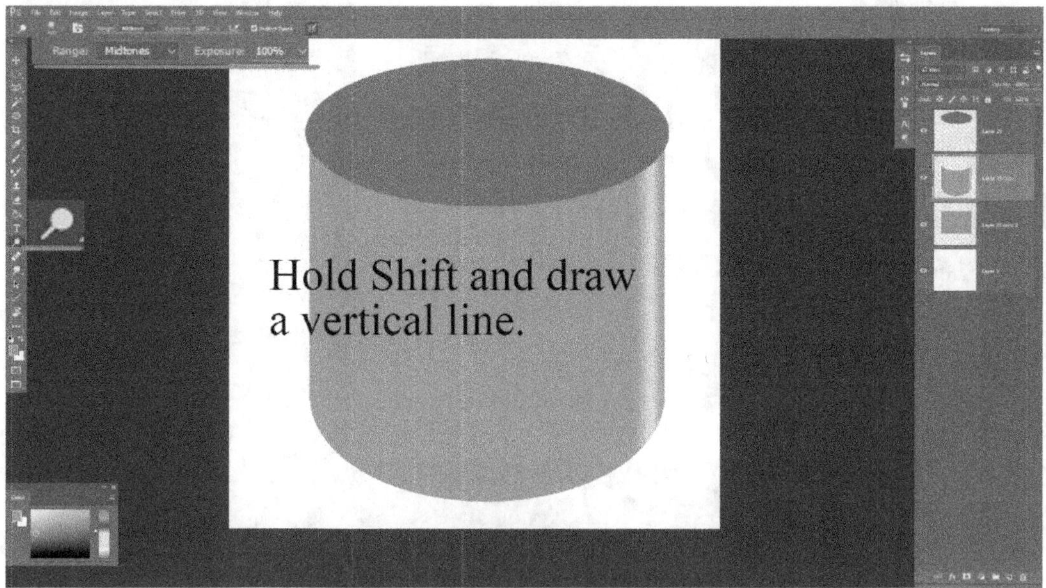

15.   Increase the brush size by pressing the "]" Key. Draw new lines until the image shown above is created.

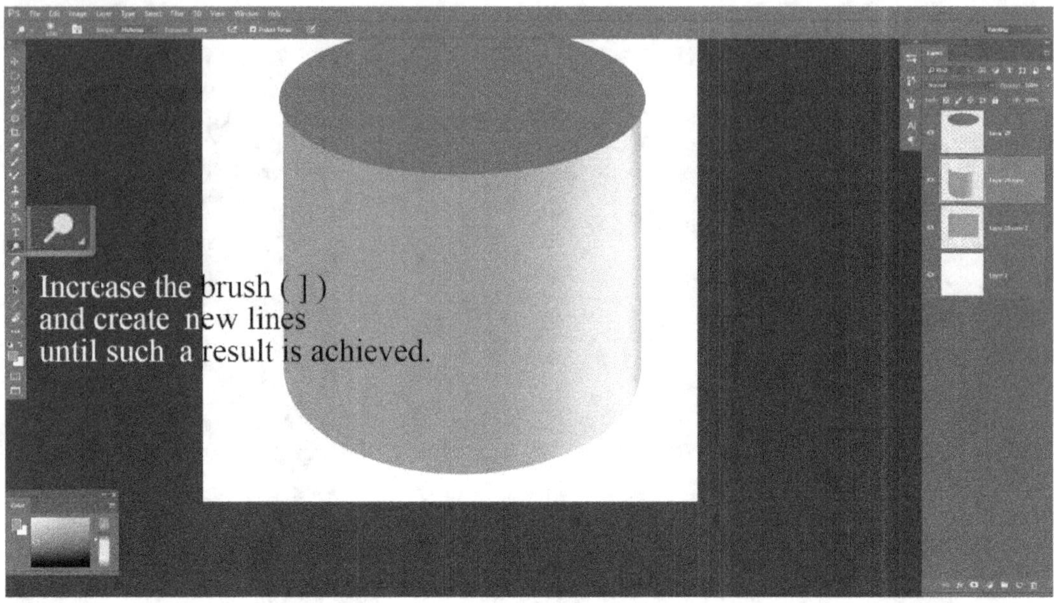

16. Use the Dodge and Burn Tools to draw highlights and shadows on the "cup". Draw vertical lines by holding the Shift Key while drawing the lights and shadows.

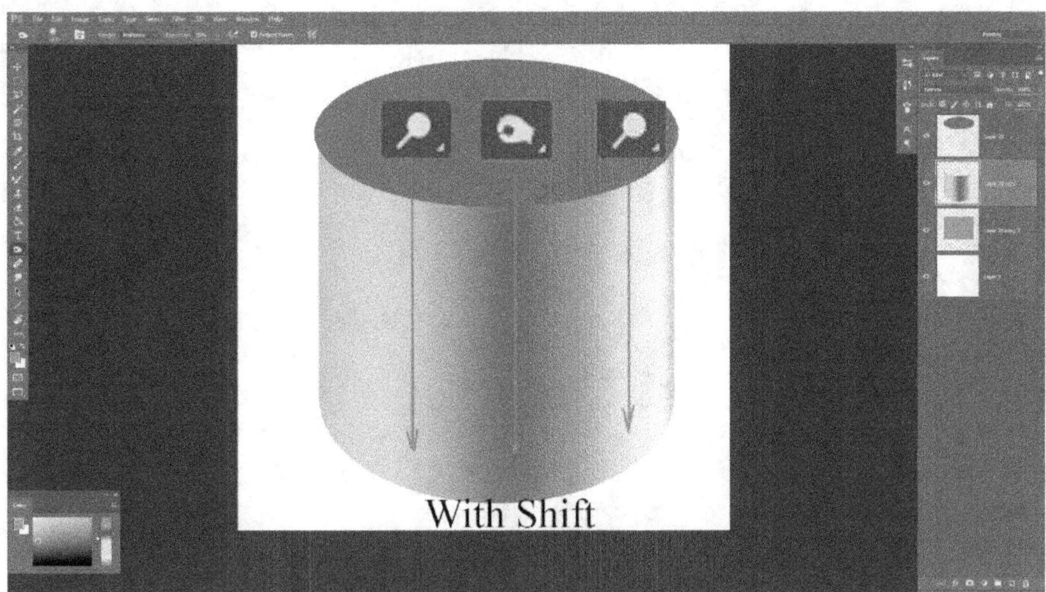

17. Click the icon of the top oval's layer. With the area selected, click the Right Mouse Button and choose "Transform Selection" on the menu.

18. Reduce the size of the selection area to the same as the width of the rectangle. Hold down the Shift Key while doing so.

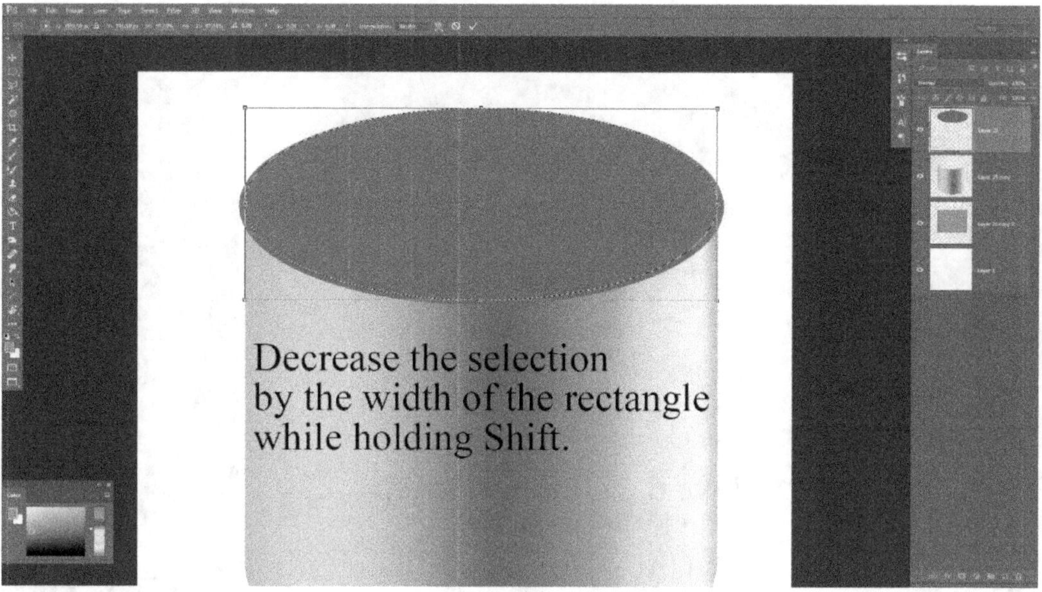

19. Move this selection area down while holding the Shift Key to make sure it is aligned with the "cup". Copy the area by pressing Ctrl+C and paste it to the same area by pressing Ctrl+V.

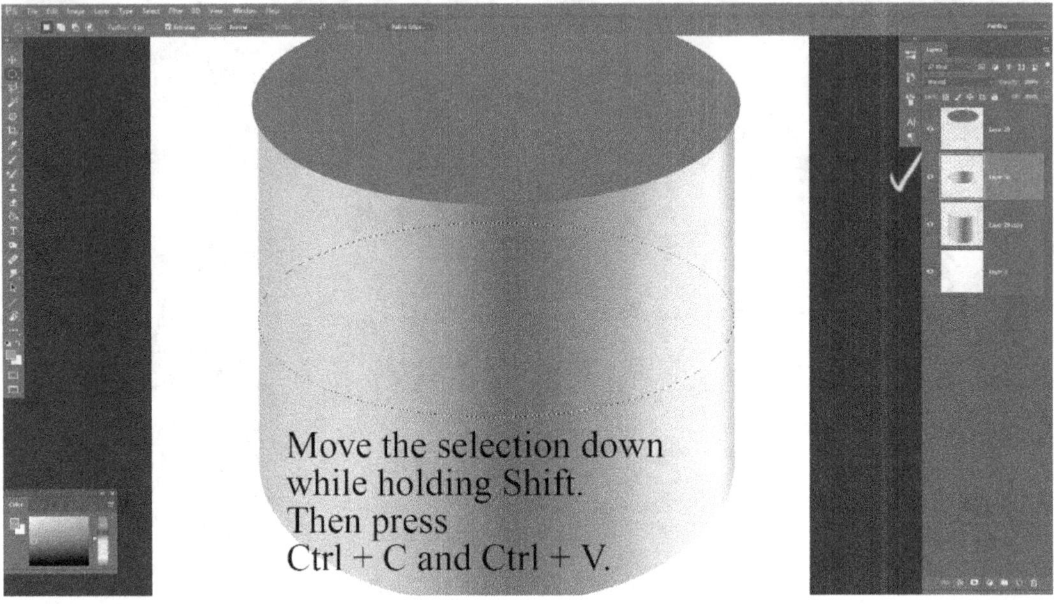

20. Press Ctrl+T and click the Right Mouse Button. Choose "Flip Horizontal" from the menu.

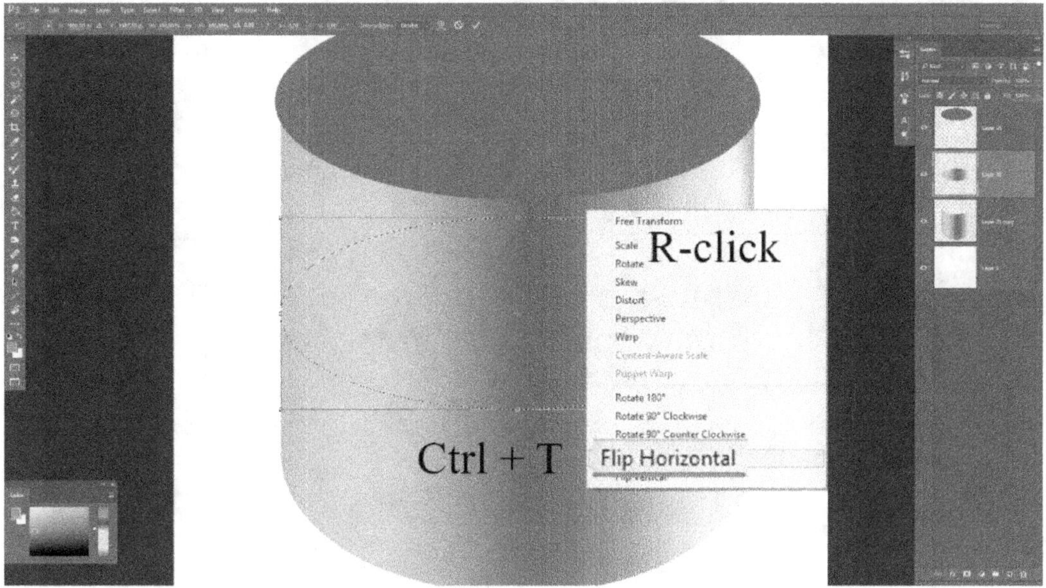

21. Move the copied area to the center of the top oval.

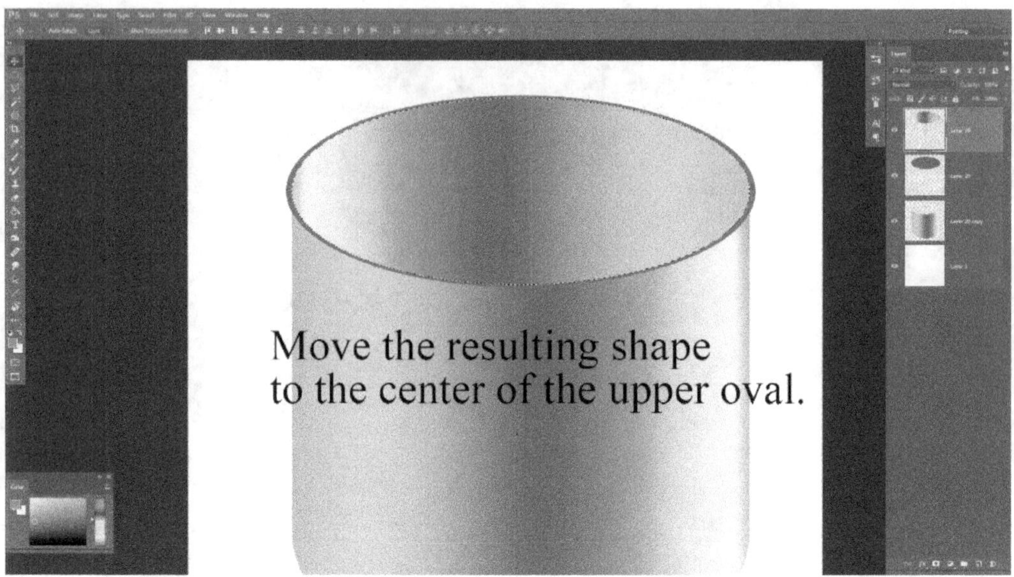

22. Lock the layer of the upper oval. Use the Brush Tool and paid the shine on the rim of the cup.

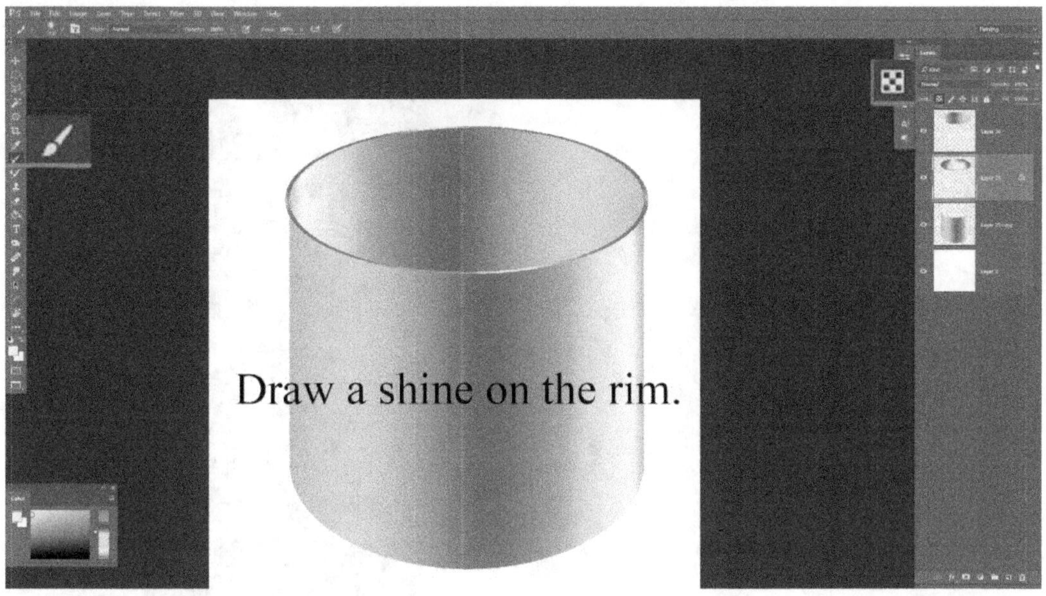

23. Lock the layer of the bottom of the cup. Draw a rounding on the bottom edge using the Brush Tool. You may rotate the canvas by pressing the R Key to make the drawing process more comfortable.

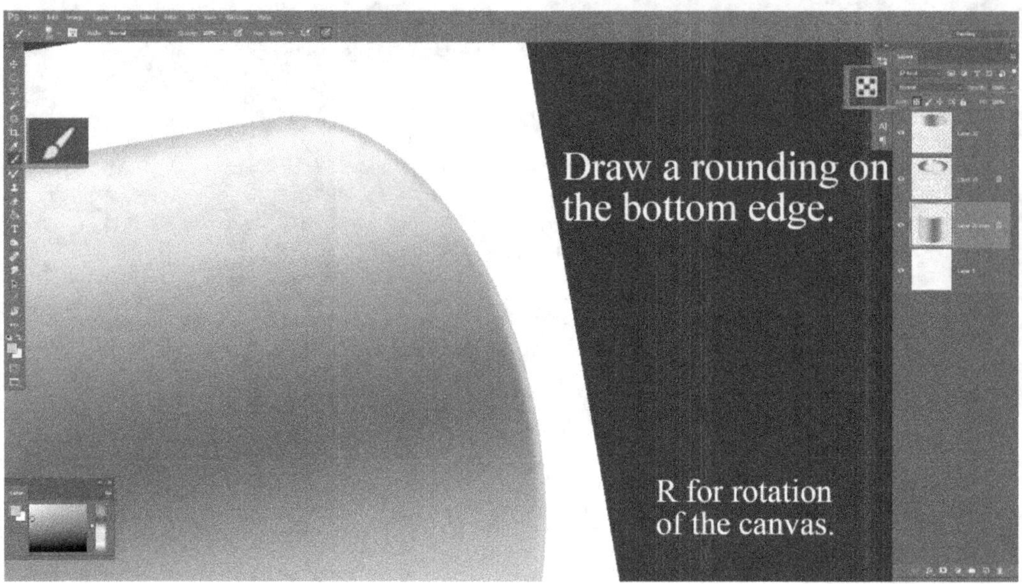

24. Draw a rounding under the upper oval with the Brush Tool. Adjust the Mode and Opacity of the tool to Normal and 14%, respectively.

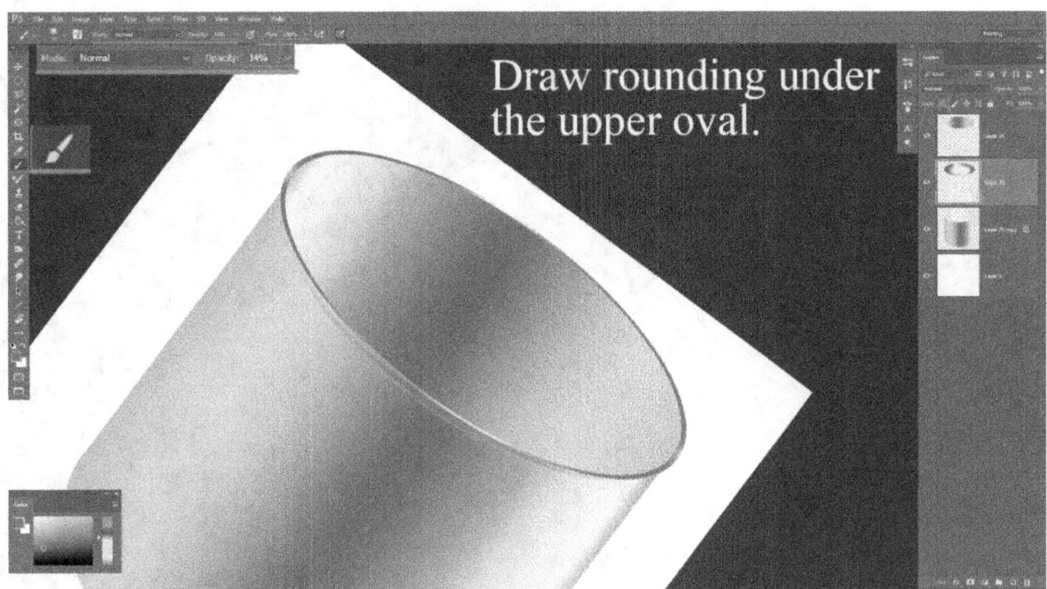

25. Lock the layer of the copied area. Draw a shadow on the inner walls of the inside of the cup with the Brush Tool.

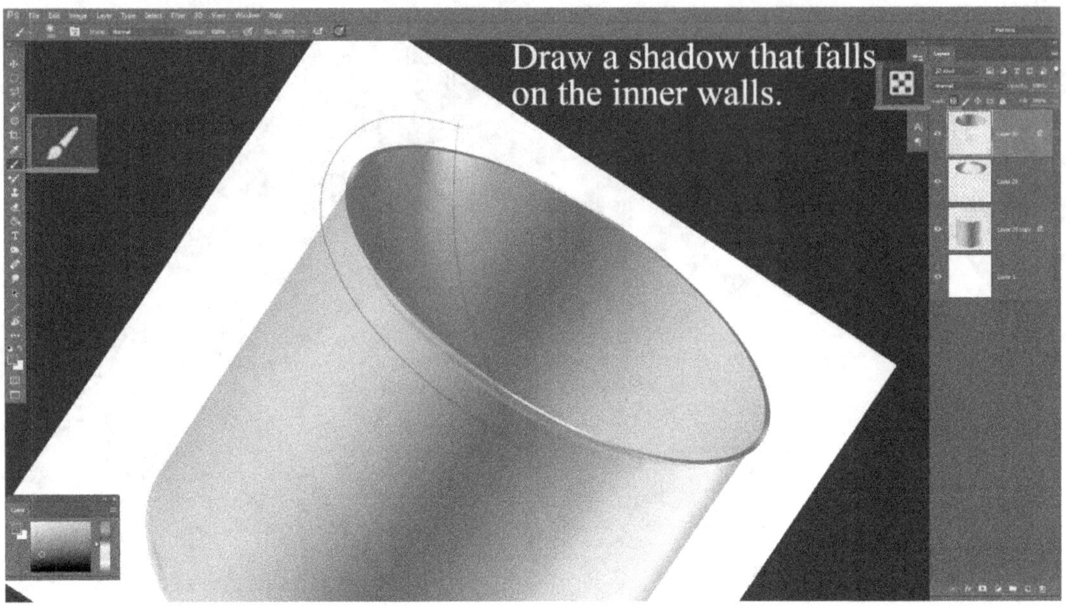

26. With the Dodge Tool set to Midtones Range and 100% Exposure, draw a highlight on the inside of the cup.

27. Unlock all the layers. Select the Brush Tool and change the Opacity to 9%. Choose the color white and draw a glare on the lighted areas.

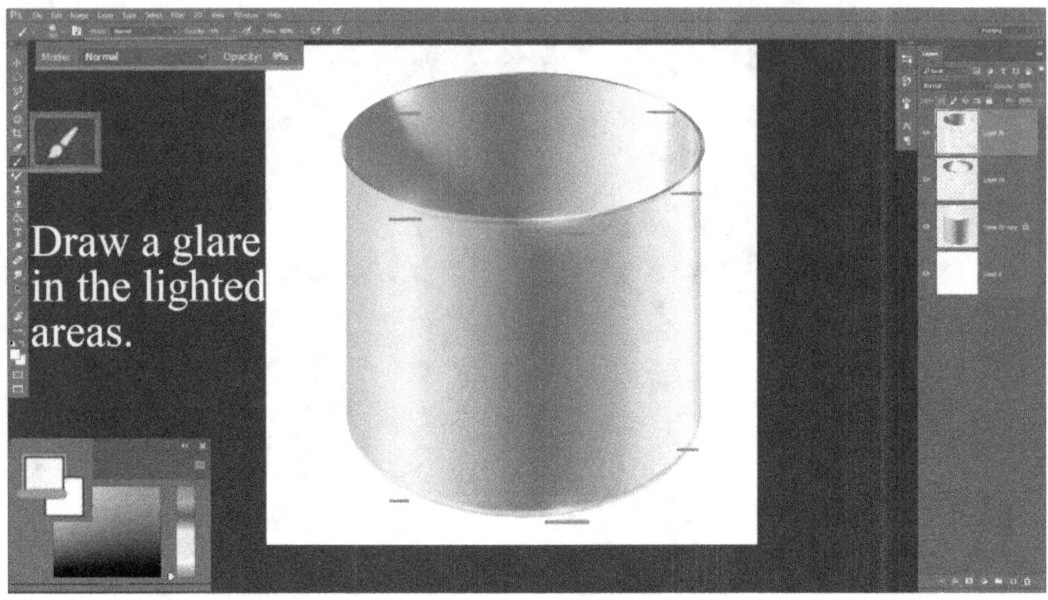

28. Select all the layers and merge them by clicking the Right Mouse Button and choosing Merge on the menu.

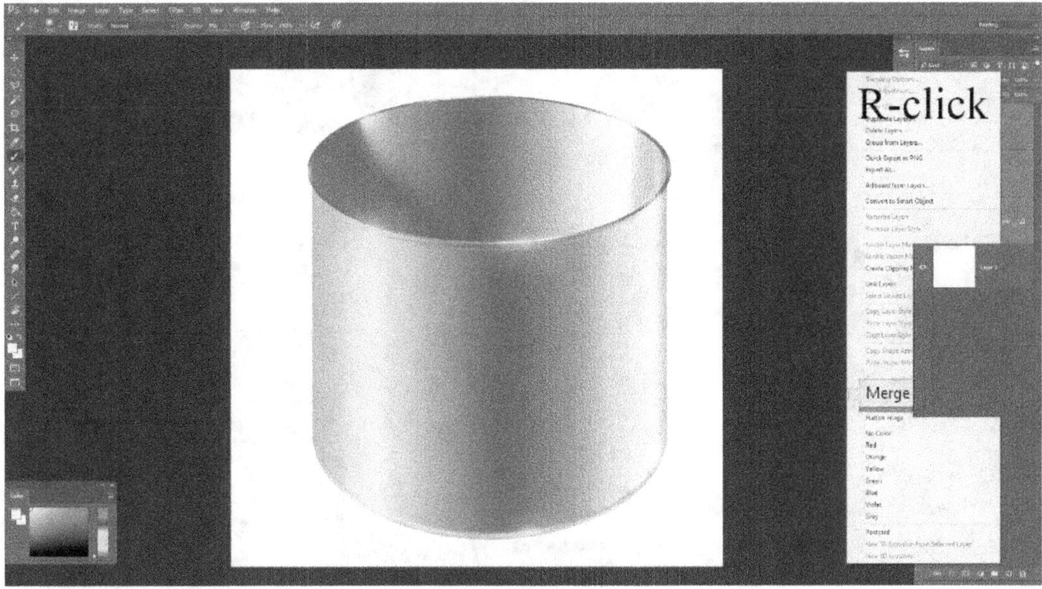

29. Press Ctrl+L to open the Levels Window. Change the middle and rightmost levels to .72 and 231, respectively.

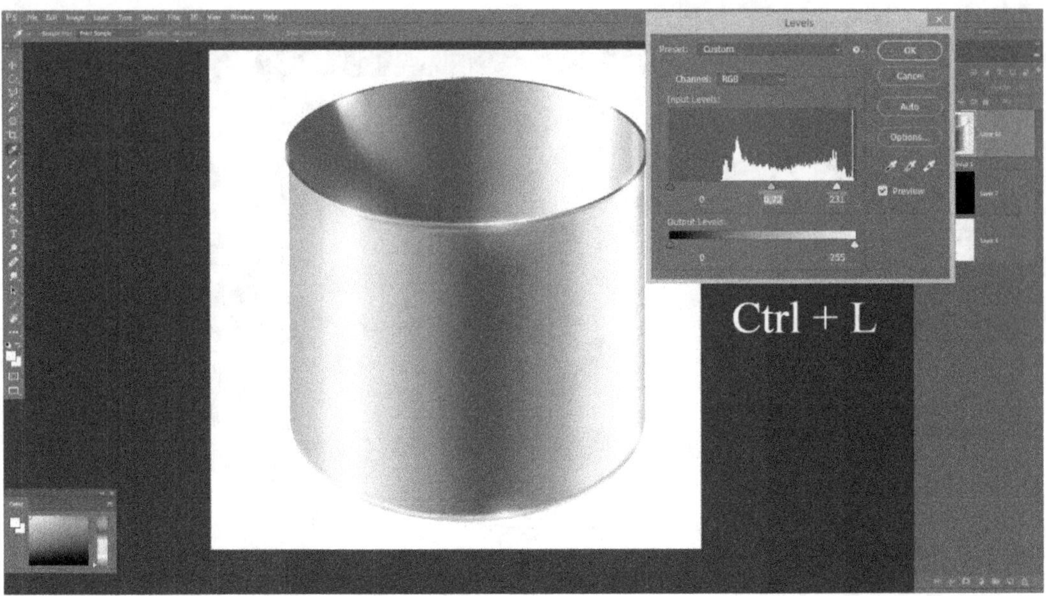

30. Press Ctrl+U and pull up the Hue/Saturation Window. Change the Saturation to -69.

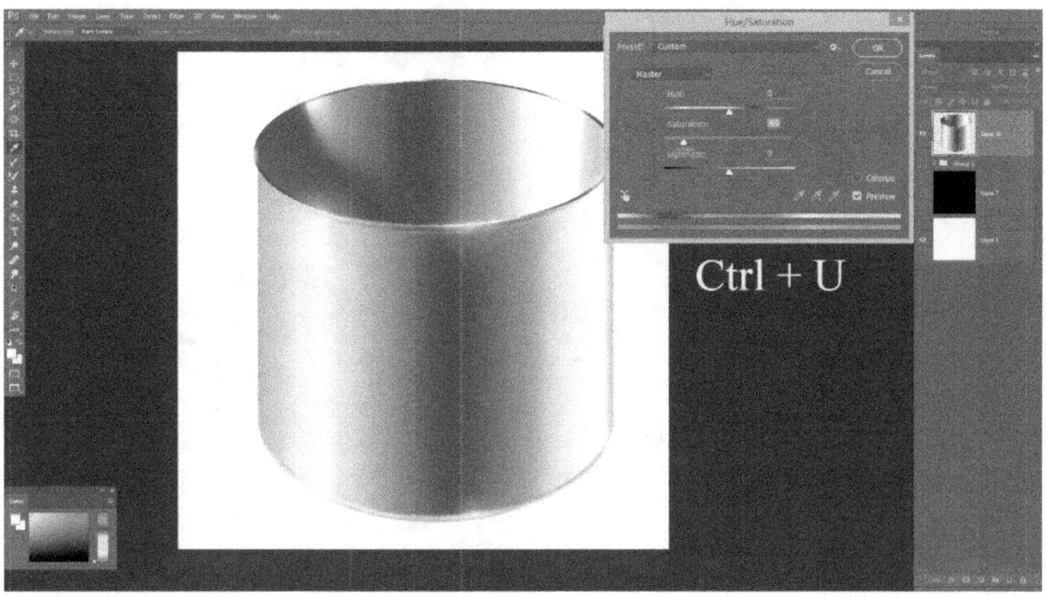

Gem

1. On a new layer, draw a sketch of any shape.

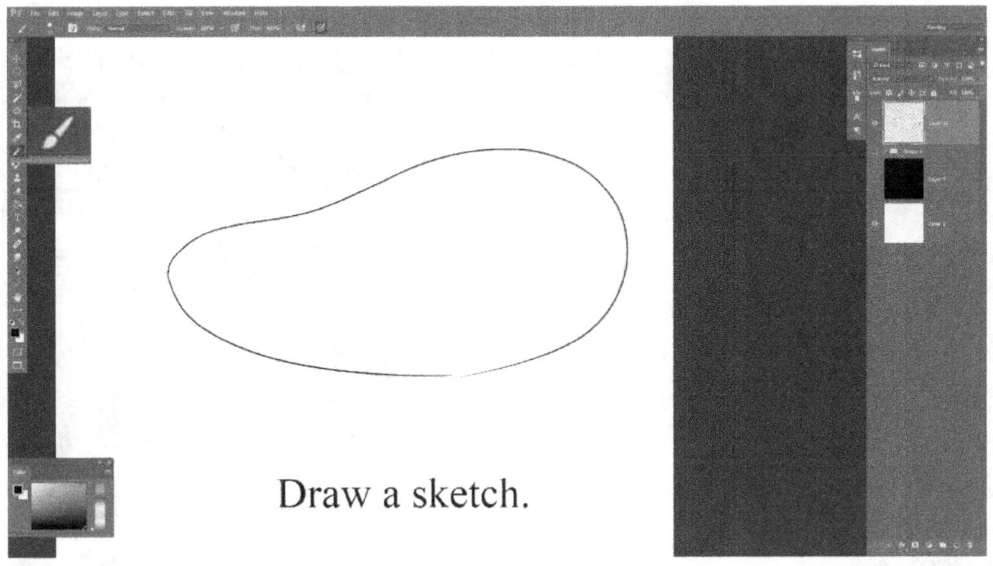

2. Create another layer. Select the Brush Tool and choose a soft brush. Paint over the sketch with any color.

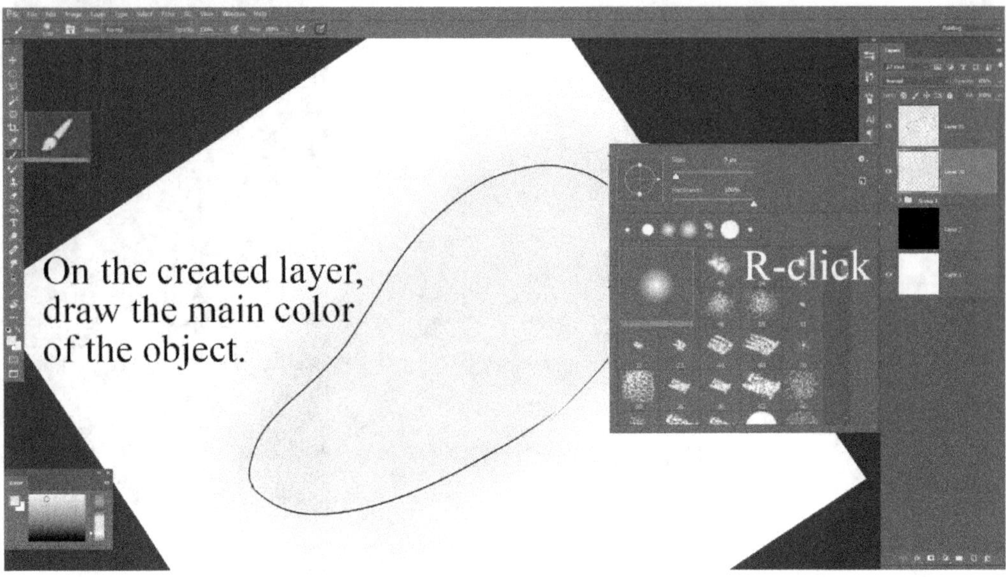

3. Draw the shadows of the shape on another layer.

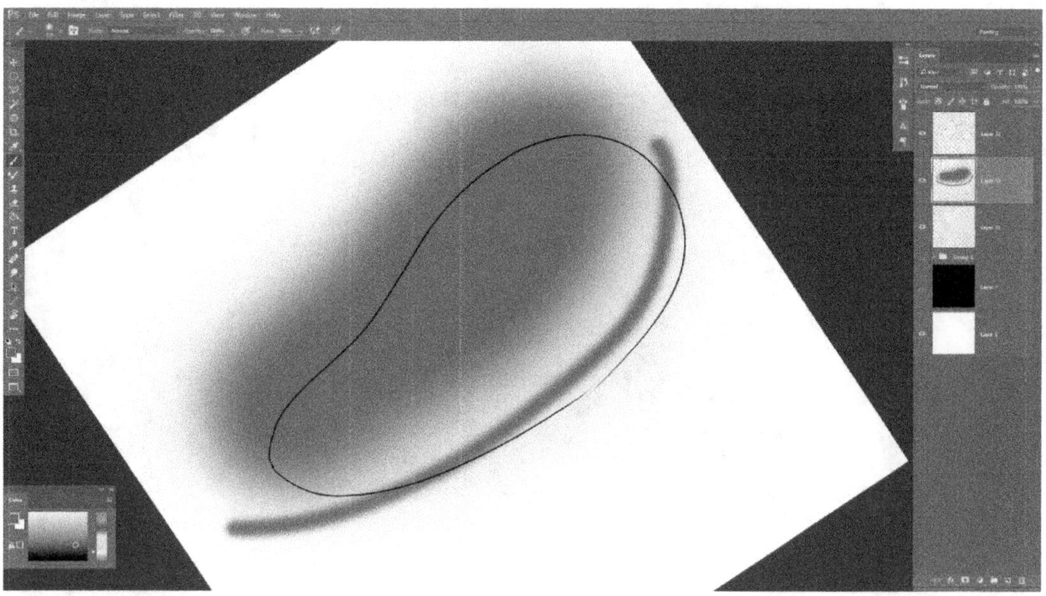

4. Select the Eraser Tool. Open the Brush Presets window by clicking the icon for it. Select the Brush Tip Shape and change its Spacing to 1%. Remove any excess colors.

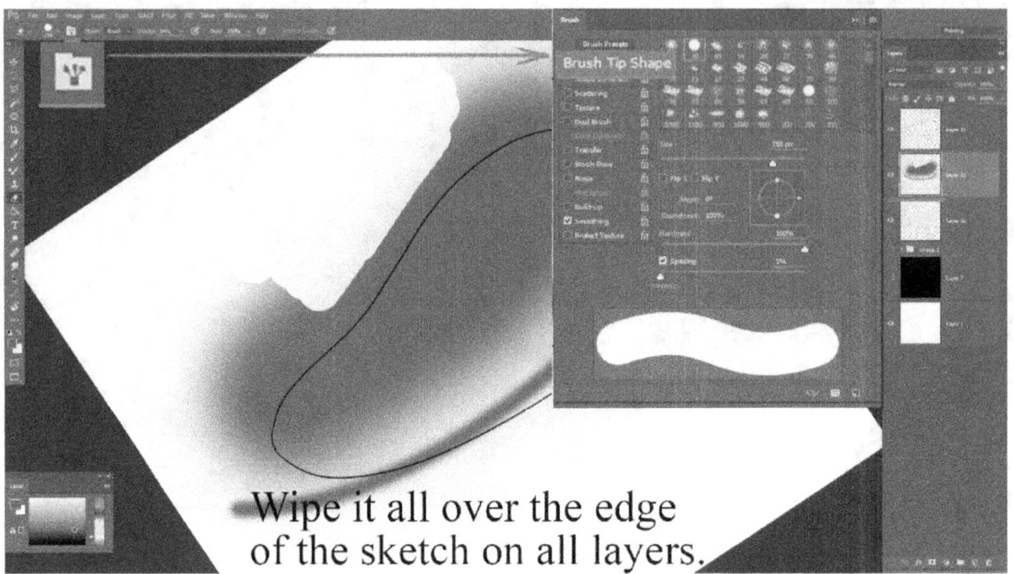

5. Choose the Polygonal Lasso Tool and mark out an arbitrary area for the reflection.

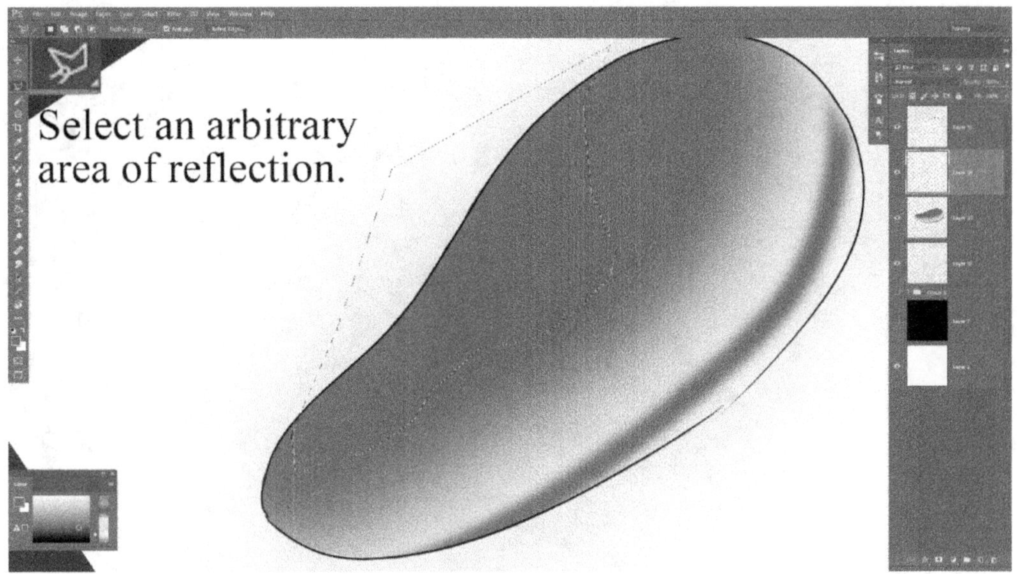

6. Click the Right Mouse Button and select "Feather..." Set the Feather Radius to 10.

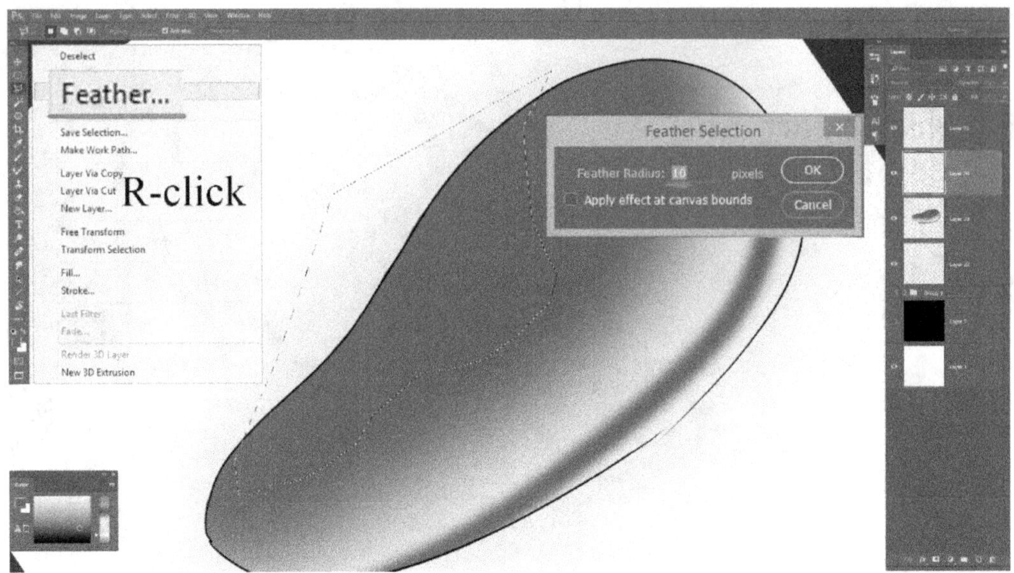

7. Make a new layer and fill the selection with a light color with the Brush Tool.

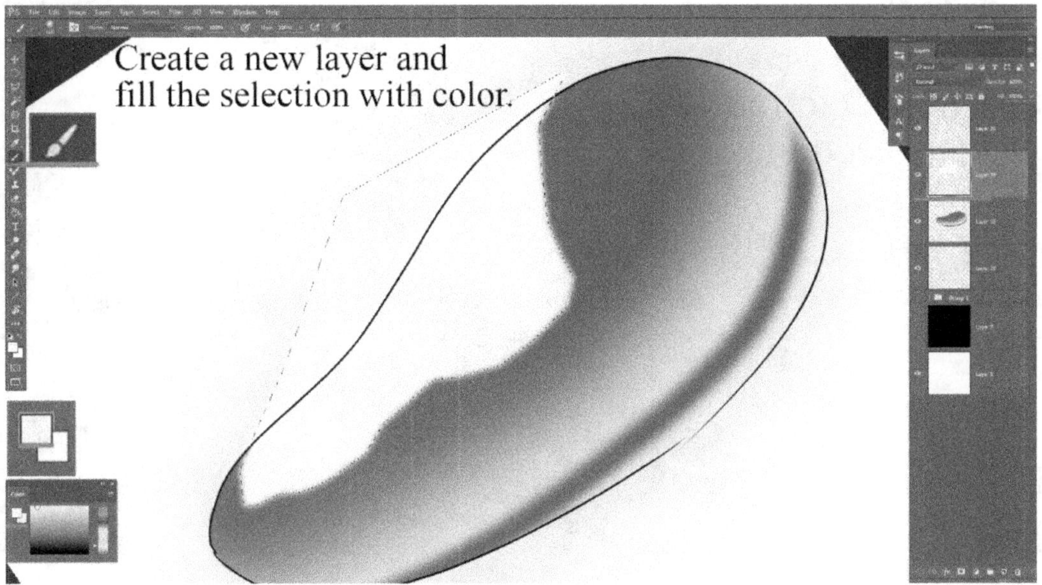

8. Press Ctrl+D to remove the selection.

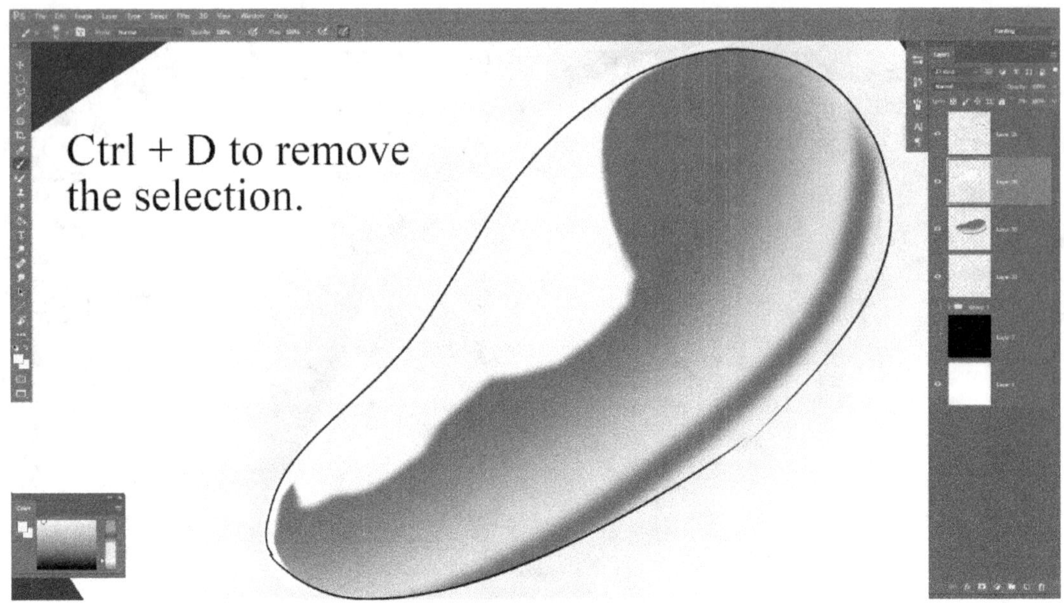

9. Select the Eraser Tool. Select a soft brush and adjust its size to 700px and its Hardness to 0%.

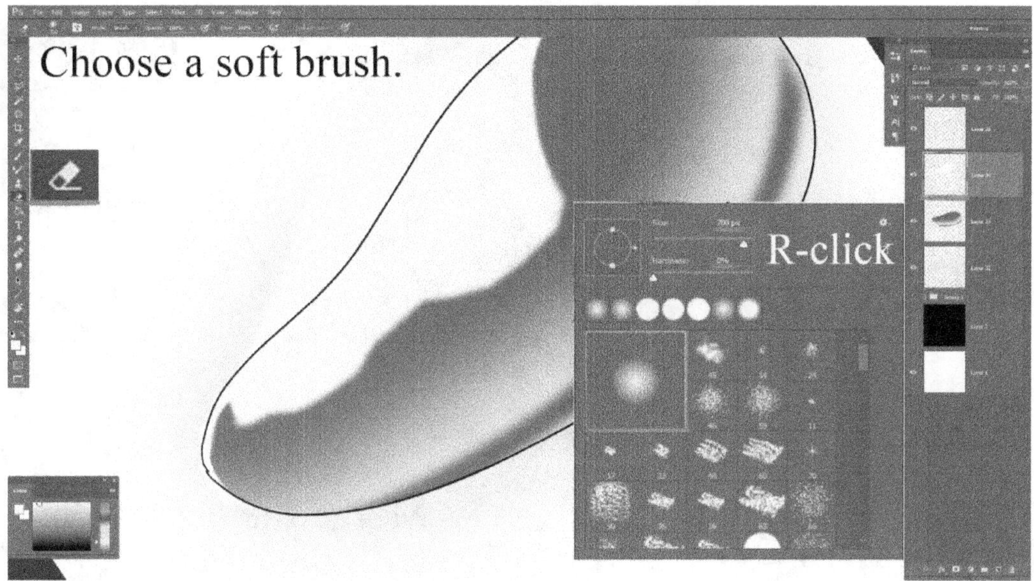

10. Soften the edges of the image and the area shown. Merge all the layers with the colors.

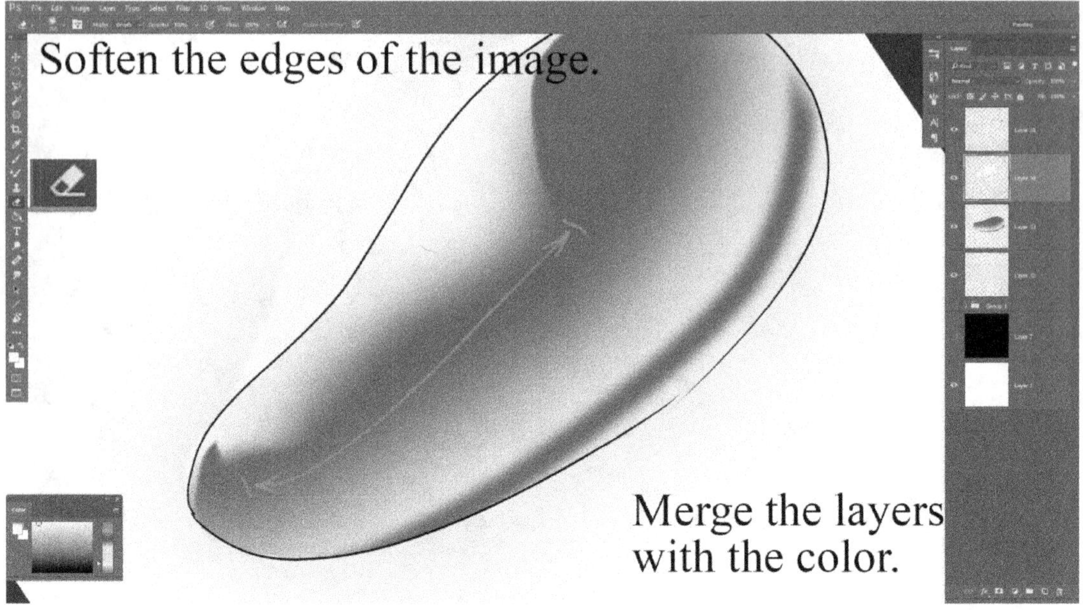

11. Select the Brush Tool and choose a soft brush. Draw a transition between the line of the sketch and the shadow.

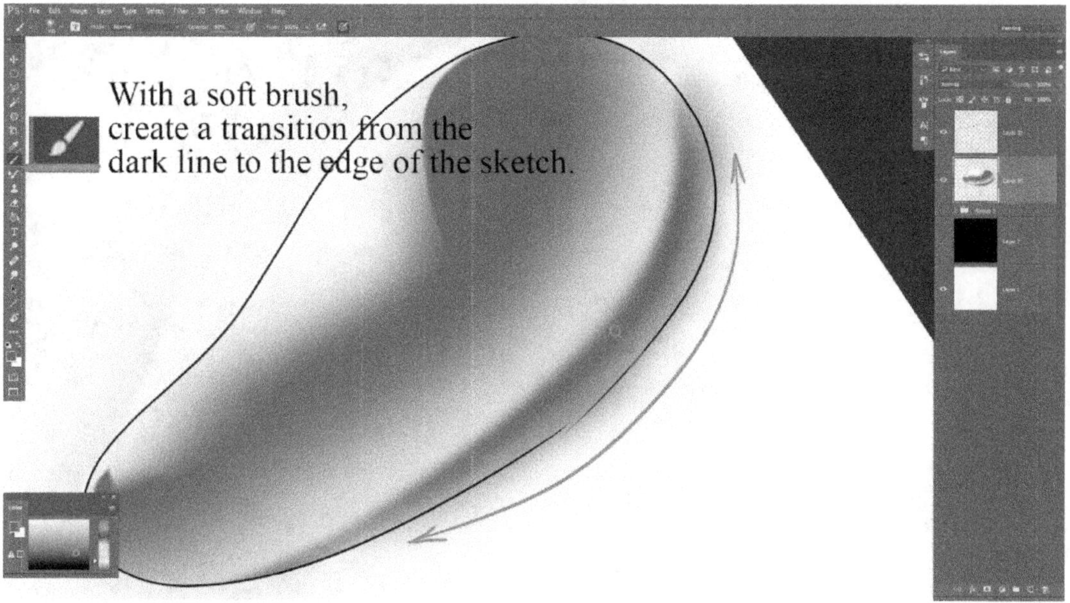

12. Select the Dodge Tool and set the Range to Highlights and Exposure to 100%. Paint over the areas shown above.

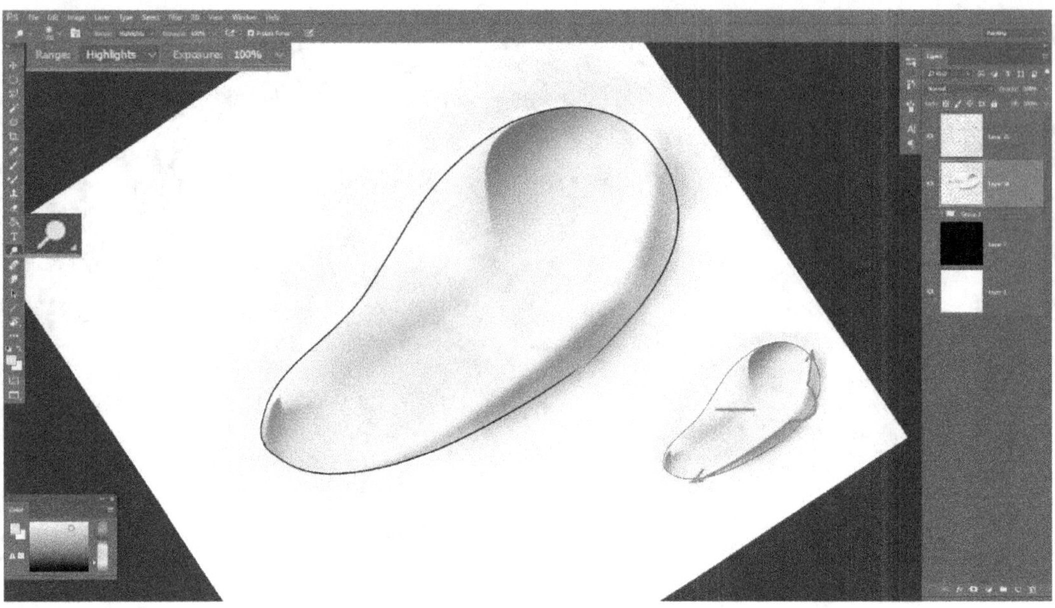

13. Press Ctrl+U to bring up the Hue/Saturation window. Change the Saturation level to -32.

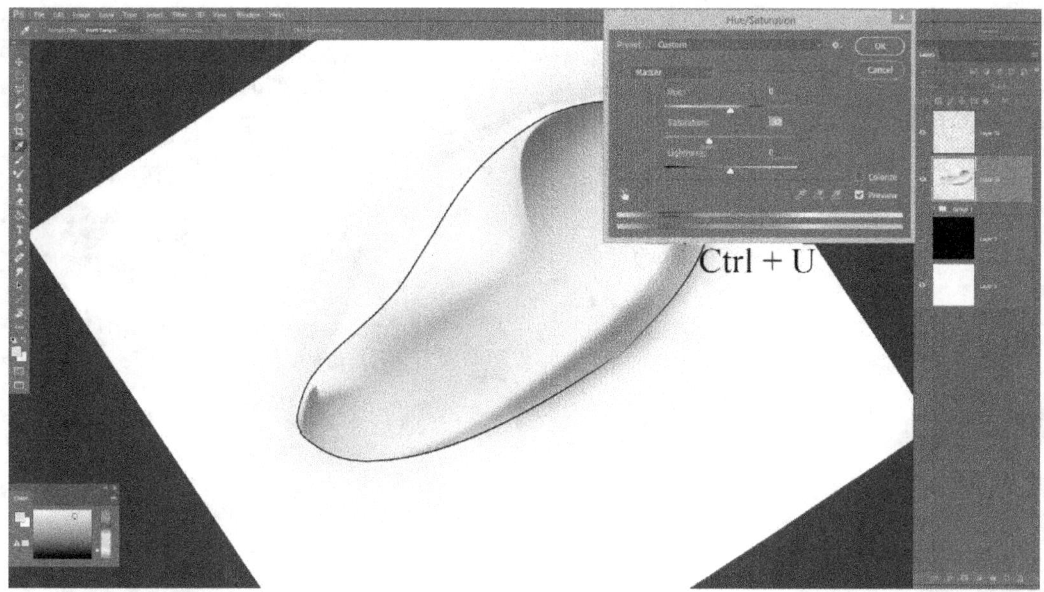

14. Choose the Burn Tool. Set the Range to Shadows and Exposure to 10%. Paint over the areas marked.

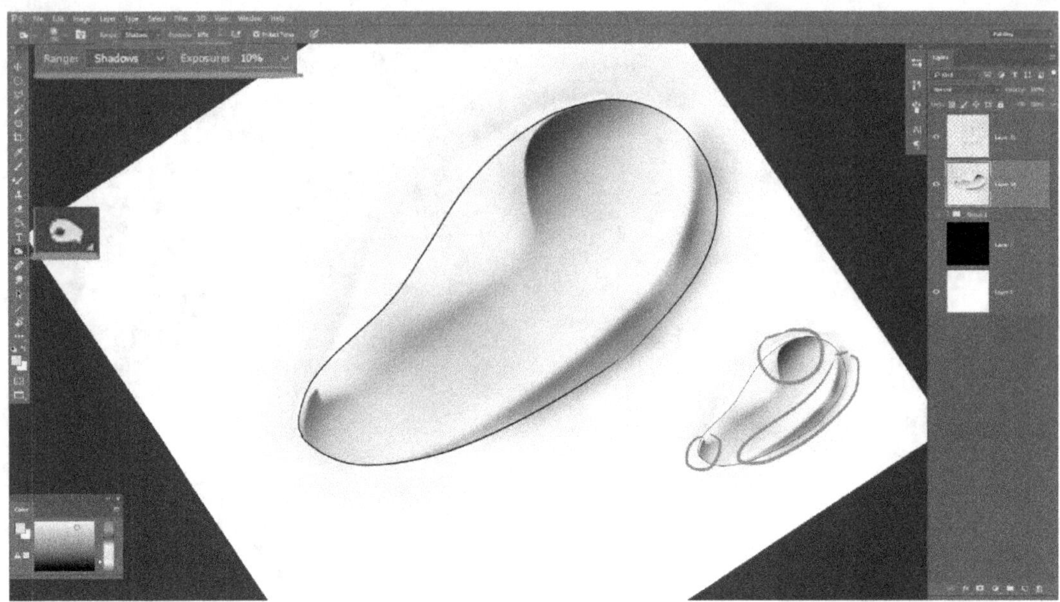

15. Choose the Dodge Tool again and paint over the marked area.

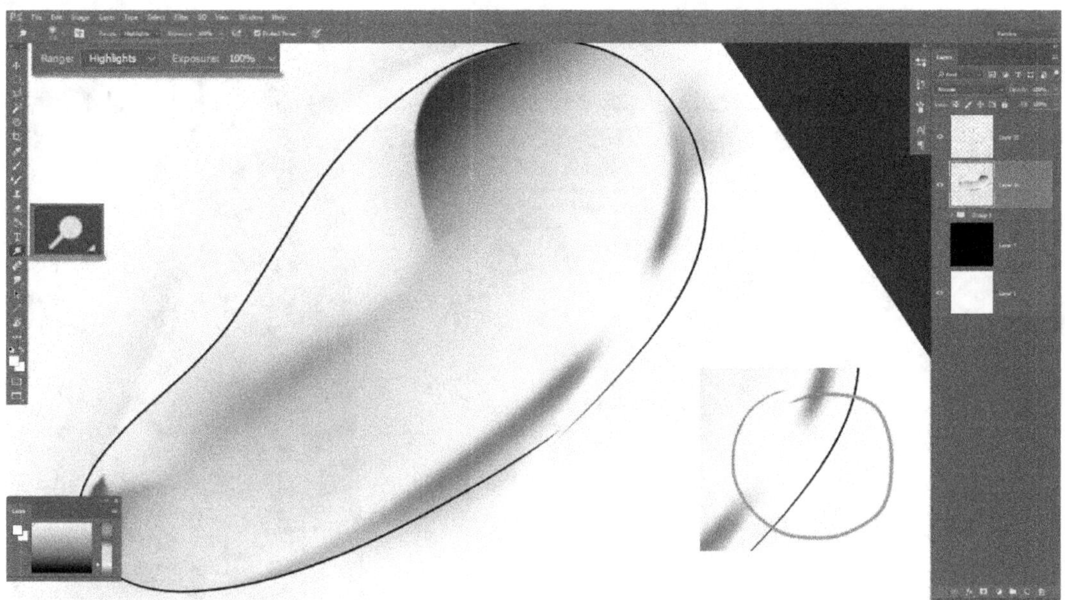

16. Use the Eraser Tool to remove excess areas of color.

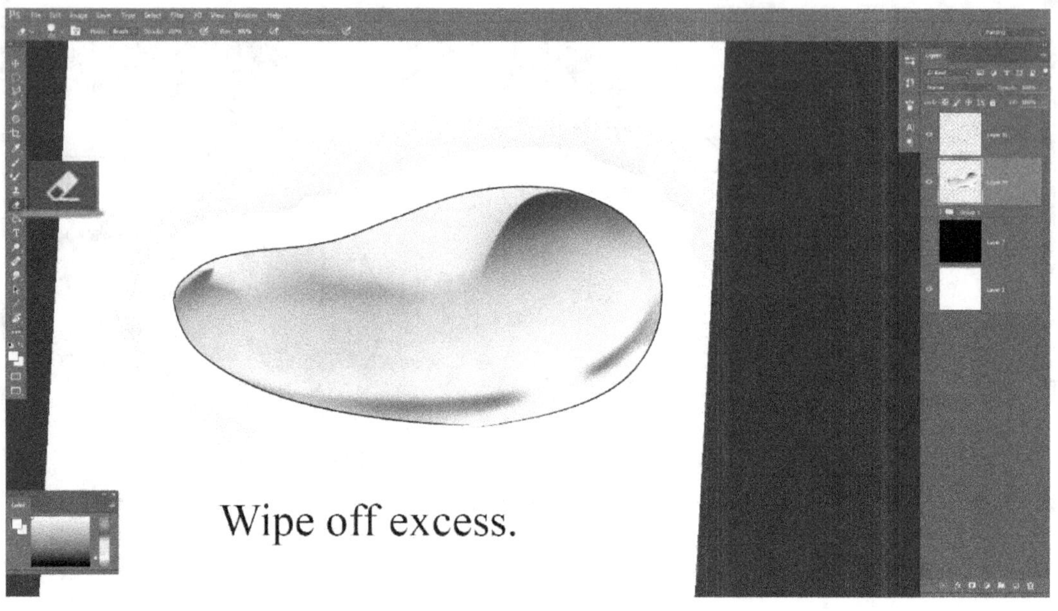

17. Use the Dodge Tool to draw highlights for the glare.

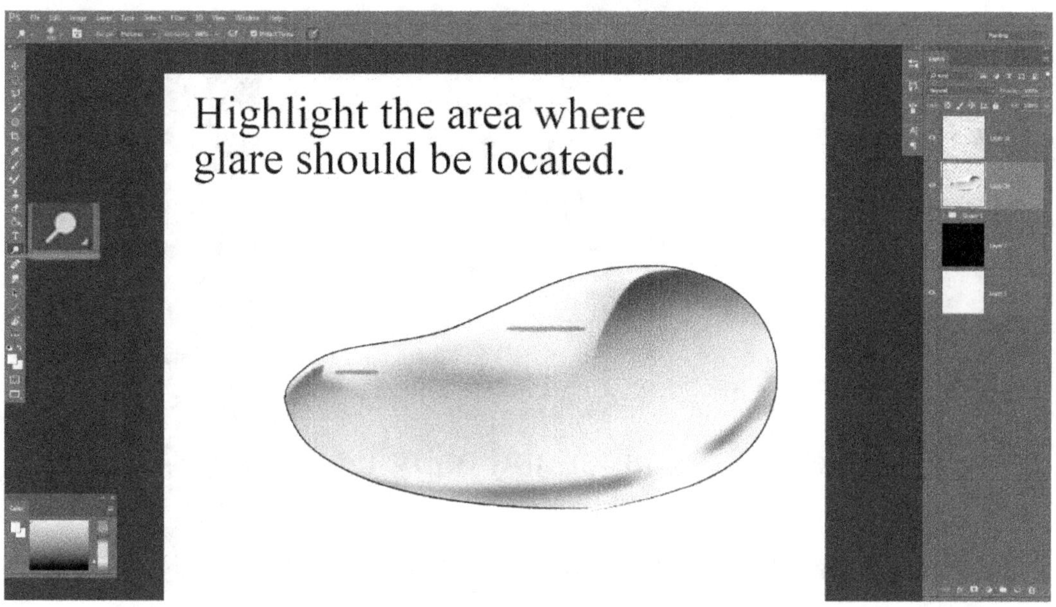

18. Move the image and make a copy of the layer.

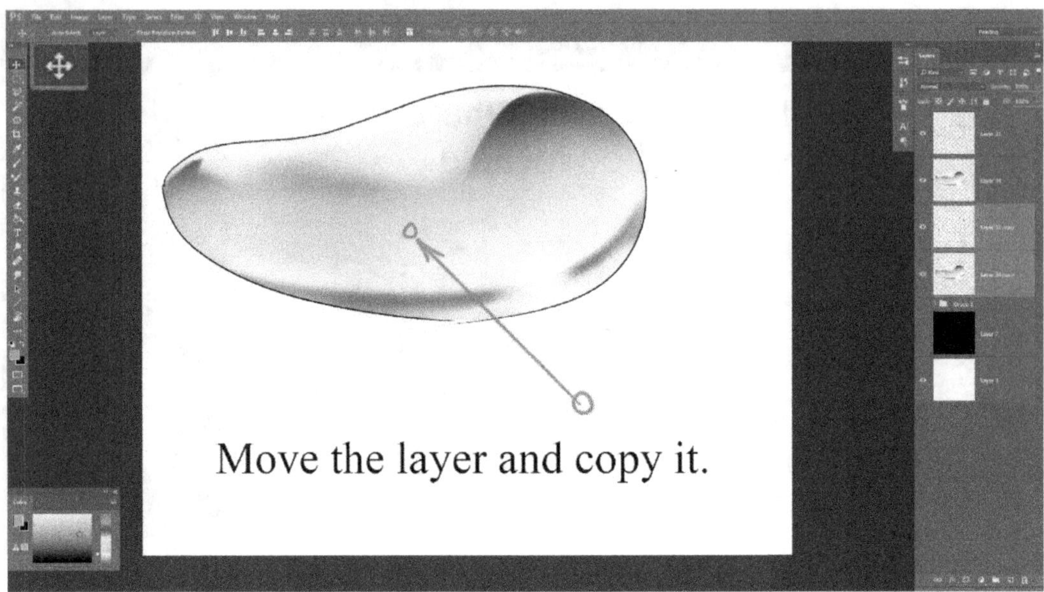

19. Press Ctrl+T and deform the copied layer as if it were a shadow.

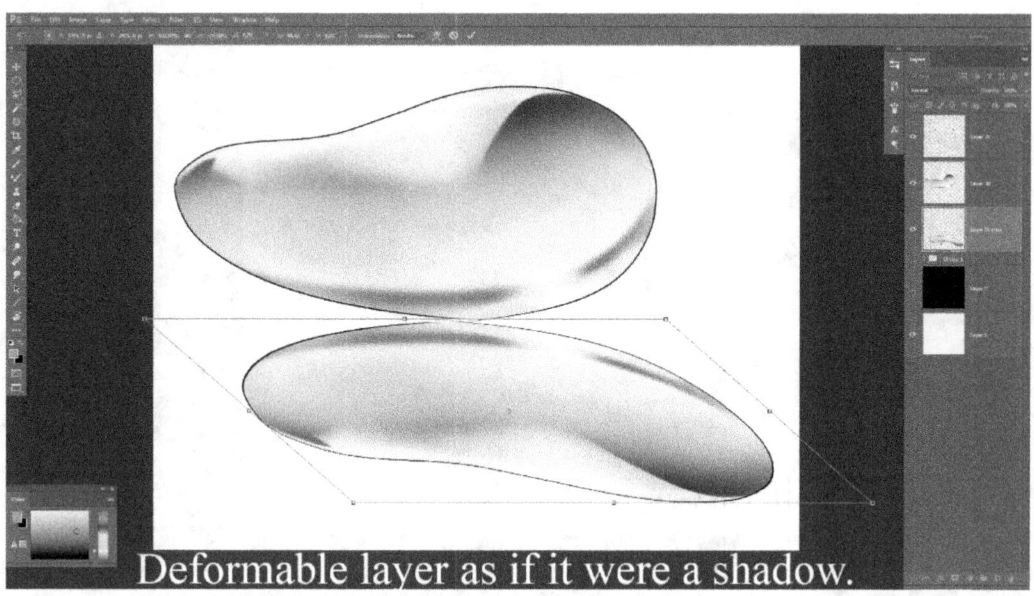

20. Lock this layer and paint it with a solid color.

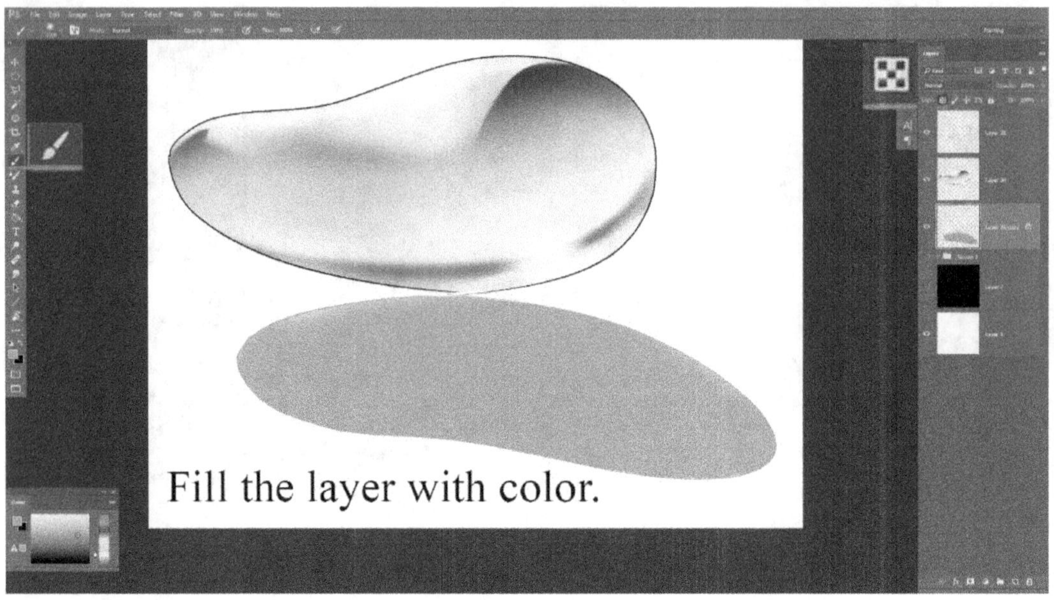

21. Use the Burn Tool to darken the areas of the shadow shown. Make sure the Range is set to Midtones and the Exposure is set to 31%.

22. Choose the Dodge Tool and change the Range to Midtones. Draw a light point over the area shown.

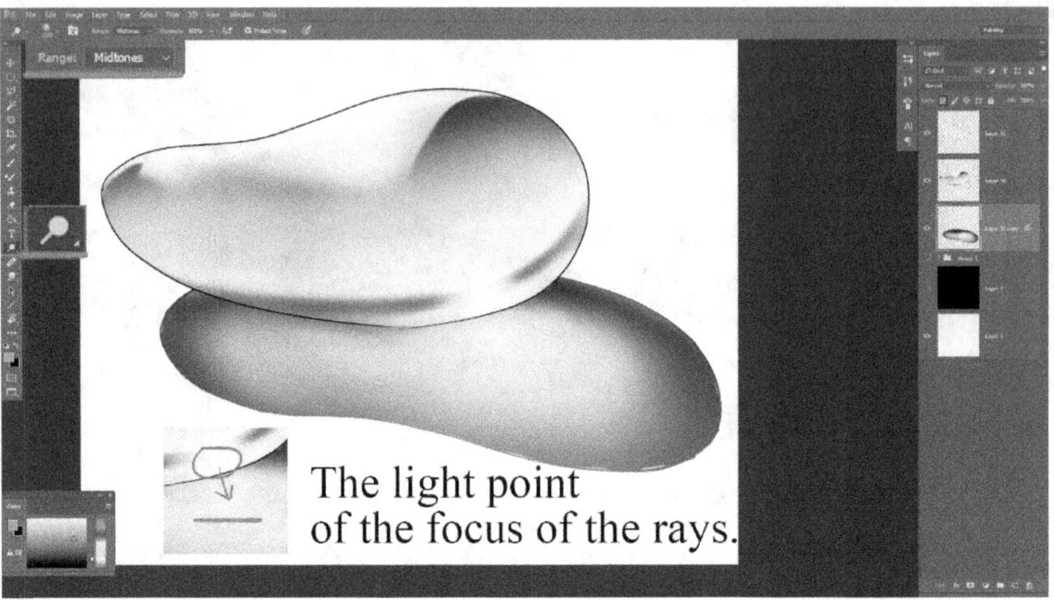

23. Lower the exposure to 25% and highlight the marked area.

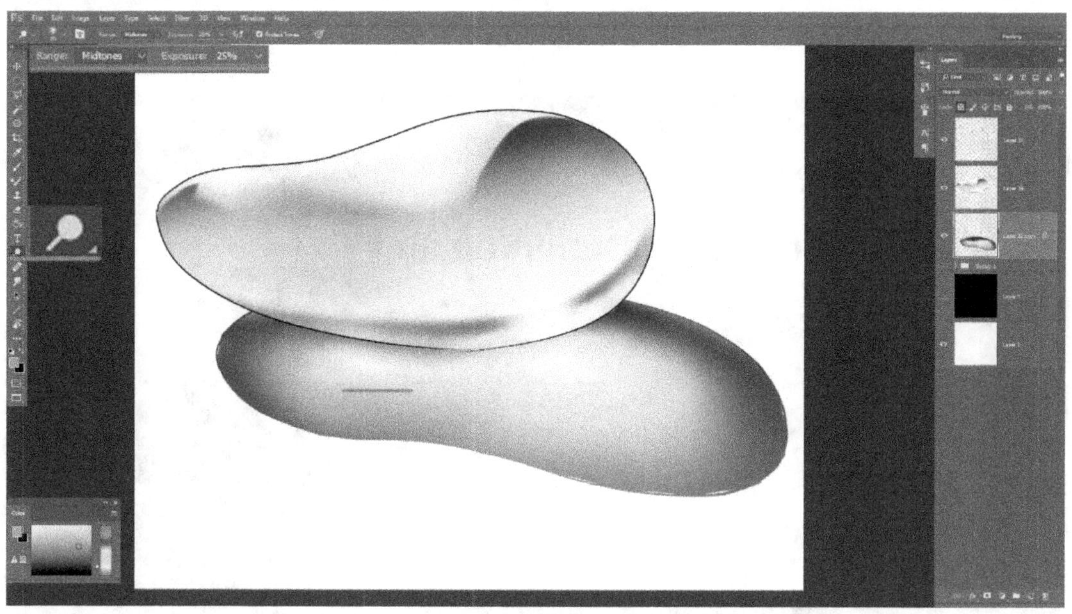

24. Mark a selection with the Rectangular Marquee Tool. Click the Right Mouse Button and select "Feather..." from the menu. Set the Feather Radius to 80.

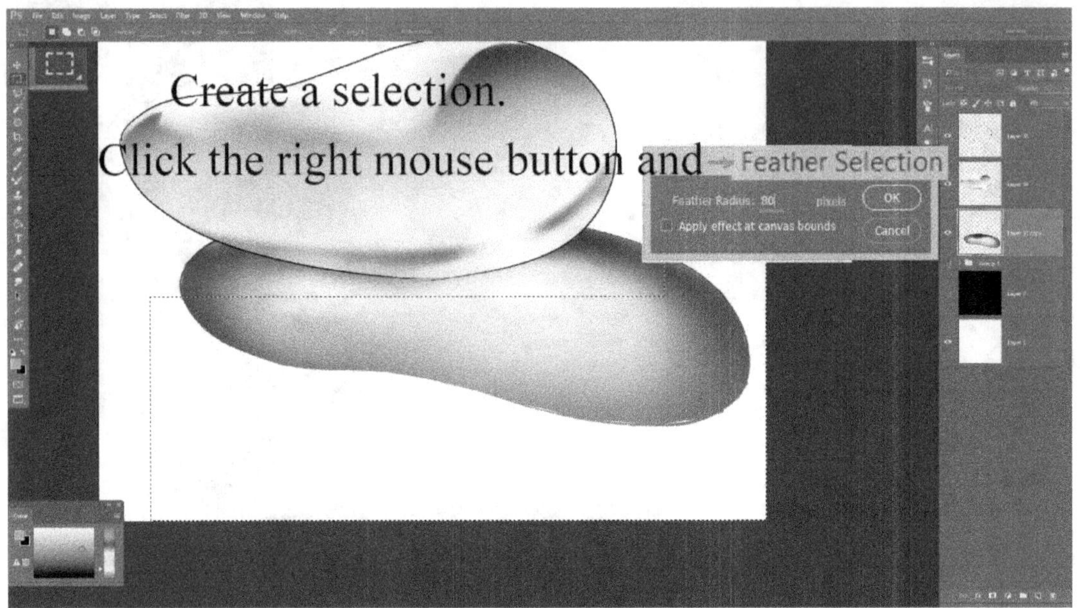

25. With the area still selected, go to Filter and choose Blur on the Menu. On the next menu choose Gaussian Blur.

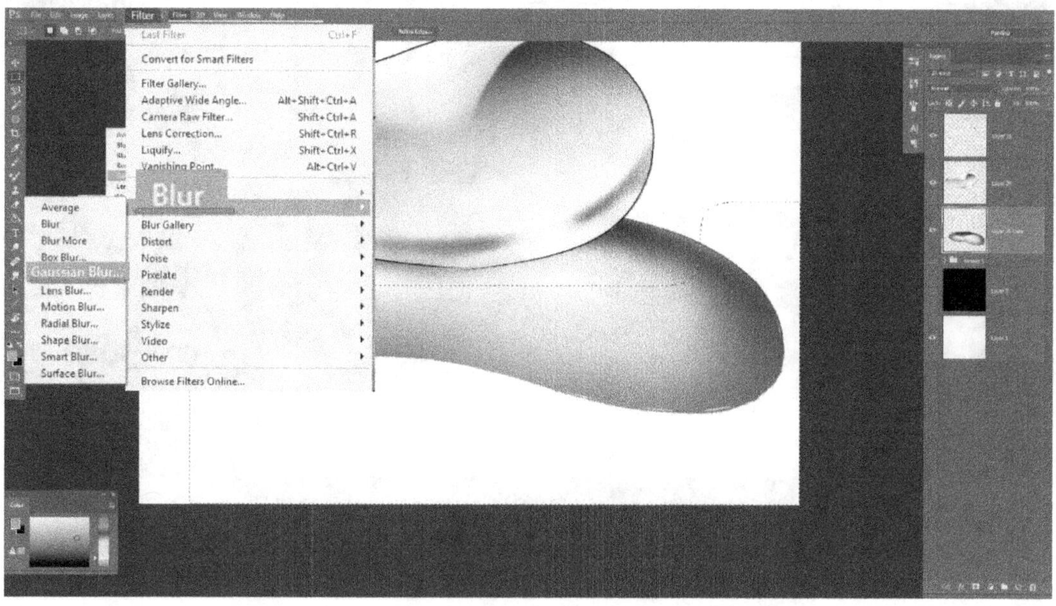

26. Set the Radius to 20.8.

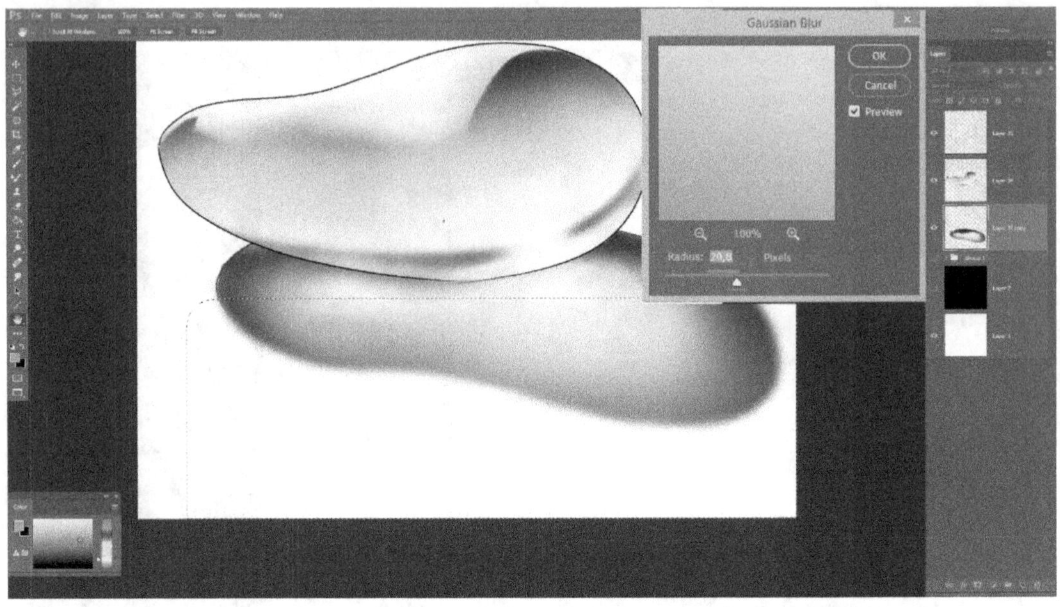

27. Create a new rectangular selection. Click the Right Mouse Button and choose Feather on the menu. Set the Feather Radius to 120.

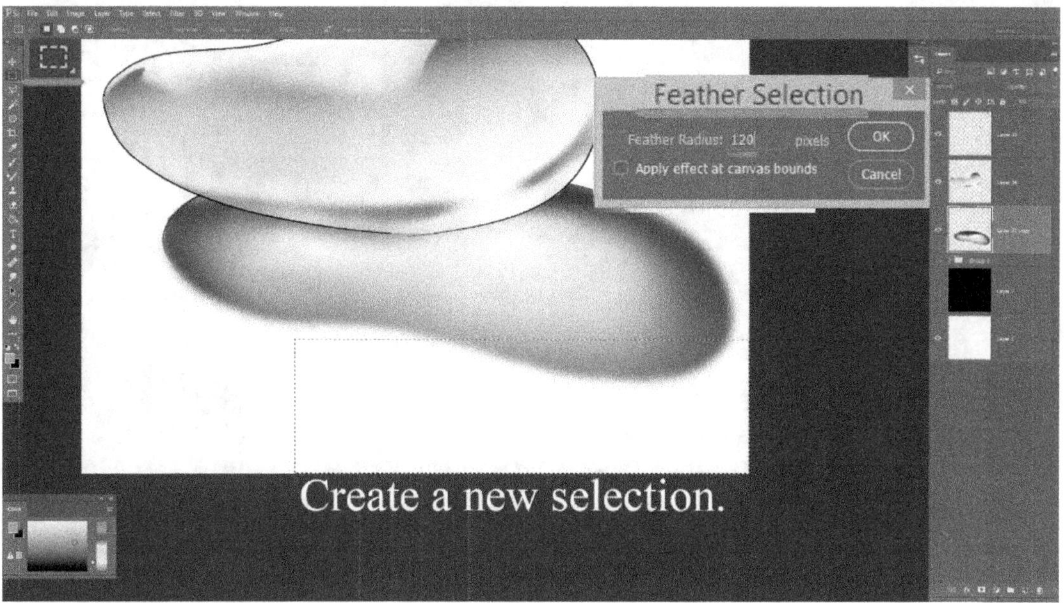

28. Apply Gaussian Blur to this area and set its Radius to 40.1.

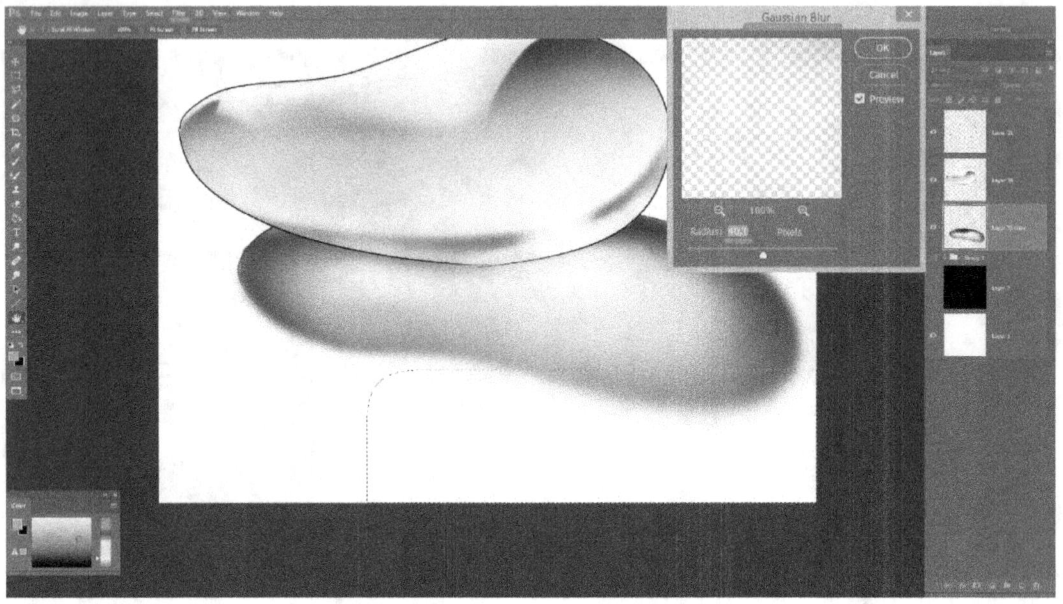

29. Use the Eraser Tool and remove a small area as shown to enhance the blur even more.

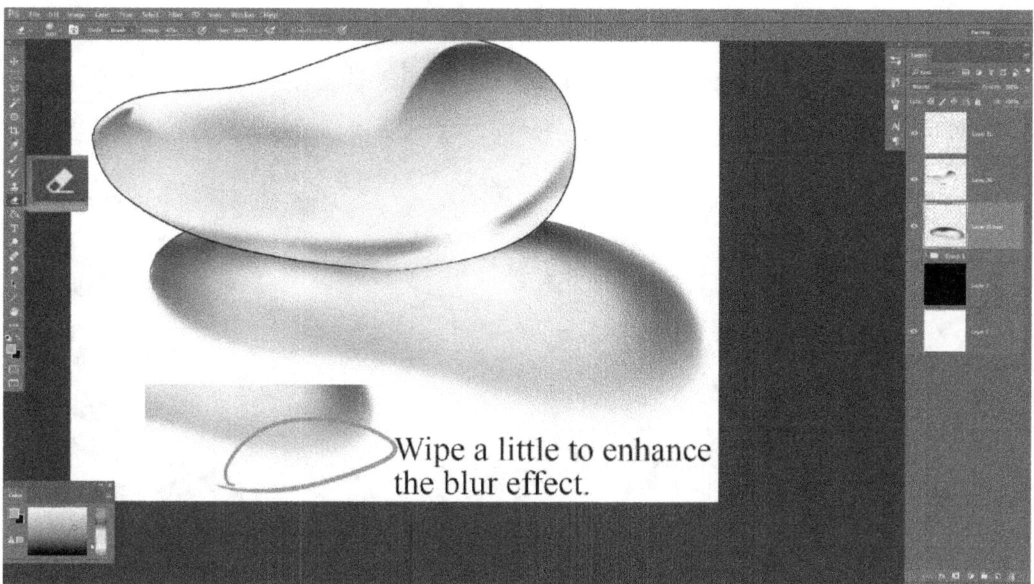

30. Select and lock the layer of the sketch. With the Brush Tool, paint over the sketch lines with a color close to the color of the object to hide the lines.

31. The object with the lines is hidden.

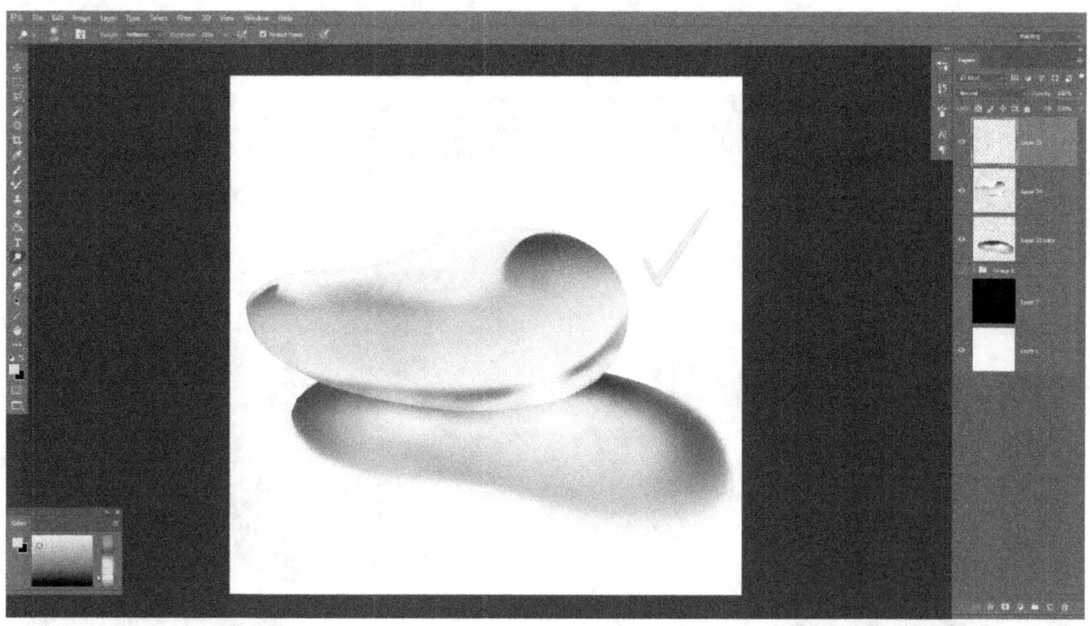

32. Merge all the layers together. Press Ctrl+U to bring up the Hue/Saturation Window. Change the Hue to an arbitrary color and adjust the Saturation to your desired level.

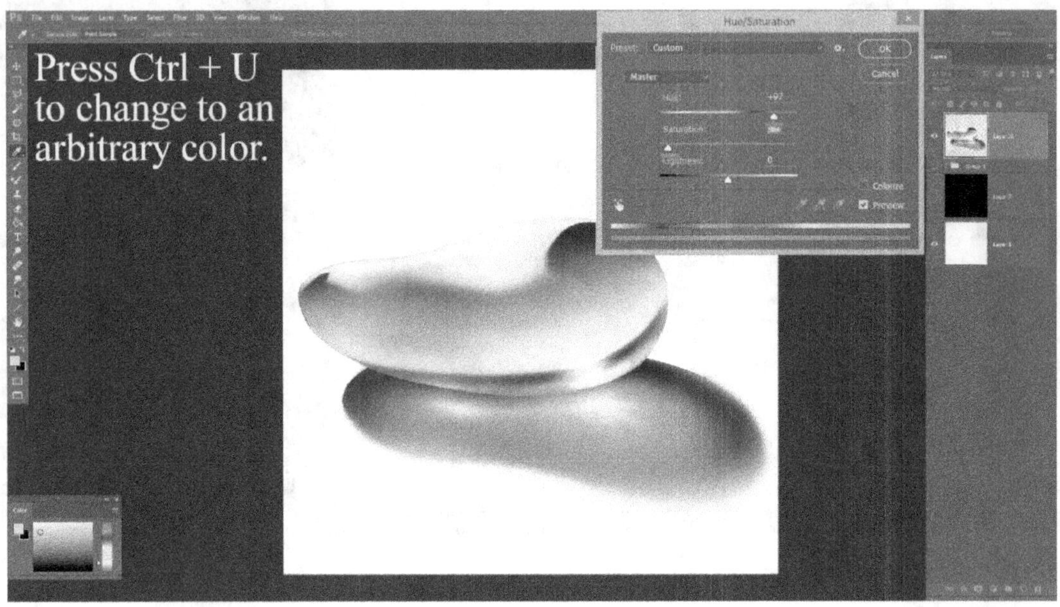

Creating 3D Images

Standing Human

1. Make a new layer. On this layer, draw the proportions of a human. Begin drawing the person by starting with the head.

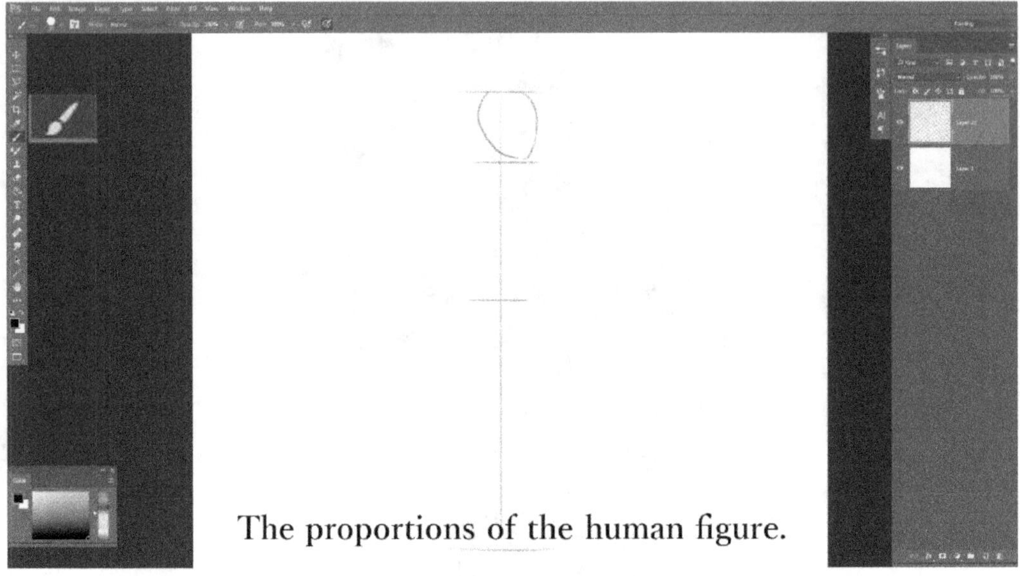

The proportions of the human figure.

2. Draw a rough outline of the shape of the man's body and legs.

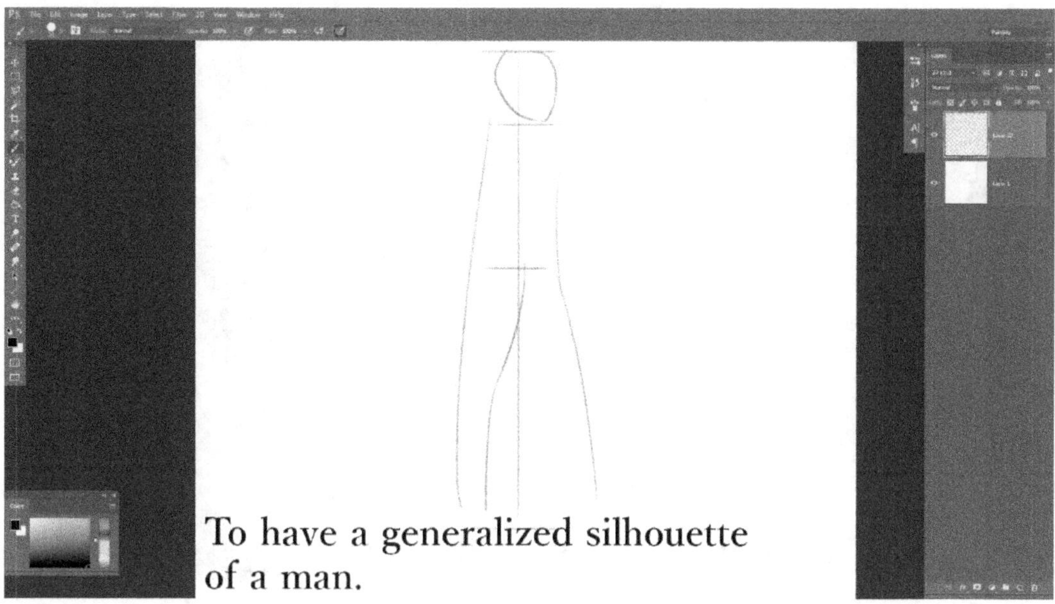

3. Add details to this rough sketch. Add as many details as you want.

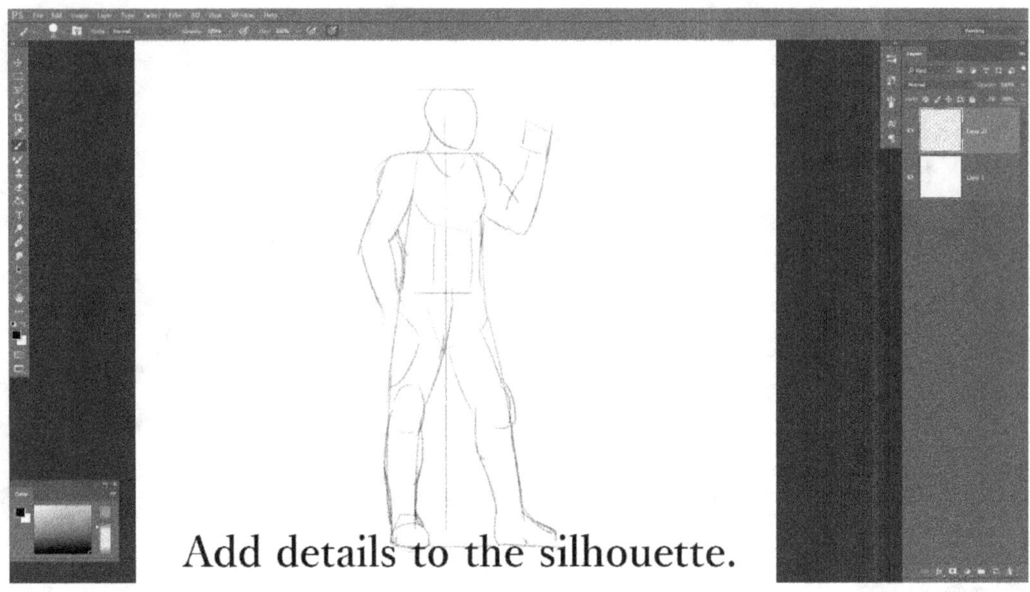

4. Add more details to the sketch. Begin drawing the hands and arm positions.

5. Once all the details of the sketch are added, remove the guidelines.

6. Press Ctrl+T to bring up the transformation box. Click the Right Mouse Button and select "Warp" from the menu.

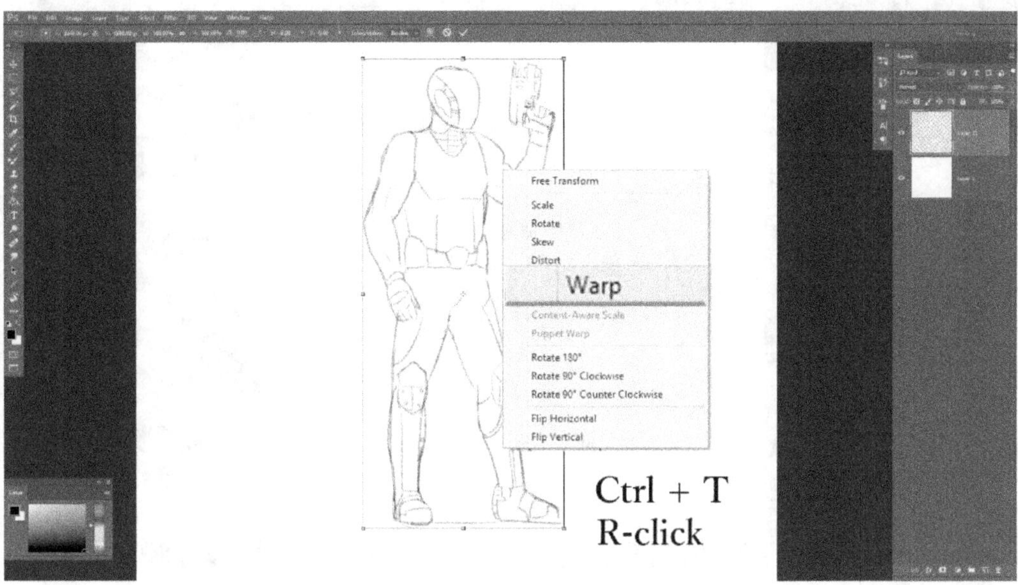

7. Add more details to the sketch. Make another layer.

8. Using the Brush Tool, paint is the colors of the sketch.

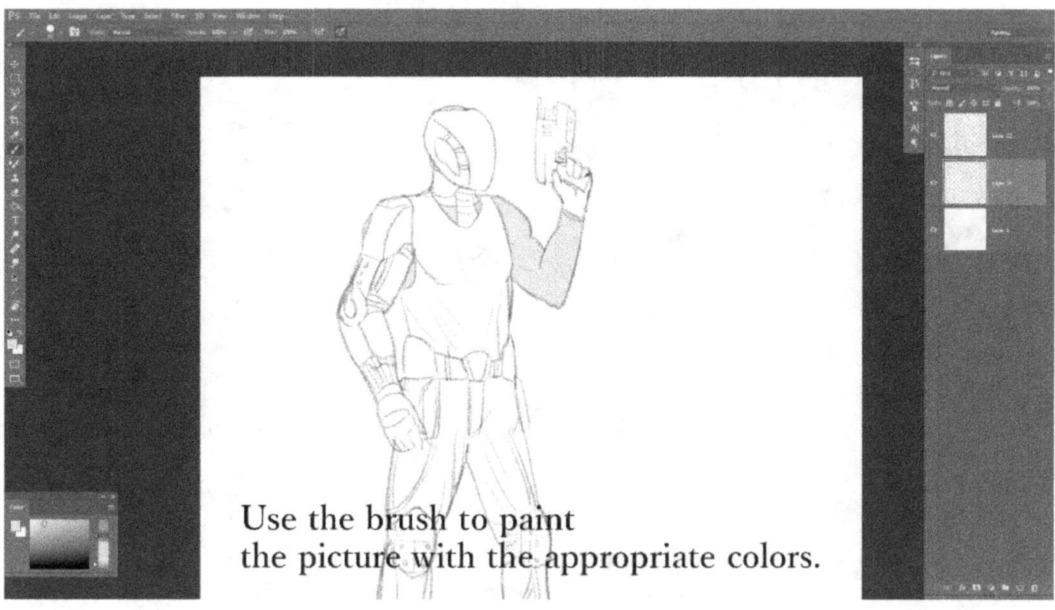

9. Fill the whole drawing with the colors you desire.

10. Adjust any errors and excess areas of color with the Smudge Tool.

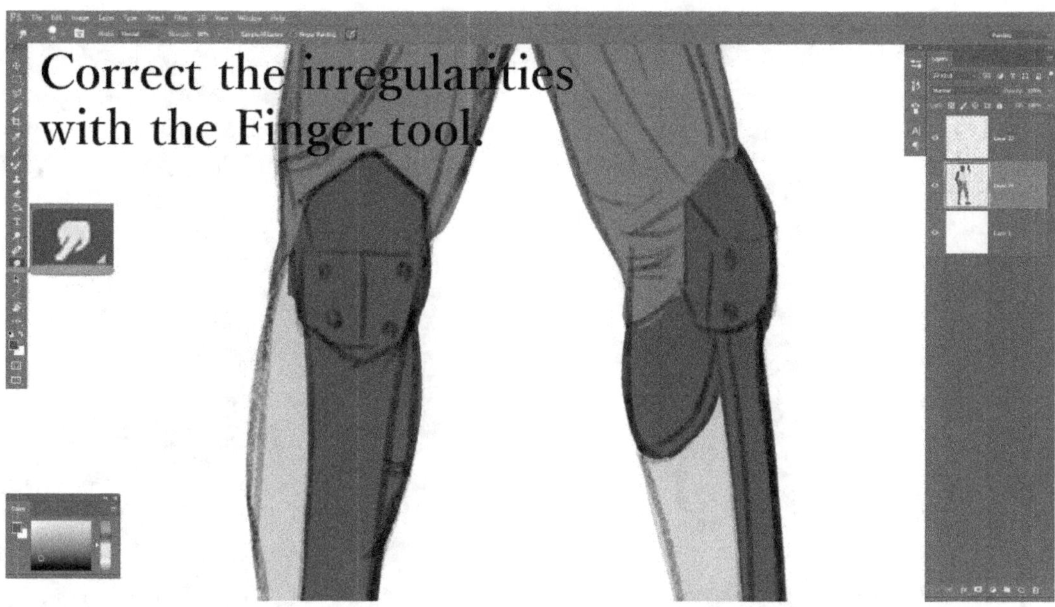

11. The figure of a man is with the adjusted and appropriate colors.

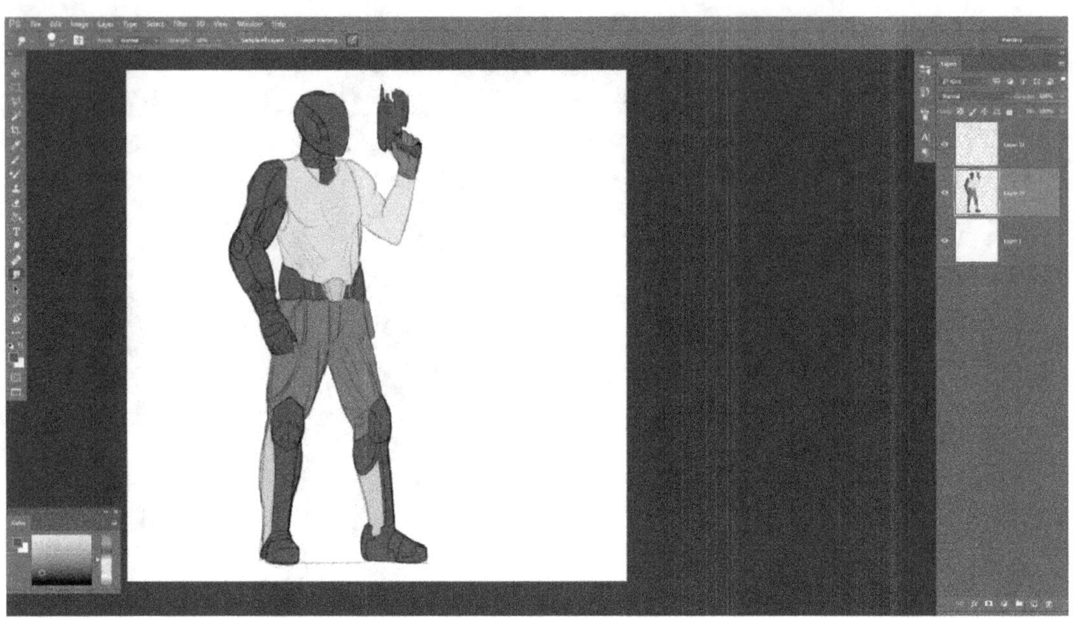

12. Lock the layer of the color. Select the Dodge Tool and draw a gloss on the face.

13. Draw highlights and shadows using the Dodge and Burn Tools together.

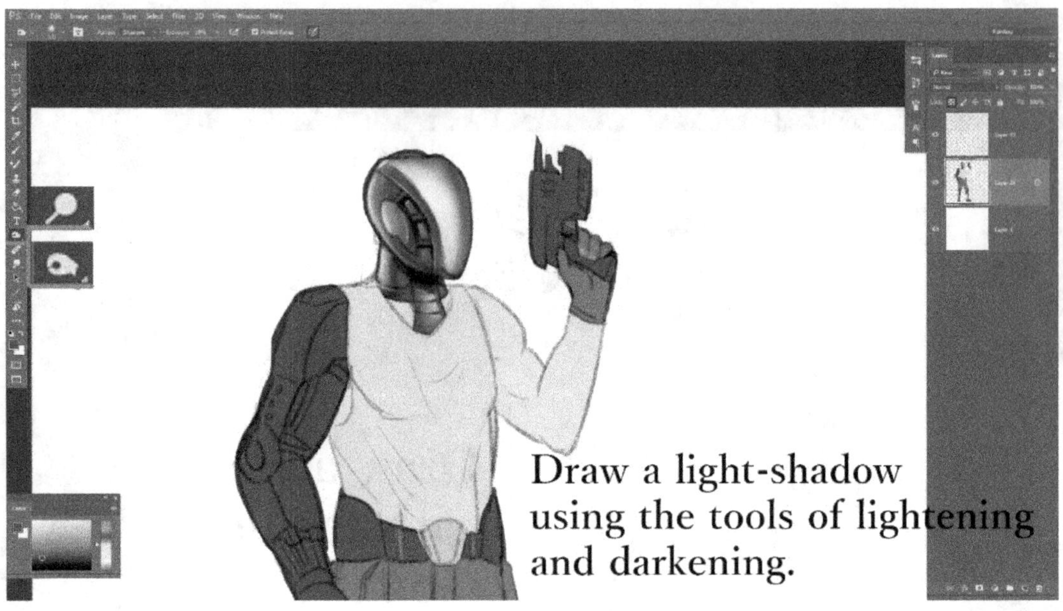

14. Using the methods used in drawing a cylinder, draw a metallic effect on the appropriate areas.

15. Adjust the strength and effect of the brush according to the part.

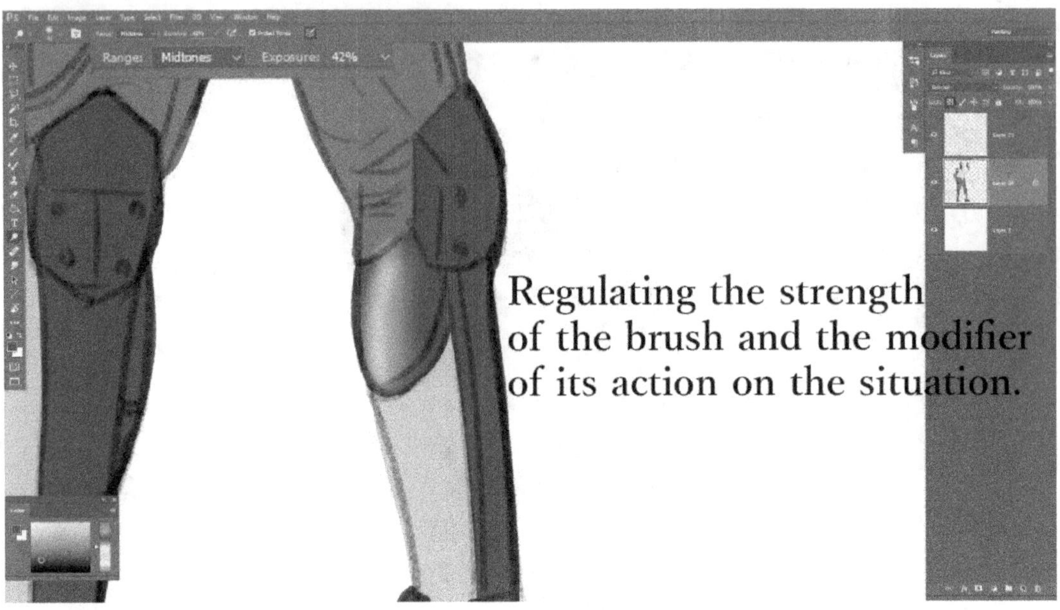

Regulating the strength
of the brush and the modifier
of its action on the situation.

16. Correct any errors with the Smudge Tool.

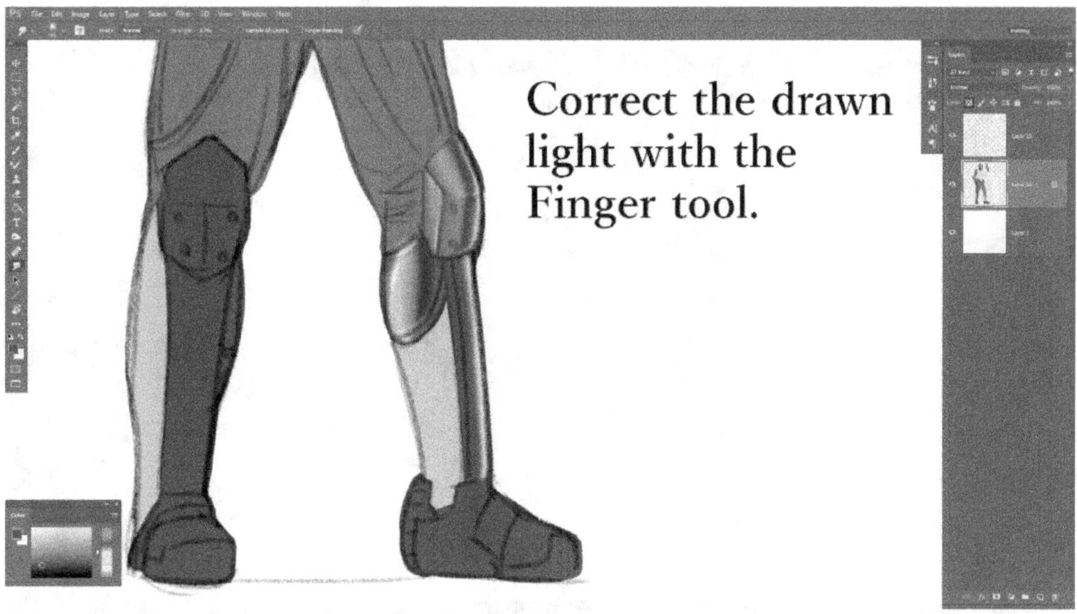

17. Use the Burn Tool with the Range set to Shadows and an Exposure of 16% to draw shadows and dark areas to add more of a metallic effect.

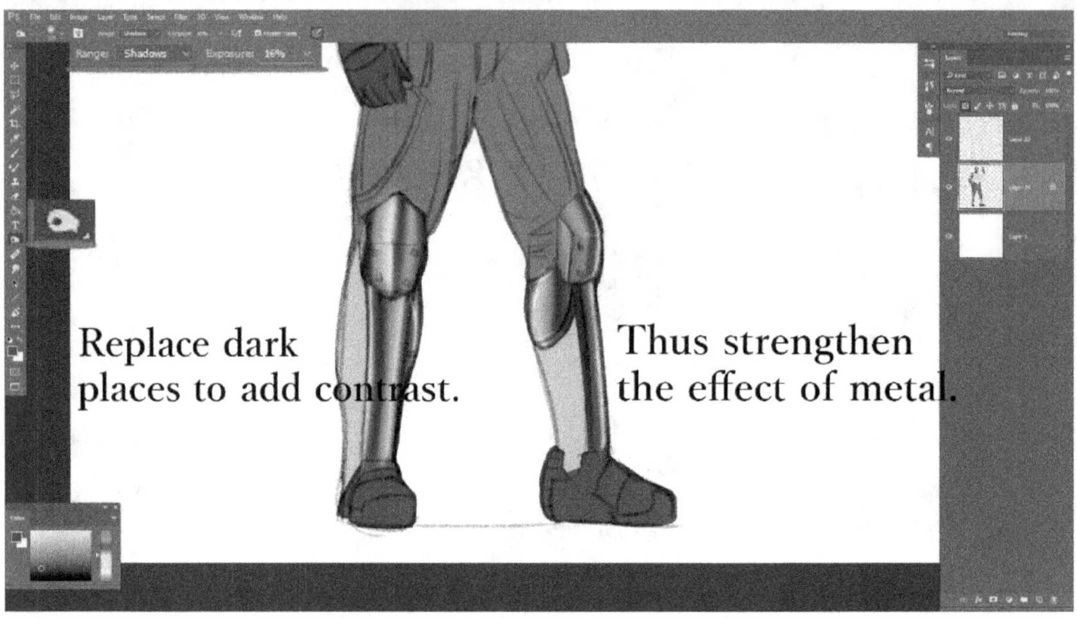

18. The drawing with the metallic areas shaded and highlighted.

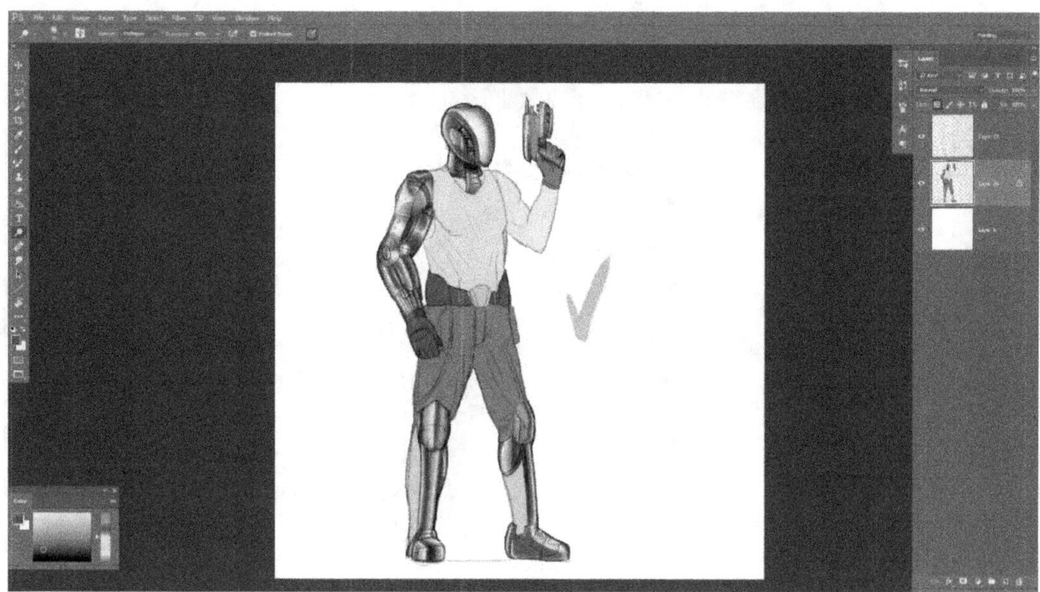

19. Use the Brush Tool in Darken Mode and 9% Opacity to add shadows to areas where the Burn Tool may not Work.

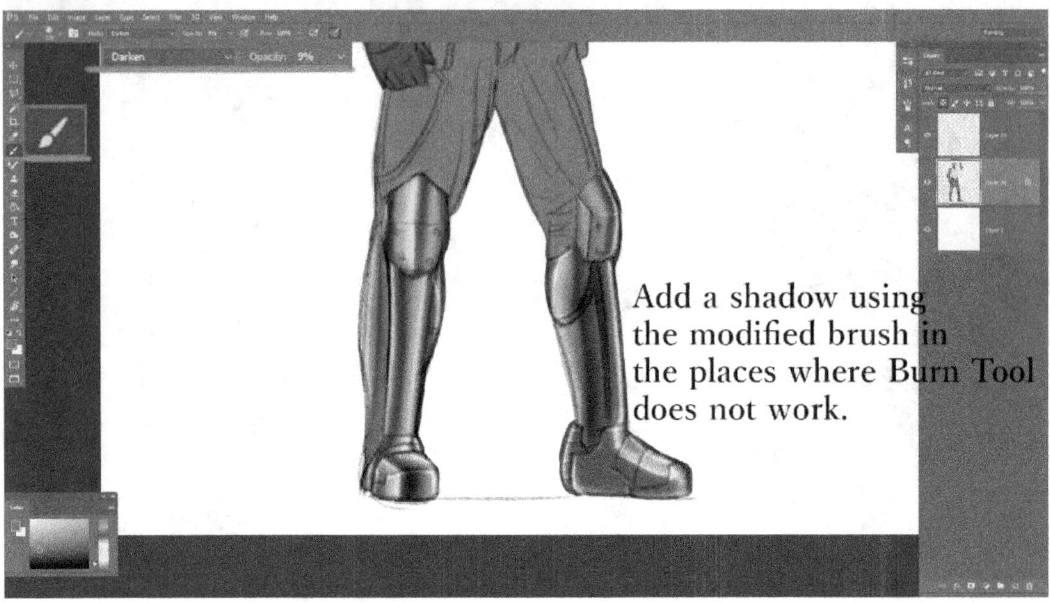

20. Adjust the Opacity to 32% and draw the creases on the man's clothes.

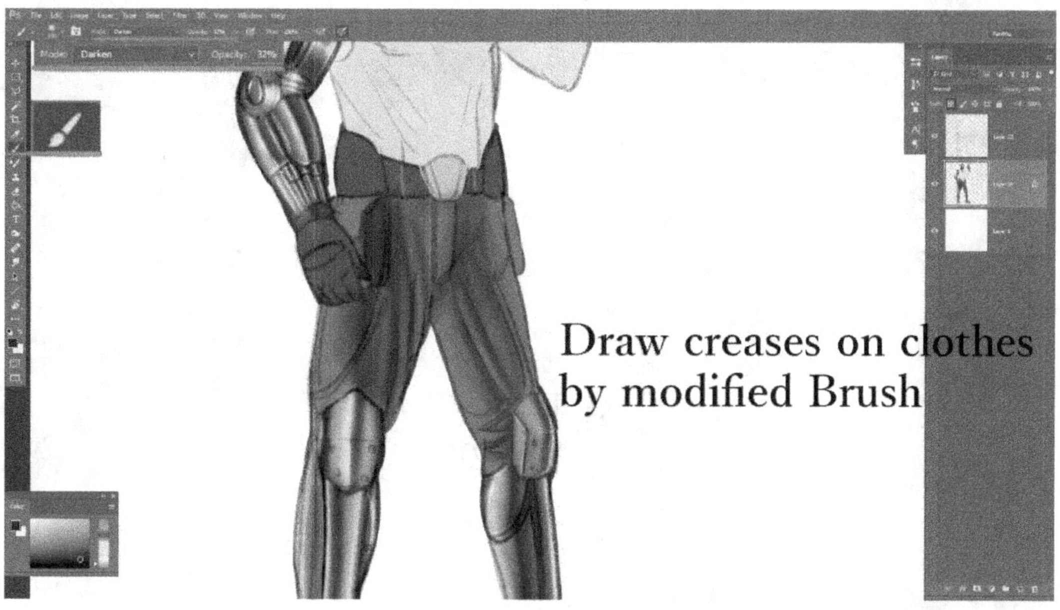

21. Choose the Dodge Tool and change its Range to Midtones and the Exposure to 42%. Paint the highlights on the skin to add volume.

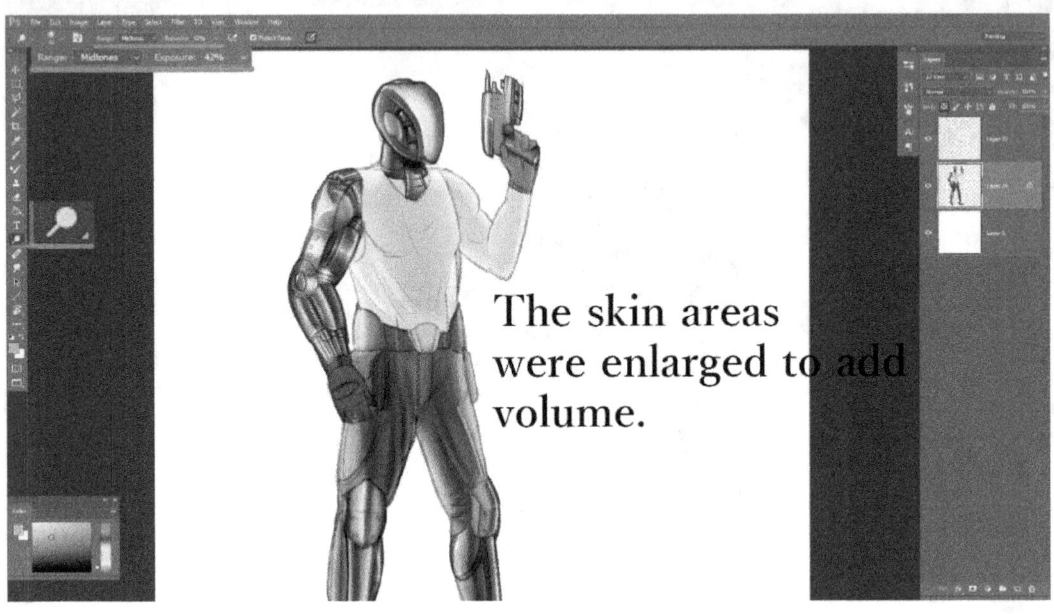

22. Using the same tool and mode, add the same highlighting effect to the clothes.

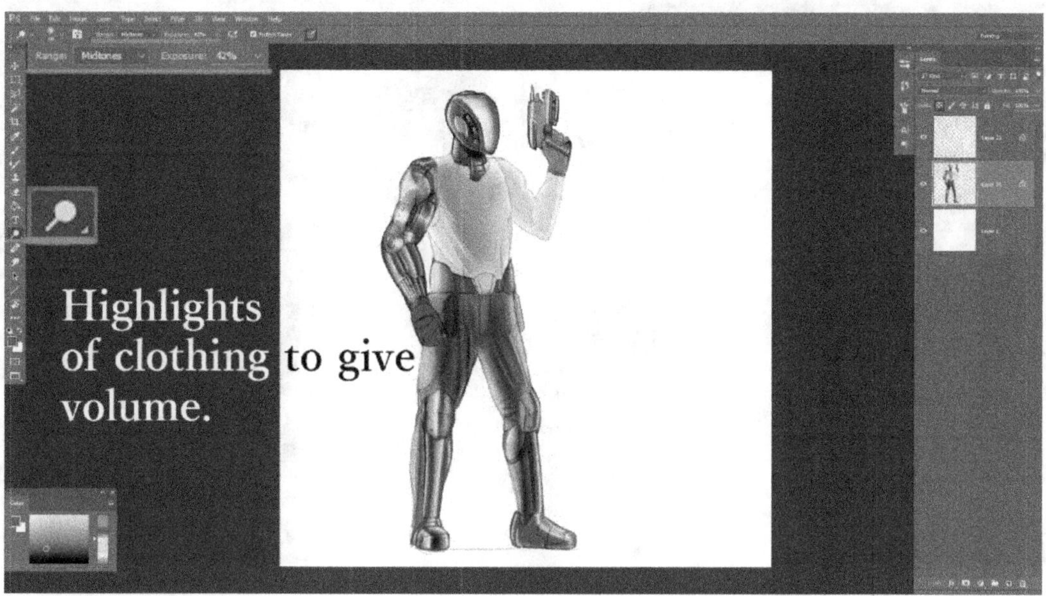

23. Press Ctrl+U and adjust the Saturation to -22.

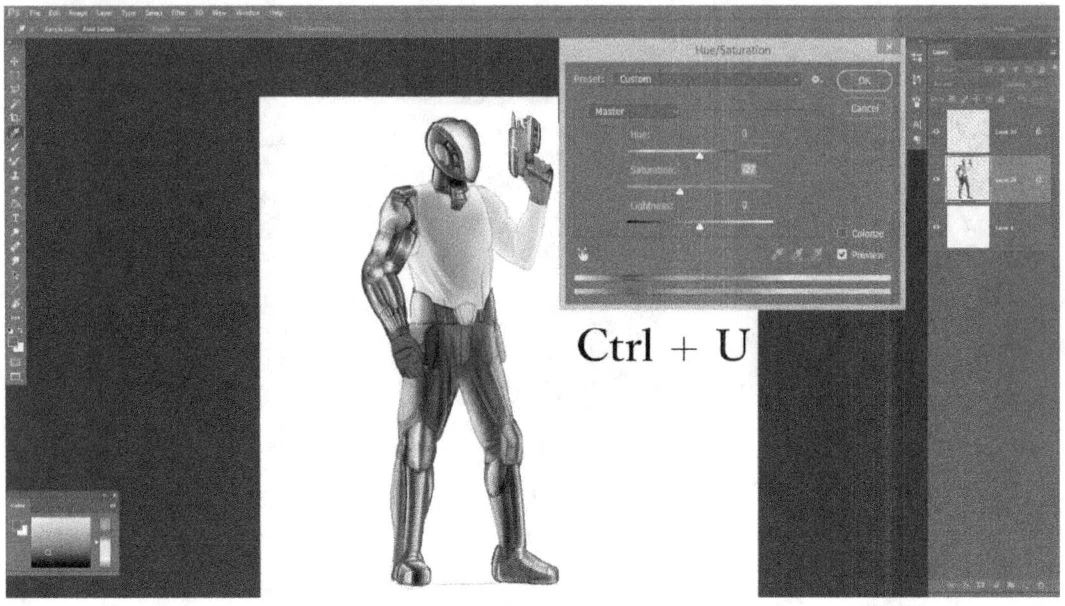

24. Select the Polygonal Lasso Tool and mark the area of exposed skin. Press Ctrl+U and adjust its saturation to -22.

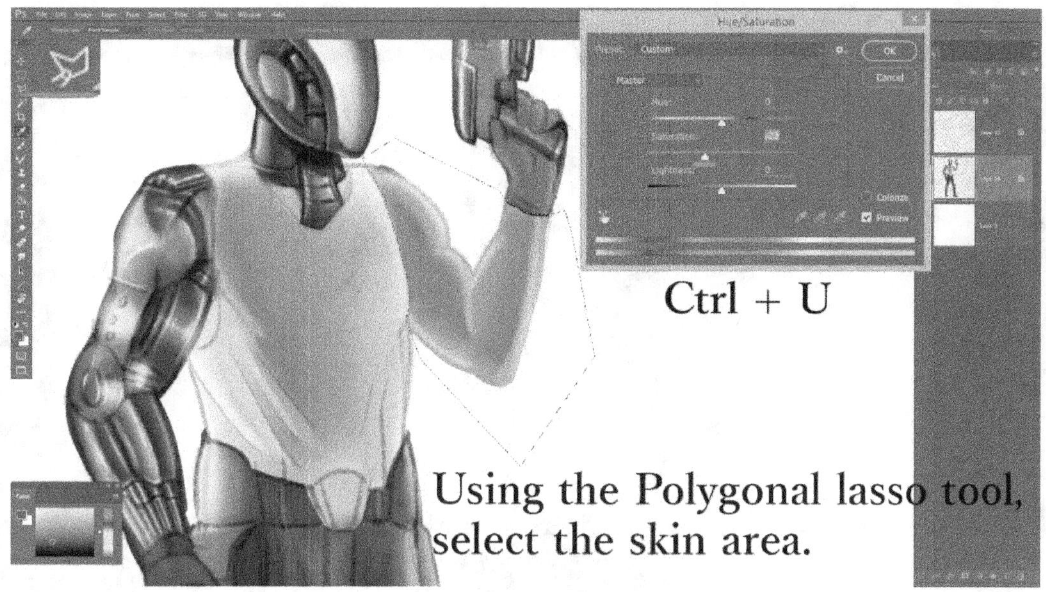

25. Draw the light sources and their reflections using the Brush Tool in Normal Mode and 10% Opacity.

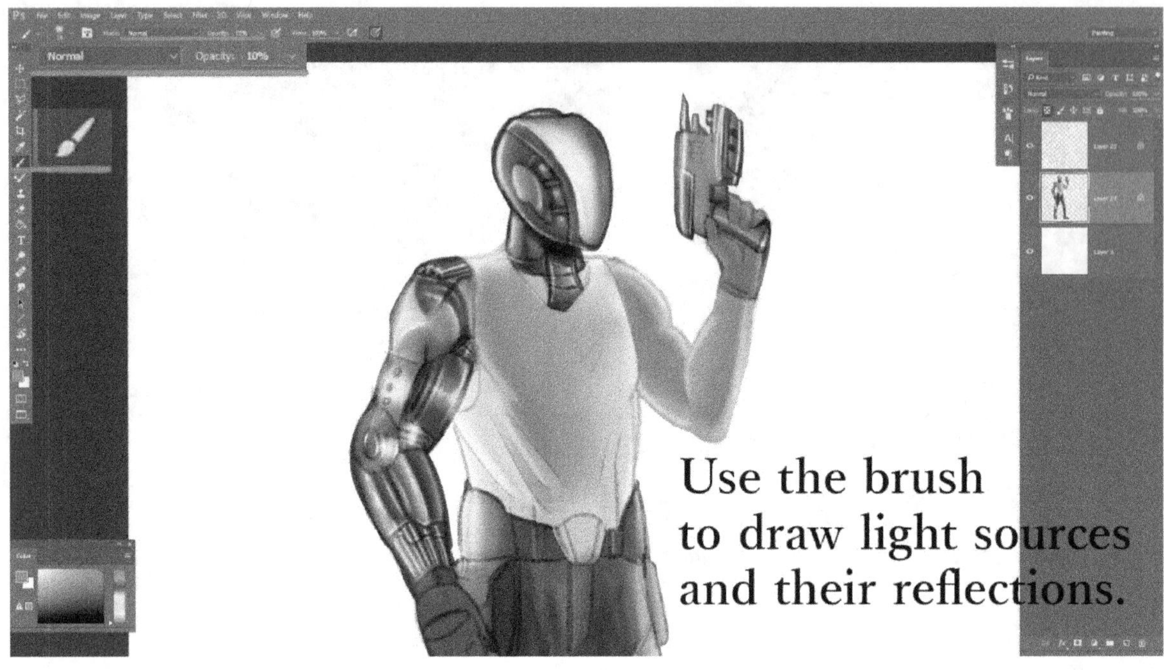

Metallic Décor

1. Draw an arbitrary patter on a new layer.

2. Press Ctrl+T on the sketch and rotate it.

3. Use the Brush Tool to draw more details to the sketch.

4. Mark out an area with the Rectangular Marquee Tool. Press Ctrl+T to pull up the transformation box. Click the Right Mouse Button and select "Warp" from the menu. Adjust the selected area to the desired shape.

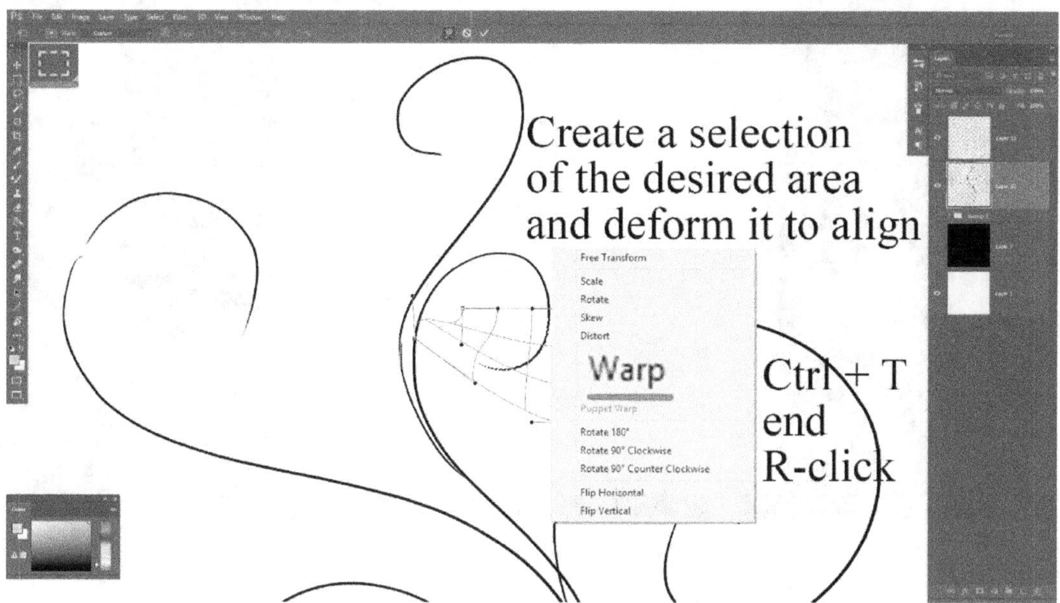

5. Do this on all the other areas.

6. Add any graphic elements you may want.

7. Draw leaves and other details of the sketch.

8. Using the Eraser Tool, remove any excess and overlapping area.

9. Lock the layer of the sketch and paint over the lines of the sketch.

10.   Fill in any closed shapes with the color.

11. The object with the areas filled in with color.

12. Thicken some of the lines of the sketch.

13. Select the Burn Tool and add shadows to create volume.

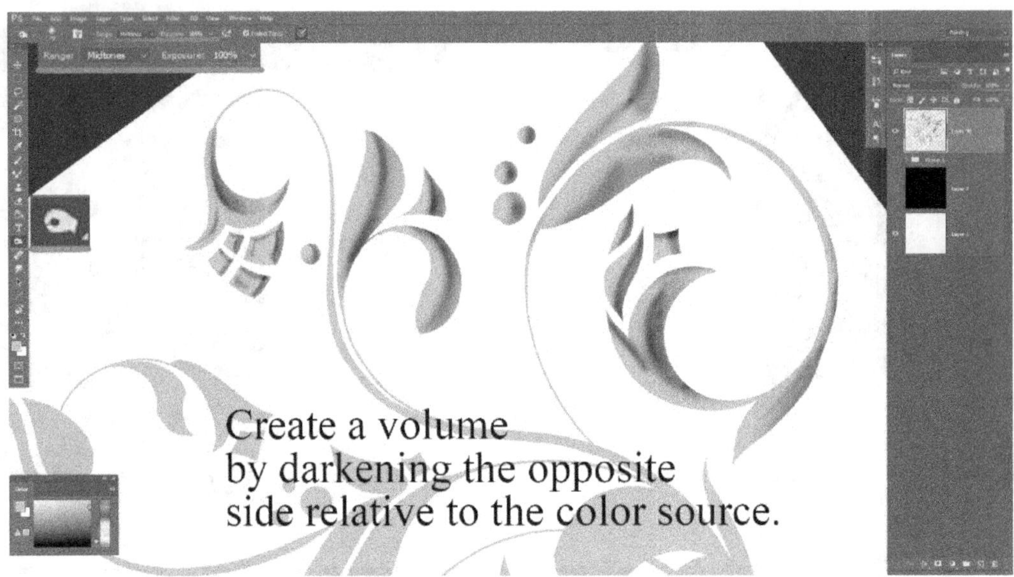

14. Apply this effect to all parts of the drawing.

15. Use the Smudge Tool to correct any blots or excess areas.

16. With the layer still locked, select the Dodge Tool. Draw highlights on the appropriate areas.

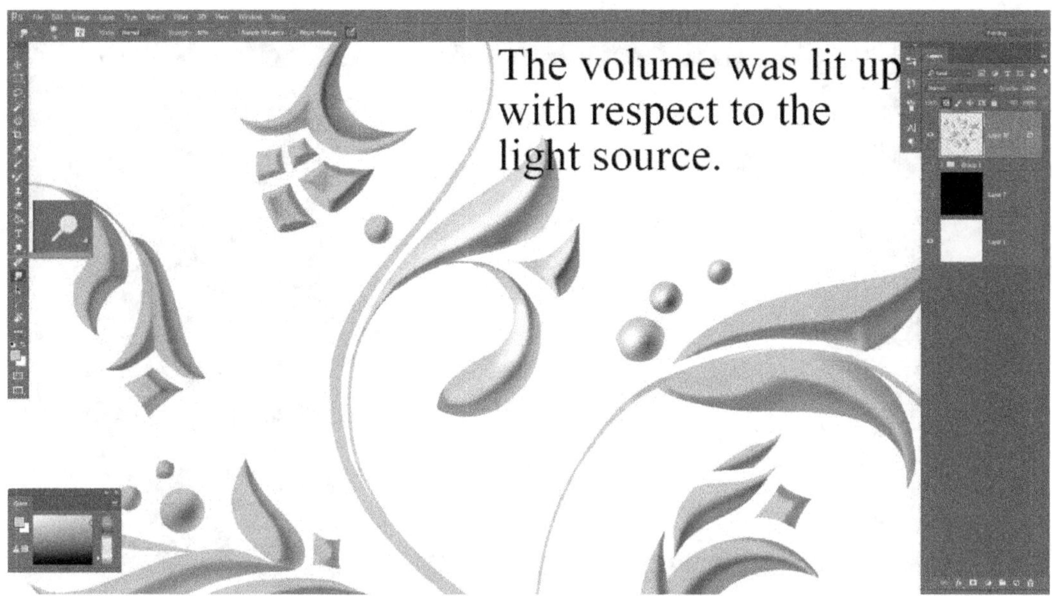

17. Add even more of a metallic effect using the Brush Tool in Color Dodge Mode with Opacity of 9%.

18. Use the Smudge Tool to narrow the shadow areas.

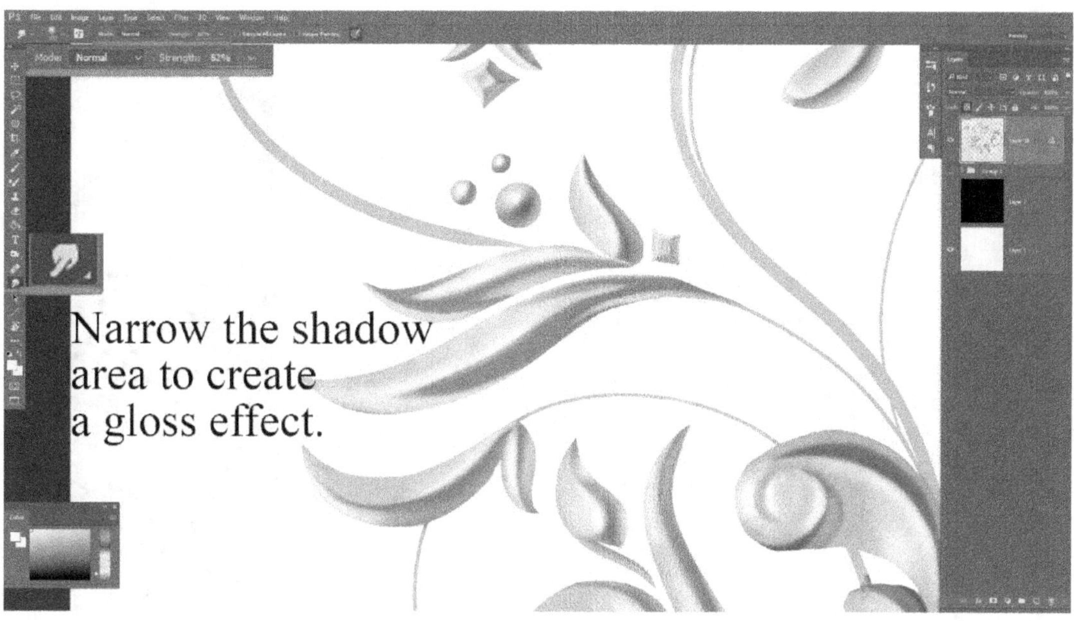

19. The drawing is with shadows and highlights.

20. Using the Brush Tool in Color Dodge Mode and 5% Opacity, add glare and reflections to certain surfaces.

21. Draw glare on the shadows as well to add more volume.

22. Make another layer and fill it with black. Move this layer under that of the object.

Sword

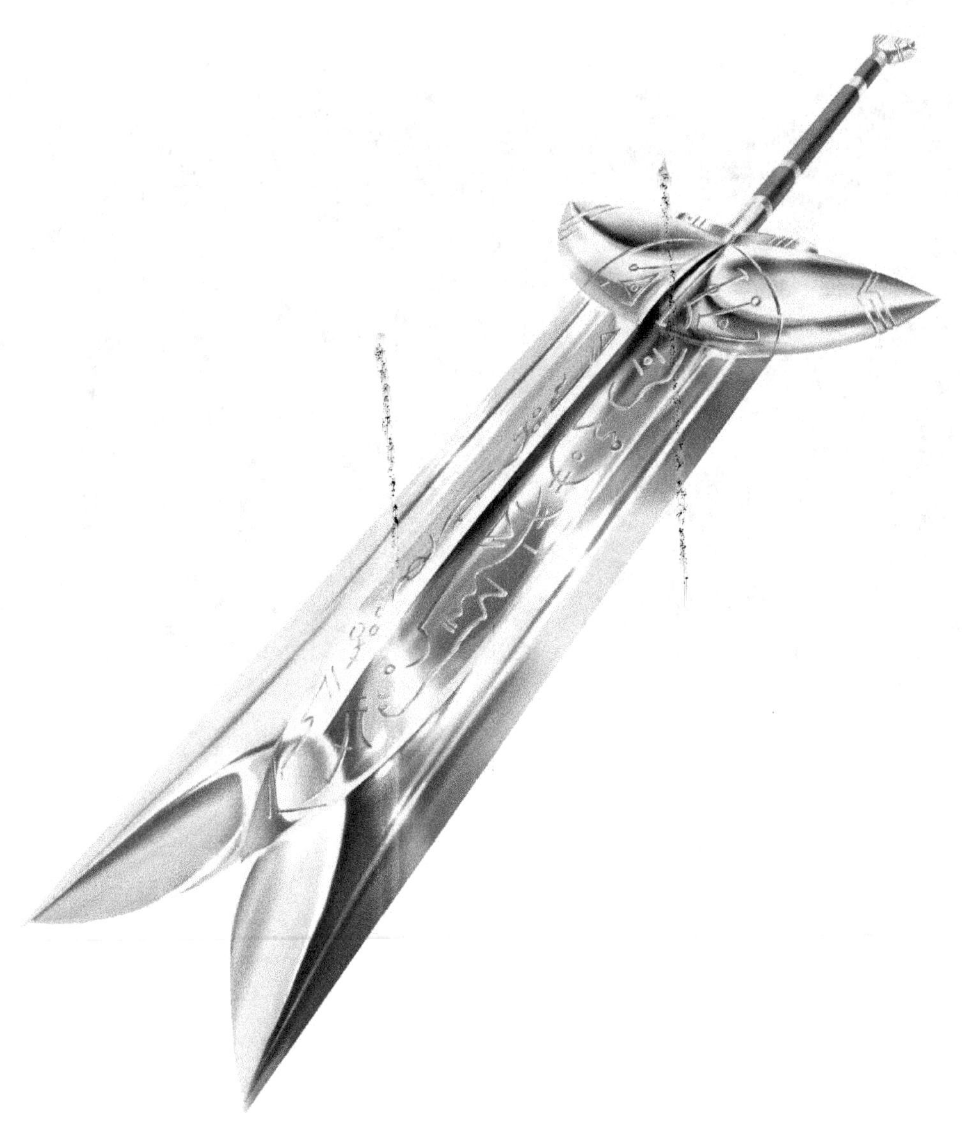

1. Make a new layer. Draw a basic sketch of the sword's shape. Hold the Shift Key to draw straight and smooth lines.

2. Draw the curves and points of the sword.

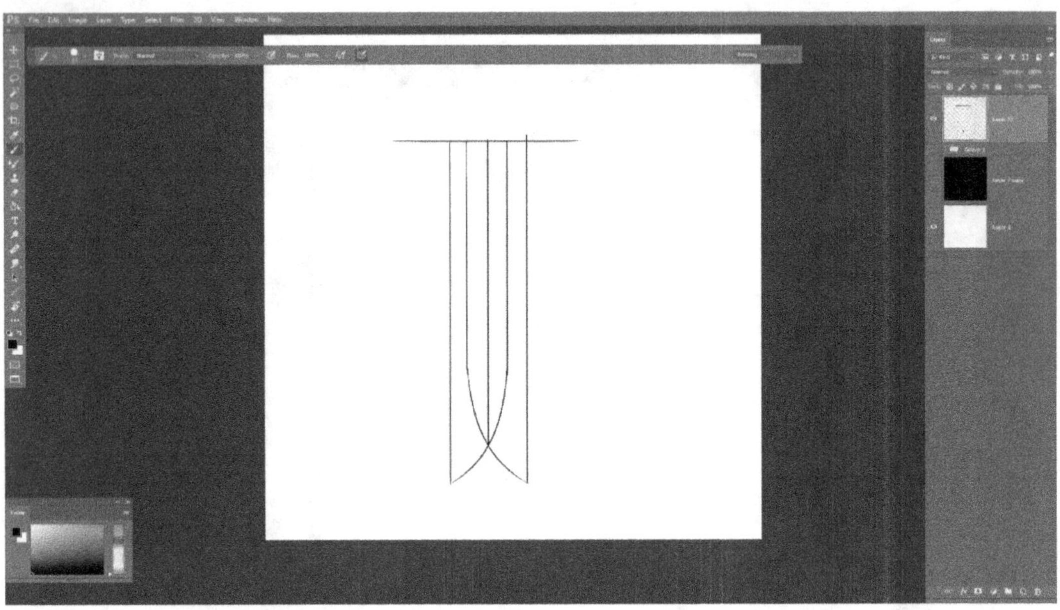

3. Draw a circular line on a new layer. Copy this layer by dragging it while holding the Ctrl and Alt Keys. Reflect the line horizontally.

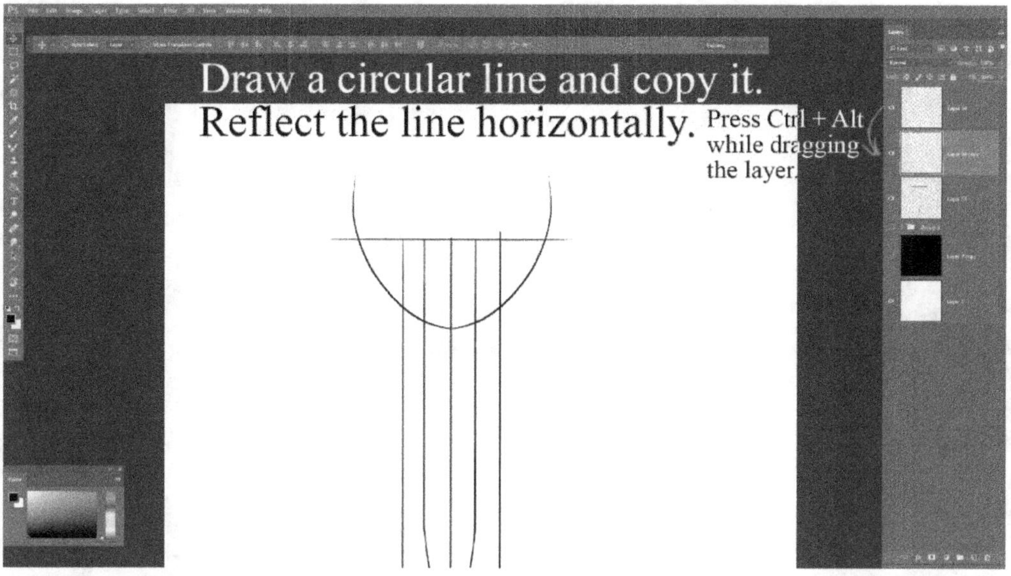

4. Merge the layers of the semicircle and make a selection around it. Press the Right Mouse Button and choose "Warp" from the menu.

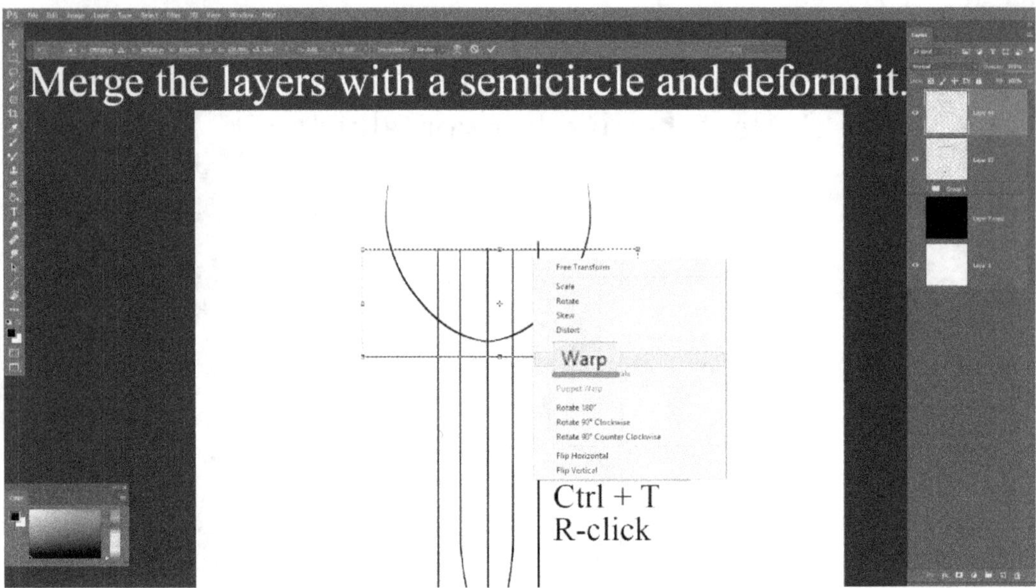

5. Make another layer and draw another circular line on it. Copy and flip the shape. Move and rotate the lines to match the lines of the sword and the previous semicircle.

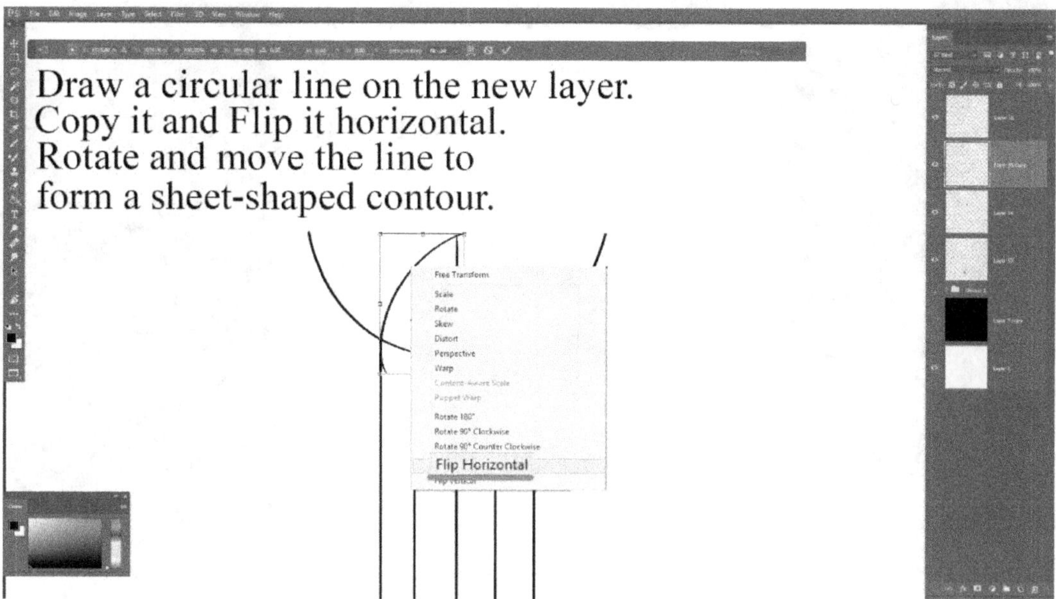

6. Select all the layers of the sketch and merge them.

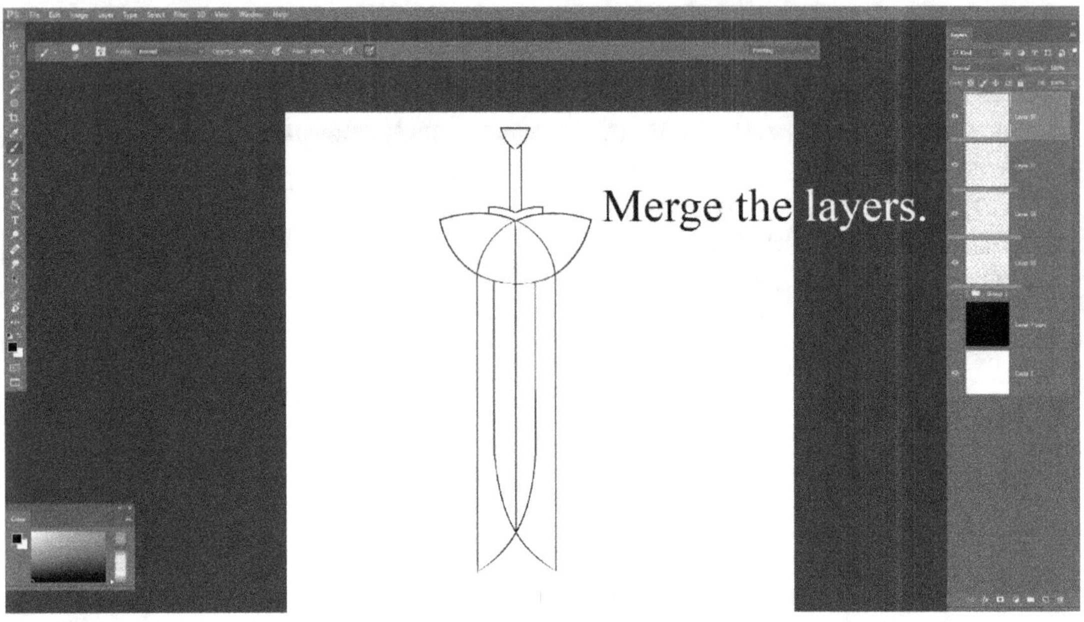

7. Press Ctrl+T to pull up the transformation box. Drag one of the bottom corners of the box outward while holding the Ctrl, Alt, and Shift Keys. Press the Enter Key to apply the change.

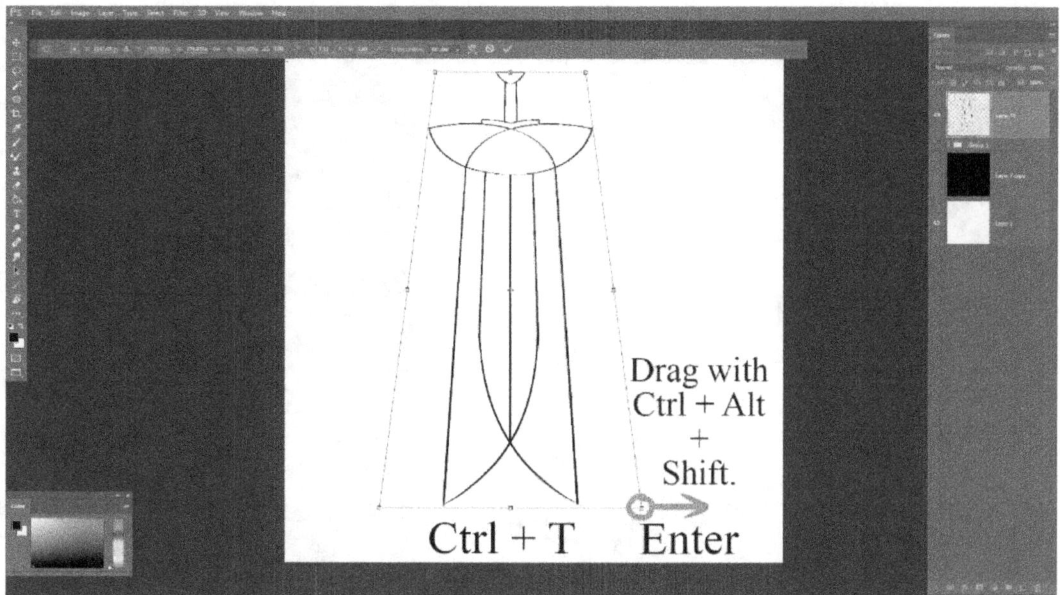

8. Press Ctrl+T again and, this time, drag the lower corner of the transformation box downward while holding the Ctrl, Alt, and Shift Keys. Press Enter to apply the transformations.

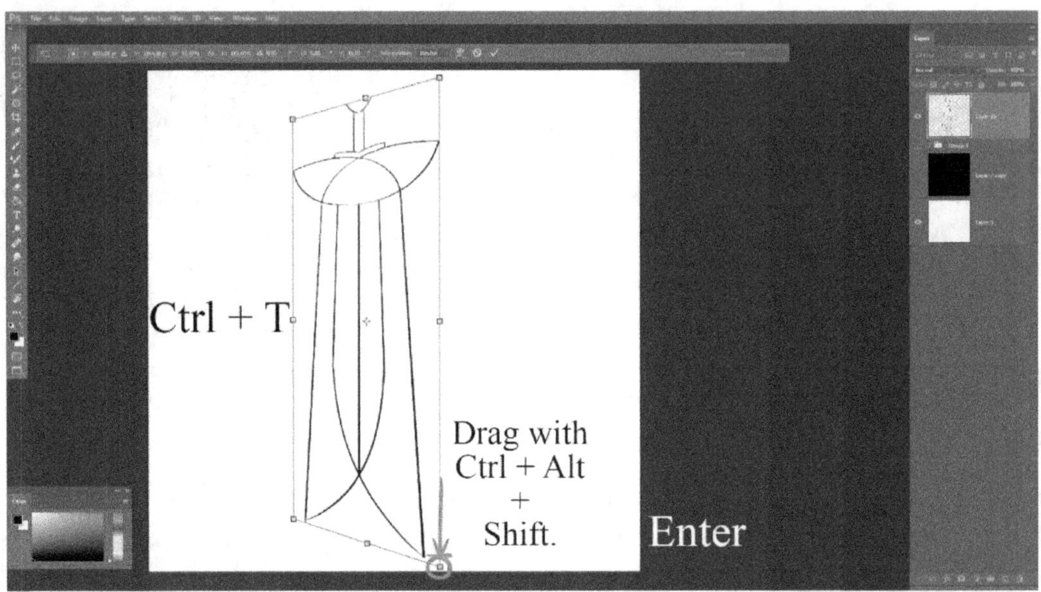

9. Press Ctrl+T again and rotate the sword.

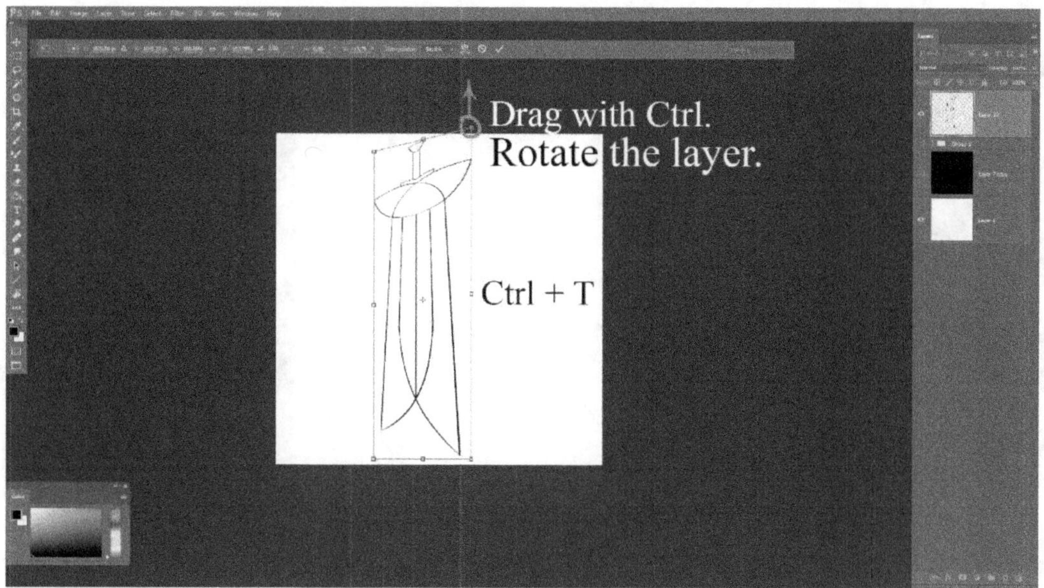

10.   The sword rotated and adjusted for perspective.

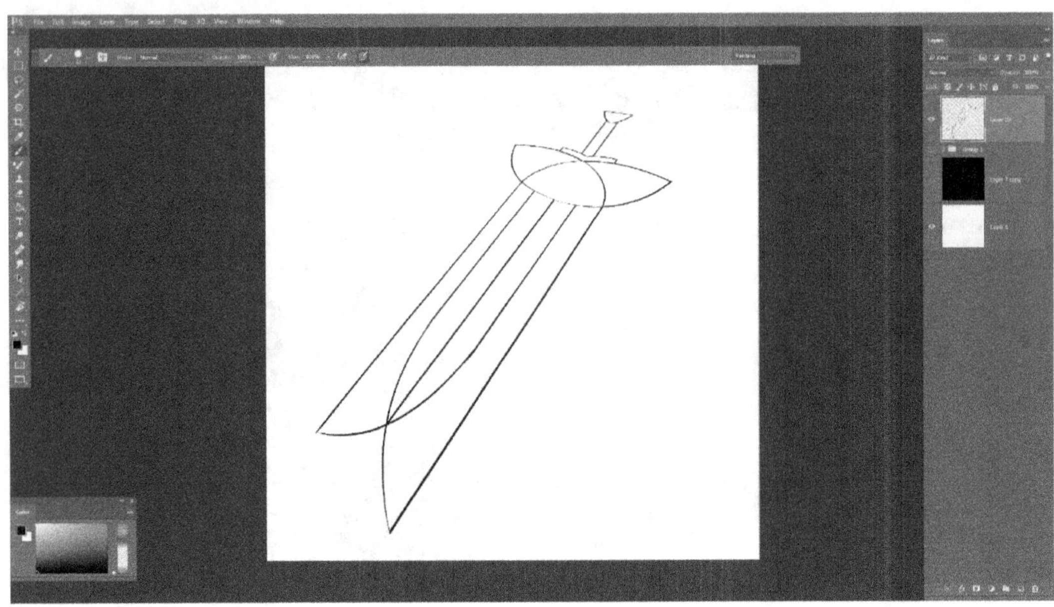

11. Draw the thickness of the handle to add a three dimensional effect.

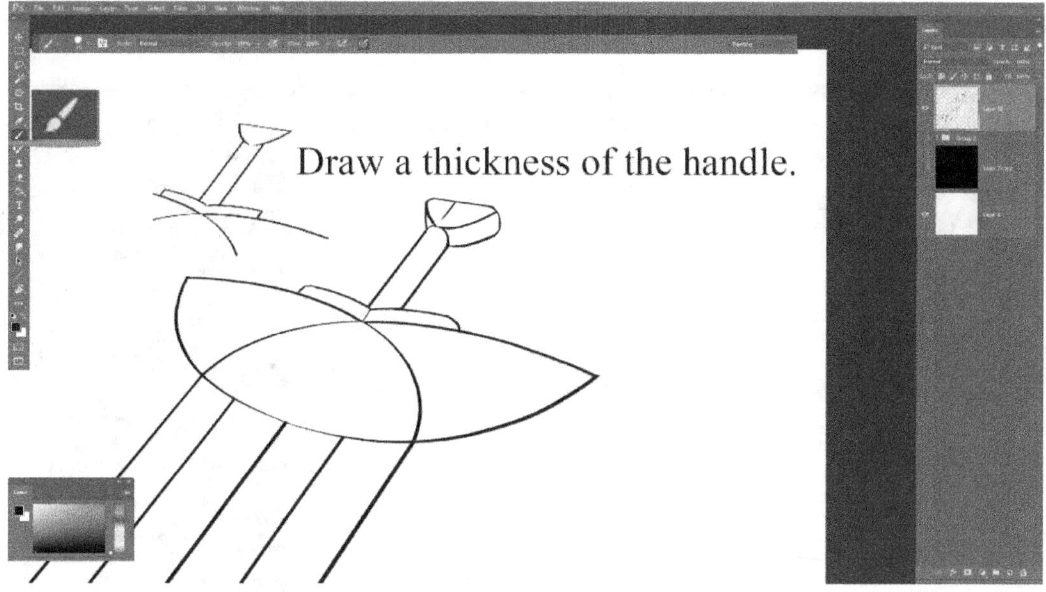

12. With the Lasso Tool, mark out the middle line of the sword blade. Press Ctrl+T and click the Right Mouse Button. Choose "Warp" on the menu and adjust the line's shape to make it appear as if it were curved.

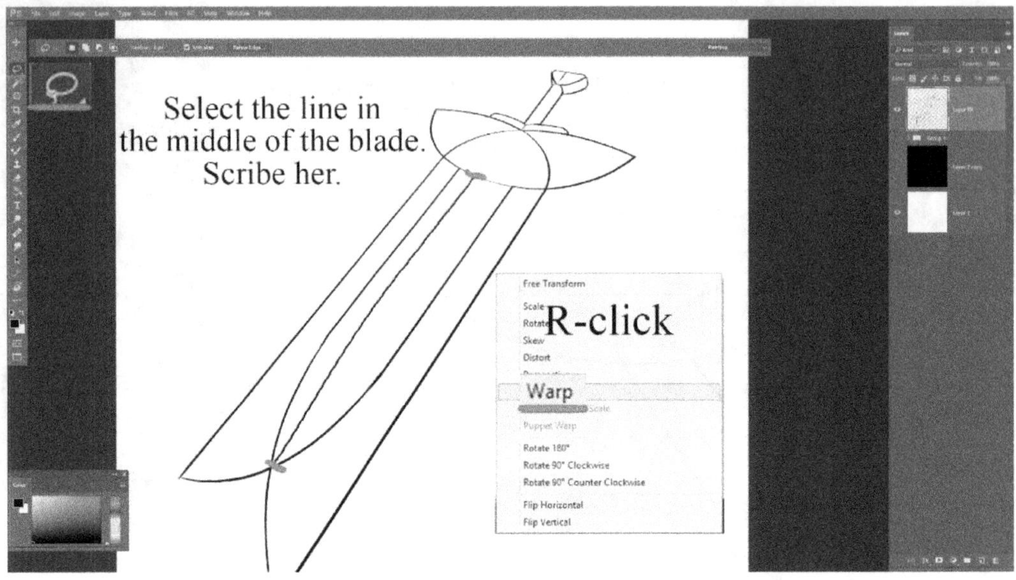

13. Select a part of the sketch with the Rectangular Marquee Tool. Move it upwards.

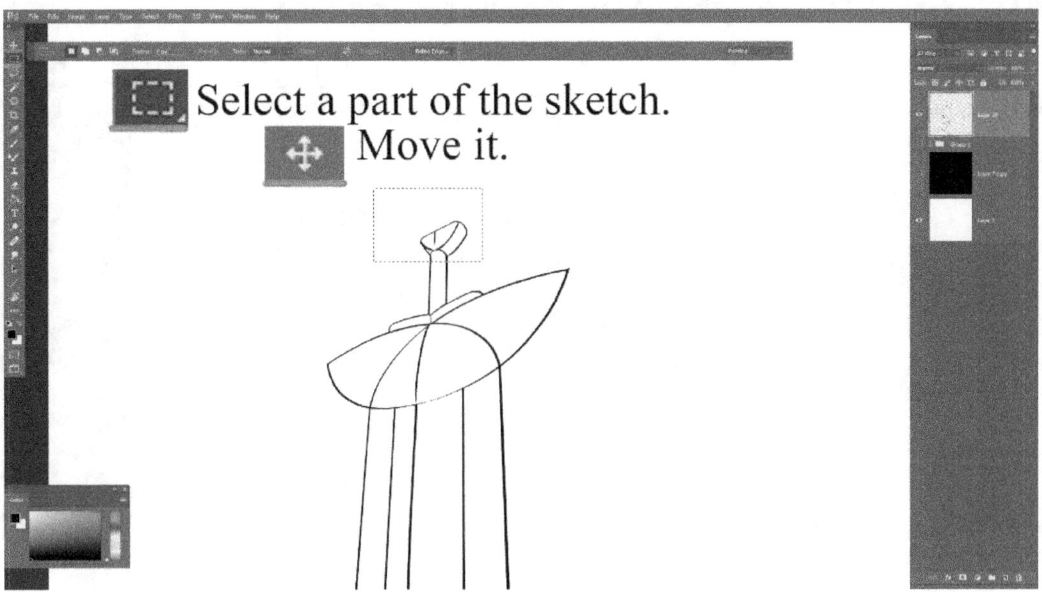

14. Select the top of the remaining handle area and stretch it vertically.

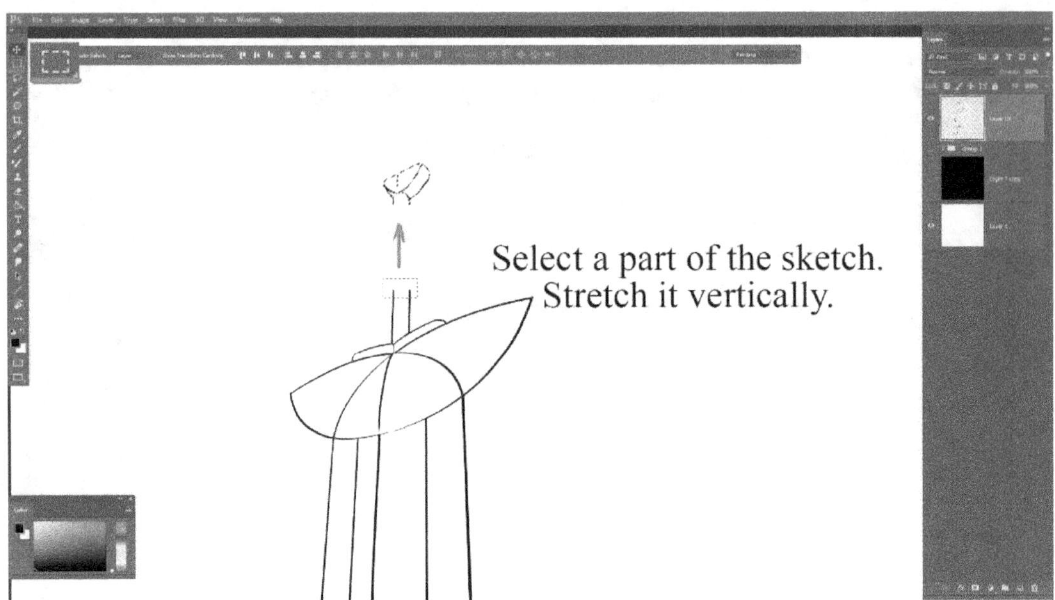

15. Press Ctrl+T and adjust the length of the handle to your preference.

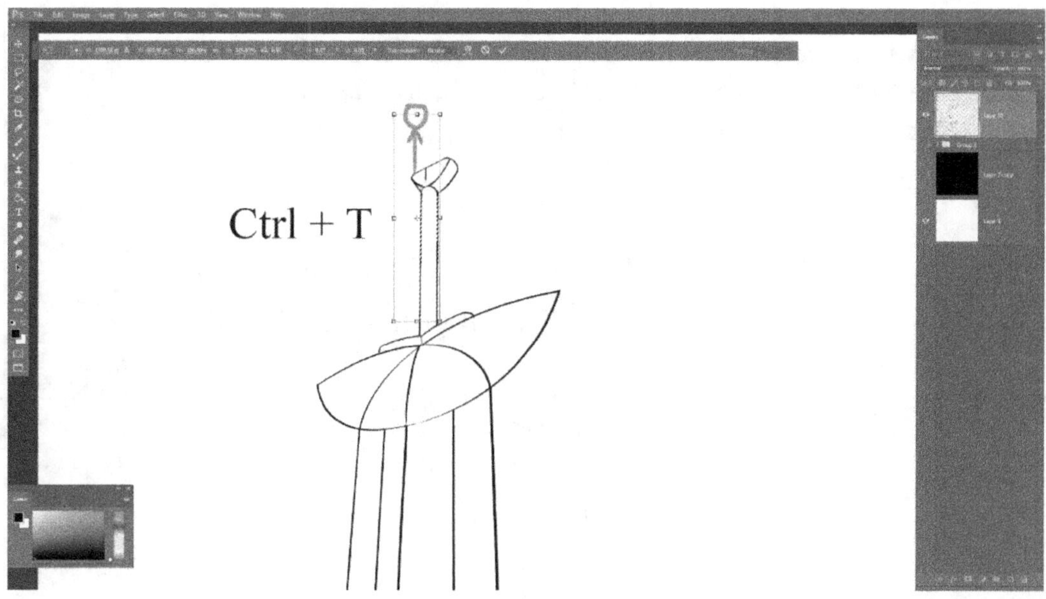

16. With the entire handle still selected, drag one of the upper corners inwards while holding the Alt, Ctrl, and Shift Keys down.

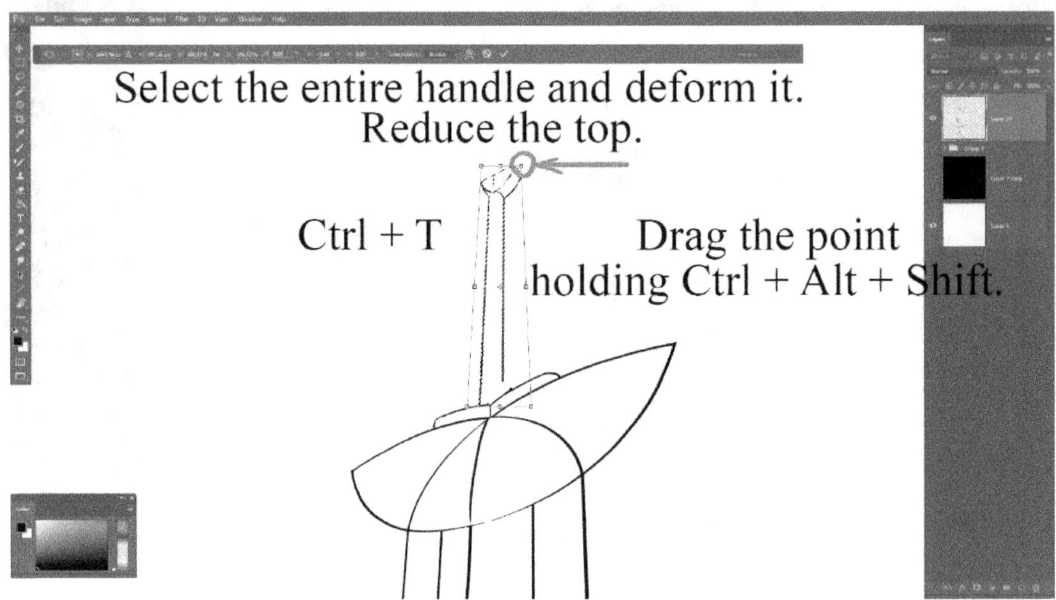

17. Make a new layer and add more details to the drawing.

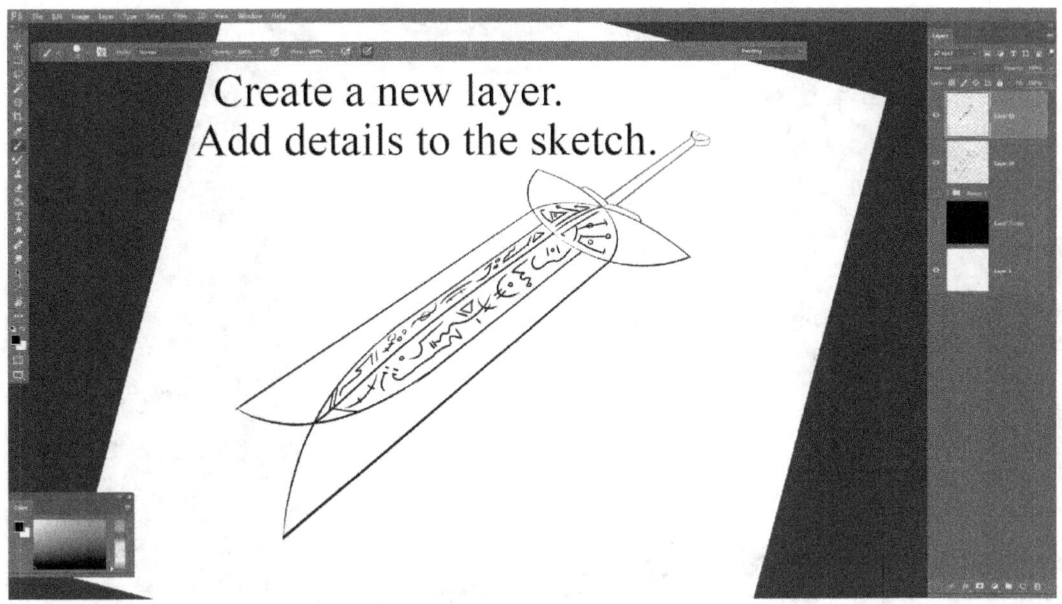

18. Add lines and details for the handle and guard as well.

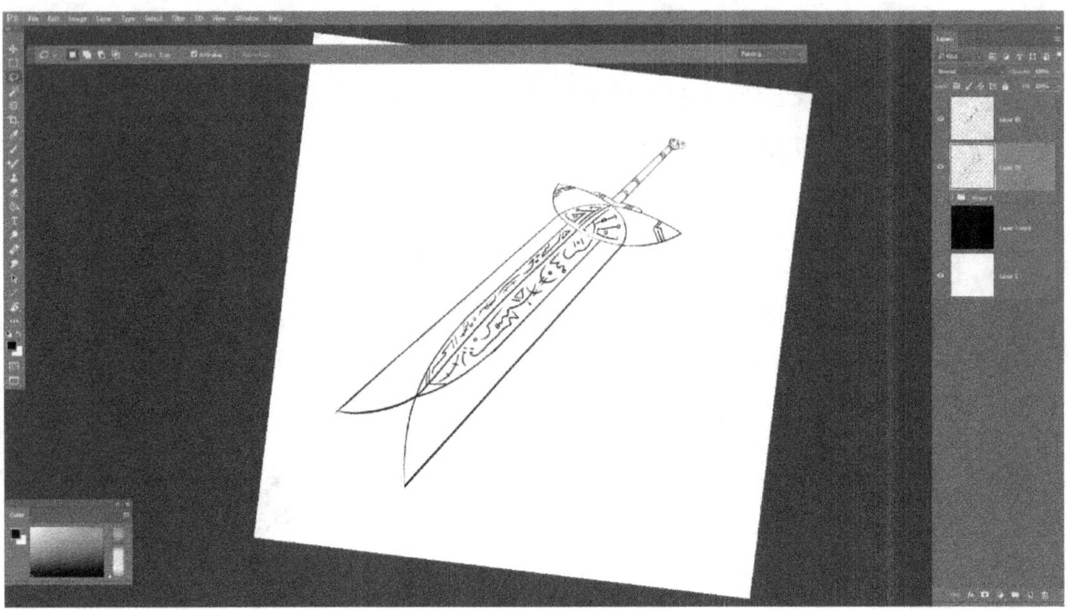

19. Make another layer. Fill the edges of the blade and parts of the handle
with the appropriate colors.

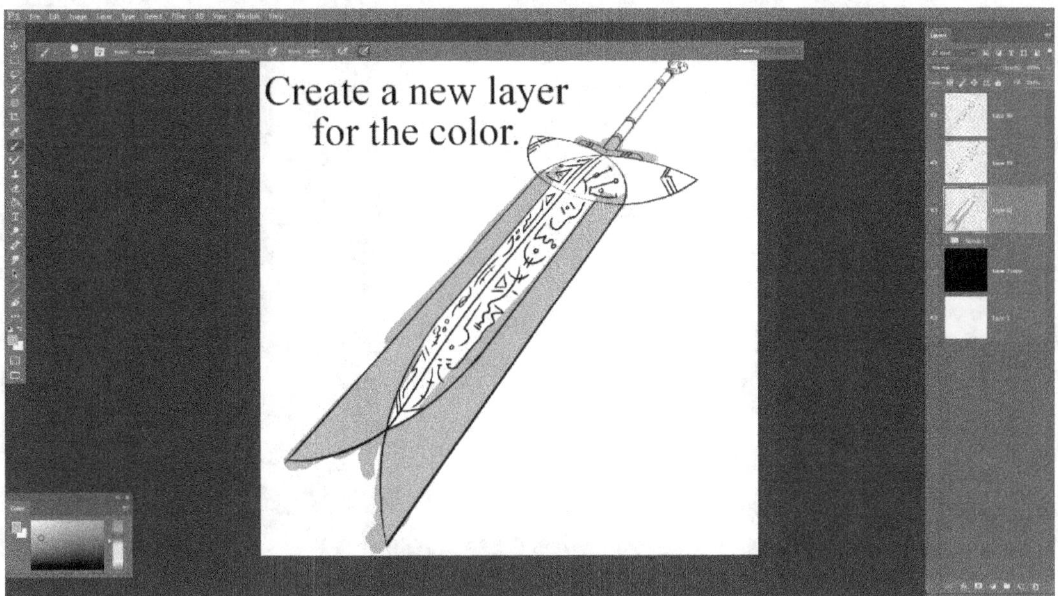

20. Make another layer for the other colors.

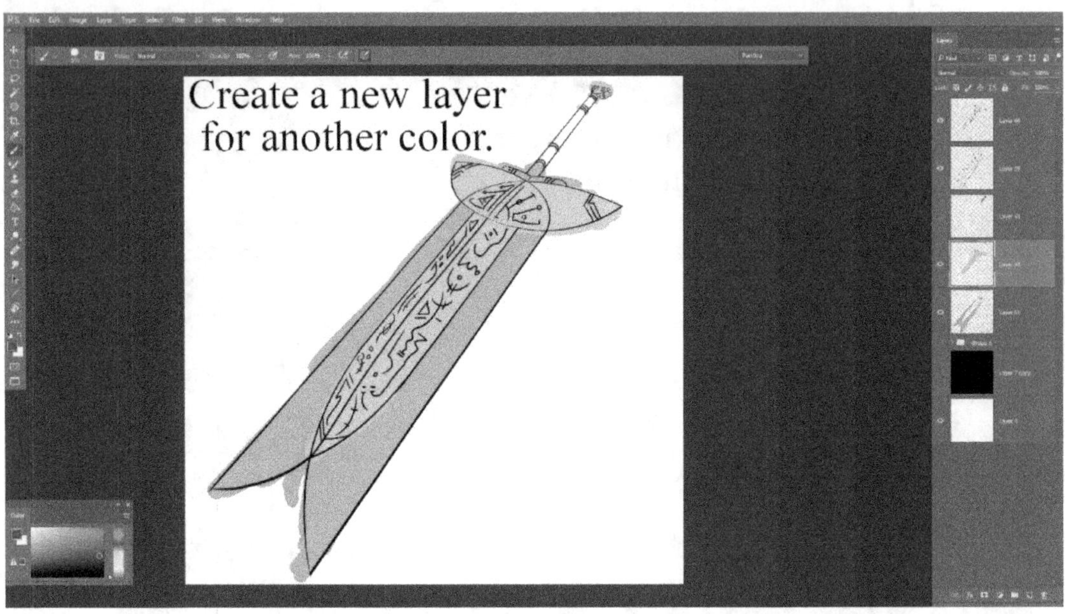

21. Use the Eraser Tool to remove any excess areas of color.

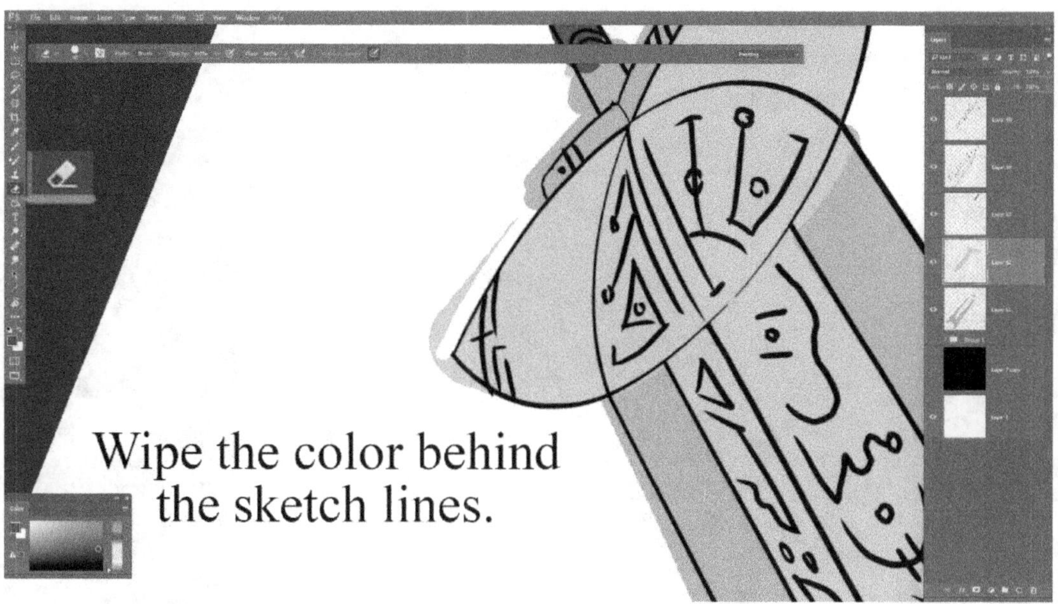

22. The sword with only some of the excess areas of color removed.

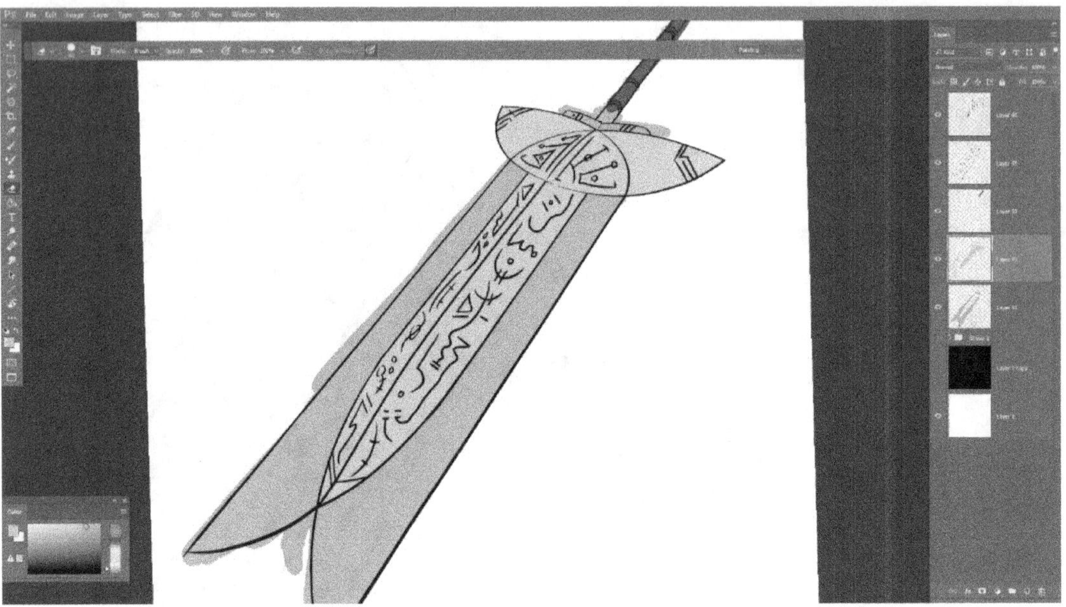

23. The sword is with appropriate and adjusted colors.

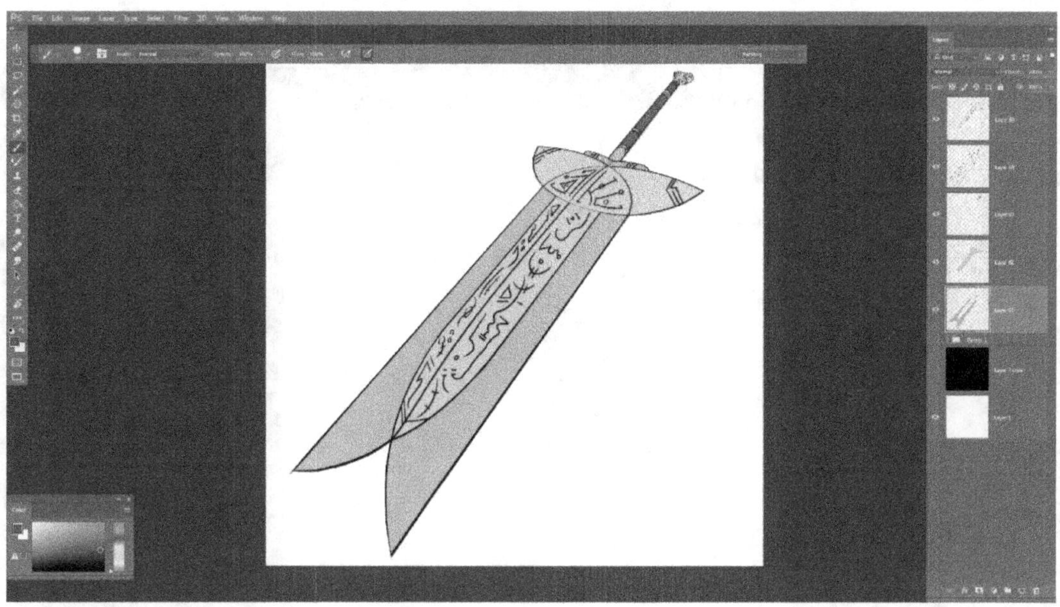

24. Select the Burn Tool and darken certain parts of the sword blade. Make sure it is set to Midtones and has an Exposure of 62%.

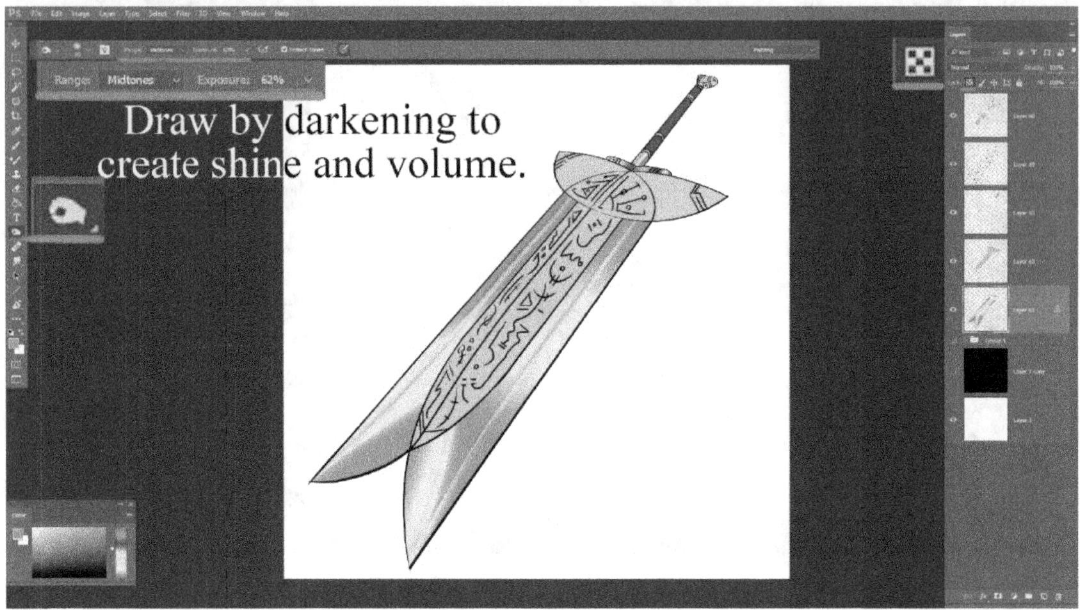

25. Select the Layer of the other color and, with the Burn Tool having an increased Exposure of 85%, draw shadows on one side of these details.

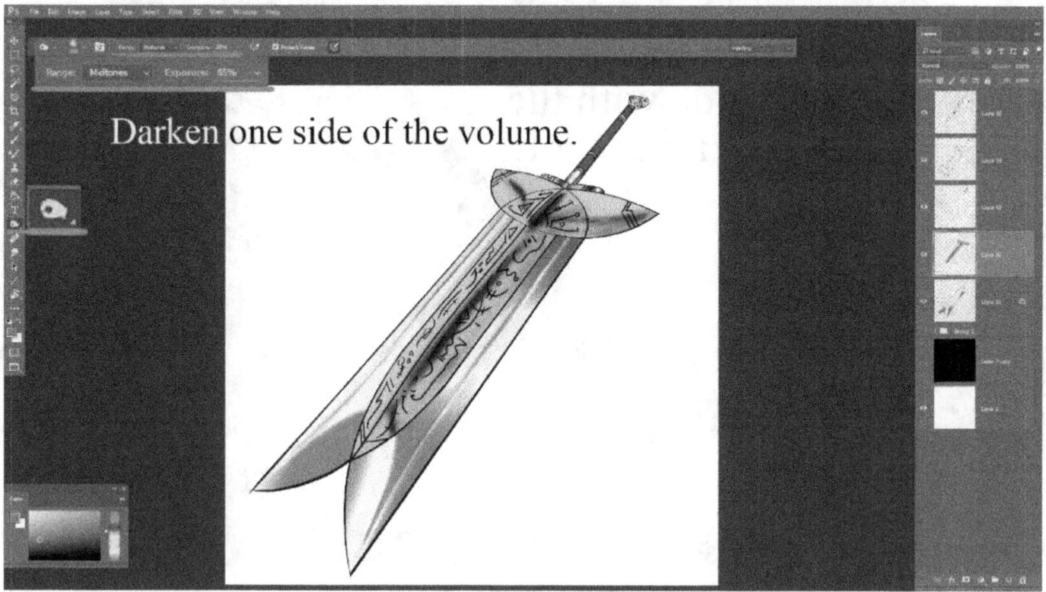

26. Adjust the areas of shadow with the Smudge Tool.

27. Select the Brush Tool and change it to Color Dodge Mode and 6% Opacity. Draw highlighted and shiny areas on the sword.

28. Draw a bit of shine on the darker side of the sword as well.

29. Select the Smudge Tool and change its strength to 76%. Edit the areas of glare and soften the brush strokes. Hide the layers of the details to make this easier.

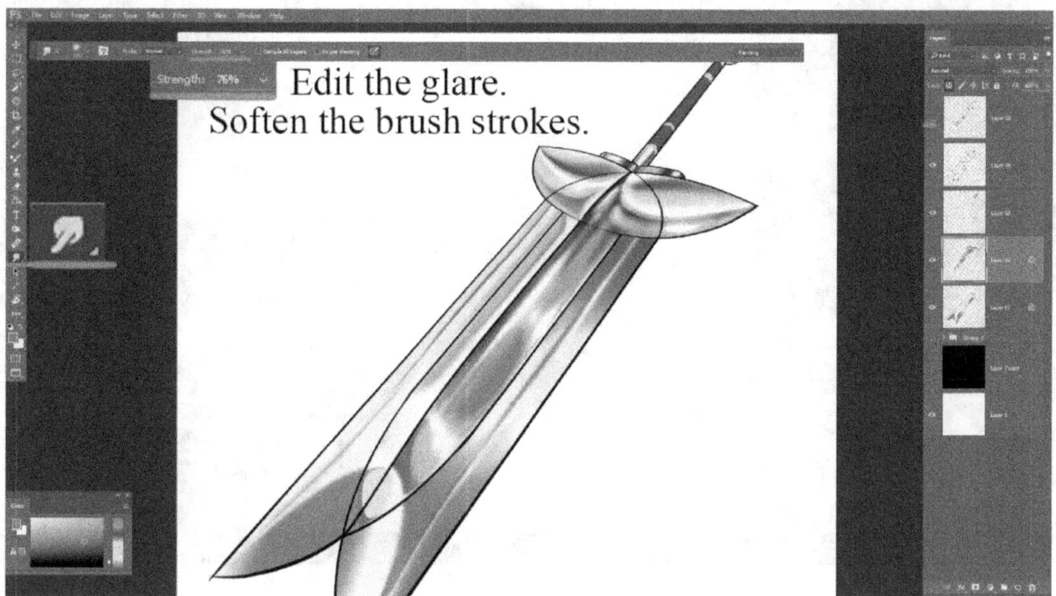

30. Lock and select the layer of the sword blade and press Ctrl+U. Adjust the Saturation Levels to -58.

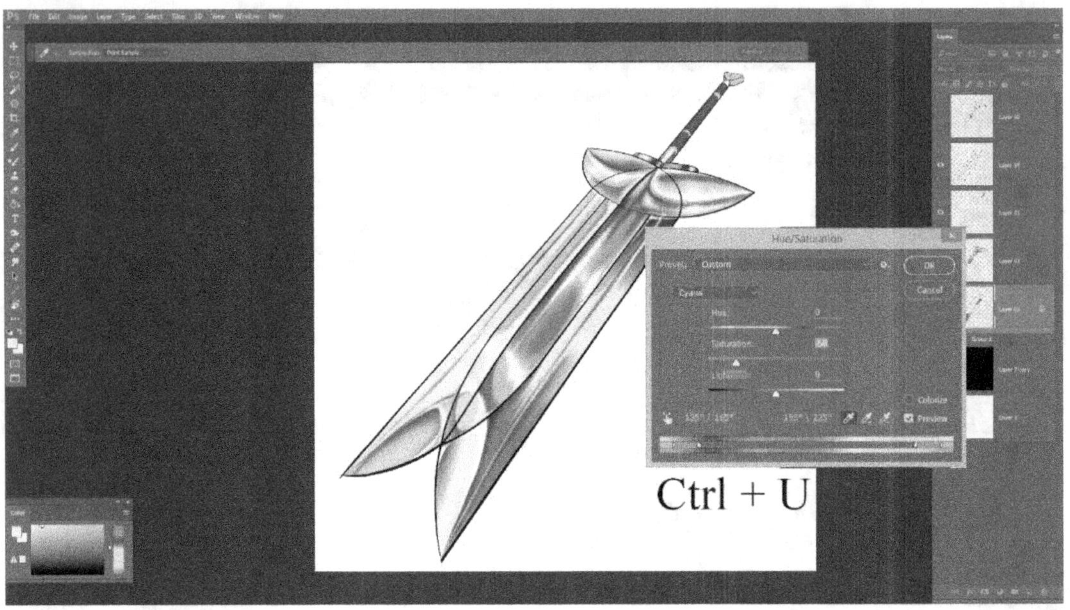

31. Press Ctrl+L to open the Levels Window. Adjust the levels to 53, 1.40, and 231 for the left, middle and right levels, respectively.

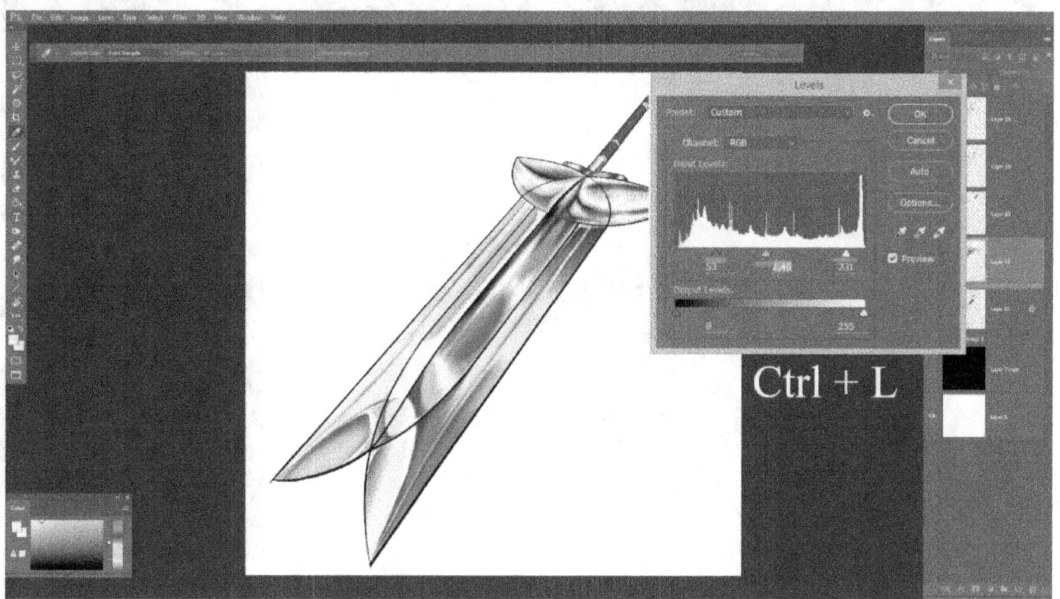

32. Draw the glare on the sword blade.

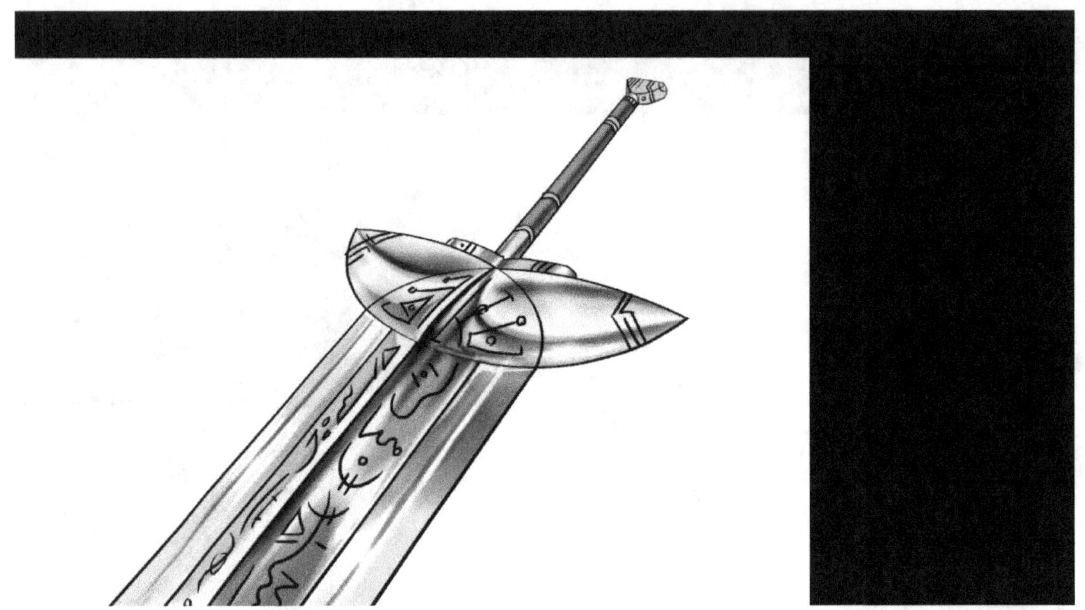

33. Draw the reflection on the points as well.

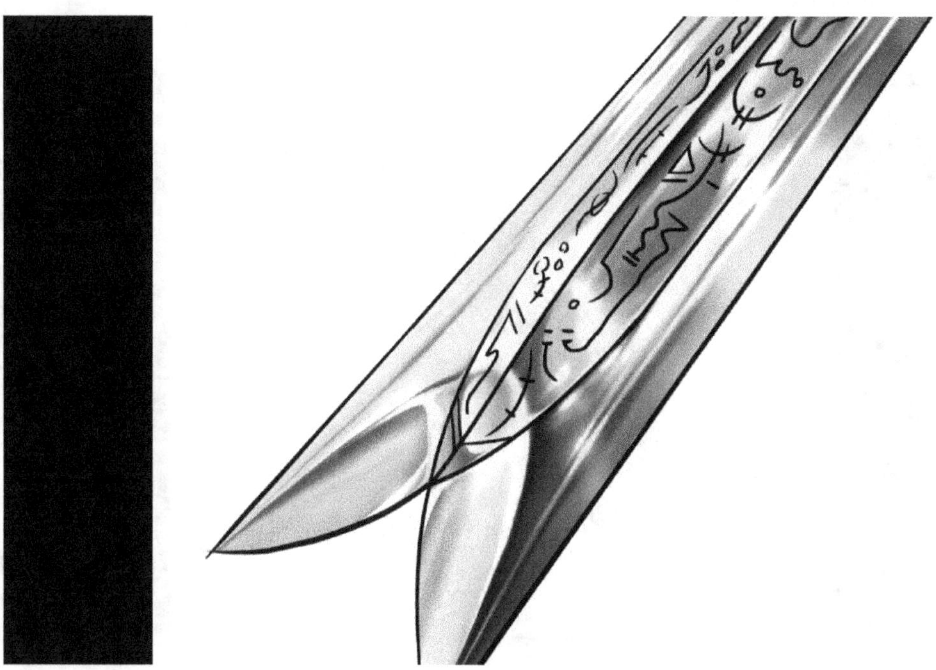

34. Select and lock the layer of the sketch lines. Using the Brush Tool, paint is over the sketch lines to hide them.

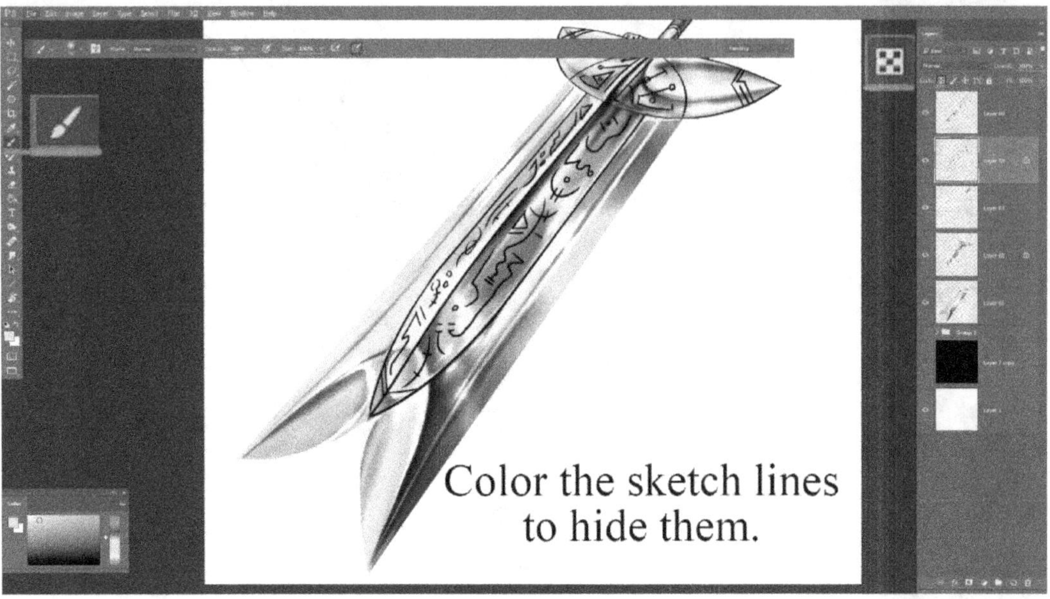

35. The drawing is with almost all the sketch lines hidden.

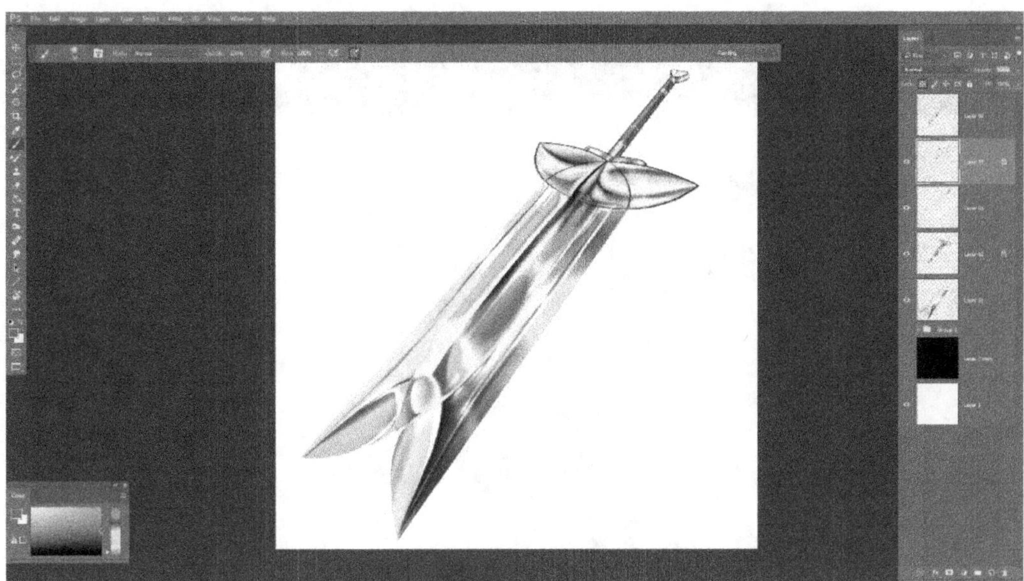

36. Make sure to use a color the same as the one next to it.

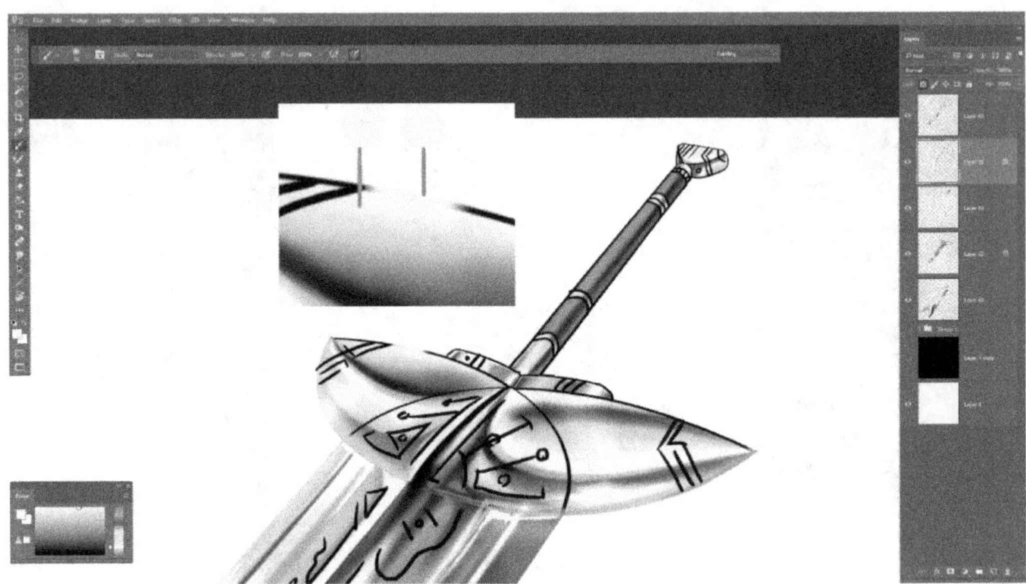

37. Paint over the lines of the other details with the Brush Tool.

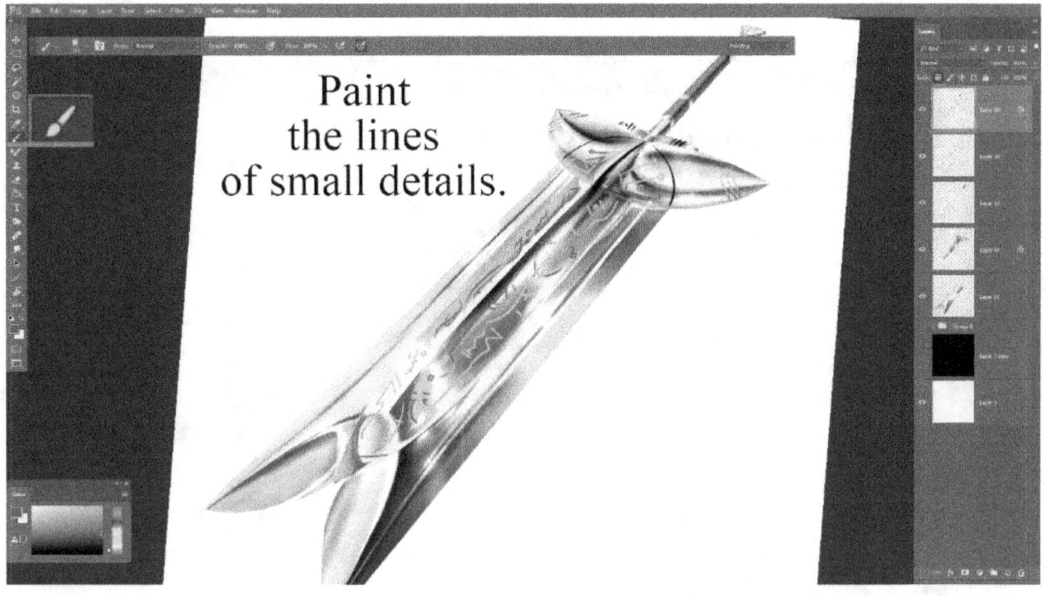

38. Press Ctrl and click on layers. Press the Right Mouse Button and select "Merge Layers" from the menu.

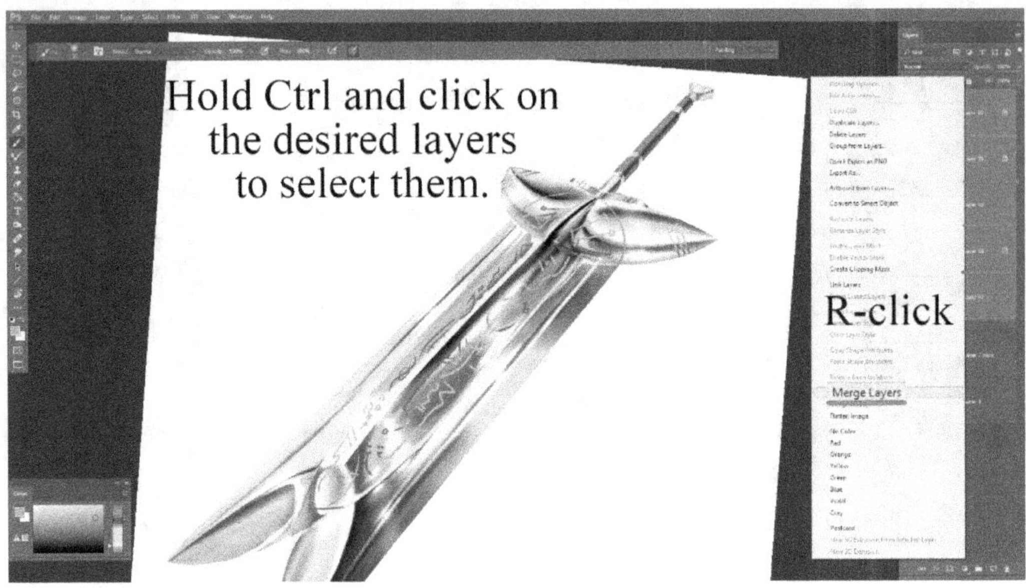

39. Draw the details and carvings on the center of the blade using the Brush, Burn, and Dodge Tools.

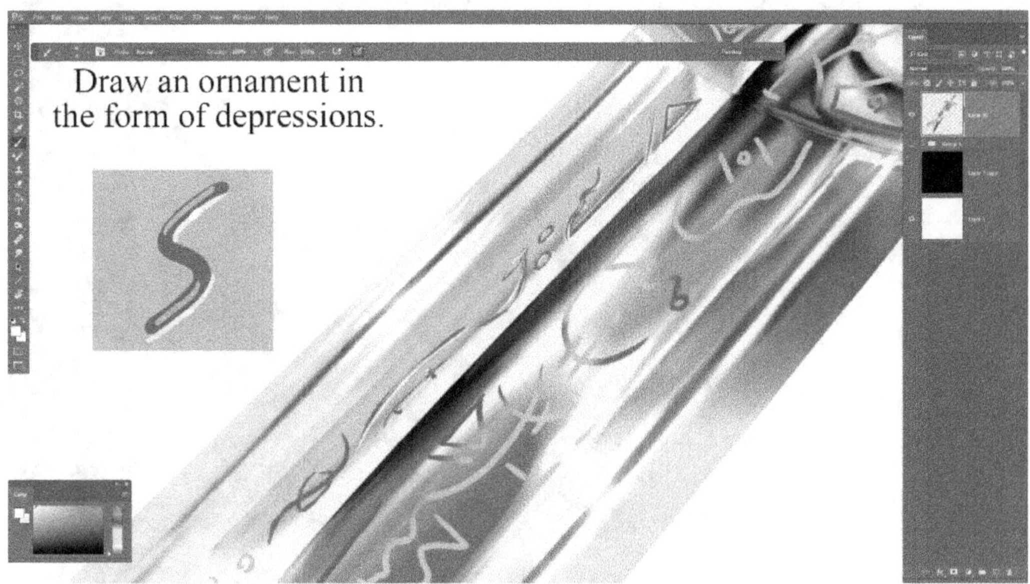

40. The guard with the areas adjusted and other those are not.

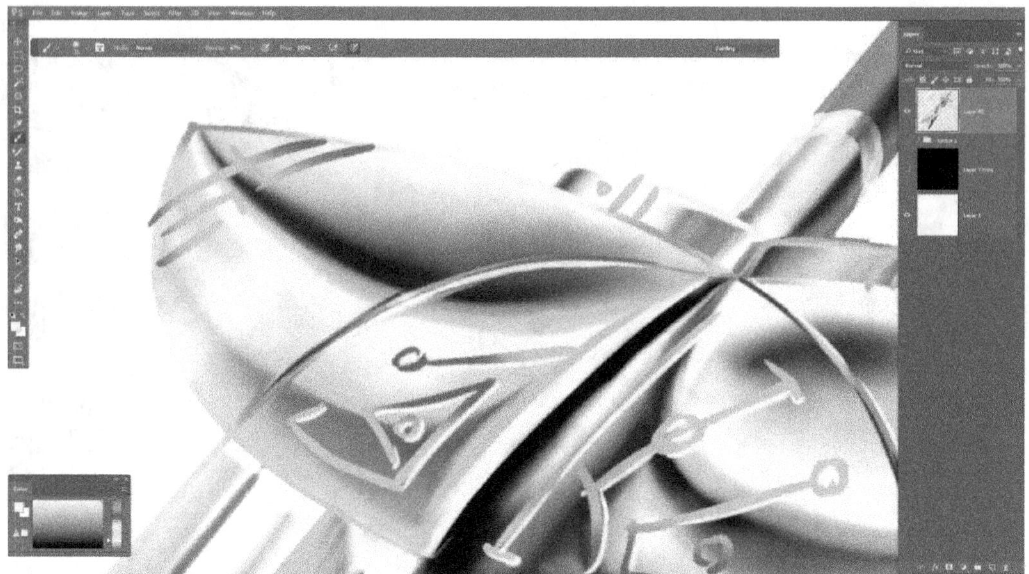

41. Apply this method to the whole of the sword.

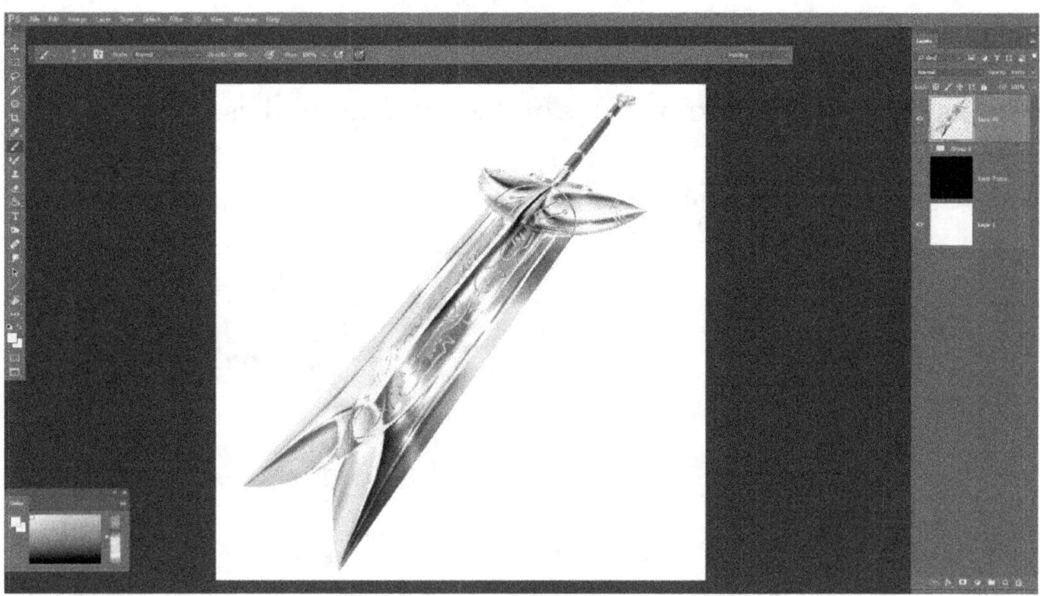

Tips and Tricks for Creating Successful 3D Images

Creating a drawing from scratch is not easy. But since there are many things around us that can be used as an inspiration for drawing, this may help make things a bit easier. In this section we will be showing you how to draw things using only a basic knowledge of the things around us.

Fantasy Planes and Spaceships

1. This is the part of the book where we give you a guide to making fantasy objects and drawings. This is useful especially when you want to draw something but do not have the inspiration you need. Begin the process by making a new layer.

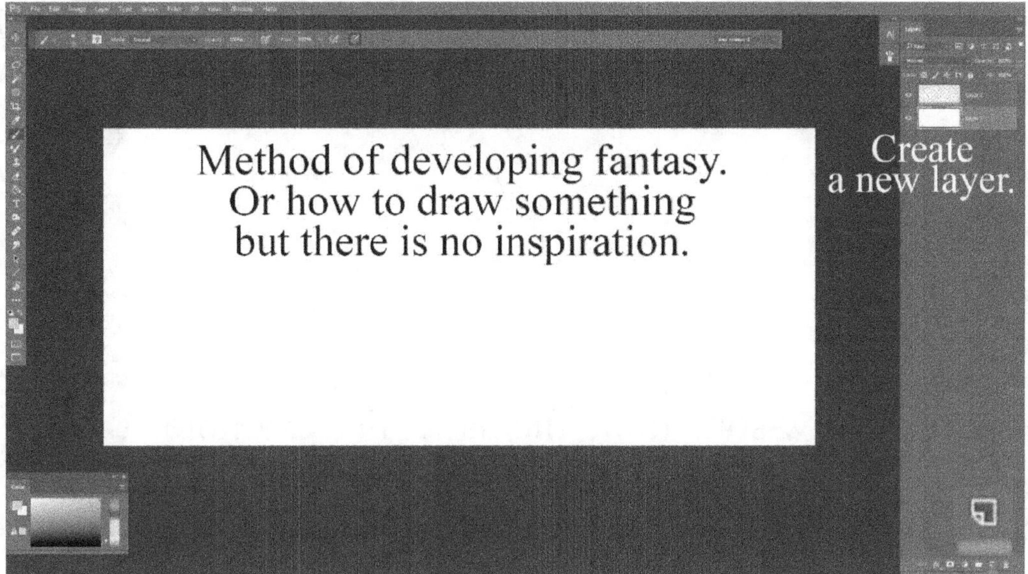

2. Draw something that fits the theme of what you want to draw. In this instance, a plane is used. You may make a sketch based on pictures of actual objects.

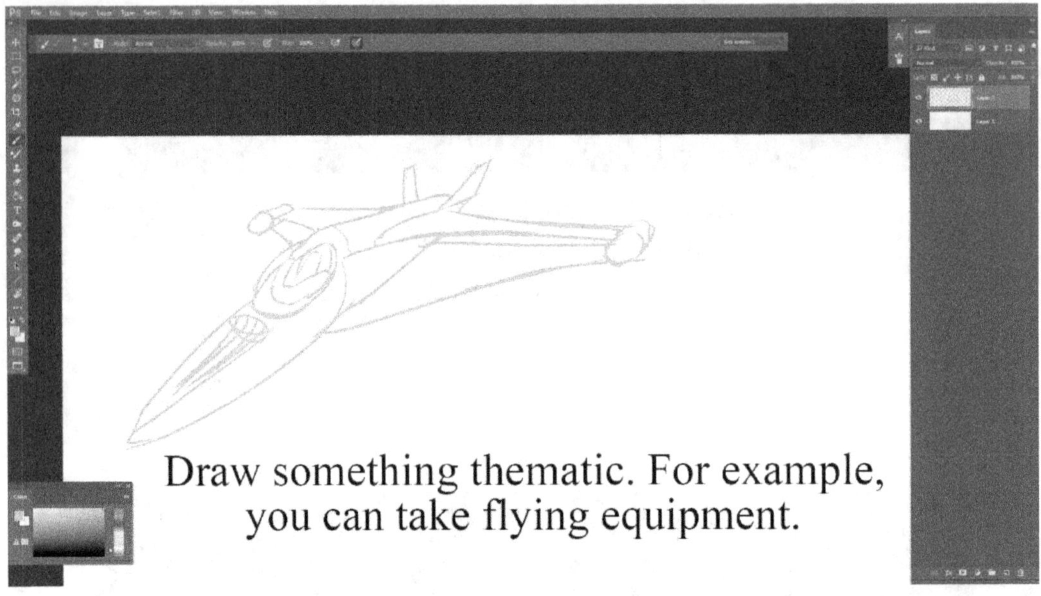

3. Take inspiration from a certain part of the first object that you may use for the same part on another object. In this case, the nose and cockpit serve as the inspiration.

The goal here is not to create a neat drawing but to form an original idea based on the thematic object.

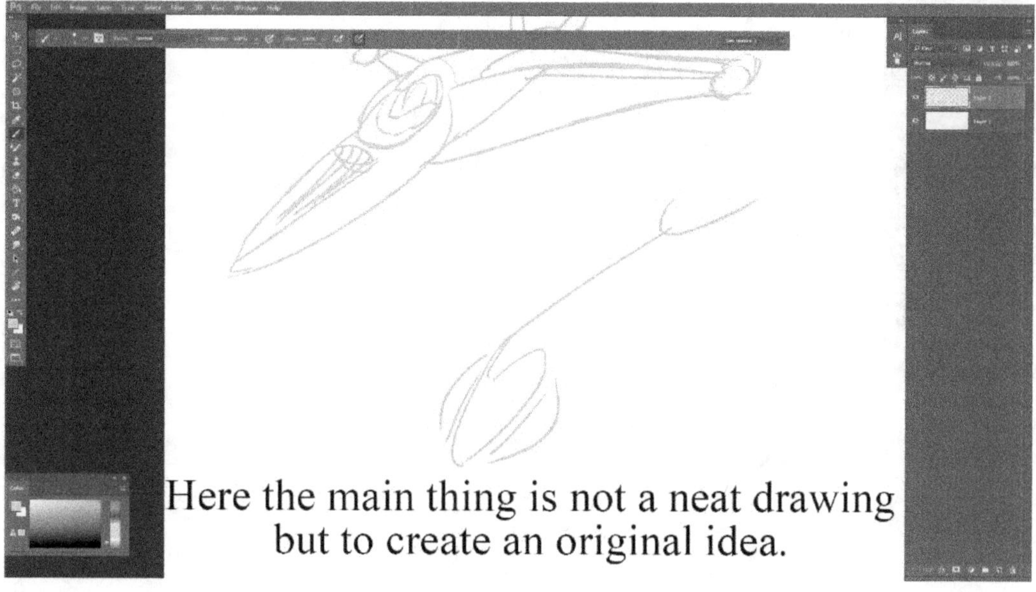

4. Continue drawing the details of the new sketch.

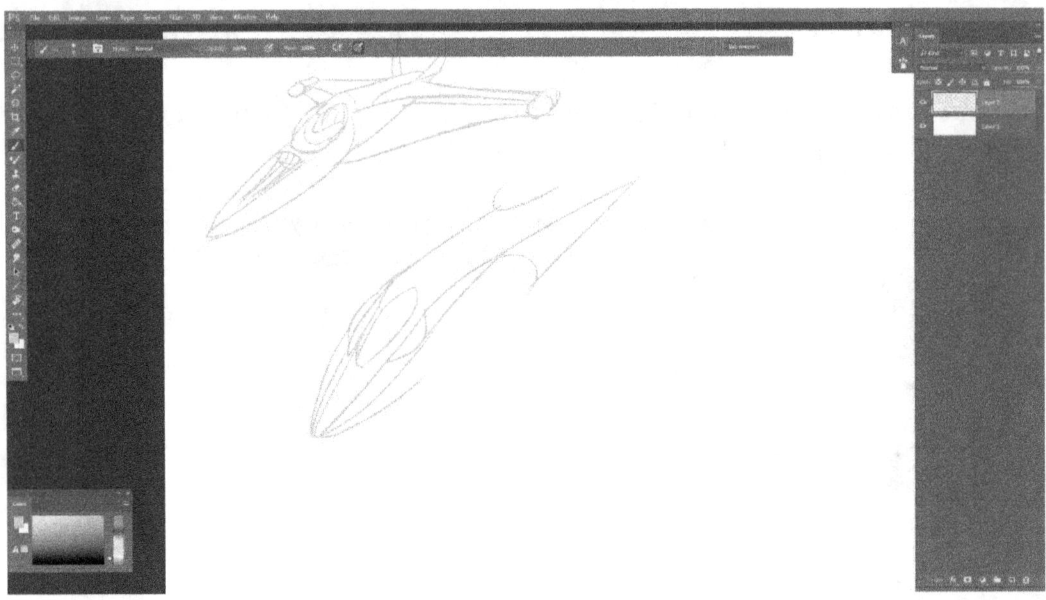

5. Add the wings of the new plane.

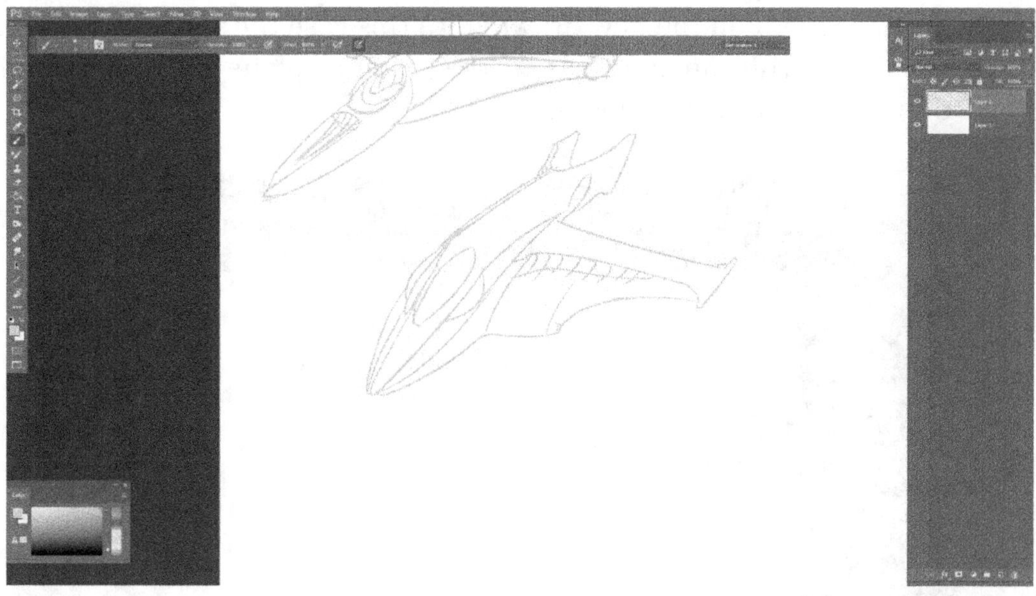

6. You may use other parts of the original object and incorporate them to the drawing. You may even combine two unconnected parts of the original object and place them on the new drawing. In this case the shape of the wing and the air inlet grille on the nose of the original plane are used to add details to the wings of the new plane.

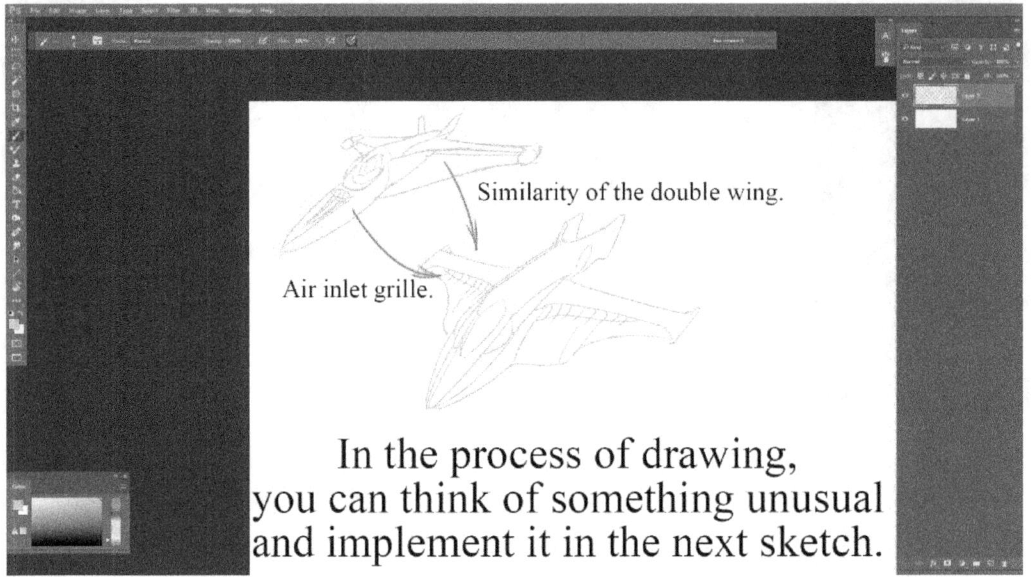

7. Create another sketch. Use perspective lines when making the sketch.

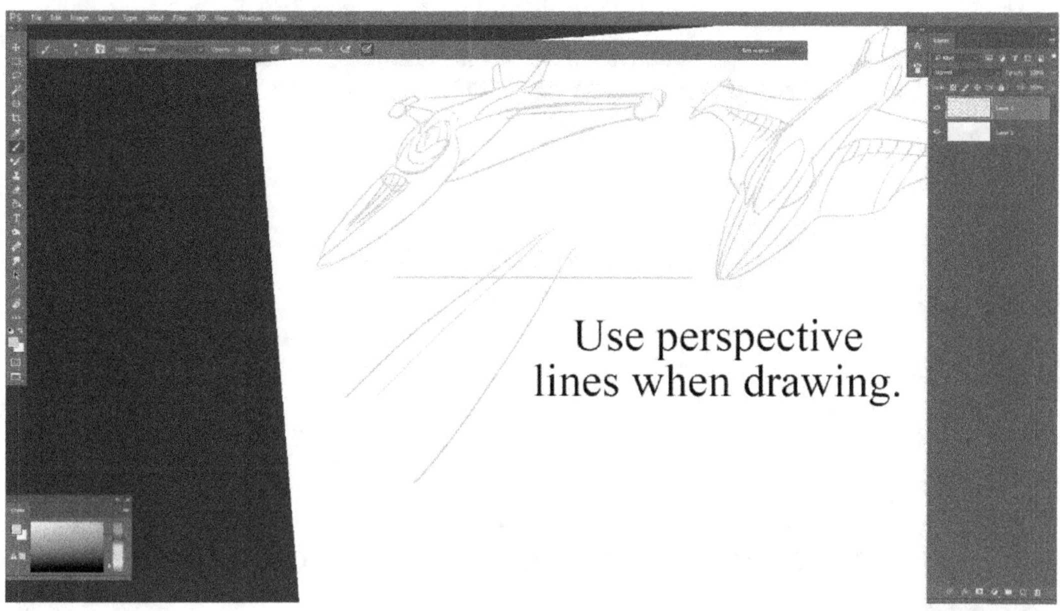

8. Draw details of the new plane. You may use any color you like for the sketch. You may even use a different color for each sketch.

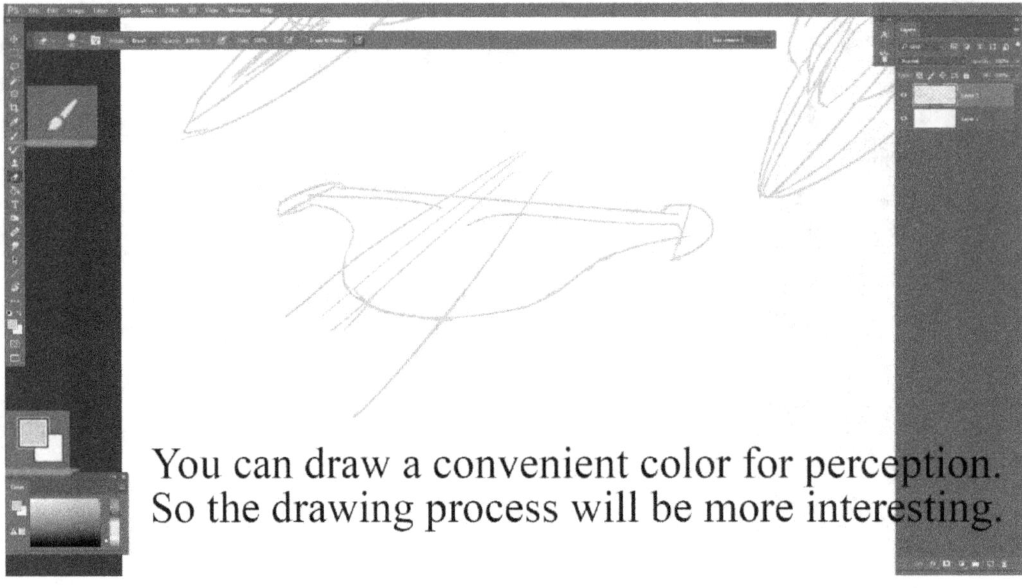

9. Draw the details and complete the drawing. The iteration of the drawing, the details and objects will appear more interesting.

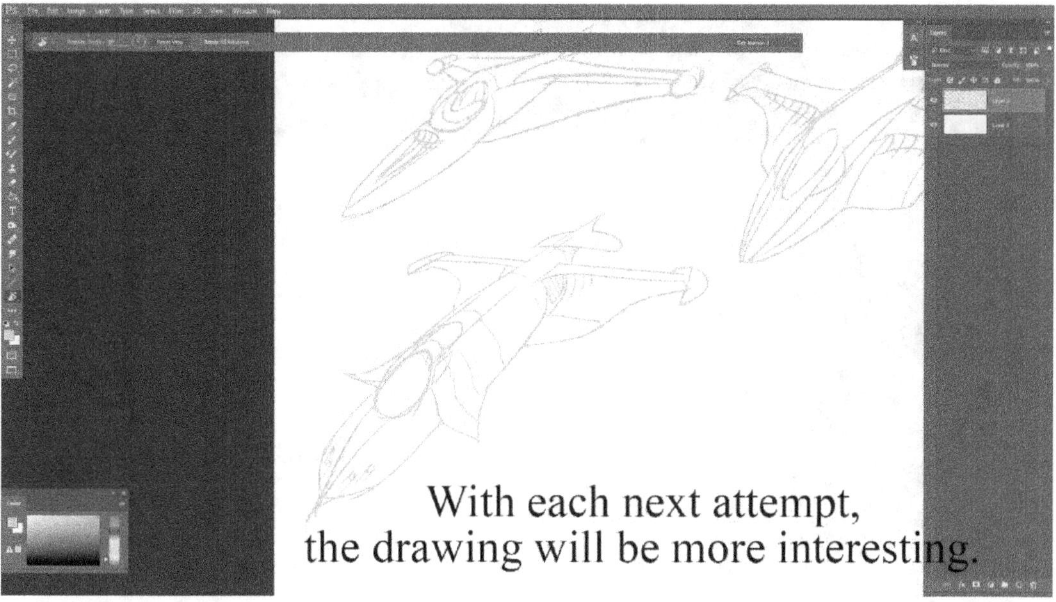

10. Use the Eraser Tool to remove any areas and items you may not like or need.

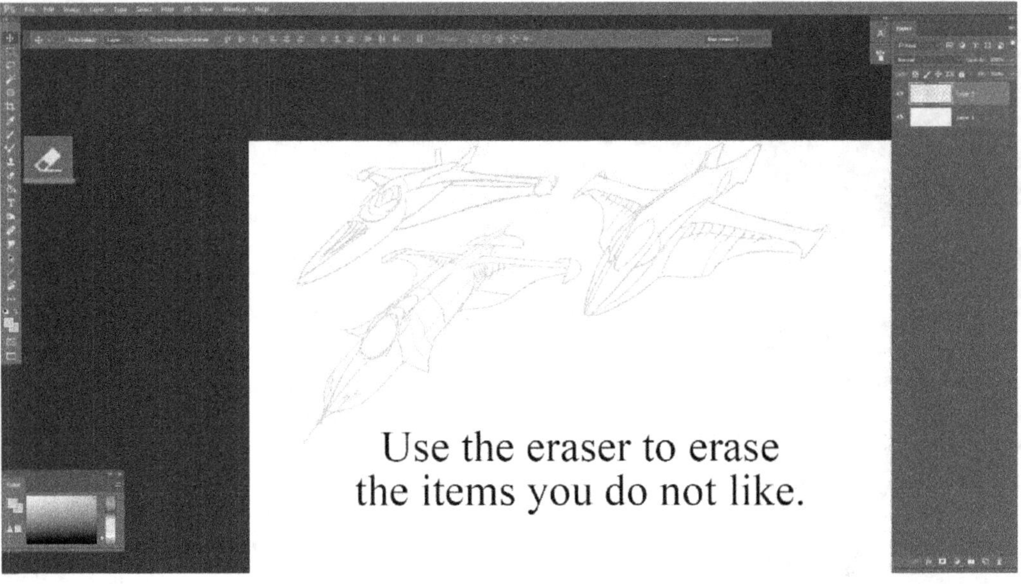

11. Begin another sketch. Incorporate parts of the other planes to this new one.

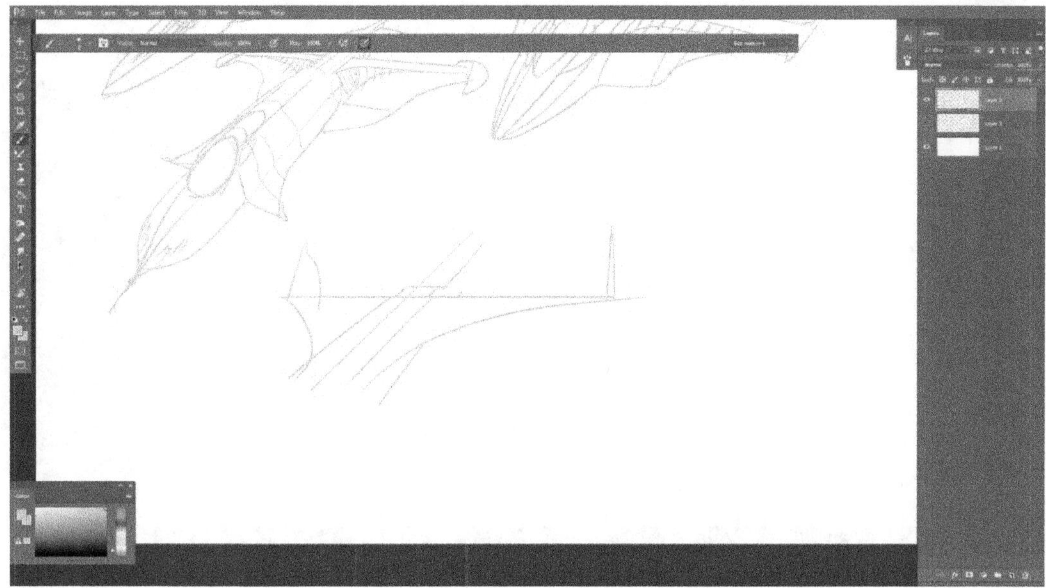

12. Add the details and ideas to the sketch as you go.

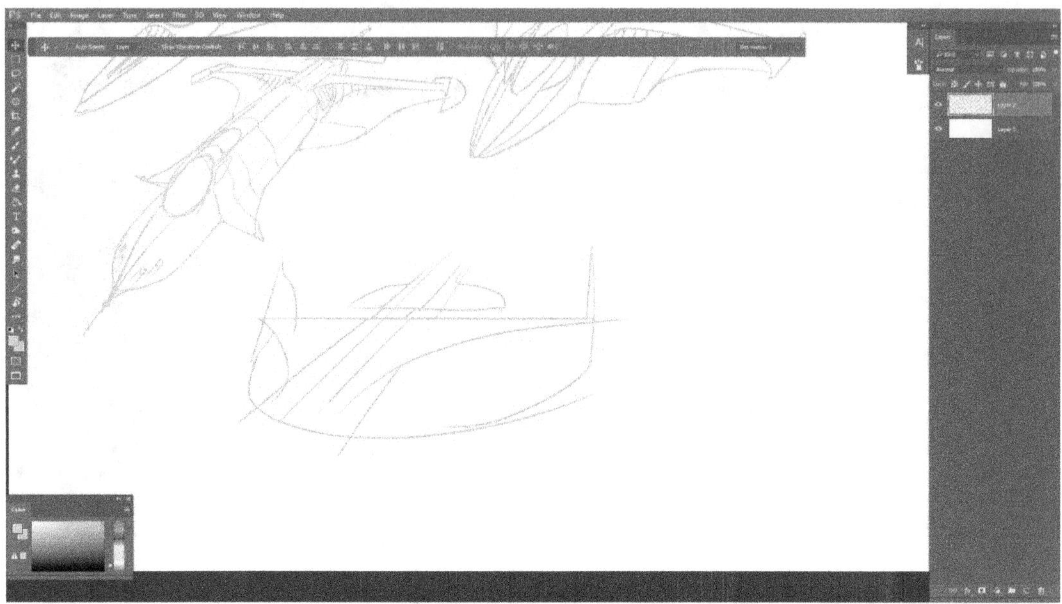

13. You can completely change the sketch as a whole. Just make sure to not get attached to just one idea.

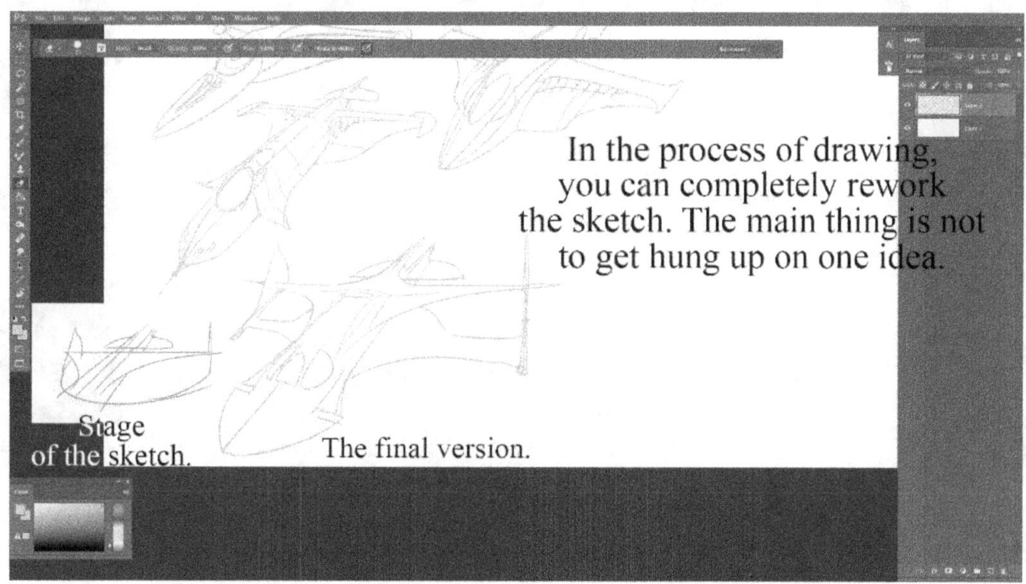

14. Draw another sketch.

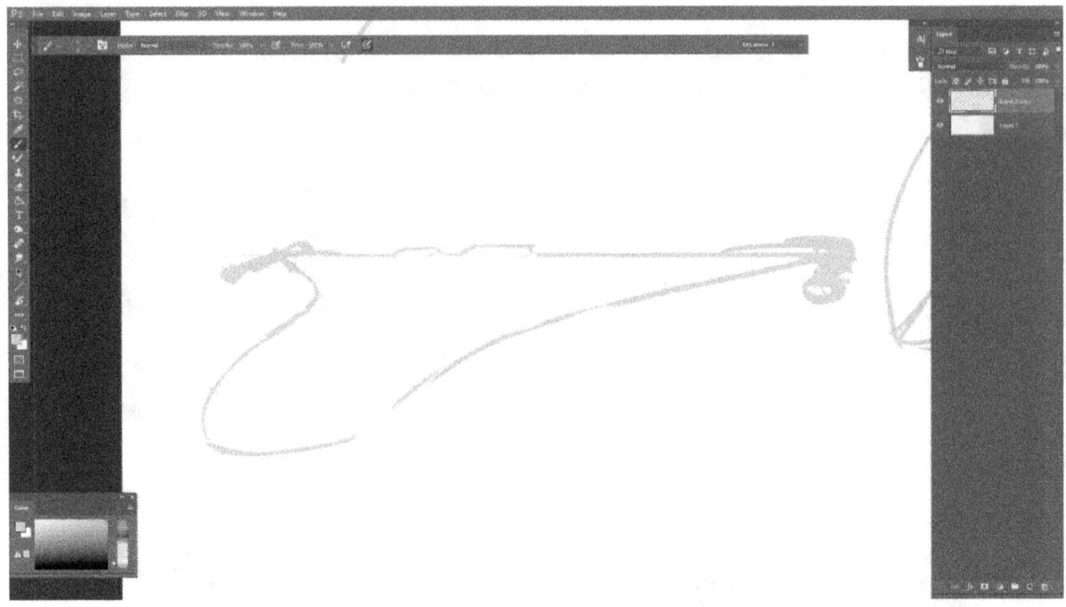

15. Draw transverse line in the object's shape. This will help with understanding the volume of the shape and may also become part of the drawing's design.

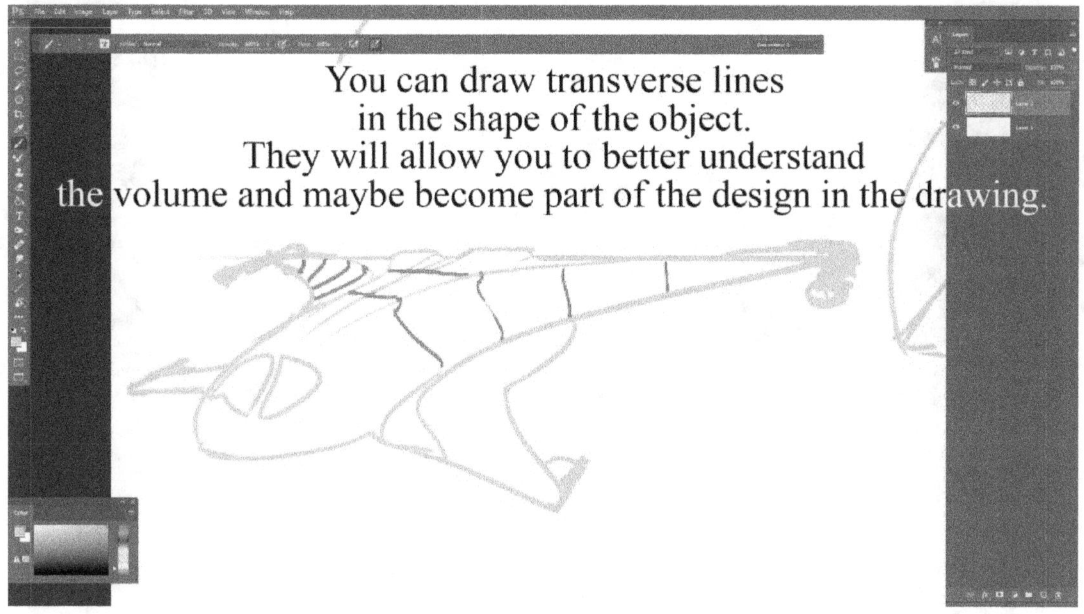

16. Add more details to the sketch.

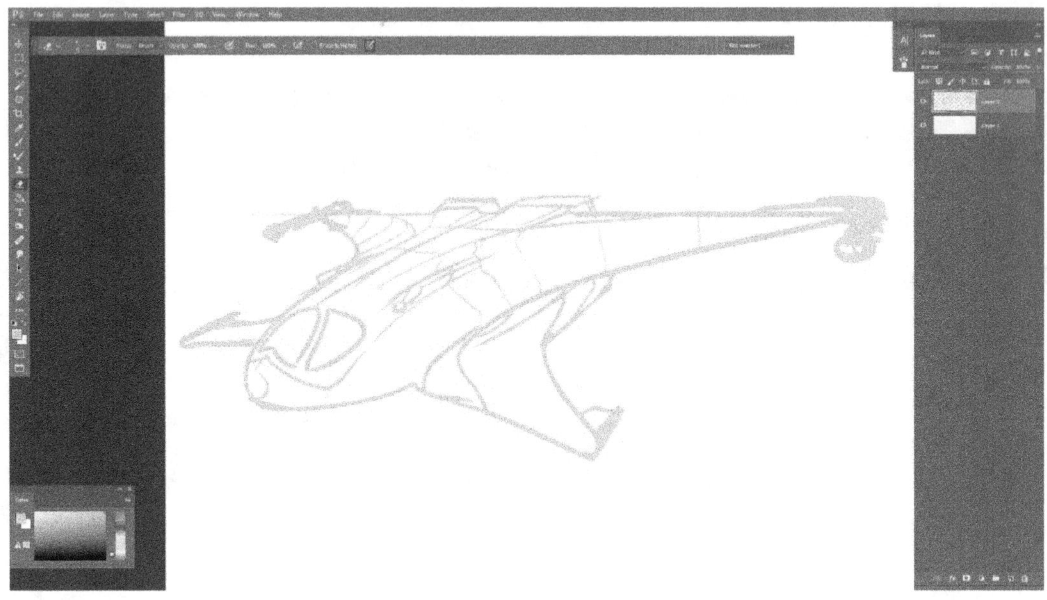

17. Begin drawing another sketch.

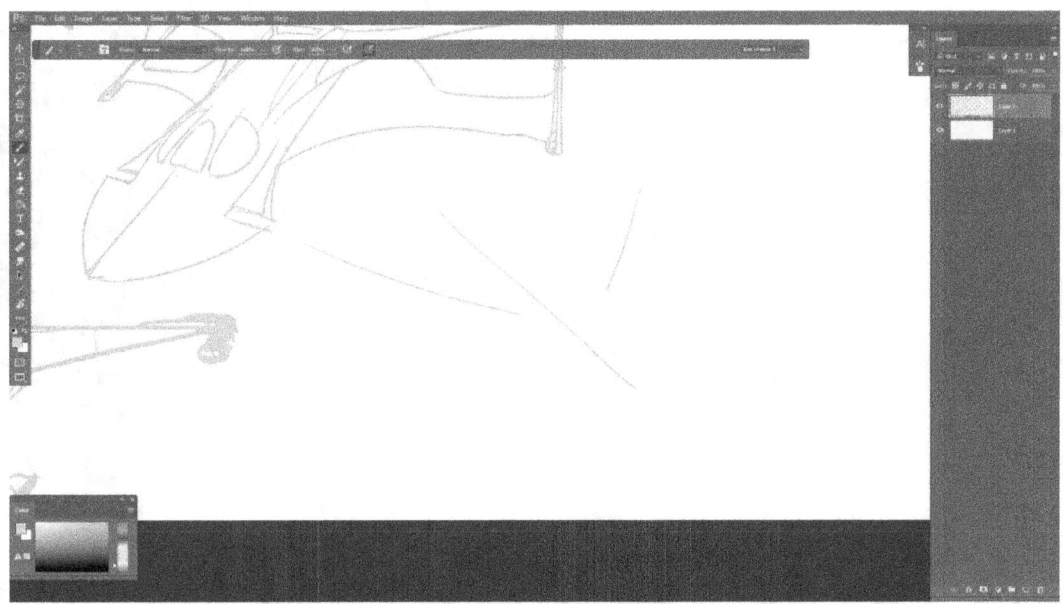

18. Draw the overall shape of the plane.

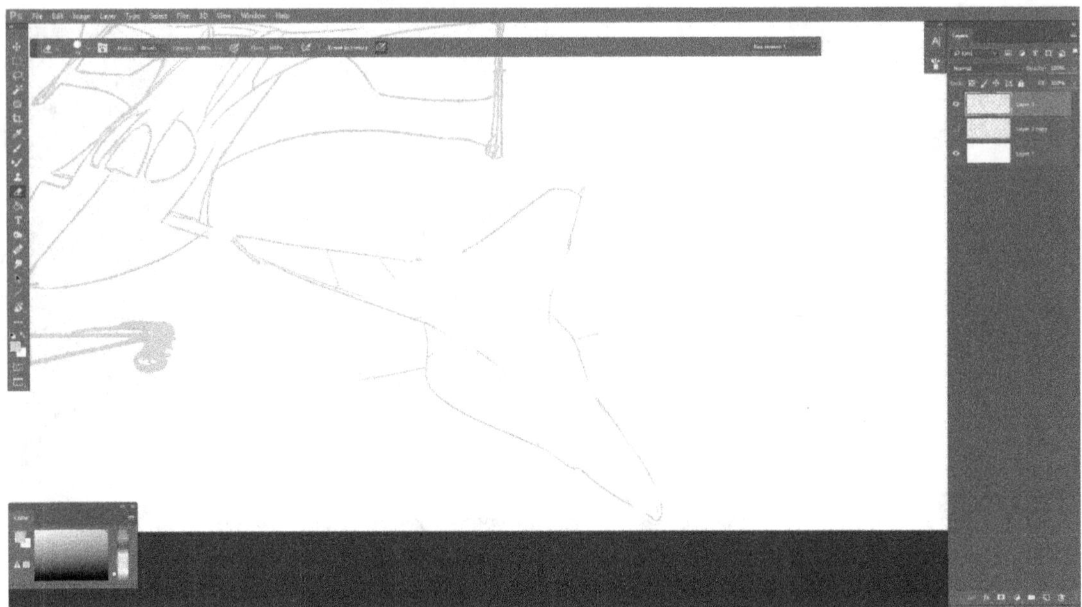

19. Add details and transverse line to give the object volume.

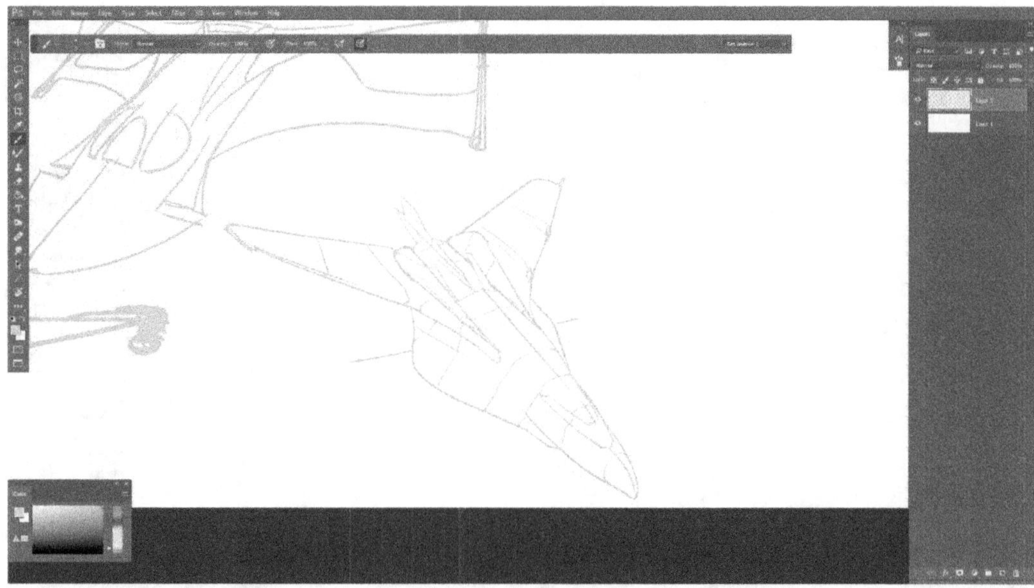

20. Begin another sketch.

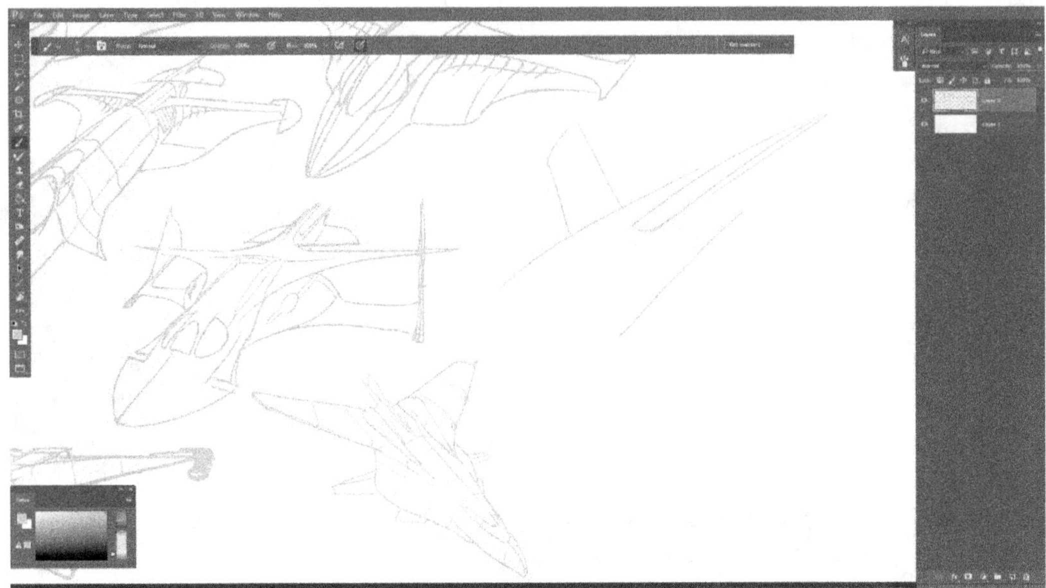

21. Always remember to incorporate some parts of the previous sketches to the new one.

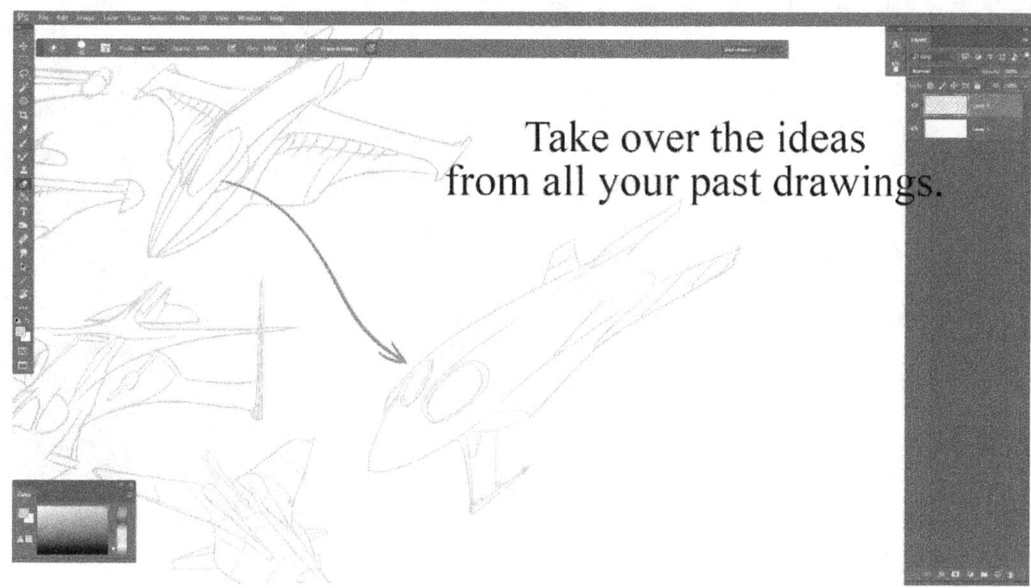

22. Add more details to the sketch.

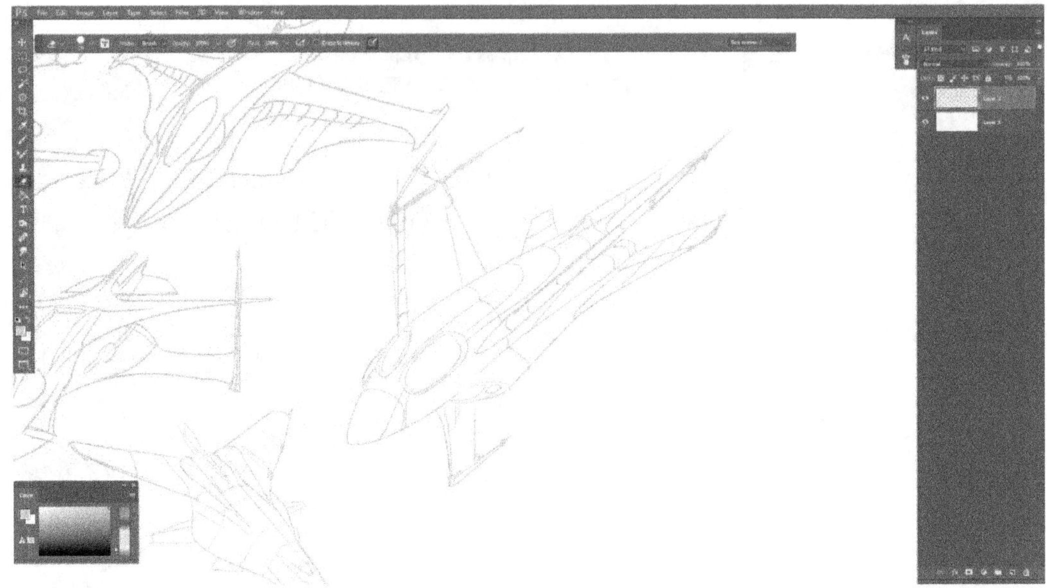

23. You may remove parts that you don't like or need from the sketch.

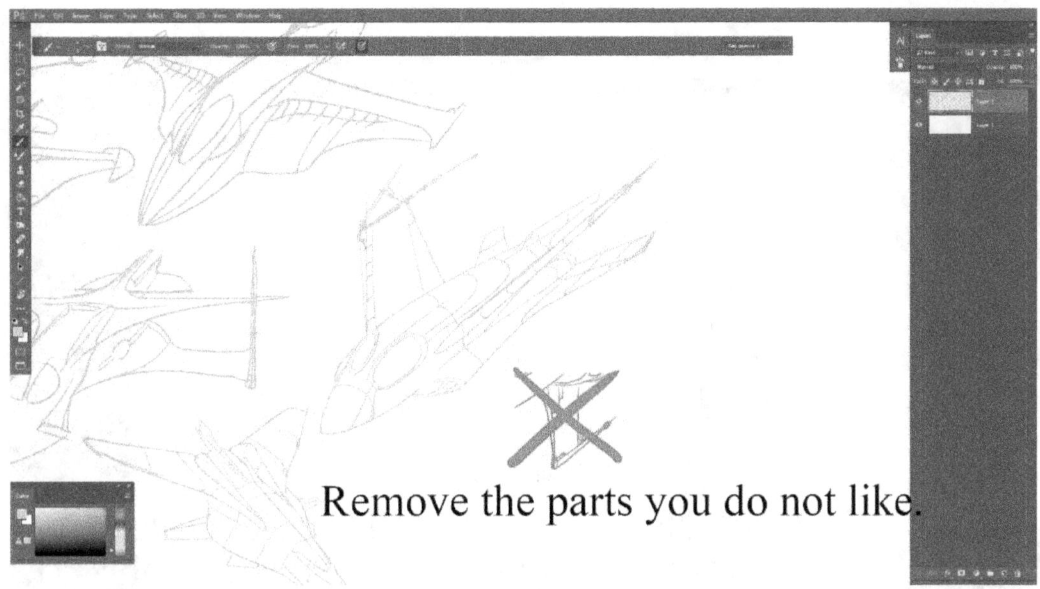

24. You can also copy certain parts of the drawing in order to create a new one.

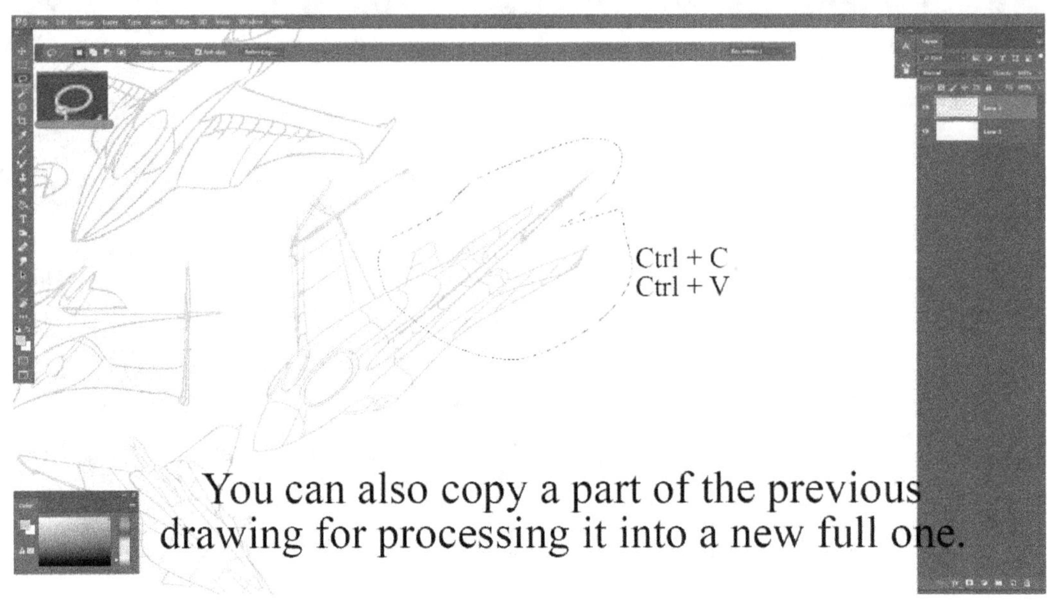

You can also copy a part of the previous drawing for processing it into a new full one.

25. Press Ctrl+T to scale the copied image.

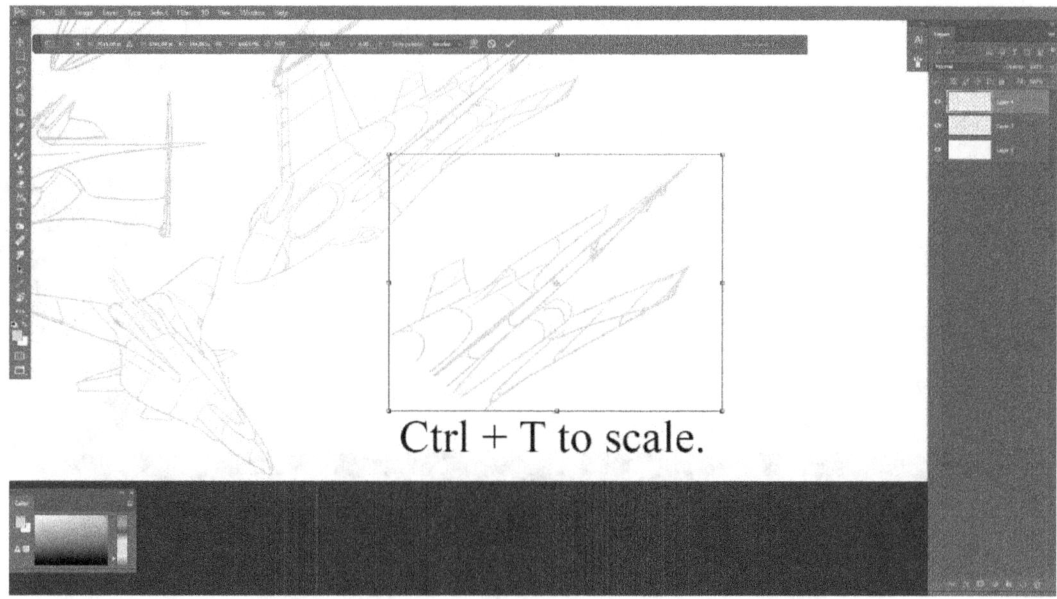

26. Add details to the new object and erase any excess parts.

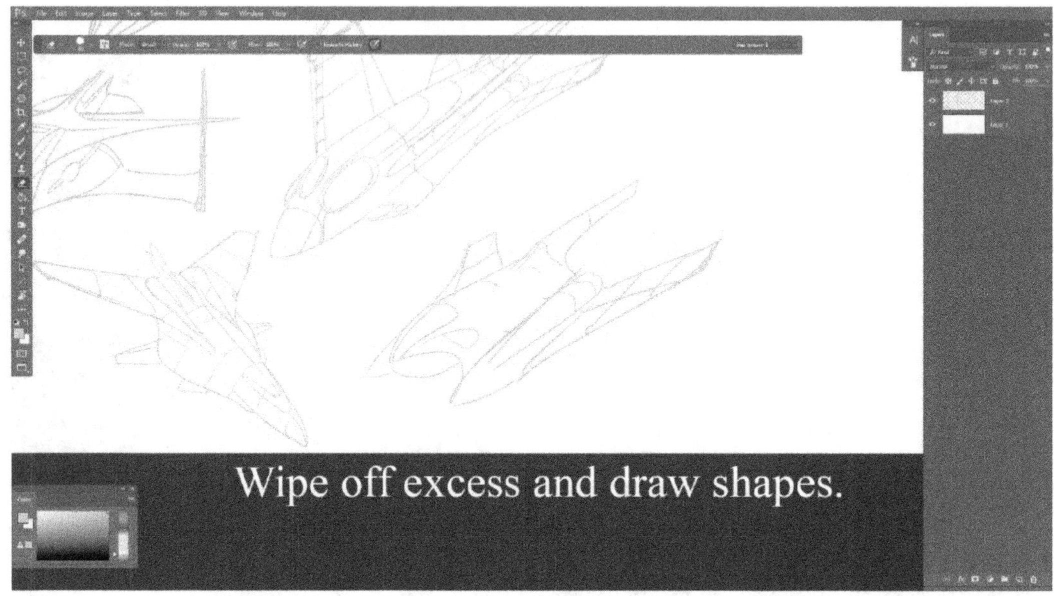

27. Add even more details to the drawing.

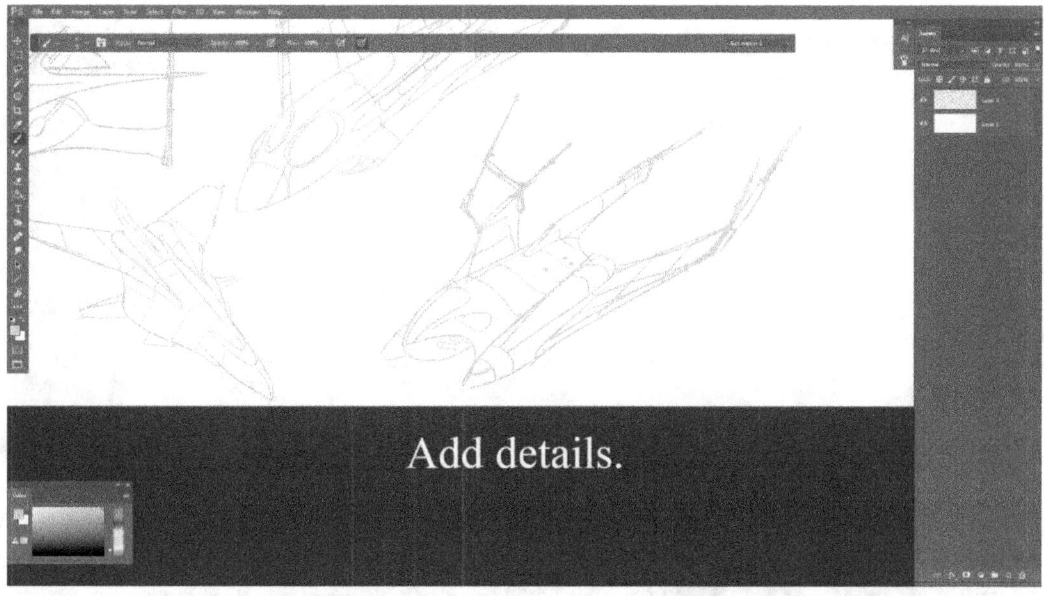

28. You can make the sketch as detailed as you want.

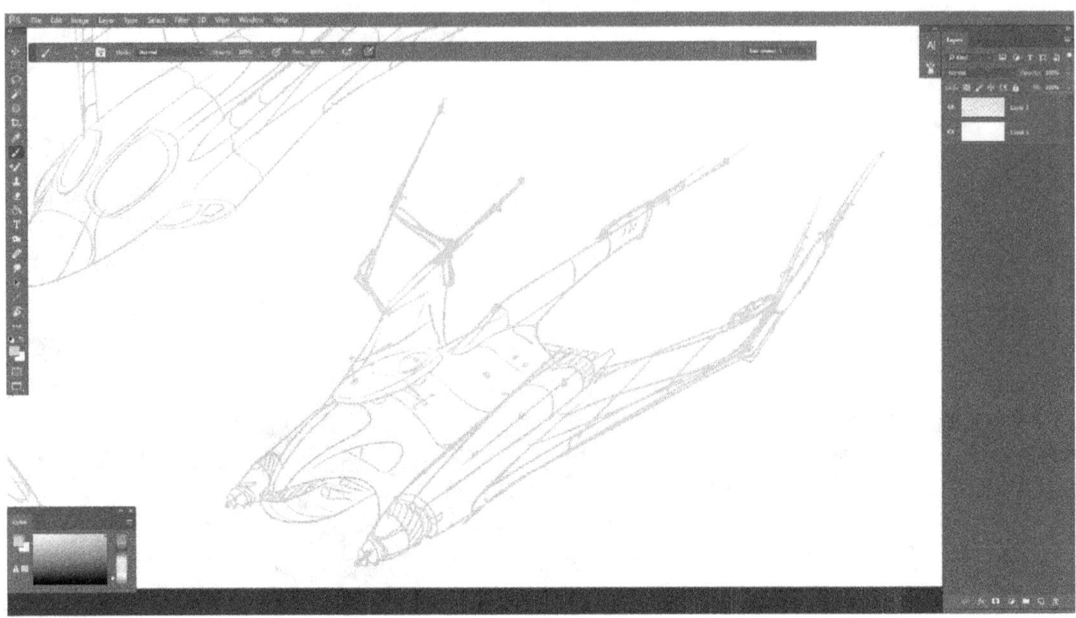

29. Continue drawing more sketches.

30. You can move the drawings around and put them on a more convenient place in the canvas. You can do this by marking an area around the object using the Lasso Tool.

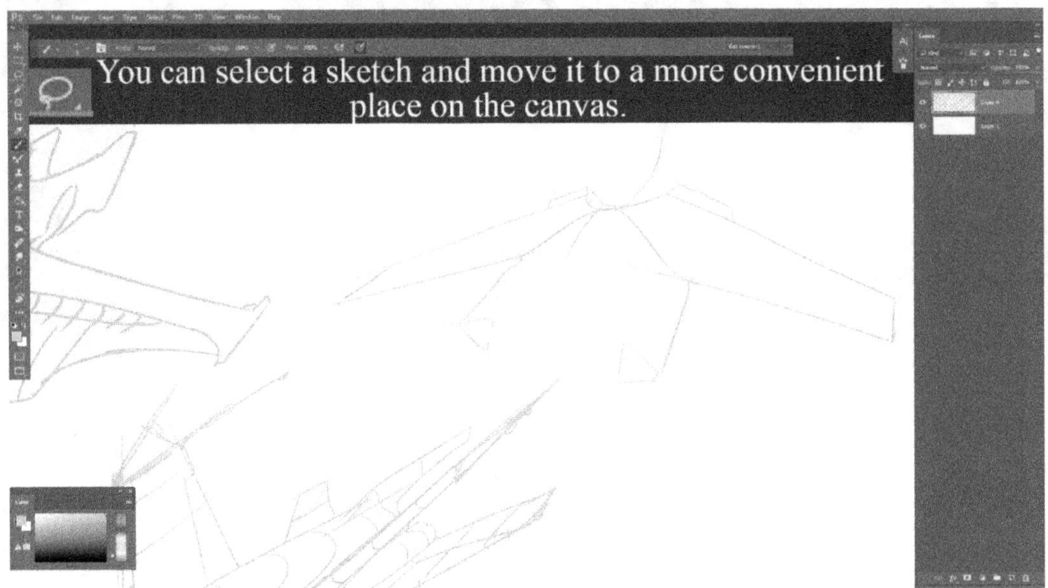

31. Add details and grilles to the drawing.

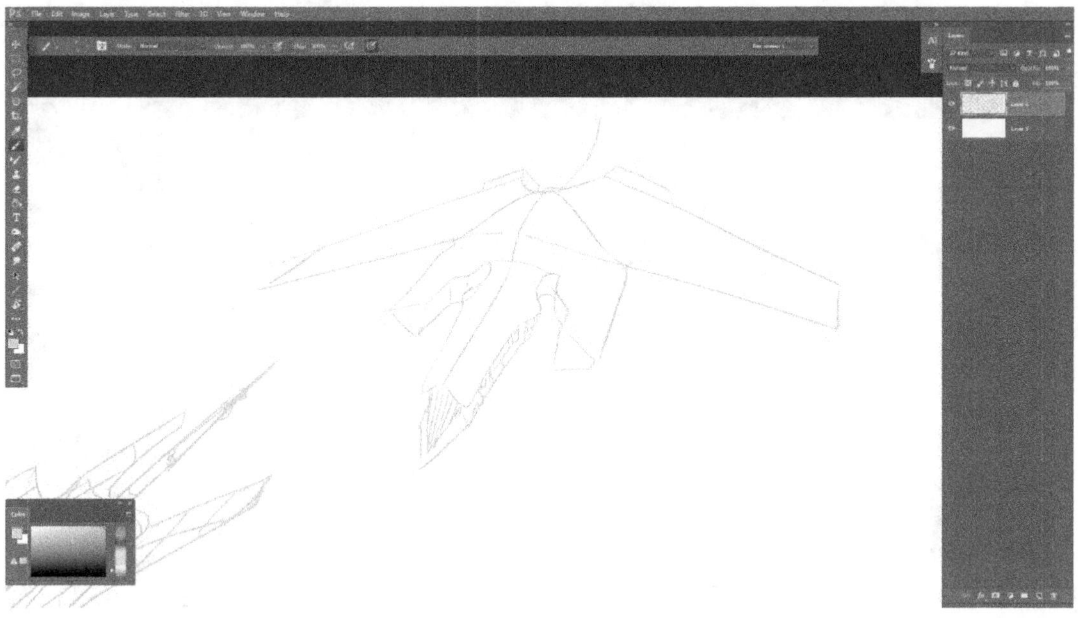

32. Add more details to it.

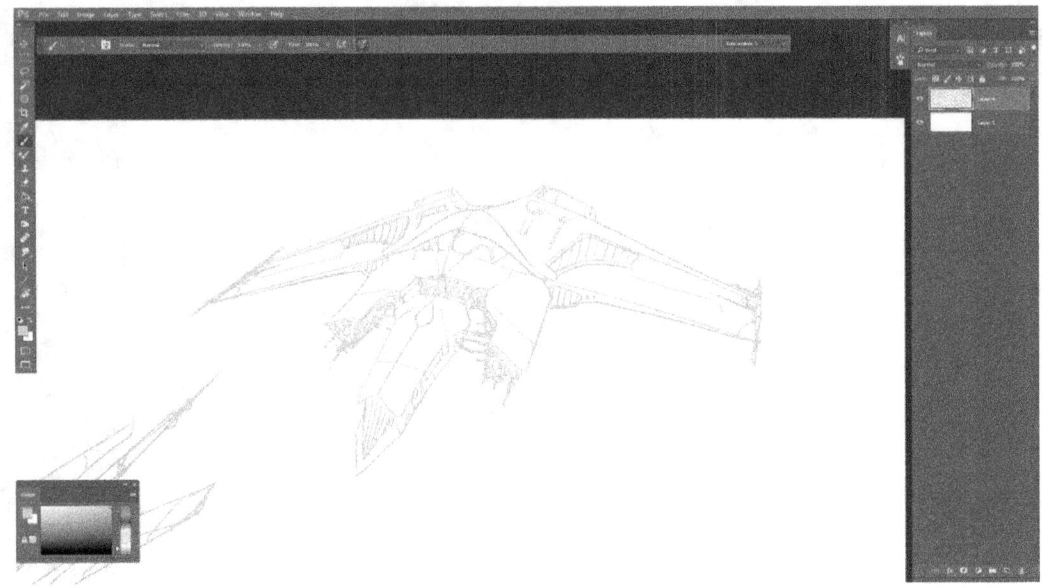

33. Make a new sketch.

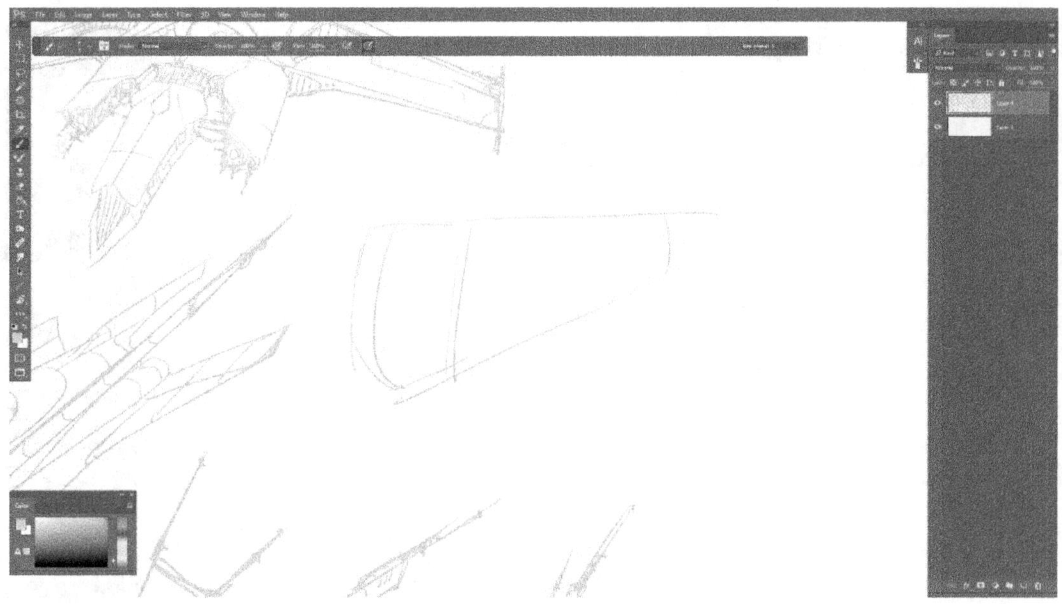

34. Add shapes and some details.

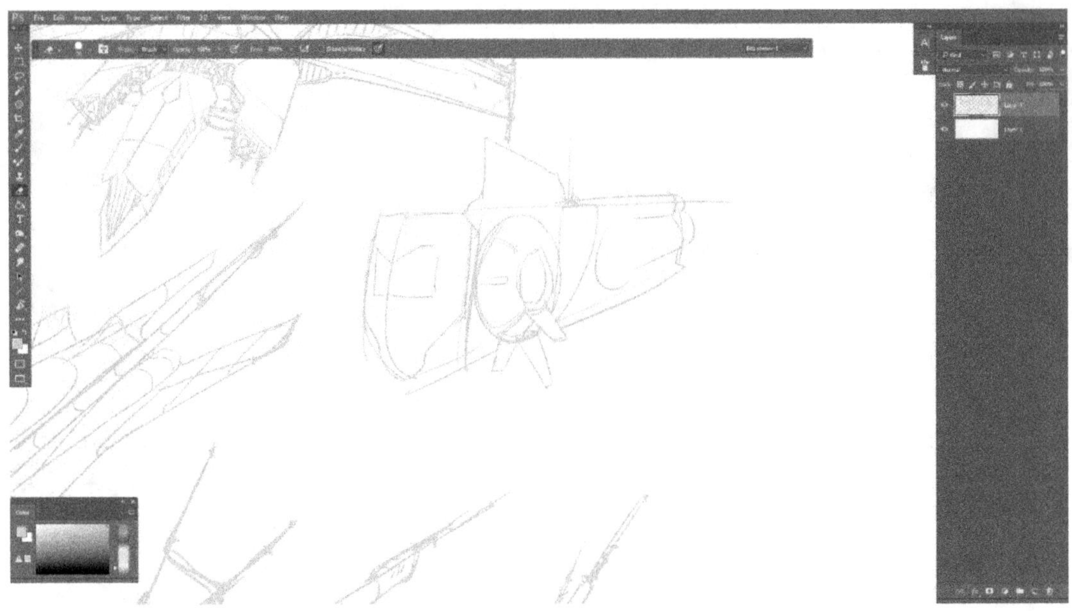

35. You may change parts of the object as you go.

36. Draw parts and shapes according to your taste.

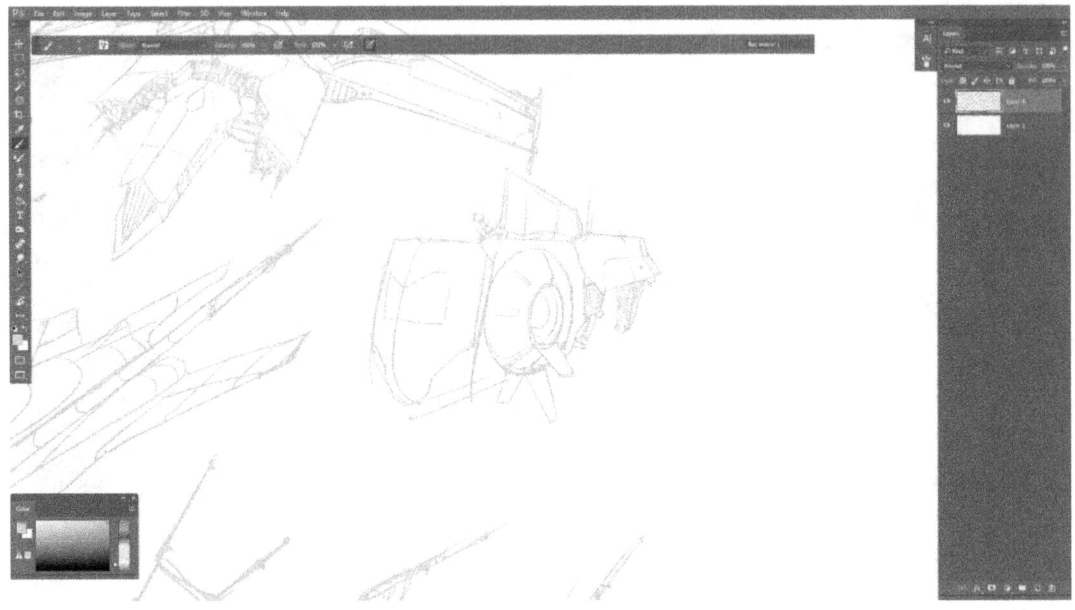

37. Add more details and volume to the sketch.

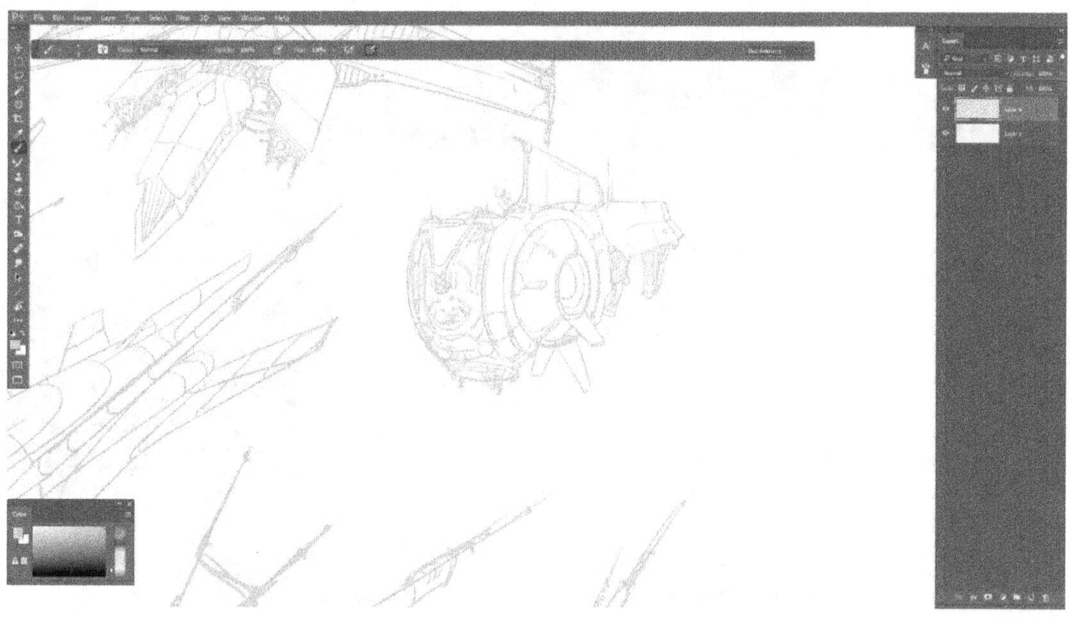

38. Begin another drawing.

39. Add the details of the overall shape of the object.

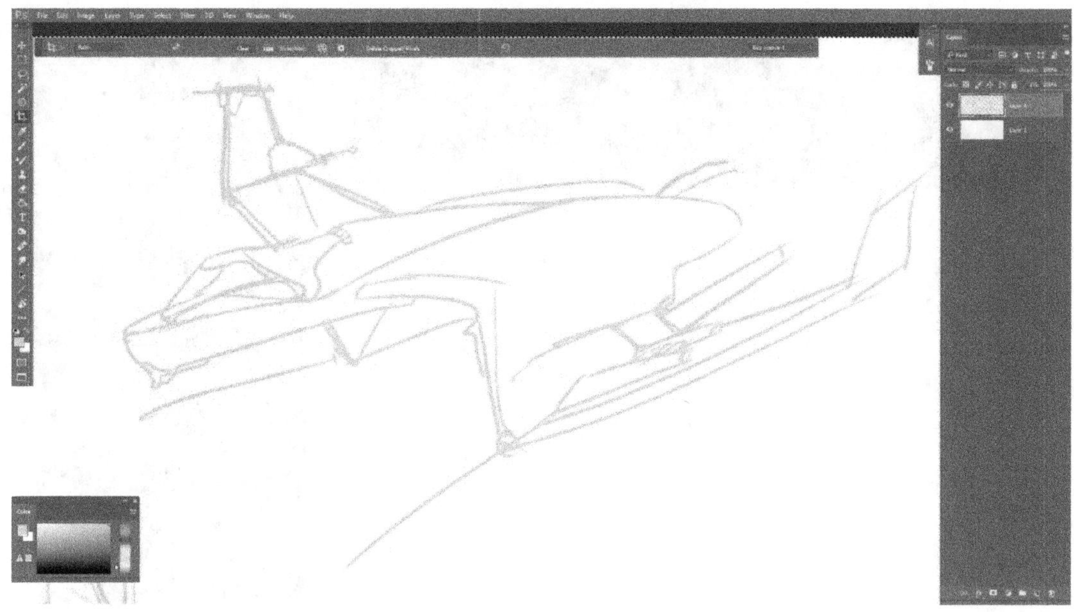

40. Add the details and volume to the object.

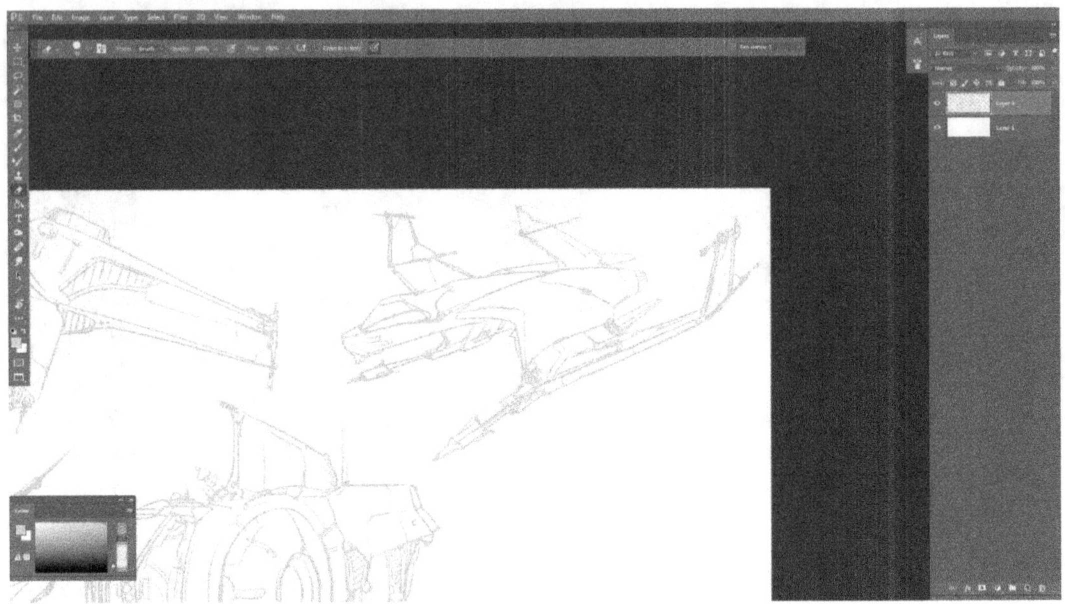

41. Begin a new sketch.

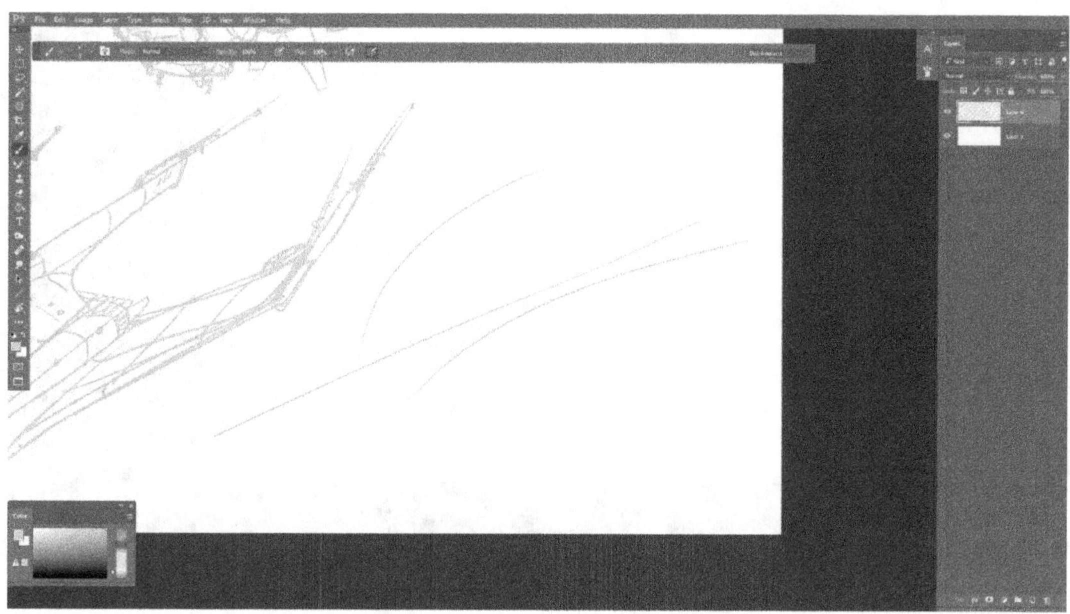

42. Draw the shape of the piece.

43. Mark out the bounds and edges of the plane.

44. Draw the details to the piece. Mark out an area using the Lasso Tool and press Ctrl+T on this area. On the dropdown menu, select "Warp" and adjust the desired area's shape.

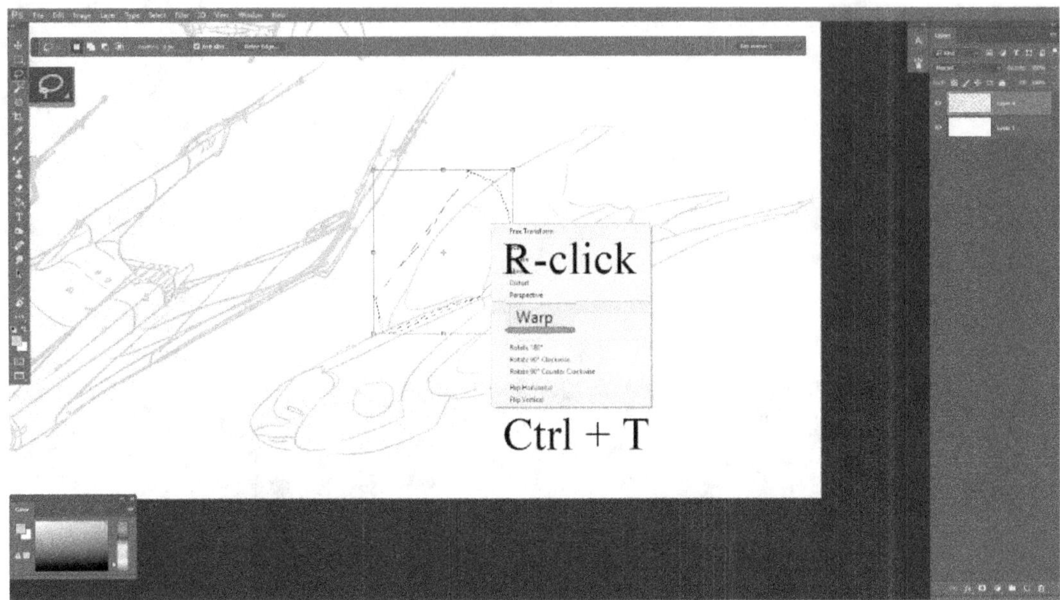

45. You may change other parts of the object using the same method.

46. Add more details to the sketch.

47. Draw the volume lines and other additional details you may want to add.

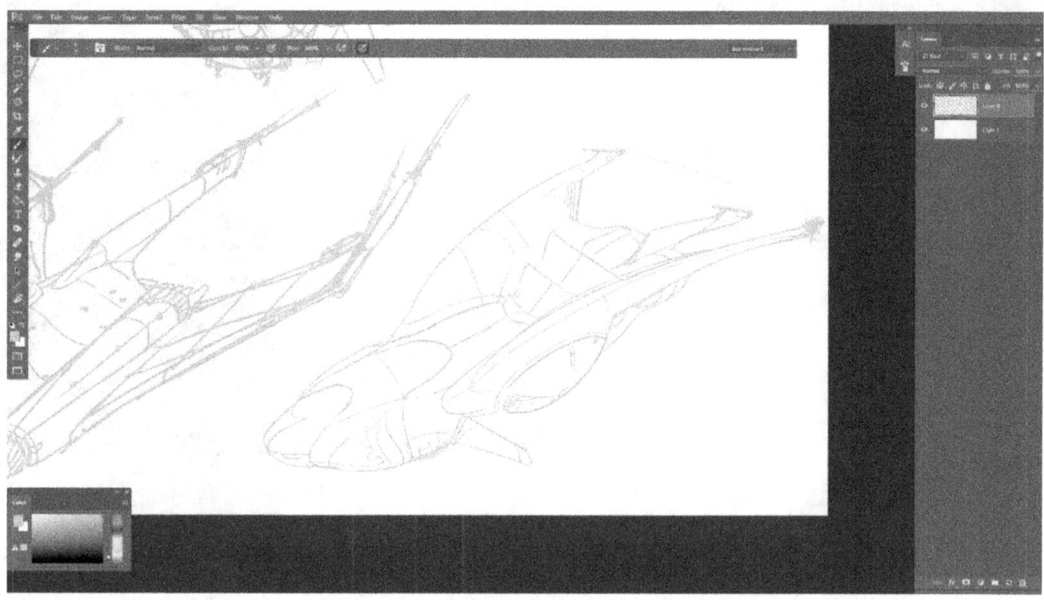

48. Draw another sketch.

49. Add details to the front of the new object.

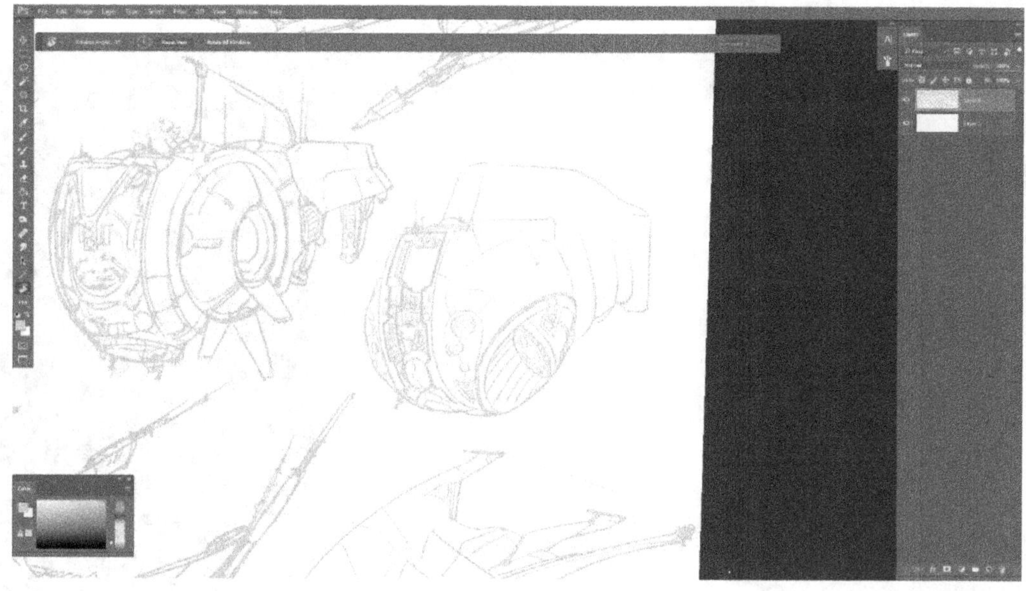

50. Add details to the rear and remove any areas you may not want on the drawing.

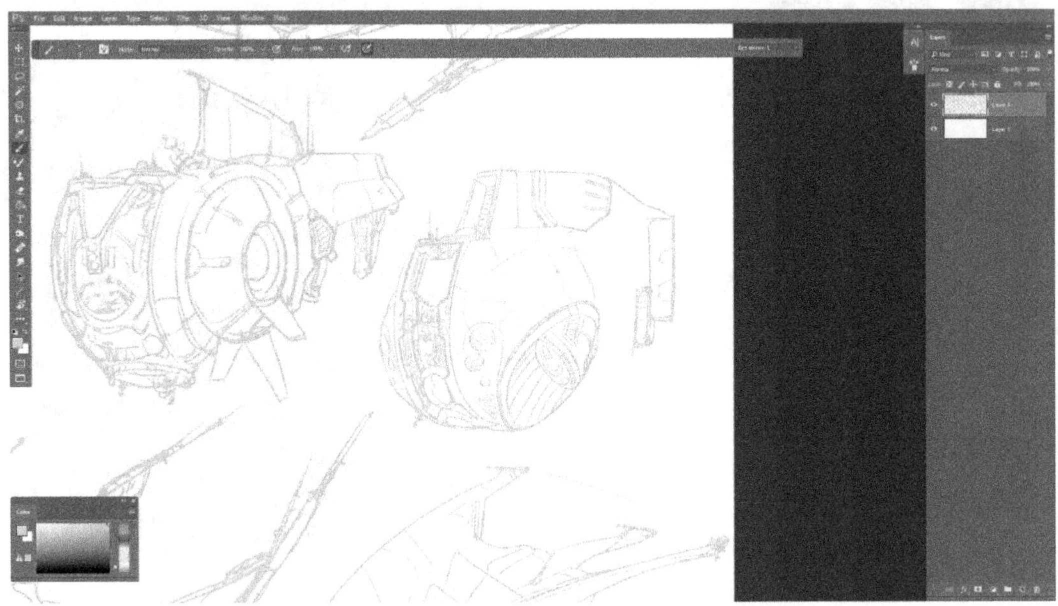

51. All the finished plane sketches are.

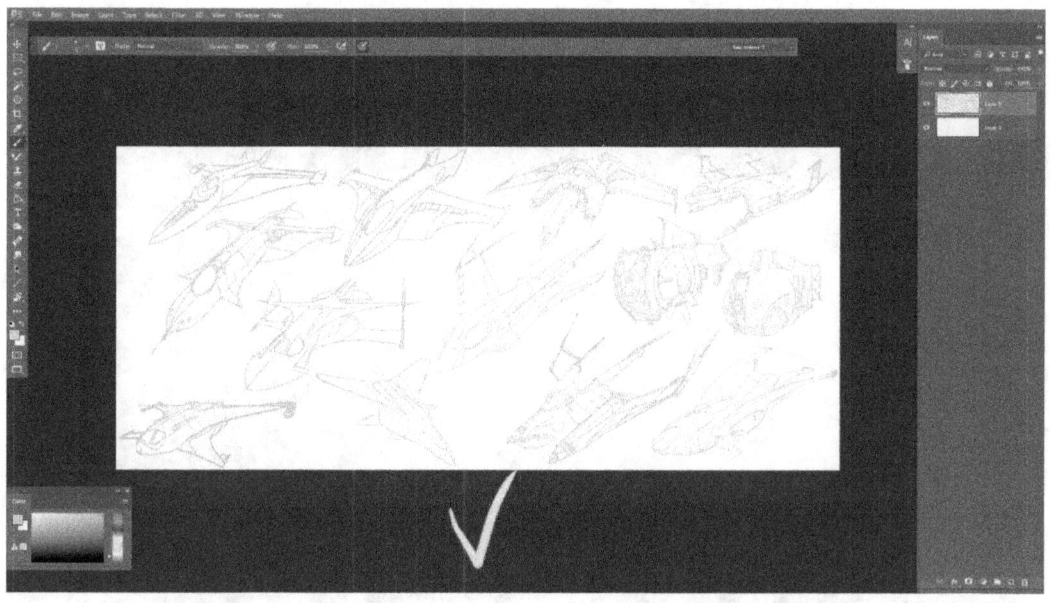

52. Press Ctrl+U and open the Hue/Saturation Window. Change the color to your desired one and adjust the Saturation to -84.

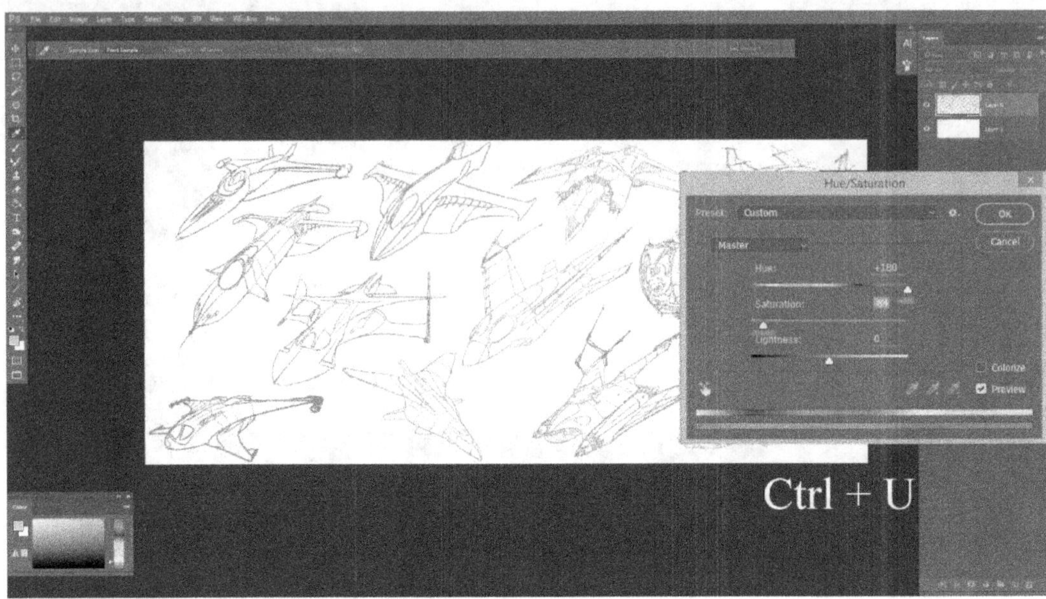

53. From the pool of sketches, select a few that, in your opinion, is successful.

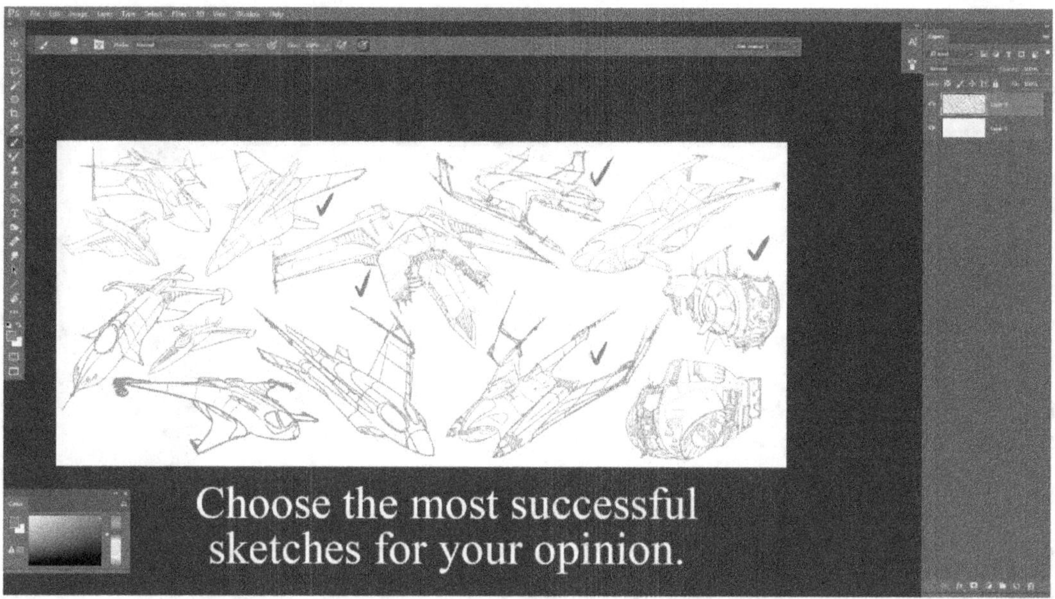

54. Select these drawings using the Lasso Tool. Cut out the desired sketches and move them to a more comfortable area on the canvas.

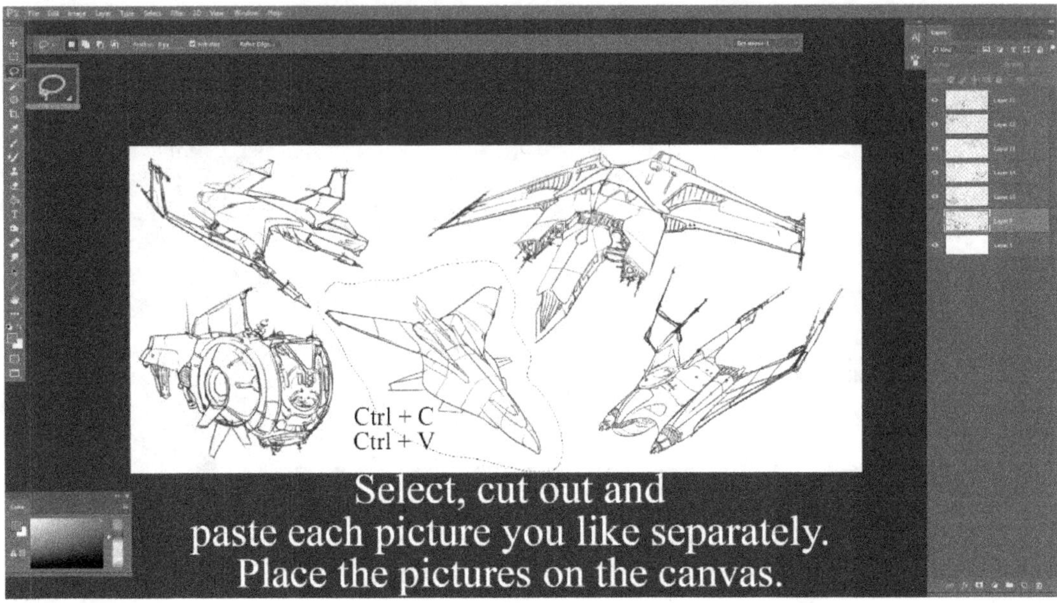

55. Make a new layer for the color. Place this layer at the bottom of every layer.

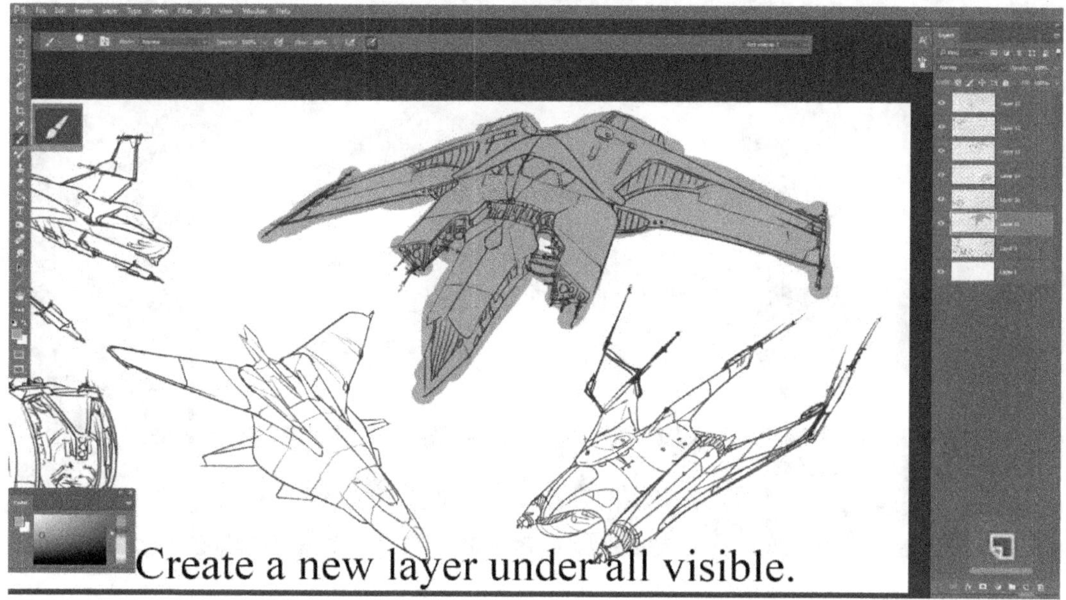

56. Fill in all the planes using the same method.

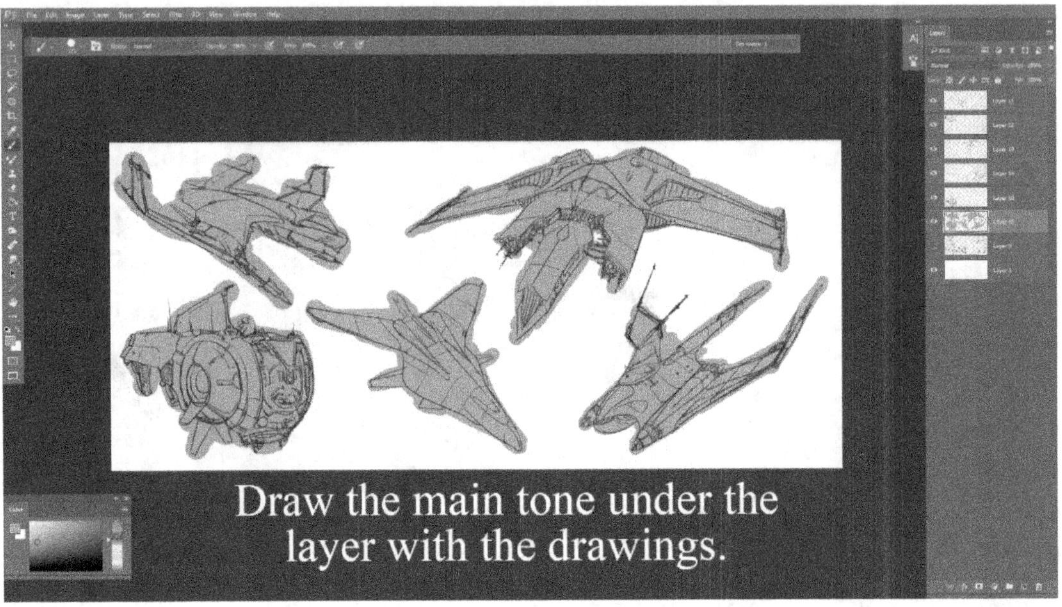

57. Remove any excess areas of color with the Eraser Tool.

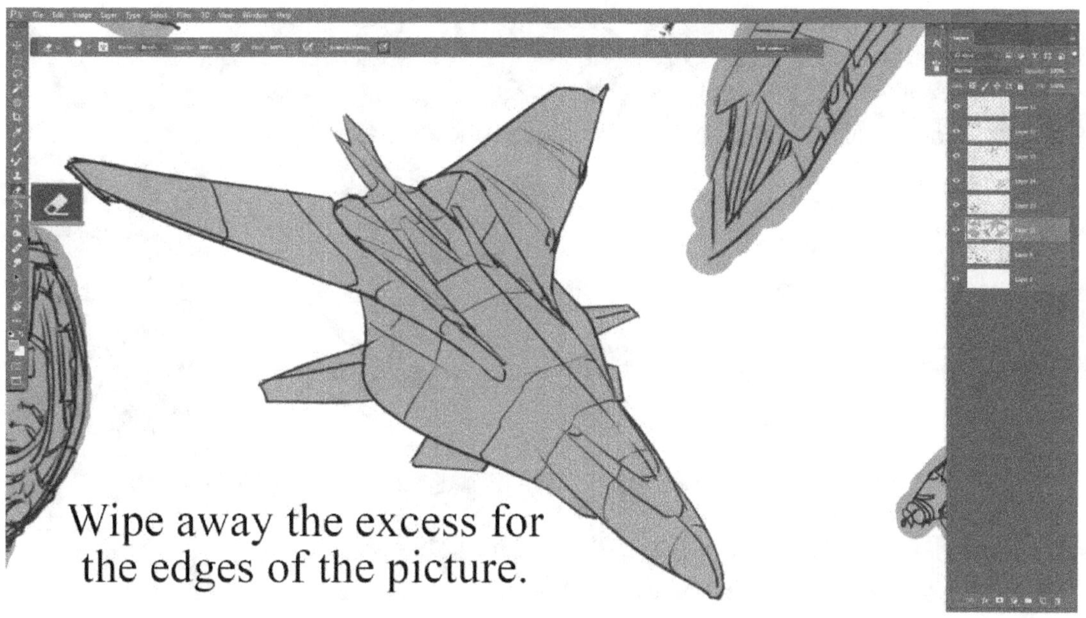

58. All the planes colored and cleaned.

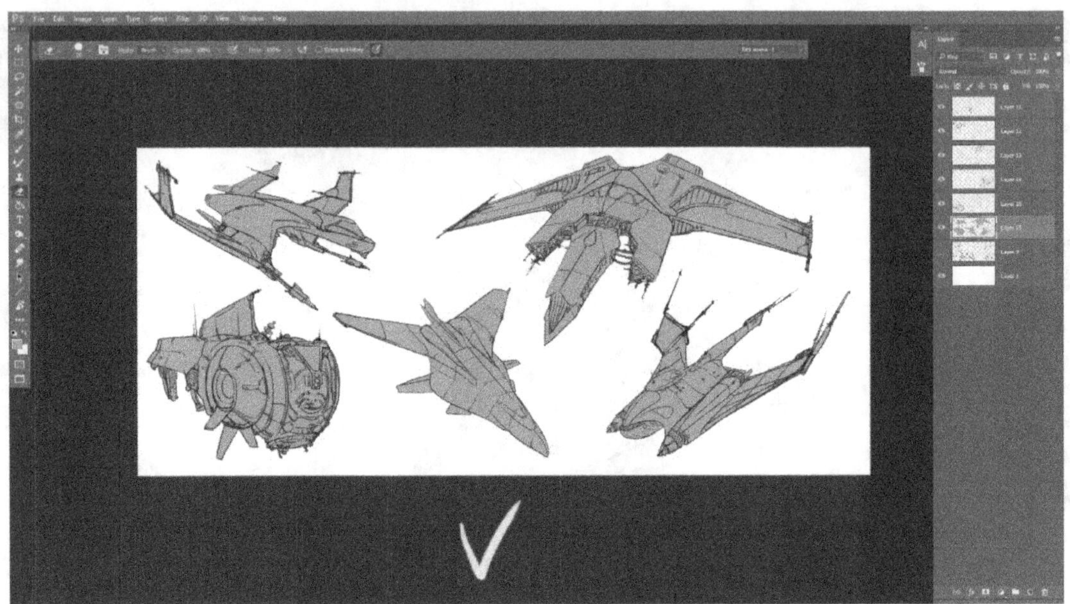

59. Make a new layer for the shades. Draw shadows and highlights to the object. Use the Brush Tool and select a darker color than the one on the planes. Adjust its Opacity to 17%. Paint the shadows on the object.

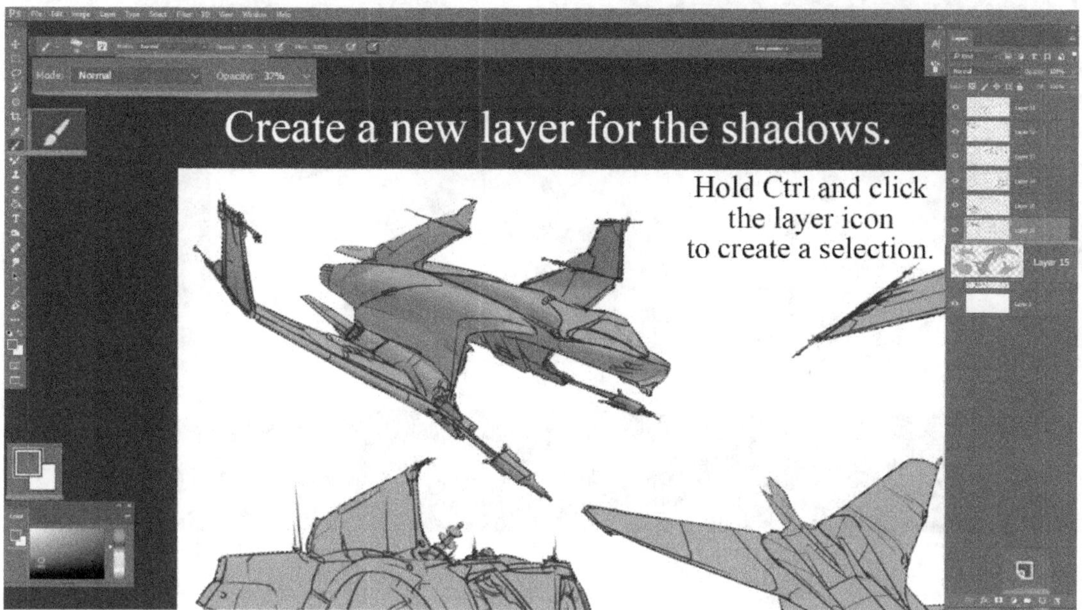

60. All the objects shaded and the lines cleaned up.

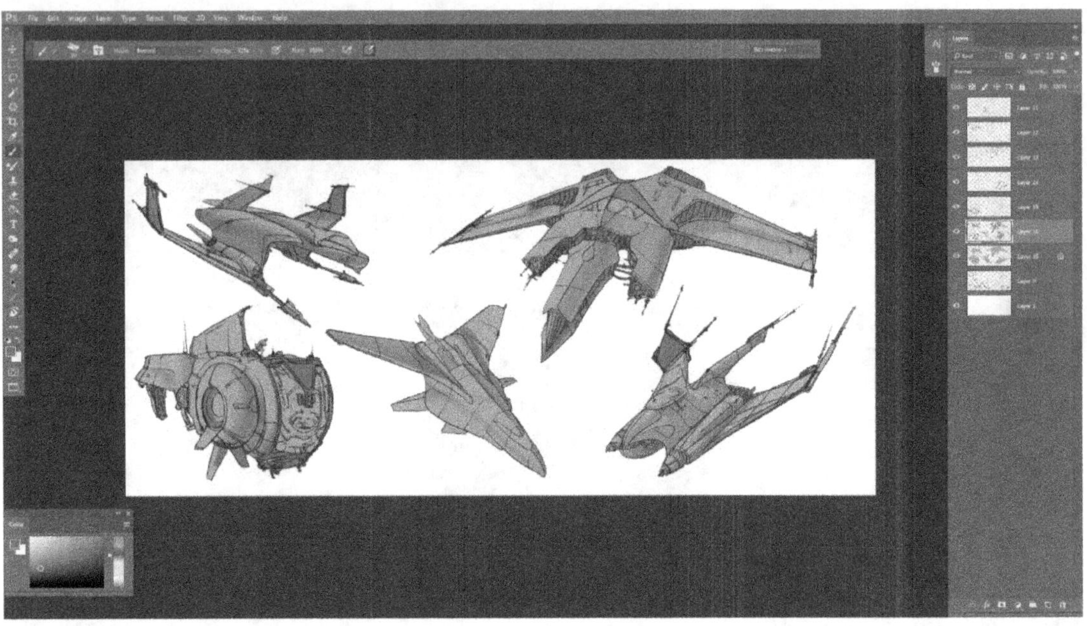

61. Once you are satisfied with the shading and highlights. Remove the selection area by pressing Ctrl+D.

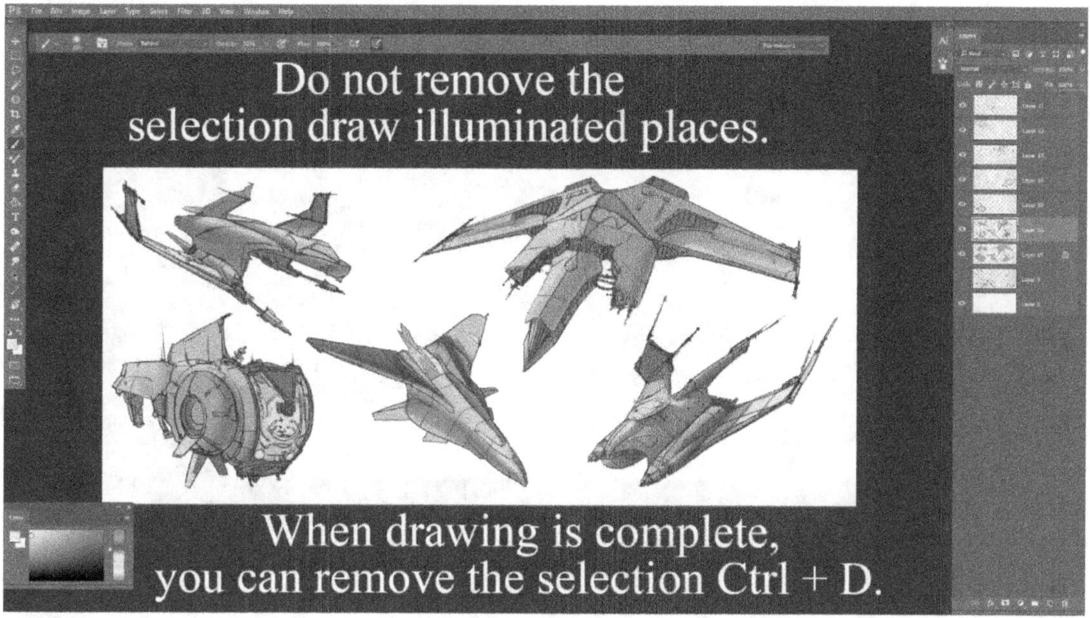

62. Change the Brush Tool's Mode to Color Dodge and the Opacity to 10%.
Draw the highlights on the areas show.

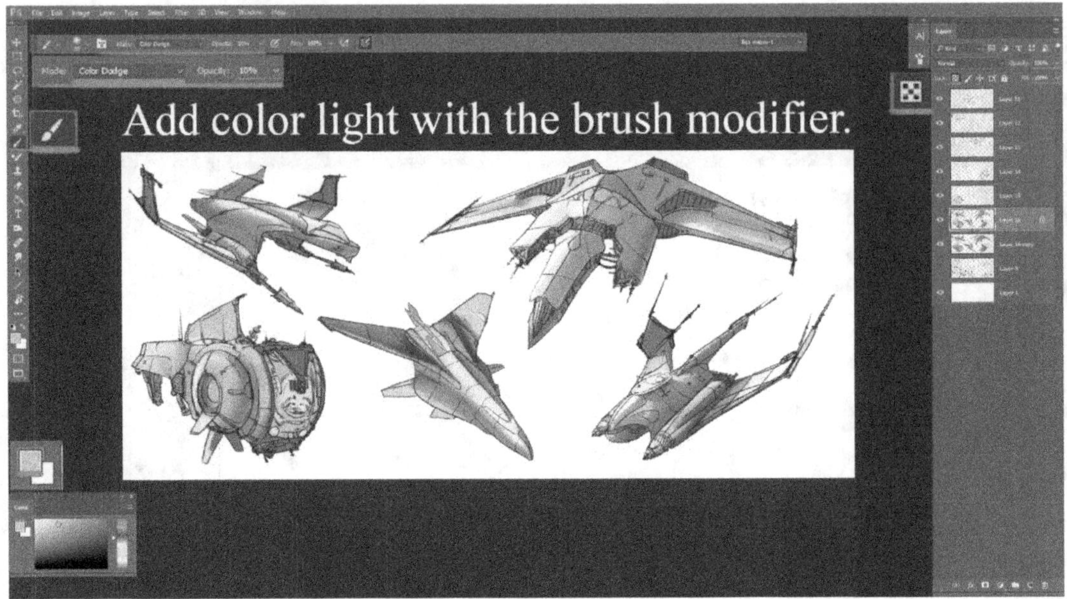

63. Add warm light sources to the sketches.

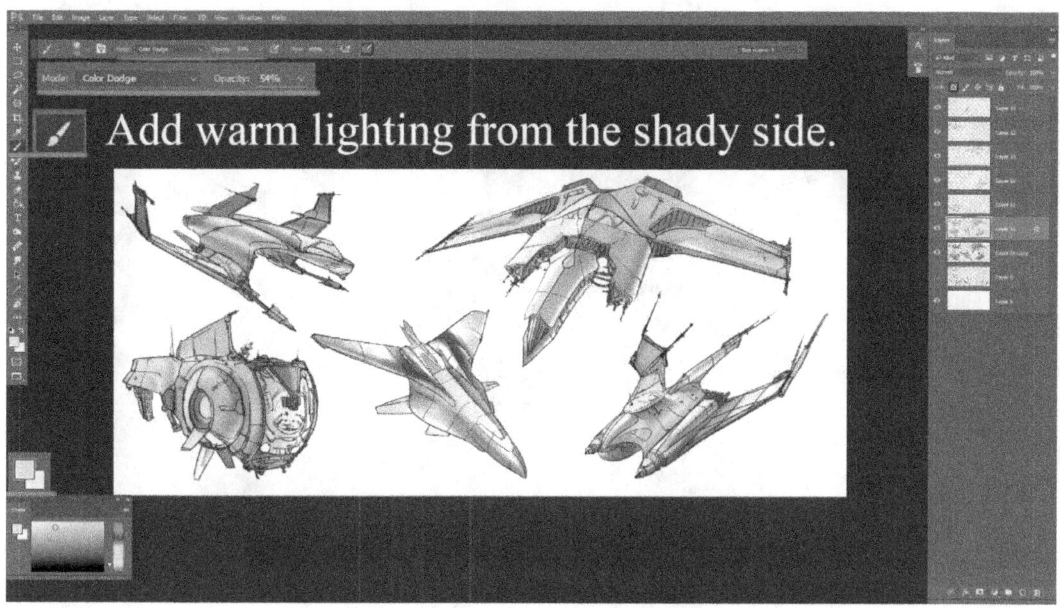

64. Add some bright areas to make a glare effect.

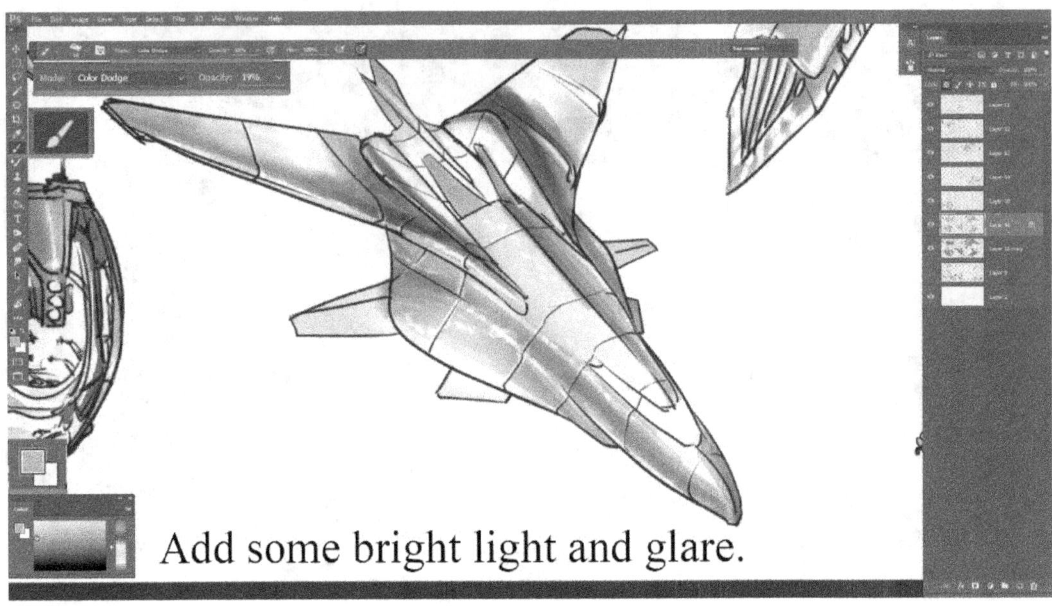

65. The drawings are with all the shadows and highlights.

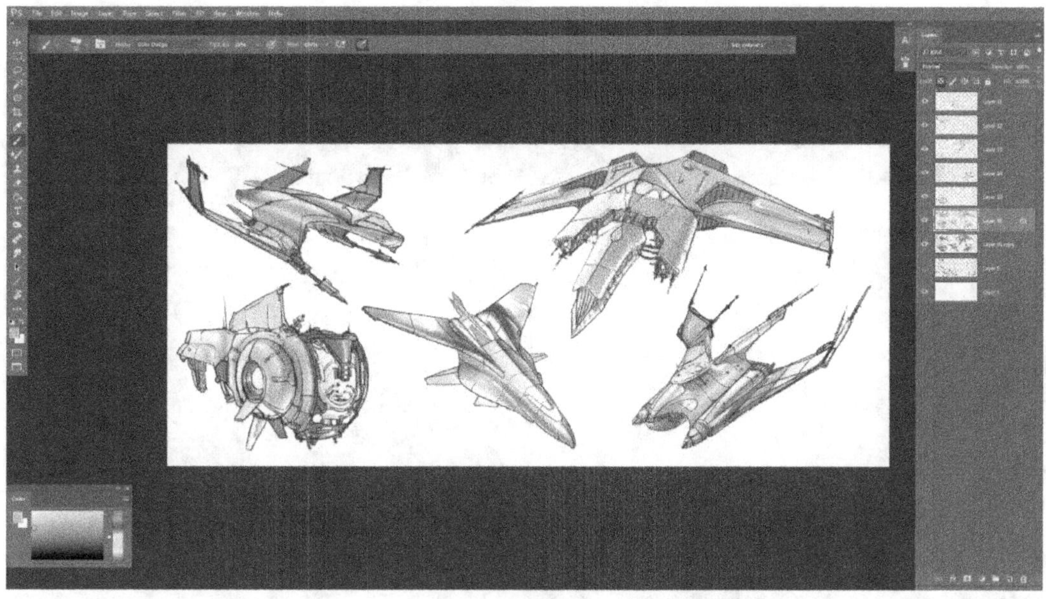

66. Use the Burn Tool in Midtones Range and 18% alcohol. Draw darkest areas of the objects' shadows.

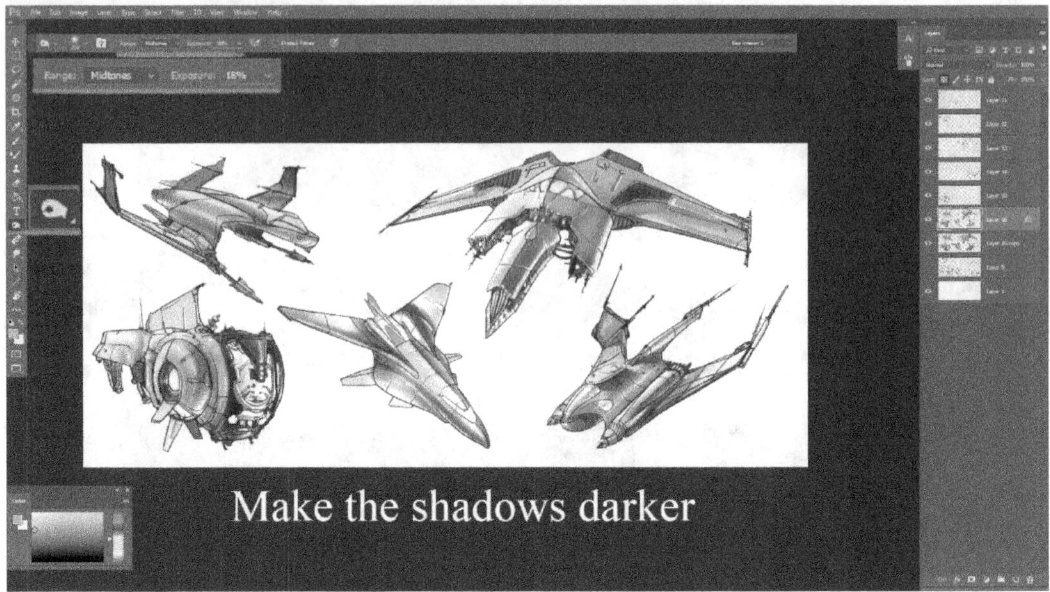

67. Select the Brush Tool and change it to Normal Mode and the Opacity to 18%. Click the Right Mouse Button and select a soft brush.

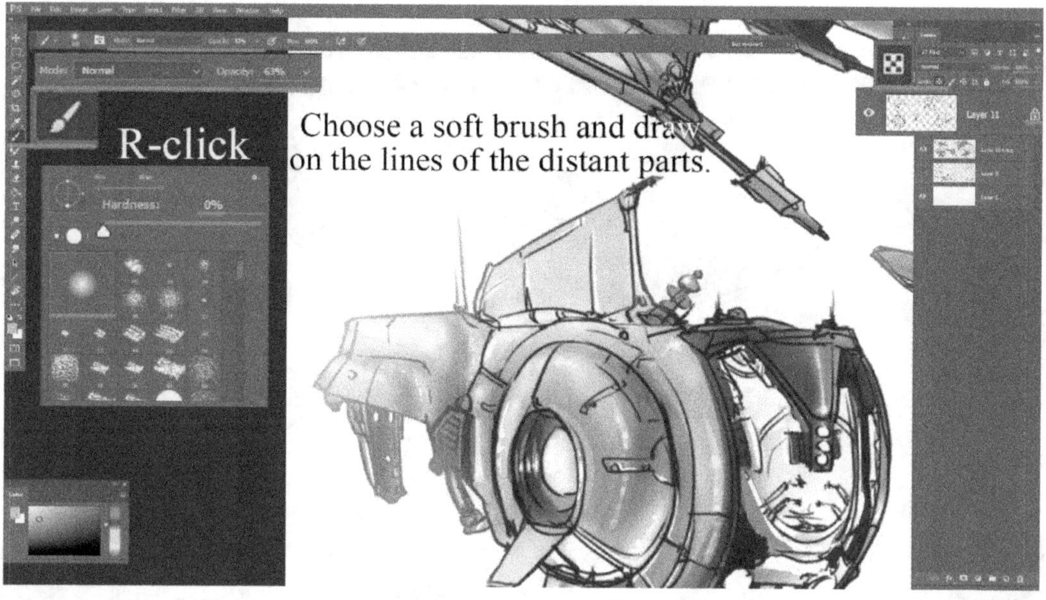

68. Select the layer of the sketch lines. Lock this layer. And paint over the lines of the sketch. Use a color close or the same as that of the part next to the line.

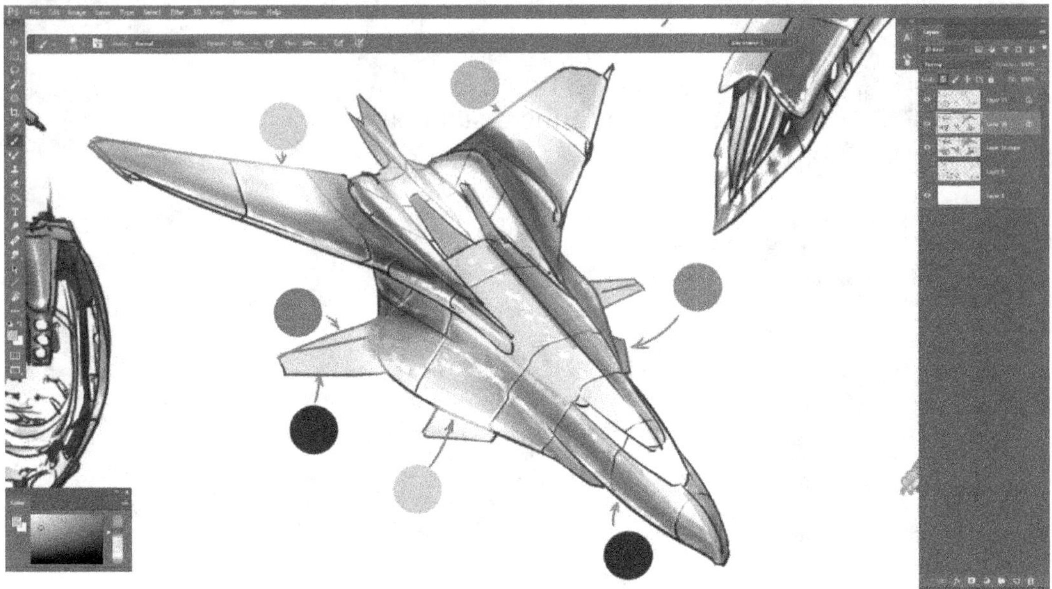

69. All the planes with the lines colored in.

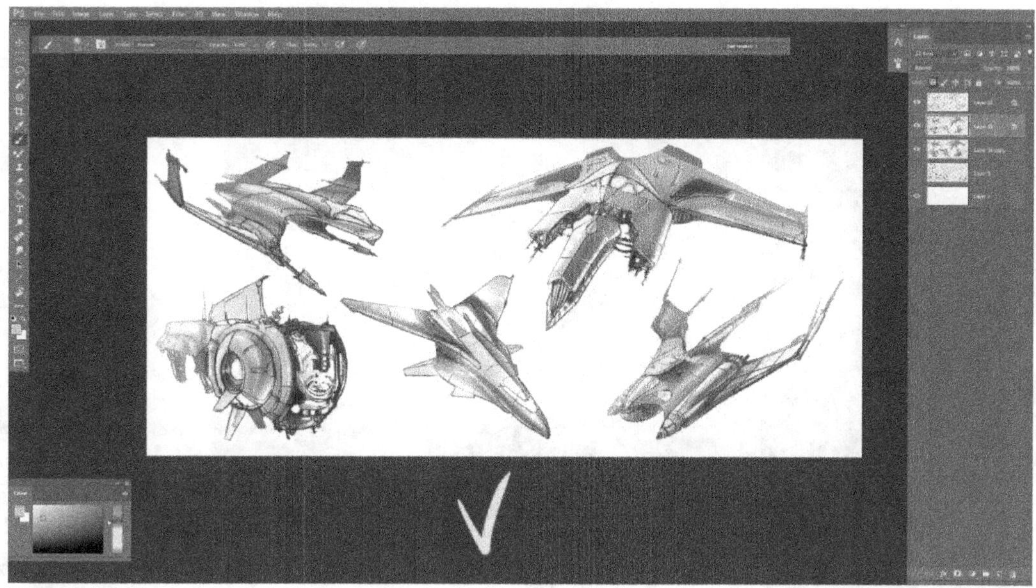

70. Use the Lasso Tool to draw an area of assumed shadow of the object.

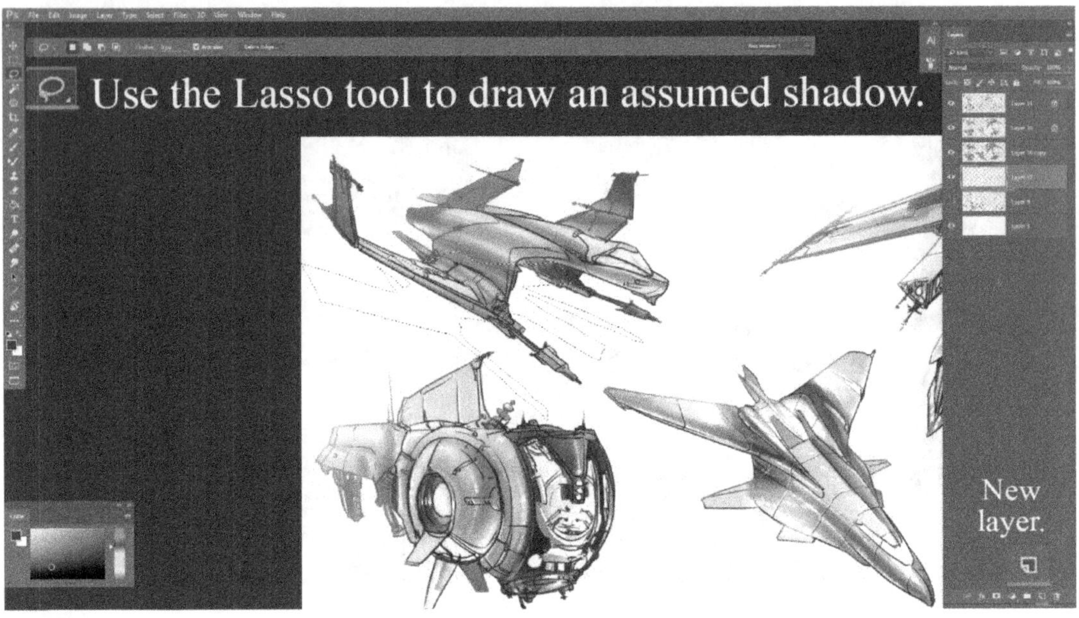

71. Use a large soft brush and paint over the areas under the object. Use the Brush Tool to paint in front of the shadows. Remove the far shadows using the Eraser Tool.

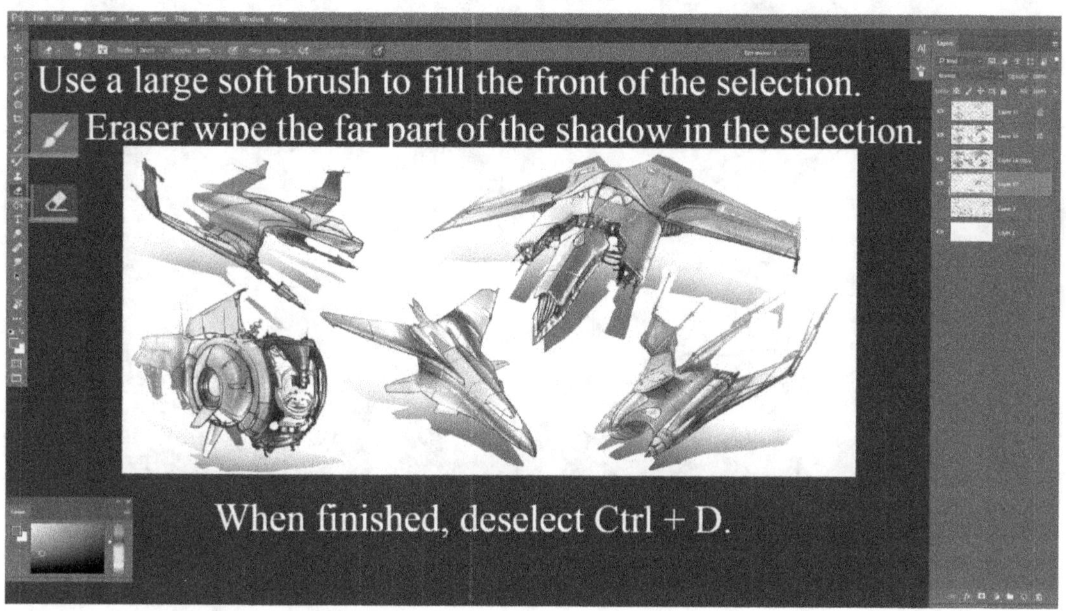

72. On the layer of the shadows draw a gradient. Choose the Gradient Fill Tool and draw a vertical line from the bottom of the canvas.

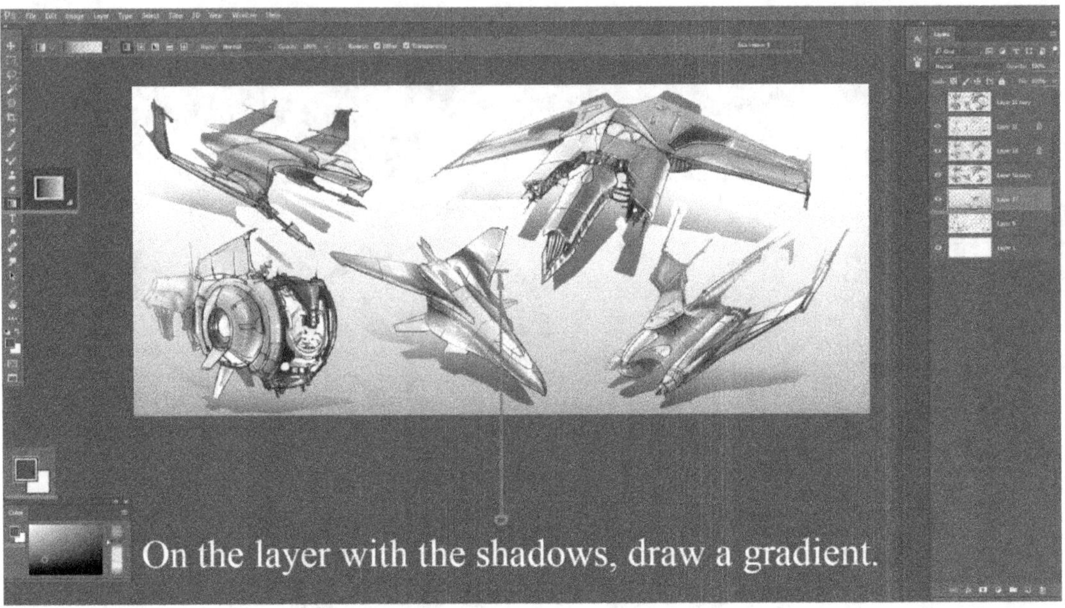

73. Make a new layer below the layer of the shadows. Mark a rectangular selection on this layer using the Rectangular Marquee Tool.

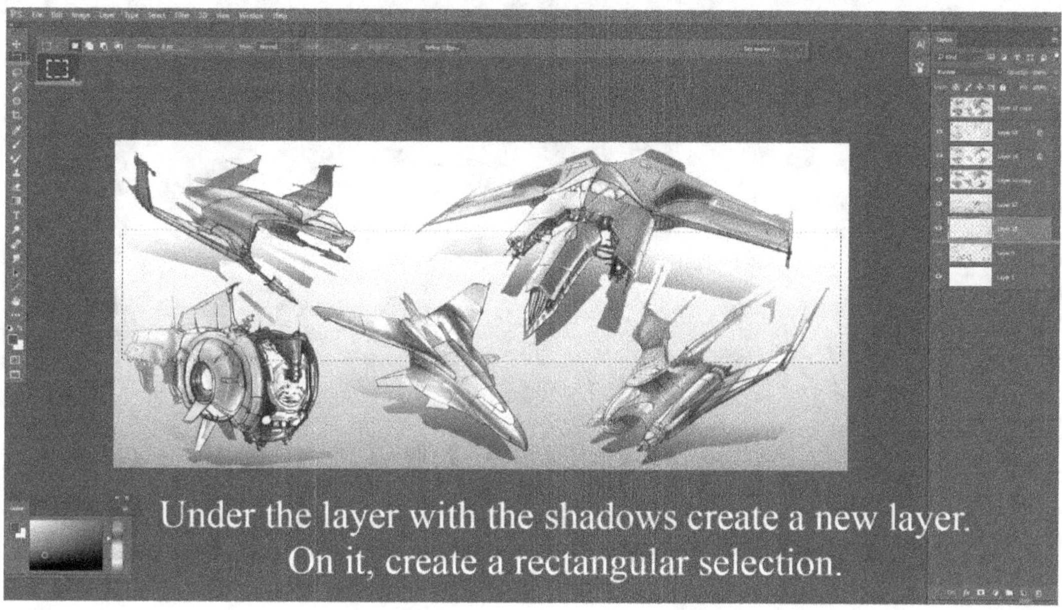

74. Fill the selected area with color.

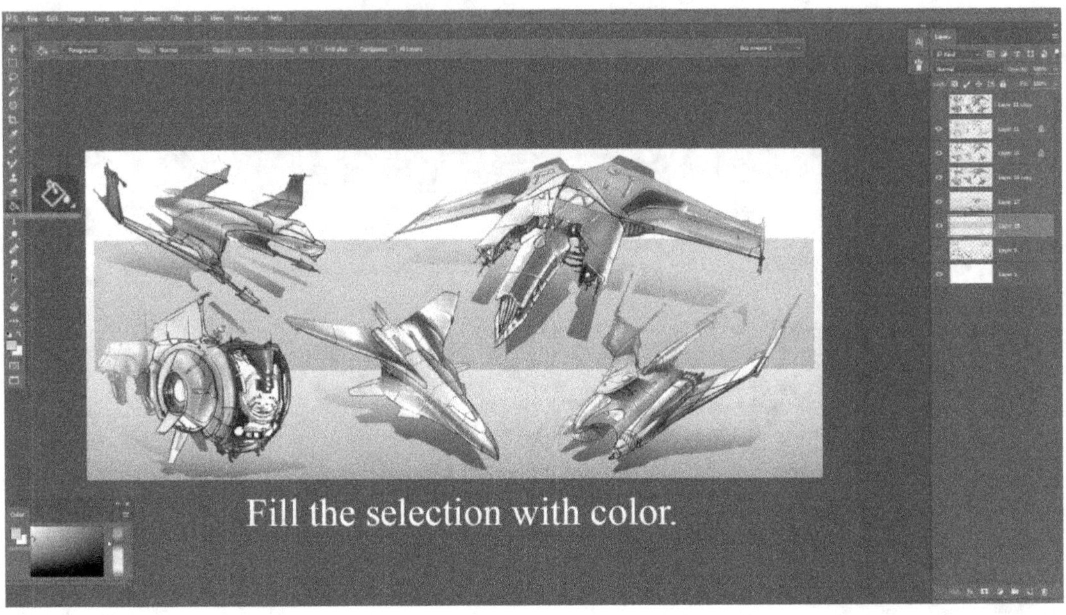

Conclusion

Painting and drawing in Adobe Photoshop is very similar to the traditional way of doing it but there are also drastic differences. Mastering this tool will take a long time to do, but it is not impossible. Just like anything in this world, anything can be mastered as long as you put in time and effort in it. And, if you love what you are doing, it will make it even more enjoyable.

Just like any other tool Adobe Photoshop needs a lot of practice for one to be proficient with it. Make sure to experiment. Find your comforts and challenge them. Make sure to always challenge yourself to be better and learn more about the tool.

Thank you!

Thank you for choosing our book. If you liked the book, please leave your feedback on AMAZON.COM

If you would like to have a bonus – **FREE BOOK,** please send the screenshot or the link of your review to this e-mail:

gloria.kemer@gmail.com and we will send you a **FREE BOOK** in PDF as a **GIFT**